JOHN IS AN UN **MAN.** 'I have to portray what I am not – a contract killer, for instance . . . The difficult part, really, is the length of time spent being the other person, and trying to remember what you said on the first meeting, or the second, or the twenty-eighth'

COMMANDER ROY RAMM IS IN CHARGE OF HOSTAGE NEGOTIATORS. 'The bleep goes, or you're phoned at home. OK, we've got a siege. What kind of siege? It's a man, it's two o'clock on a Saturday morning, the man's gone crazy. He's come home, found his girlfriend in bed with another guy, he's produced a knife, he's threatening to kill everybody in sight . . . When the bleep goes it could be anything'

DETECTIVE CHIEF SUPERINTENDENT EILEEN EGGINGTON WAS AMONG THE FIRST SIX FEMALE SPECIAL BRANCH OFFICERS TO BE TRAINED AS AN AUTHORISED SHOT. 'I was then being employed on protective duties, unarmed. And I enjoyed it, I have to say. I found there were practical difficulties to carrying the firearm, because it had to be kept in a handbag and therefore the drawing of the weapon was more difficult.'

ABOUT THE AUTHORS

Robert Fleming is a television documentary maker. His early career was in light entertainment – he was the first director of *Ready, Steady, Go!* Since then he has made films on a wide variety of subjects, including a profile of Cardinal Hume, the bicentenary of *The Times*, the Big Bang (the financial revolution in the City of London), and *This Sporting Land*, a series on the social history of sport. Several of his programmes have received awards.

In 1987 he and his wife, Marion, formed Argo Productions and, apart from a documentary for Channel 4 on the paedophile clinic, Gracewell, he has concentrated on programmes about the police. These include the series *Flying Squad* (1989) and *Murder Squad* (1992), both of which attracted over 12 million viewers.

Fleming's remaining ambition is to score 100 before lunch against Australia, at Lords.

Hugh Miller was born in Scotland but has lived for more than twenty-five years in Warwickshire. He is the author of a number of books, among them *The Silent Witnesses*, a study of forensic pathologists, the bestselling *Casualty* and the acclaimed Mike Fletcher crime novels. He also wrote *Seaforth* and *Seaforth 2*, the novels of the BBC television serial of the same name. His work has been translated into most western languages.

Hugh Miller lives in Warwick with his wife Nettie.

ROBERT FLEMING
WITH HUGH MILLER

SCOTLAND YARD

A SIGNET BOOK

SIGNET

Published by the Penguin Group
Penguin Books Ltd, 27 Wrights Lane, London w8 5TZ, England
Penguin Books USA Inc., 375 Hudson Street, New York, New York 10014, USA
Penguin Books Australia Ltd, Ringwood, Victoria, Australia
Penguin Books Canada Ltd, 10 Alcorn Avenue, Toronto, Ontario, Canada M4V 3B2
Penguin Books (NZ) Ltd, 182–190 Wairau Road, Auckland 10, New Zealand

Penguin Books Ltd, Registered Offices: Harmondsworth, Middlesex, England

First published by Michael Joseph 1994
Published with revisions in Signet 1995
1 3 5 7 9 10 8 6 4 2

Typeset by Datix International Limited, Bungay, Suffolk
Set in 9.75/12 pt Monophoto Plantin
Printed in England by Clays Ltd, St Ives plc

To Marion
wonderful wife, co-director and everything else –
who now goes to sleep counting policemen

Contents

Illustrations

(*Copyright holders are indicated in italics.*)

Preface to the Paperback Edition

The Metropolitan Police is in the throes of the biggest reorganisation in its 166-year history. Some of the changes forecast in the hardback edition of this book have already taken place and there are many more to come.

Many of these changes are intended to devolve responsibility from Scotland Yard to five newly created areas, each run by an Assistant Commissioner. The work of the Met's own restructuring team, combined with the findings of the Sheehy Report and the Audit Commission Report, has meant that hundreds of middle- and senior-ranking officers have left the service in what has been, and will continue to be for some time to come, a difficult, painful and challenging time for the Metropolitan Police.

To my great regret, the publishers have accepted legal advice which has meant that the names of some convicted criminals have been removed from this edition.

Foreword

My association with the Met began seven years ago
when, as a documentary maker with Thames Television,
I rang 230 1212 and said that I would like to make a
film about them. By luck my timing was right. Sir John
Dellow was in charge of Specialist Operations and he,
with the full backing of the Commissioner, Sir Peter
Imbert, was looking to improve the image of the Met by
opening doors previously closed to the media.

As a result, I spent three months observing the Flying
Squad at Tower Bridge before filming the series that
was transmitted in February 1989. At first I was treated
with suspicion by men who had serious doubts about
their work being shown on television. To some I was a
creature from outer space, and always remained so. But
others I found I could work with and so I began an association with the Met that has, so far, lasted seven years.

'The Stockholm Syndrome' is a police term, often
used in kidnaps, when, through continual exposure, the
criminal and the victim lower their resistance to each
other. In my relations with the police, it is a trap that I
have tried to avoid, but it has not always been easy. Not
surprisingly, in an organisation of 46,000 people, I have
come across all types of people, from highly intelligent
high-flyers to a few depressing dinosaurs.

But, overall, one cannot fail to be impressed. After
seven years of working closely with the Met, the tradi-
tions and standards of professionalism and dedication

that have made Scotland Yard the most famous name in the world of crime detection are what I remember most vividly.

A close second is the way in which so many people, police and civil staff, were extraordinarily helpful, both with the writing of the book and the making of the television series. I am only sorry that some of the 'back-room' departments have received less coverage than I would have liked, due to restrictions of space. I am well aware that their work is every bit as important as the more glamorous squads.

After Sir Peter Imbert and Sir John Dellow retired, their successors, Paul Condon and John Smith, continued to open doors for me that had never been opened before. Historically, many squads, in particular Special Branch, Criminal Intelligence, Crime Operations and the Force Firearms Unit, have always kept film makers and authors very much at arm's length, but with firm approval from the top every department in Scotland Yard has been accessible.

I would like to be able to say that I have written this book myself, but I have not. Scotland Yard is too big and, simultaneously, I was producing the television series. I was, therefore, particularly lucky to have Hugh Miller as my co-author. For almost a year he has ploughed through hundreds of thousands of words that I sent him as transcripts of over 120 interviews, along with all the newspaper cuttings, books and endless tapes containing my often incoherent 'impressions'. His achievement in disciplining this mountain of material into a coherent structure is extraordinary, and I am deeply indebted to him.

ROBERT FLEMING
London, November 1993

Organisation of the Metropolitan Police Service

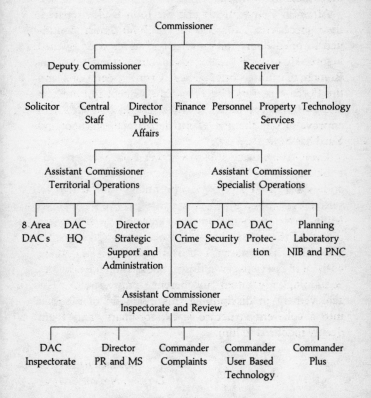

Introduction

Scotland Yard is the headquarters of London's Metropolitan Police. Some sections have national responsibilities, for instance the Anti-Terrorist Branch, but by and large the Yard is the headquarters of the Met. It is not, as many people believe, a police station. The familiar building fronted by a revolving sign in Broadway, Victoria, is strictly an office block; its call sign, CO, which appears on the shoulder badges of its uniformed officers, stands for Commissioner's Office.

The Metropolitan Police District is divided into eight geographical areas. The principal administrators are the Commissioner, the Deputy Commissioner, the Receiver (the most senior civilian in the Service) and three Assistant Commissioners. They form the senior management group, known as Policy Committee, and all work from Scotland Yard.

Each of the eight Metropolitan Police Areas is under the control of a Deputy Assistant Commissioner, who works directly to the Assistant Commissioner of Territorial Operations at Scotland Yard. The Yard provides support for the Areas, as well as policy and operational guidelines. A number of specialist squads and departments also come under the auspices of Scotland Yard, but not all of them are under the same roof. Although New Scotland Yard is officially the office building at number 10 Broadway, many of its departments work from buildings throughout Central London.

The Metropolitan Police District

A total of 46,000 people work for the Metropolitan Police; 28,000b are police officers, the remaining 18,000 being civilian employees. Approximately 4,000 people work in the headquarters block in Victoria

The building is a monument to the 1960s, and, even by the architectural standards of its time, it is uninspired. Floor after floor of box-like, cheerless offices mirror the commonplace exterior and its entire absence of personality.

In 1782, forty-seven years before the formation of the London Police, a new road was driven through the Palace of Whitehall area and the old buildings were demolished. Little and Middle Scotland Yard were replaced by Whitehall Place. Great Scotland Yard remained. In 1829 the London Police Force was created through an act of Parliament introduced by Sir Robert Peel, the Home Secretary. The headquarters were at 4 Whitehall Place, with a servants' entrance in Great Scotland Yard. The servants' quarters were turned into a police station, and soon the men of the division were referring to the station by the name of the little street it faced. In 1890 a new building was opened, on the Thames Embankment; it was called New Scotland Yard. Today it is referred to as the Norman Shaw Building, after the architect who designed it. The move to the present building at 10 Broadway was made in 1967.

Scotland Yard's reputation is worldwide. The Receiver, Graham Angel, recalls being reminded of this when he complained about having a hard day on a European Community police committee.

'A Foreign Office colleague told me I should realise how lucky I was. Policing and the SAS were the only two topics on which our European partners were interested in hearing how the Brits operated.'

The structure of this book is based upon the accompanying chart showing the hierarchical organisation of the Metropolitan Police Service. The two principal operational departments are Territorial Operations and Specialist Operations, the three others being Inspection and Review, the Receiver's Department and the Deputy Commissioner's Executive, which is really three smaller departments grouped under the authority of the Deputy Commissioner. Recently the first of a new generation of 'super' Regional Crime Squads was formed, intensifying fears in certain quarters of a move towards a national police force. The new South-East Regional Crime Squad, which went into operation in April 1993, combines three squads to make a single force with 600 detectives and ancillary staff covering thirteen police forces in Greater London, the Home Counties and East Anglia. Further amalgamations are planned in the north-east and the south-west, reducing the nine existing Regional Crime Squads to five.

The national direction being taken by the new squads is emphasised by the South-East Squad's HQ being in the same complex of offices as the National Criminal Intelligence Service (NCIS).

Commander Roy Penrose, Coordinator of the South-East Regional Crime Squad, said the merger would create an impetus to deal with organised crime and give the police a greater capacity to target serious criminals who are becoming increasingly mobile.

'Within the new South-East region, arguably four-fifths of the national organised crime is catered for,' Penrose said. 'I say that because the more affluent one of our archetypal criminals gets, the more he wants to move out into the greener pastures of the commuter belt around the M25. So if you accept that London is largely contained within the M25, then if you take almost a thirty-five-mile span around it, most of them are there. And in all our jobs we are seeing that there are Liverpool connections, Glasgow connections, Birmingham connections, but it all seems to be controlled from here in London.'

Bill Taylor, Assistant Commissioner, Specialist Operations, says there will always be a range of criminals operating nationally; 'So I think it's right to say that, in order to meet the threat effectively, you probably need an organisation that captures the national picture and is able to tap into the variety of activity going on in different forces.'

Taylor pointed out that the Regional Crime Squads do not work to NCIS. 'Roy Penrose reports to a management committee of Chief Constables of the constituent forces. He doesn't report to NCIS and he's not tasked by NCIS. NCIS just provides him with an intelligence service, in the same way that it provides a service for the Metropolitan Police, a service to Hertfordshire and so on. But in the future you could have the situation where NCIS and the RCS could come together as one organisation.'

Simon Crawshaw, Director of Intelligence at NCIS, explained how the establishment of NCIS affected Scotland Yard.

'NCIS took direct responsibility for the Interpol Office, the National Bureau of Interpol for the UK. It had been housed in Scotland Yard and was traditionally staffed by officers from around the country. But to all intents and purposes it was run by Scotland Yard, and the British representative of Interpol has traditionally been a senior Metropolitan Police Officer, up until the time that it was moved to NCIS. The British representative then became the Director General of NCIS.

'The other major move out of Scotland Yard, physically, was the National Drugs Intelligence Unit – it's now formed into the Drugs Division of NCIS. The National Office for the Suppression of Counterfeit Currency was a national function operated and run by the Metropolitan Police. That moved to NCIS.'

The National Football Unit, set up to look at football hooliganism around the country, also became part of NCIS.

'The only other main area that changed was in the field of organised crime,' Crawshaw said. 'It was recognised that there was expertise in international organised crime and crime groups held within a unit which was part of Scotland Yard's Criminal Intelligence Branch (SO11). The people with the expertise on groups like the Mafia and the Triads, and a number of analysts also engaged in that work, moved into NCIS.'

The introduction of NCIS has, in some areas of crime, reduced Scotland Yard's role.

The year 1993 saw more changes in the Metropolitan Police than at any time since the foundation of the service in 1829. Three major studies, in particular, created widespread reverberations.

One: On 28 June, presenting his White Paper on Police Reform to the House of Commons, the Home Secretary Michael Howard announced, among other measures, his intention to create a police service for the twenty-first century with, as its key, a new partnership between police and public to present a united front in the fight against crime.

Two: A Royal Commission on Criminal Justice was established on the day that convictions against the 'Birmingham Six' were quashed; the Home Secretary said that the Appeal Court decision, together with others, raised serious issues of public concern. The Commission's report suggested that police investigations were insufficiently thorough, and that questioning of suspects was often rambling and not focused on the real issues. It recommended that detective training and training in investigations should be overhauled, and that police performance should not be assessed unduly on arrest or conviction rates, but rather on quality.

Three: The controversial Sheehy Inquiry into the Police Service made 272 recommendations which, had they all been implemented, would have had a major impact on every police service in the country.

The Metropolitan Police are always keenly aware of the criticisms levelled at them, and a recurring theme of this book is the way they make efforts to change before change is imposed on them from the outside. Some criticisms, however, have inspired little more than distress.

'The damage to morale has been enormous,' said the Commissioner, Paul Condon. 'I've been in the service twenty-six and a half years, and I have never known a single event during that time knock the wind out of the service the way that the perpetration of Sheehy did. I was out of the country on the Wednesday when the report came out. I flew back to England on the Saturday, was handed Sheehy literally as I got off the plane, read it all on Sunday, came in to work on Monday, made some phone calls, spoke to people, and morale was right on the floor. It was as if Constables and Sergeants had been punched in the stomach – had the wind taken out of them. They knew there would be reform, but they thought somehow it was to do with management and senior officers and maybe allowances, so they just weren't psychologically prepared for it. They are not dinosaurs, they are not arguing for the status quo, they know there's got to be change, but they need to sense that it's fair, and they don't have that sense at the moment.'

Much to the relief of the Met, the Home Secretary ignored many of Sheehy's more controversial proposals.

Condon thinks that the service as a whole is desperately unsettled. They need three things, he says: they need to feel understood, they need to feel appreciated, and they need to feel supported.

'If I take the understanding one first,' he said, 'I think there is a feeling that politicians in particular and the media want to over-simplify policing and say there's more crime, therefore the police have failed. Even the youngest cop knows that's an over-simplification. So they want to say things like, "Well, Commissioner, why can't you get the world to understand it is more complicated? There is more crime because there are more cars; there are more things to steal in most places; family life is breaking down, there is more ambiguity around moral issues." And they want the Commissioner and the service to be able to say to the wider world – please understand, crime isn't as simple as you think.'

They feel under-appreciated, Condon said, because of statistics like one in his first annual report which showed that during the previous year nearly 12,000 Met officers were injured on duty. Of that number, 3,400 were physically assaulted, and of those over 100 had bones broken or were stabbed. Furthermore, in the eighteen months prior to the report being published, three police officers were murdered.

'And in terms of support, they believe that the criminal justice system just doesn't support their effort. On things like Disclosure, we've had to abandon major cases. In terms of understanding, appreciation and support, the average cop feels confused at best and let down at worst. And they want me, as the new Commissioner, to change that dramatically.'

Condon found some laudable areas in the report of the recent Royal Commission on Criminal Justice, but he says it fails to address some of the central problems.

'A recent MORI survey showed that confidence in the criminal justice system is in danger of collapsing,' he said. 'In excess of 80 per cent of those surveyed thought the system hampered the police in doing their job. Those are some worrying trends. I do hope there will be a very lively debate about the criminal justice system, and that we get a Criminal Justice Bill that looks at not just the needs of suspects but the right of society to protect itself. So things like Disclosure, the right of silence – I have some very strong views about those, and I hope we have a good debate about those issues. At *The Times* one-day conference on the Royal Commission, I pointed out that we have had to abandon over sixty major cases of drugs, armed robbery and other offences, because we could not risk divulging informants, undercover police work or technical devices. I just don't see how that can be in the public interest.'

Assistant Commissioner Bill Taylor has the same misgivings.

'A lot of time and effort and energy, quite properly, has been spent on looking at police and policing,' he said. 'I think some of that energy now needs to be put into some of those areas of criminal justice which make the policing of the country more effective. I mean some of the obvious things, some of the things that were looked at by the Royal Commission. There are some impediments to effective policing, for example the Disclosure issue, which is a very big issue, and which has probably worked to the detriment of the criminal justice system. It has reduced our ability to get at the truth.'

Taylor believes the system is bristling with irregularities. 'We are investigating, we are not interested in prosecuting any more; we are just interested in getting to the truth, and the anomalies go something like this: the Serious Fraud Office, if they are investigating fraud, can require people to give an explanation under penalty, but we can't do that in cases of rape or murder. If you infringe the law in your vehicle, I can write to you and require you to give information under penalty. If the investigation concerns a rape or a murder, I can't write to you – not unless there has been an infringement of the road traffic legislation. Now that really needs sorting out.'

Public concern over the rising crime rate, poor arrest figures and the apparent diminishing of police capability has led, inevitably, to changes in the overall police image. But the changes vary with viewpoint, and the Commissioner does not feel the police are losing public support.

'We are one of the Aunt Sallies that are there to be knocked,' said Condon, 'but at the same time the dear old British public are essentially fair in forming a judgement about us. I can go anywhere in the world and say I'm the Commissioner at Scotland Yard, and there is almost a reverence about British policing, about what it stands for. So the British public, I think, still support us, and we are respected abroad for what we are and what we stand for.'

He is not so confident about the media.

'We have lost a lot of ground with the media. I accept that totally. I don't criticise the media for it. I feel an obligation as Commissioner to try and make a difference, to be accessible, to talk through policing issues and so on. And I actually sense the British public have more or less had enough of police-bashing. They just don't believe some of the hype they read or see. I sense that maybe the mood is ready to swing back in our favour.'

One of Scotland Yard's most senior policemen, not wishing to be quoted, says that areas of London are out of the control of the police. Condon does not agree.

'I dispute totally any notion that anywhere in London is out of control or a no-go area. I think that's pure hype. I've travelled extensively, and I believe that London is one of the safest capital cities in the world. That still applies.'

Does the Met have the resources it needs to maintain an efficient police service?

'No Commissioner will ever feel he has enough,' Condon said. 'If I had thousands more police officers then I could do a better job than I am doing now. But, equally, if there were thousands more teachers and doctors and nurses the same would be true in other areas.

'I've just had on my desk the crime figures for the first six months of 1993, and we are making progress. Our huge Bumblebee initiative across London seems to be making headway – reported burglaries are down 3 per cent for the whole of London. We haven't seen figures like that for over a decade. Reported burglaries on domestic properties are down 4 per cent.'

Newspaper reports suggest that the Metropolitan Police has one of the lowest crime clear-up rates in the United Kingdom. The figures, Condon pointed out, do not necessarily give a clear or particularly accurate picture.

'Our overall clear-up rate for violence against the person is 62 per cent – over six out of ten crimes of violence we clear up. Sexual offences, 59 per cent – again, six out of ten. Murder is even higher, the clear-up rate varies from 70 to 80 per cent. It's only when you get into the bulk issues like burglary, where our clear-up rate is 12 per cent, and motor-vehicle crimes, where it's a low clear-up rate, that you get down to an overall clear-up rate of 16 per cent.

'Now, what we are doing, as Bumblebee has shown us, is arresting the active burglars. In the past – and in some provincial forces now – those burglars were persuaded to admit lots of other offences. In London now, by and large, it's one arrest, one clear-up . . . The Met has never been into that in a big way. We have put our efforts into victim care and genuine detections, and over the years that has worked against the Met. But I think more and more provincial forces now are adopting Met practice. So I don't think the Met has got anything to fear in terms of productivity or clear-ups.'

International comparisons can be hard to make when talking about clear-up rates. Condon said the only safe statistics are based on the numbers of police officers. A telling fact there, immediately, is that we have the smallest ratio of police officers to population of virtually anywhere in Europe.

'I think it's only Portugal that has a smaller number. If you take France, with roughly the same population, they have something approaching two-thirds more police officers than we have here – well over 200,000. Places like Germany, Holland, Italy, they have far more police officers to members of the population than we have. That reflects two things: one, the law-abiding nature of our public, and two, the very strong bonds between the police and the public here which allow us to police with a much smaller number.'

Condon is clear about his priorities. Foremost is a determination to make people feel safer living in London.

'I see us making efforts on terrorism, burglary and so on, issues that affect feelings of safety. Second come the quality-of-life issues. I want to put more police officers on the streets, because people feel good about that, it does improve the quality of life. More police officers on the streets means less vandalism, nuisance, yobbish behaviour, all the things which can affect people's quality of life. Thirdly, I want people to have renewed confidence in the integrity and the ethics of the police. Those things all interact. So it's safety, quality of life, confidence in the police. I believe I can impact all three of those issues.'

A perennial cause for concern is that the police investigate their own alleged crimes and misdemeanours. Condon said he would welcome an effective alternative, if anybody could show him one.

'I am not closing my mind to it, I am just saying I look forward to an alternative that will work. It may be that the nearest we would get would be seconding police officers full-time to some sort of national complaints agency, where they would work totally under the supervision of independent people. My resistance isn't one of defending turf, I just need to see what the value added is, how a new system would work.'

Public expectations of the police, based on fictional stereotypes like Dixon of Dock Green and DI Reagan, are simply unrealistic and unhelpful, Condon says.

'The only way we can take policing forward and develop it and maintain trust and confidence, is to hold the line on ethical policing. If we do that then you can't have a DI Reagan [in the television series *The Sweeney*]. You can't have the ends justifying the means. The community must understand what they can and can't have from policing. They can have courageous police men and women, they can have intelligent police officers, absolutely loyal and committed police officers; they can't have corrupt police officers, they can't have violent police officers, they can't have police officers to whom the end justifies the means.'

Condon explained what he means by ethical policing which must apply, he emphasised, from the Commissioner all the way down to the youngest recruit.

'It is believing in a set of standards about policing, about doing things right every time, about not bending rules, about not being violent and using only reasonable force, about treating everyone with respect and dignity, regardless of who they are, what they are. That's the backbone of all we do.

'I'm not asking for my people to be saints, I'm not asking them to do anything; what they want me to do is endorse ethical behaviour. They want me to say to them, look, it's all right, chaps, to be ethical, it isn't soft and it isn't weak to be ethical, it's actually all right and necessary.'

He has no doubts about the ethical standards of his people in Anti-Terrorism, Special Branch, Robbery Squad or Criminal Intelligence.

'If you look at some of the toughest jobs that police officers have to do with some of the most difficult criminals in some of the most violent situations, that's where you'll find the highest ethical standards, because they know that nothing else will do. They know the quality of the legal advice these people will get. They know there is no end to the lies and the confusion that those top-end criminals would visit upon policing. Those cops have learnt by hard experience that nothing but the highest ethical standards will do. Jack Reagan would not survive in the Robbery Squad. He certainly wouldn't survive in the Anti-Terrorist Squad. They are top-flight professional cops. So if ethical policing can work at that level, sure as hell it can work at day-to-day street level.'

On the subject of the George Dixon-style policeman, Condon said he had never met one, although he believed that a number of his early colleagues had Dixon-like traits.

'The Met I joined in '67 was great fun, and I enjoyed it, and it was the foundation upon which I built my career. But there were things about policing in those days that were fairly rough-and-ready and just wouldn't be good enough nowadays.

'The system was much simpler. Police officers took their own cases to court. The paperwork was simpler, too. Let me be frank, the potential for being less rigorous about the quality of evidence was there. I don't think there was the ethical rigour that there is now. There was an awareness that corruption was about . . . I honestly believe now that that corruption has gone. There may be the odd bad apple, but the feeling that there was a bit of institutional corruption around, that has gone, thankfully.'

There is a recurring argument inside and outside the police service about the precise role of the police officer in today's society. It is an argument which tends to boil down to the 'Thief Takers or Social Workers' issue.

'Only 20 per cent of what a police officer does, even today in London, is crime-fighting, law-enforcement in the truest sense of the phrase,' says Assistant Commissioner Peter Winship of Inspection and Review. 'A lot of the calls are for help, for a different kind of policing role that many of the public, I think wrongly, believe us to be engaged in.'

Commander George Churchill-Coleman of the Fraud Squad has no doubts about the fundamental police role.

'The primary objective of the police service is to prevent and detect crime, and my feeling is that we have moved away from those primary objectives into areas I would term as secondary policing. They may be seen by some as laudable – looking at victim support, counselling individuals and so on and so forth – all of these things would be fine if we had infinite resources and could do them all. We can't.'

The Commissioner, for his part, believes in the art of the possible.

'It isn't a stark choice between hard cop and community cop,' he says. 'Life isn't as straightforward as that. I deal with the things which are within my power and my range and my scope. I cannot do a great deal for the homeless in London. I cannot do a great deal for the unemployed. I cannot do a great deal to keep families together. I cannot do a great deal about moral teaching within families, churches, schools and so on. That doesn't mean I am not in favour of schools programmes, community programmes, sector policing – all of those things I sign up to and support. But I suppose, at the end of the day, it's a balanced question of what the police are there for.

'I believe the police are there to deal with society as it is, to set standards, to enforce a moral framework, but I do not believe they are there to fundamentally change society. I do not believe we are there in a social engineering role, to somehow design crime out of the community . . . That's a role I want to give to politicians, to Parliament, to a whole range of agencies, as well as the police. It's the art of the possible: what I can achieve in London with 28,000 police officers looking after seven to eight million people and nearly a million crimes a year. So I'm saying let's live in the real world and use police resources ethically and to the best effect, across a range of issues with limited resources.'

Over the last three years one incident has caused much controversy and sadness inside Scotland Yard.

On 12 December 1990, the *Sun* carried a front-page story claiming that Assistant Commissioner Wyn Jones had taken 'freebie' holidays from the controversial Cypriot businessman Asil Nadir, and had done 'unofficial work' in vetting Nadir's security men. Jones went on leave at that time and has not returned to duty since.

The Home Office has long ago accepted that the *Sun* story was false but, in the words of *Observer* correspondent David Rose, 'it set in motion a juggernaut, which no one was prepared to stop: a five-month investigation by nine officers; a four-week tribunal chaired by a QC; further interminable argument among lawyers.'

The charges against Jones have mostly collapsed. Those which remain allege no financial corruption or any improper business links. They concern occasions when he is alleged to have used his car unnecessarily; an 'unnecessary' night in a hotel following a meeting, plus some very complex technical claims about foreign trips. There is no suggestion that Jones pocketed an extra penny of expenses. One of the so-called 'progressive tendency' of young university-educated officers at Scotland Yard has been quoted as saying that Jones was the most radical Assistant Commissioner in the history of the Met, and that his downfall was a 'stitch-up'.

Deputy Commissioner John Smith said, 'Wyn Jones is a very good friend of mine, as he was of the last Commissioner's. He seemed to have been either loved or disliked, one of those persons who encourages the stark opposites in emotions. He was a very good Assistant Commissioner who did a number of innovative things in ways that other people couldn't.'

SPECIALIST OPERATIONS
Introduction

Deputy Assistant Commissioner David Veness explains his concept of what Specialist Operations Crime is all about. Broadly he works to preserve London's way of life against the threat of crime to order, economy and the social structure.

'I'm like a forest ranger up a tower watching for the signs of forest fires, the fires in question being threats of serious crime moving towards the capital. I oversee specific and major cases – that's relatively unusual, because the cases are usually dealt with by others. I only intervene when there's a need to bring together various branches and skills and co-ordinate them.'

Veness has a direct responsibility to oversee highly delicate cases such as kidnap, extortion and product contamination, and to work with the victims and the appropriate police agencies to manage the crises.

Veness says that terrorism is number one in his top three crime priorities in London. 'It's a crime in which I do not have direct operational involvement,' he said, 'but we're enormously keen to provide our resources to support those combating it.'

Number two is burglary; armed robbery is number three. 'Armed robbery in its generic sense – the use of guns by bank robbers, or criminals robbing betting shops or off-licences, the use of guns in so-termed contract killings, and the use of guns more generally throughout society. It comes down to a danger I keep referring to, the fact that we've got a property-based crime problem in London, and I'm trying to prevent it becoming a violent-crime problem, and the quickest way for it to move is at the barrel of a gun.'

Commander George Ness, on the other hand, believes the focus has shifted from property-based crime.

'In the thirty-five years since I became a police officer,' he says, 'I think one of the main changes is a move away from property crime. There used to be an awful lot of things like stolen lorry loads and serious warehouse break-ins. I think to a degree that's gone.'

He agrees armed robbery is a serious problem, but believes it is being controlled.

'There's still armed robbery, but we've cut the incidence drastically because we've gone into target hardening – making things harder to steal – with the security companies, and because the Flying Squad has been effective in taking out some of the major players.'

Veness and Ness are both seasoned policemen from different professional backgrounds. As a Detective Inspector at Bow Street, Veness gained a scholarship to Trinity College, Cambridge, emerging as a BA and Master of Law. In November 1991, at the age of forty-three, Veness was promoted to DACSO Crime and took command of the specialist crime squads at Scotland Yard. These are International and Organised Crime (SO1), the Fraud Squad (SO6), Crime Operations Branch (SO10), Criminal Intelligence (SO11) and the Force Firearms Unit (SO19).

George Ness is Commander SO1, SO8 (Flying Squad), and SO19. He describes himself as an East End, West End, North London detective. He was in the East End as a Commander from 1986 to 1990, then moved to Scotland Yard to take over Flying Squad and the Regional Crime Squad. He assumed his present responsibilities in 1992.

When travelling abroad David Veness encounters a certain amount of misunderstanding: many people do not grasp the proper function of Scotland Yard. 'The first few minutes are always spent explaining that it is the headquarters of the Metropolitan Police and that, whilst we have certain national interests, there are others with clear national responsibility, like the new National Criminal Intelligence Service, and our world really exists within the confines of the M25. But they cloud over and don't believe you, and still are convinced that you work with Sherlock Holmes and that it's all a much darker secret than that, and they smile knowingly.'

In relation to the Metropolitan Police Areas, Veness says he is effectively a supporter. He is a leader of squads within Scotland Yard, but all their work resonates with what is being done on Area at the level of serious criminal investigation. He has to identify emerging crime problems and identify resources that can usefully be employed to help combat emerging crime.

To a degree, the many departments of Specialist Operations do not necessarily function as one, because their jobs are quite specific and they work within the broader plan of the Metropolitan Police. 'How we try and coordinate, so there is little friction and as much benign activity moving in one direction as possible, is to cluster into families. My family is the crime family.'

The Crime Operations Group (SO10) act as his confidential secretariat. 'Then there's Criminal Intelligence, and then the Force Firearms Unit. That's the crime family. Then there's an identifiable protection family, an identifiable security family, and a forensic family which is almost in two parts, the laboratory and the photographic fingerprint side, and if you want to be complete there's the Criminal Records side as well.'

The families are in many ways independent pillars which come together on an everyday basis in order to serve the Metropolitan Police as a whole.

As DAC (Crime), Veness bears the brunt of vociferous criticism of the high crime rate.

'We enjoy a very happy position compared with a great many other capitals around the world. To the amazement of almost everybody else, we are an unarmed police service. That is because there is not, at the moment, an overwhelming need to respond in an armed way to the level of crime that we've got. Now that's an enormously important statement, and it puts us apart from the levels of crime that exist pretty well everywhere else in the world. They've not only got armed police forces, they've got armed private security as a routine, so I think we need to view London in the context of where it sits within the world.'

But that, he was quick to add, does not mean anyone has cause to be complacent about the poor detection figures.

'There is a great impetus to put policing at the localised level and to force resources on to the street, because that's what the public want, they want reassurance, and they find reassurance in the presence of a uniform. At the same time we have burgeoning serious crime problems – there's armed robbery, there's counterfeiting, there's fraud on a grand scale, there's money laundering, there's everything associated with drug trafficking and worse to come. Now, we must look at those two sets of facts alongside each other. At the moment localised policing is in the ascendant and has the political will behind it. I find that slightly unimaginative, and my own preference would be for a rather more balanced perception that recognises what serious crime can do to society.'

He believes there is a lack of political will addressing itself to the upper end of the crime problem. The reason, he believes, is that serious crime like fraud or money laundering is not seen as a pressing issue, it is insidious. But if those crimes are disregarded they actually have a far more damaging effect on the social structure.

To do the job that he and his people are supposed to do, he could use twice as much of everything. 'I need twice as much in terms of rewards to informants, in terms of technical resources, and I could use twice the number of men and women that I've got at the moment.'

It ought to be a *sine qua non*, he says, that the criminal justice system is at the heart of the Metropolitan Police fight against serious and organised crime. In his judgement that is not so true as it should be.

'We are going through a phase where the criminal justice system is less of a factor in the serious villain's mind than it was ten or certainly twenty years ago.'

And that, he believes, is because, although nowadays the methods of investigation and interrogation are far more effective than they used to be, a battery of 'democratic' measures aimed at making the law fairer to the accused have effectively reduced the ability of the police to get convictions in court.

Disclosure is a particularly severe obstacle to criminal prosecutions. 'I think it is unhelpful if informants think that routinely they will be exposed by the process of criminal trials, because that may see the end of informants. They are absolutely critical, and there is no detective, no lawyer and no judge in the world who has ever come to a different conclusion after years in this business.'

Commander George Ness says, 'It was a lot easier in the old days to arrest and process criminals and to take cases through the courts. Now every case is a battle. Every case has with it a packet of paperwork. The Criminal Prosecution Service are an inhibiting factor, and they have made the whole system much more clumsy. This business we're going through with Disclosure is absolute nonsense – well, it's not a nonsense, it's founded on the highest of principles, that if there is evidence that will tend to affect the verdict on someone being prosecuted, then those facts must be available to everyone. That's laudable, we must all support that. But the process of Disclosure and making sure everything is looked at is so cumbersome, so time-consuming and so inhibiting that it's contributing to the whole legal system grinding to a halt.'

Another concern is the credibility of police in the light of several recent well publicised appeals which exposed police malpractice. George Ness sees a reversal in the shape of EPIC, which stands for Evidence Priority Implementation Committee. EPIC looks at methods the police use in giving evidence, and analyses why some police evidence is disbelieved.

'We're looking at all sorts of ways to build integrity factors into police evidence, so that scurrilous things that did not happen cannot be alleged by the other side.'

In a recent speech Veness touched on the topic of advance signs in serious and organised crime, and he identified Eastern Europe as the next area of major concern for London.

'One can look around the world and see where the major threats are coming from,' he said. 'They come from the cartels of South America, with the drug trafficking that is taking place through Southern Europe and, increasingly, through other European capitals and ports.

In referring to Eastern and Central European and, indeed, to Russian criminals, I was highlighting the dangers of arms trafficking, because, although the Russians have done extraordinarily well in keeping together the infrastructure of the Red Army, there has inevitably been a spillage in weaponry and, not only that, there is an enormous amount of weaponry available within Russian criminal society. We know that some of that is haemorrhaging westwards, and in London, where we have just a limited number of firearms within our criminal community, just a few more could actually change our life more significantly than in Amsterdam or Paris.'

Veness' remarks were underscored in August 1993, when armed police in London seized twenty-six weapons, among them several from Eastern Europe.

Ness, too, can foresee a dangerous criminal imbalance in Britain emanating from the political and social changes in Europe. 'This idea of free movement with a hard boundary is all very well in theory, but I'm not so sure it's going to be as effective as it should be in practice. In free Europe we're going to have problems with the people who have been deposed from Yugoslavia, Turkey, places like that. Some of them will come here, some will organise and some will commit offences. There's a great deal of what we call organised crime in what was the old USSR, and I think we'll get some of them over here.'

We are a soft target, he says. 'Our policemen are not armed, we've got a criminal justice system that is creaking and is totally ineffective, we haven't got room in our prisons for all the people we would like to lock up. This is still a fairly well-off country, there's quite a lot of money about.'

So what can be done? Veness says the Metropolitan

Police can take steps to assist their colleagues on the ground in the European capitals. 'We've already begun sending officers over to Eastern Europe and Russia. We will continue that and we will welcome their officers here, in order to ensure their systems of policing become as effective as possible, given the enormous difficulties they face.'

The presence in London of criminal rings and syndicates originating abroad is a cause for relentless vigilance on the part of Specialist Operations.

'The Chinese Triads, not surprisingly, prey mostly on the Chinese community,' Veness said. 'I suspect we are not as aware as we might be of the degree to which the Chinese community suffers extortion at the hands of the Triad groups.'

He says that nobody quite knows what is going to happen with the Triads. 'Some of us are fearful that if there are great changes in Hong Kong in 1997, then we might see some more Triad-associated people coming into the UK.'

The Yardies, a Jamaican criminal organisation operating in the United Kingdom and the USA, are unusual as a crime group, according to Veness. The pyramidal and hierarchical structures detectable in other groups is very elusive in their case, almost invisible. They are also a worry in the broader context of policing London, because the use of firearms appears to be prevalent among them, almost as a routine of their drug and inter-dealer activity.

'Now if you've got the presence of violence,' Veness says, 'and violence reinforced by guns in the inner-city communities where there may be a significant immigrant proportion in your population, then you've not only got a crime problem, you've got a broader violence problem, and you've also got a potential social disorder problem.

We need to treat the Caribbean criminal particularly seriously.'

Penetrating the Yardies is very difficult, Ness said, because they are not just ordinary young men from Jamaica. They are fearsomely distinctive.

'It's no good saying, "That officer is black, therefore we'll ask him to penetrate that group," because he'll stick out like a sore thumb. By and large he's born in the UK, he's decent, he's respectable. These people aren't. The difference would show. I think we need to do something about penetrating them, though. We need to be more proactive.'

Ness believes the difficulty in tracking down armed robbers today lies in the way gangs will divide and regroup in different combinations for different crimes.

'If there's a group of ten or twelve people who are armed robbers by profession, "project" people as opposed to one-off jobs, you will find that three or four of that group will come together to do something, and perhaps on another occasion it will be a different three or four doing it.'

There is still a territorial element in serious crime in London, but Ness says it is nothing compared to the old days.

'There's no real dispute over territory. There may be a dispute over fields of operation, like drugs or pornography, and they may defend their right to deal in that kind of crime, but there's not the same degree of geographical division and defending of territory that there used to be. I mean, the Krays were the East End and a bit of the West End, the Richardsons were clearly a South London gang. I don't think that exists any more.'

Reverting to the topic of drug trafficking, Veness says the gun in the hand of the trafficker is the most dangerous element of the illegal drugs scene.

'The dealers in crack, the suppliers, the importers, are violent people, very, very violent people. They have access to lots of guns and they will shoot each other and anybody else who gets in their way.'

Taking that into account, along with other indicators of an increase in the use of firearms in crime, Ness believes that the Metropolitan Police will eventually have to be armed.

'I think it's inevitable,' he says. 'We've now got ARVs [Armed Response Vehicles] which are one of my responsibilities. We've had them for two years. Five years ago, if you'd said, "Let's put some policemen who are permanently armed, or have permanent ready access to firearms, on the streets on a twenty-four-hour basis," people would have thrown up their hands in horror and said, "No, we can't do that." I think when the ARVs we have are no longer sufficient to service our needs we'll go for more. If the level of gun violence being offered to officers and citizens goes up, and we say we want an armed policeman there within five minutes, that really means an ARV on each Division, and once you have got that, it's but a small step to saying that all police officers should be armed.'

Veness believes that he and his people have a responsibility to be vigilant observers of the threat from international organised crime, and that a special group should be formed to address the responsibility.

'In broad terms, I would see such a group functioning on a three-by-three system, which would need strategic and policy direction. The first tier would address the delicate issues of confidentiality, privacy and individual liberty. The second might have to address specific areas of criminality such as the Latin American drugs threat, and that may well spawn activity at a third level which is looking at specific targets, criminal structures and criminals, to see what could be done to disrupt their activities. So that's the first set of three. The other three would be what could actually be done in terms of the attack, and again I would see criminal structures and identified organisations being the first tier of targets. The second tier would be actual individuals whose activities are prominent within those structures. Thirdly, we would need to address broad preventative issues, what could be done within society to make our defences better. That's the three-by-three approach that we broadly envisage.'

Talking of the work of SO10 (Crime Operations Group) and SO11 (Criminal Intelligence Branch), two departments which operate well away from the limelight, Veness says they take the police to a stage of criminal activity and the workings of criminals where they interrupt, interdict and disrupt at a much earlier stage than has been the case historically. They also take a broader view, they look for a wider scheme of criminality rather than responding to one-off criminal acts.

'So we present the totality of villainy before the courts, rather than the isolated incidents. It's enormously important that one should see it in context. Some colleagues are suggesting that by the year 2000 the whole approach will be proactive, supported by intelligence. I'm more cautious, I think we need to persist on the broad front.

'By the year 2000 we will run combined operations between London and Moscow, but that does not mean that the broad aspect of crime that affects the average person who lives and works in London is going to be impacted by a factor of 80 per cent or 90 per cent by these innovations. If I'm fortunate I will get the resources to move into key areas of criminality. In terms of the serious crime that affects violence within inner cities, I would also hope to be as proactive in intelligence and in an innovative way as is possible.'

Veness says that many people still subscribe to the sentimental myth that the Metropolitan Police practices of twenty-five years ago were more reliable and down-to-earth than those being used and proposed in today's technological era. Yet twenty-five years ago corruption was widespread throughout the Yard, and corruption within the police has the potential for doing the most damage to the service.

'The officer who pursues a path of corruption seeks to do so in an atmosphere of closeted confidentiality,' Veness says. 'The technical era destroys that confidentiality because the very systems portrayed as intrusive are also intrusive into corrupt activity. The chances of the product of that material, and thus the nefarious behaviour, becoming known to other officers are thereby enhanced.' Widespread technical control, he argues, virtually rules out corruption.

Veness points out there is a consoling fact, besides the widespread use of technology, that separates the present era of policing in London from that of twenty-five years ago.

'Nowadays wrongdoing among police officers is brought to our notice by other police officers,' he said. 'Twenty-five years ago, it was brought to our attention by criminals.'

SO 1

International and Organised Crime

The range of work that SO1 tackles includes illegal immigration and deportation, war crimes, cheque fraud, jury protection and arts and antiques crime. On the surface it would appear to be a ragbag of police roles, with no obvious links.

Detective Chief Superintendent Tom Glendinning points to a central logic. Officers skilled at investigating major crime often have to consult specialists; specialists, in their turn, have occasion to tap the knowledge of people experienced in handling broad-scale crime. In SO1 these needs are brought together under one organisational umbrella.

'The reality of it is that someone somewhere has got to be flexible. Someone has got to take on that investigation that doesn't fit comfortably with any others – and we attract a large proportion of those investigations.'

Perhaps six or seven 'families' of organised criminals dominate the major part of high-profit crime in London, and while there is no longer a team within SO1 specifically targeting them, Glendinning says they don't entirely escape the attention of his officers: 'We do, from time to time, attack some of these groups.'

SO1(1), the Reserve Squad, had its origins in the old Murder Squad, who used to assist other police forces who lacked the capacity or the skills to deal with major crimes. Today, a stated function of SO1(1) is to provide a reserve, headed by senior detectives, to investigate offences of murder and other complicated or confidential inquiries within the Metropolitan Police District, the rest of the United Kingdom, or internationally.

SO1 are quite often called to foreign countries. A team consisting of a Detective Superintendent, a Detective Inspector, a Detective Sergeant and often a specialist (e.g., a pathologist), can be mobilised within a day, if necessary, although two or three days would be more typical. 'We provide help where they have serious investigations to carry out – murder, say, perhaps serious assaults, even corruption.'

'We also go to crimes at sea,' Glendinning said. 'If it's a British registered ship, and if we are requested, then we investigate major crimes on ships.'

On home territory the Reserve Squad often carry out investigations within Government departments. They are sometimes asked to review old cases on behalf of the Home Office – one such was a review of the Craig and Bentley case.

'A current investigation,' Glendinning said, 'concerns a large number of the Jewish community in London receiving a Christmas card containing anti-Semitic material. It will take a considerable time to investigate.'

The reason this case is dealt with by SO1(1) rather than an Area Major Investigation Pool (AMIP) is that the investigation is likely to be widespread, complicated and quite probably intensive, three factors which suit the case particularly to the resources and expertise of the Reserve Squad.

'We are also responsible for supervising jury protection,' said Glendinning. 'We have to protect the jury *and* investigate allegations of attempts to coerce them. Cases usually involve people of some substance from within the various criminal enterprises. They take precautions to ensure that any subsequent investigations are unlikely to be successful.'

The protection of juries is carried out by uniformed officers, who are supervised by officers of SO1. Glendinning did not want to go into the details of how jurors are 'nobbled'.

'The reality is that some of it is very, very sophisticated. Clearly we have direct threats to juries. We have had more than just a hint that substantial amounts of money have been offered to jurors to return favourable verdicts. Some of it, though, is much more subtle than that.'

Another responsibility of SO1 is to investigate criminal offences that happen in any of the Royal residences within the Metropolitan Police district. 'We've had thefts, we've had intruders. Fortunately they are very, very rare and that's the way we want to keep it.'

An outpost unit working within SO1(1) are the Chemist Inspection Sergeants, a group of eight Detective Sergeants commonly called the Chemistry Sergeants.

The Arts and Antiques Squad also comes under SO1(1). It is one of the smallest operational squads in Scotland Yard, consisting of only three officers with three civilian auxiliaries, although they can call on other detectives.

In 1984 Arts and Antiques was disbanded, because the police felt that other categories of crime had a higher priority. Distinguished quarters of the arts and antique trade campaigned for the squad to be reinstated; in 1989 the squad was re-formed with two officers who had received two weeks training at Christie's.

Glendinning agrees that the squad is unrealistically small, even allowing for the occasional supplementary help.

'But I think we have to assess the need against our

resources, and try at least to achieve some middle ground, so that we satisfy the art world's demands, and the demands of the general public in London.'

(1) RESERVE SQUAD

Formerly known as the Major Investigation Pool, the Reserve Squad encompasses a whole range of police work, from the investigation of serious crimes both at home and abroad, to jury protection and the operation of the Arts and Antiques Squad.

One of the Reserve Squad's most remarkable cases in recent years was the murder of Dr Robert John Ouko, the Kenyan Foreign Minister, who disappeared from his home at Koru, near Lake Victoria in Western Kenya, on the night of 12 February 1990.

Detective Sergeant Ken Lindsay described the background. 'He had come back at the beginning of February from a trip to America with the President of Kenya, Daniel Arap Moi, and several other MPs,' says Lindsay. 'They had been given a week off to go home and have a rest. Ouko went missing on the Monday night and was found dead on Friday morning in scrub land about three miles from his home. The body was badly burned and there was evidence of a single gunshot wound through the head. Initial investigations by the Kenyan authorities suggested Ouko had committed suicide. The public in Kenya were not satisfied with that, and as a result Scotland Yard were called in to investigate.'

The SO1(1) Reserve Team was headed by Detective Superintendent John Troon and his deputy Detective Inspector Graham Dennis. They were assisted by Detective Sergeant Ken Lindsay and Detective David Sanderson from the Scotland Yard Science Laboratory. A pathologist, Dr Ian West, was also part of the team.

Ouko's death had triggered serious unrest; he was a leader of the Luo tribe, the second largest in Kenya, and students from the tribe led riots in the streets of Nairobi, openly blaming the Government for Ouko's death, which had been officially declared a suicide. As soon as the Scotland Yard Team arrived the pathologist, Ian West, carried out an autopsy on Ouko's body. His findings left him in no doubt that this was a case of murder.

'There were a number of factors which led him to say this,' Lindsay explained, 'but the main one was that the shot to the head would have killed Ouko instantly; there would have been no chance for him to set fire to himself afterwards.'

The civil unrest began to settle down as word travelled that the Scotland Yard team were treating the death as murder. The team based themselves at Kisumu, on the edge of Lake Victoria, where the entire top floor of a hotel served as their offices and accommodation. A team of ten or twelve Kenyan police officers were assigned to help them.

'Only two or three of them were competent,' said Lindsay. 'The main worry we had about them was that, although it was a confidential inquiry, and we were reporting directly back to the Commissioner in London, the Kenyan police were reporting back to their immediate supervisors. So we couldn't make a move without other people knowing about it, and I think without a doubt all our phones were bugged, and probably our rooms.'

The investigation was fraught with minor intrigues and deceits. The Kenyan Commissioner of Police had assured the Scotland Yard team that theirs was the only investigation into Ouko's murder, but in fact the Kenyan Special Branch were carrying out an investigation of their own.

'Almost every witness we interviewed was interviewed again soon afterwards by Kenyan Special Branch. They didn't want us to find out anything that was going to embarrass them. On one occasion we were about to arrest four people and interview them, but the morning before we got to them the Kenyan Special Branch arrested them and locked them up for five days for rumour-mongering. That was how it went nearly all the way through.'

In spite of poor cooperation and blatant obstruction, the Scotland Yard investigators uncovered a startlingly clear picture of corruption leading up to Robert Ouko's murder.

'He was probably the only honest man in the Kenyan Government,' said Lindsay. 'He had a reputation for being honest, he wouldn't take a penny – I think Ouko was respected and trusted by Margaret Thatcher and the Americans, and I think he was a problem. At the time he disappeared he was due to deliver a report on corruption in Kenya to President Moi.'

Among those on whom suspicions of corruption centred were a government minister and Heziaki Oyugi, the top civil servant and the Head of State Security. 'It was said of any corrupt deals done in Kenya that 15 per cent would be paid to the minister: in fact his nickname was Mr Fifteen Per Cent. And then 10 per cent would go to Oyugi on top of that. These were probably the figures Ouko was going to report on.'

The SO1 Team's inquiries revealed that Oyugi had been in the vicinity of Ouko's home just before he disappeared; at interview he denied it, but there was positive proof. Attempts to interview the minister were not successful; even when firm appointments were made, he simply ignored them. Eventually both Oyugi and he were arrested, with several others, after the Scotland Yard Team gave evidence to the Kenyan Commission of Inquiry.

'The minister was sacked,' Lindsay said, 'although I believe he's still an MP, and Oyugi was sacked as Head of State Security. The man whom we believe was Oyugi's runner is at present charged with murder. He met us from the plane, he was everywhere with us, and he reported back to Oyugi. Every time we saw Oyugi, he was there. If we wanted to go anywhere Oyugi provided the transport and his runner would go with us.' Oyugi was also charged with murder.

The investigation by Scotland Yard, which became increasingly difficult, went on four months. In the end there was virtually no cooperation from the Kenyan side, so it was decided, because the obstructions made it impossible to move forward, that the team should withdraw, complete their report and give it to the President. That was what they did, and following the delivery of their findings President Moi set up a Commission of Inquiry in Nairobi.

'Oyugi has since died, of motor neurone disease, in a hospital in London,' said Lindsay. 'Nearly a dozen people who were witnesses in this investigation have also died. One of the first deaths was that of a driver, who gave very important evidence about the movements of Oyugi's runner, and about the fact that his car was in use at the time of Ouko's disappearance. His car had been used but the petrol consumption and mileage had not been recorded. The driver died from poisoning, although obviously we've never investigated that, and the Kenyan authorities say there was nothing suspicious.'

The minister spent fourteen days in prison, then he was released without charge. His runner is the only person now in prison in connection with Ouko's murder.

It was obvious that the Scotland Yard investigation stirred up unforeseen trouble in Kenya, and in the end their presence was a severe embarrassment. This could hardly have been what the authorities had in mind when they invited the Yard to investigate.

'I think they believed that when Scotland Yard detectives went out there,' Lindsay said, 'they would turn round and say Ouko's death was a suicide. When that didn't happen I think they were shocked. And having called us out there they were stuck with us. We went about our investigation and they did not like it at all.'

While Lindsay is convinced that President Moi had no part in the death of Robert Ouko, it was clear from many aspects of the case that dishonesty among the authorities was widespread, and there was blatant tampering with evidence.

'In some photographs of the body there was a gun by the head, in others there was no gun,' Lindsay said. 'When a gun was located it was dusted for fingerprints and a partial print was found. It was sent to Nairobi for further examination, but by the time it got to Nairobi there were no fingerprints on it. John Troon ordered that the gun be sealed and not test fired, so that it could be sent back to London for examination. But they did test fire it, they ruined the evidence.'

Even when the Scotland Yard team asked to see the test-fired bullets, they were sent three bullets that had been fired from a different gun. The degree of tampering in the case almost amounted to farce. The body had been moved after death even though it was claimed that it had not, and the Kenyan pathologist, Jason Kaviti, had made out no fewer than three separate death certificates in the name of Dr Robert Ouko, each with a different cause of death. It was also found that Kaviti had told lies, and it was not until the Commission of Inquiry that he changed his mind and agreed that Ouko had not committed suicide after all.

'At the end of Kaviti's evidence,' Lindsay said, 'the judge in charge of the Commission of Inquiry said something like, "We can't stop you investigating deaths, Dr Kaviti, but when you go away from this inquiry, please stop falsifying death certificates."' Jason Kaviti is still Kenya's senior pathologist.

While the team was in Kenya, Lindsay said, the local people seemed to think that Scotland Yard officers came from Scotland. 'In fact I was the only Scottish person there. When we walked down the streets of Kisumu people would come up and shake hands with us, and they would clap as we were walking down the street doing our shopping. When we were driving along in a car, people on the street and standing in bus queues would wave and clap as soon as they saw us drive past.'

The team virtually became household names, Lindsay said. 'Although people didn't really know who we were, or what we did or what not, they trusted us 100 per cent to find out what happened. They had a great belief in us. They had no belief whatsoever in their own police or their own Government.'

Other cases illustrate the variety of investigations carried out by the Reserve Teams of SO1(1).

On 12 November 1974 a distressed young woman, dishevelled and bleeding from head wounds, ran into a Belgravia pub and shouted, 'He's murdered my nanny! My children! My children!'

She was Lady Lucan, the wife of Richard John

Bingham, Earl of Lucan. Later, Lady Lucan said that her husband had beaten the nanny, Sandra Rivett, in the basement of their home, and then attacked Lady Lucan when she intervened. Sandra Rivett died of her injuries. Since that day no one has been able to trace Lord Lucan.

'Things hadn't been going well in the family,' said Detective Superintendent Alec Edwards of SO1(1). 'He wasn't getting on with his wife, he had a drinking habit and a gambling habit. He had moved out of the family home to another address, but there were still nasty telephone conversations between them. On the night of the murder it would appear he thought the nanny had left for the day. The light had been removed in the particular area of the house where she was attacked.'

The nanny was beaten about the head with a lead pipe. The accepted theory is that, in the gloom, Lord Lucan mistook her for his wife. Lady Lucan walked into the same area shortly after the nanny was attacked and found herself being beaten about the head. After a few moments it stopped and Lady Lucan recognised the attacker as her husband. He carried her back to the bedroom and bathed her wounds. She broke away from him and ran to a local pub for help. When the police arrived at the house Lucan had disappeared. Subsequently, an inquest named him as the murderer of Sandra Rivett.

'The case is still open,' said Edwards. 'The policy has been that it will remain open until he is found, or until he is proved to be dead. The Press still publish reports of people claiming to have seen him in various parts of the world. There is still some family interest, too – his son has been trying to have his father officially pronounced dead, with a view to settling the trustee estates. That's still going through the courts.'

Edwards says it is hard to have an opinion about the case. 'Certainly after the murder he laid low for some days, we can prove he went to stay with some friends. After that it's open to speculation. I would suggest that if he did stay alive, then he is outside of the UK, possibly somewhere like Australia, South Africa, somewhere that's fairly easy for a fugitive to hide away and keep from being noticed.'

Fifty or sixty times a year, Edwards estimated, something will happen – an alleged sighting or some other small possible development – to make him or other officers take another look at the case papers.

Many people believe Lucan took his own life. He wrote to the family suggesting that he might be on the verge of doing himself harm, and in a letter to friends he asked them to look after his children, going on to indicate that he did not expect to see them again.

Examining the investigative papers, Edwards finds that opinion is sharply divided. One camp believes Lord Lucan committed suicide close to the time he disappeared, while others think he lived on for many years and might still be alive. Edwards believes he is still alive.

'I've read the papers through and through again,' he said, 'and, apart from that ambiguous note, there's nothing to suggest to me that he ever committed suicide.'

And when a fugitive is alive, Edwards believes, there is always a chance of catching him. Every alleged sighting of Lucan that appears to have substance is followed up; if the report comes from abroad then the checking is done through Interpol, or police-to-police with the country in question. Sightings have been reported and investigated throughout Europe and in various states of Australia, as well as in Zambia and Zimbabwe in central Africa, and in Botswana in the south.

'The investigation is becoming one of the longest-running on Scotland Yard files,' Edwards said, 'although the Jack the Ripper case is probably the longest.'

Lucan was not well resourced at the time he disappeared. 'He was in considerable debt. For some time his only source of income had been from gambling.'

A plausible theory is that friends looked after Lucan for a long time, keeping him away from public view, and eventually the ageing process produced its own disguise. To provide themselves with at least a notion of how he might look now, Scotland Yard have photographs of Lucan to simulate the natural changes over a twenty-year period.

Edwards acknowledged that his chances of ever solving the Lucan case are remote. But he does not take that personally. 'The case goes with the office,' he said. 'If I don't sort it out, somebody else will come along and try.'

A case investigated by Edwards in 1990 involved the murder of former Great Train Robber Charlie Wilson at his home in Marbella, on Spain's Costa del Sol.

'Wilson had been released from prison some years earlier,' Edwards said. 'He'd sold up in the UK, moved down to Marbella, and was actively engaged with other people down there, mostly in drug dealing.'

On 23 April Wilson and his wife, Pat, were joined by friends to celebrate their thirty-fifth wedding anniversary. Later, in the early evening when the friends had left and only Wilson and his wife were in the house, there was a ring on the doorbell. Wilson was preparing a salad in the kitchen so Pat answered the door. A young man with a baseball cap pulled down over his eyes, a Londoner by his accent, asked to see Wilson. Pat called her husband and he came at once; he and the visitor exchanged quiet words, then walked across the patio in the direction of the barbecue. Pat Wilson remained indoors. After a few minutes she heard raised voices, then two loud bangs.

She ran outside and saw her husband staggering towards the pool with blood spurting from a wound in his neck. He collapsed by the pool and died almost at once. The attacker had meanwhile escaped over the garden wall.

An examination of Wilson's body revealed that he had been kicked hard in the testicles. When he doubled over a vicious punch broke his nose. He was then shot twice at zero range with a Smith and Wesson revolver; one bullet entered his neck and severed the carotid artery, the second was fired into his mouth and came out through the back of his head.

'The case is still under Spanish jurisdiction,' Edwards said. 'What happened was, like so many cases we pick up, the body was returned to the UK so the local coroner could hold an inquest. In this case Westminster were the authority. Since this was a British subject killed out in Spain, the coroner asked us to look into the case on his behalf and report back to him for the inquest. Which we did. I went down to Marbella and discussed the matter with the local police, and over a period of time we conducted our own investigation. What emerged was, we had two British subjects, also involved in drug smuggling, who were suspected of carrying out the execution. One kept watch while the other did the shooting.'

No one has ever been arrested or charged with Charlie Wilson's murder, although the Spanish police believe the killers are two young Englishmen who had escaped in 1989 while being transferred from Albany Prison on the Isle of Wight to Blundeston in Suffolk. At the time of their escape one had been serving thirteen years for armed robbery and the other was doing nine years for fraud and drug offences. When Pat Wilson was shown a picture of one of them in London, she said she was 60 to 70 per cent sure he was the man who killed her husband.

'But there are one or two other people still outstanding,' Edwards said. 'We'd like to interview them and hold identity parades, should they come to the notice of the police. But the matter will still have to go back to Spain – they have the jurisdiction over the case.'

Chemist Inspection Sergeants

Eight Detective Sergeants, one for each Metropolitan Police Area, enforce the regulations governing pharmacists and the storage and trade in dangerous drugs at their retail premises. The officers, usually known as chemistry sergeants, have the task of checking the drug registers in chemists' shops to confirm that dangerous drugs on the premises have been obtained legally, and that amounts issued to customers are covered by doctors' prescriptions.

'Chemists are like everybody else – there are people within the profession who are not playing the game,' said Detective Chief Inspector John Butler, who heads the Chemist Inspection Sergeants' department and the Arts and Antiques Squad. 'They can have more prescription drugs on the premises than they should have.'

A current investigation involves temazepam, a sleeping drug which can become highly addictive. 'It's used in Glasgow and some other cities in the north as a substitute for heroin. Because it's a prescribable drug, the chemists can get it legally. Some of them have been buying it in large quantities and taking it up to Glasgow and other places, selling it there and making large profits. Cocaine is another thing; they can have it legally on their premises, and some of them have been selling it off or using it themselves.'

There are no particular legal loopholes that permit the abuses. If the Chemist Inspection Sergeants were able to look at the books more often than they do – at present they aim to make one visit a year to each chemist's shop in London – levels of dishonest trading would shrink, although some fraudulent methods of record-keeping are harder to detect than others. The problem is widespread and appears to be growing. The cash transactions in individual cases highlight the attraction in this branch of crime. 'In the temazepam investigation there have been seven arrests,' Butler said, 'and we're talking about four or five million pounds' worth – and that's just one case.'

Some investigations start because of tip-offs, others arise directly from inspection of the books. Chemist Inspection Sergeants are arresting pharmacists at the rate of approximately one a week. Those usually involved are from smaller businesses, and in general there is no indication that the illicit trade is organised. There is evidence, nevertheless, that small-time *ad hoc* organisation does take place.

'The temazepam case was organised in the sense that a group of chemists dealt through a non-drug dealer in large amounts,' Butler said. 'That's not what is usually meant by "organised" crime, this was organised only in the sense that people got together and operated for a single purpose.'

Arts and Antiques Squad

Butler has no doubt that, next to drug trafficking and the arms trade, art is the biggest area of international crime. And yet he sets out to combat it with one Detective Inspector, two operational officers and three civilian assistants.

During 1991 and 1992 the Arts and Antiques Squad was involved in the recovery of stolen art works to a total value of £13,348,000. Among the property recovered was a quantity of silver stolen from premises in New Bond Street, a Brueghel worth £2 million stolen from the Courtauld Institute, four Korans stolen in Rhodes, and three paintings worth a total of £2 million stolen in transit between London and Portugal.

'It has been said that the Arts and Antiques Squad is very much élitist,' said Butler. 'I don't think that. My view is that arts and antiques are just commodities like any others. Mr Smith in Brixton has probably got property that is dear to him, maybe something that's been passed on from his father, or medals, or something that was given to him in retirement. We have to reduce crime in that area as much as we do in the area of priceless jewellery or paintings worth millions.'

Butler believes that for the squad to function at maximum efficiency an adequate database should be in place, listing everything from missing chairs worth a couple of hundred pounds to works of art worth millions. It happens that the Arts and Antiques Squad already has the beginning of a fine database. It is called ACIS (Article Classification Identification System). ACIS, which costs less than £1,000, is a computer program which runs on a normal PC and stores information on stolen articles in files from which data can be retrieved at speed. Additionally, ACIS displays a small coloured picture (or icon) of any stolen item in the database; this can be blown up to a full-size colour image on the screen, or printed out with a laser printer as a coloured picture on paper.

At present the Arts and Antiques Squad has only a London brief, but Butler would like them to become a national squad. The database will go a long way towards making that possible.

Without prime-quality data to hand, Butler believes, the service on offer can only be sub-standard.

'We don't get much cooperation from the art world, and the reason is because we haven't been very useful or helpful to them, and any time they've tried to help they've either got their fingers burnt or come away with mud on their faces.

'There must be warehouses full of stolen property, but nobody knows it's stolen. And down here we wouldn't know it was stolen if it was stolen up in Cumberland, for example, even if they told us.'

At the time Butler spoke, a number of Italians were buying up art in London, and a telephone call had set inquiries in motion.

'The implications are that they are spending Mafia money, or drugs money. And this comes just after an inquiry we've carried out that links the Mafia with art and drugs.'

Art purchase, especially of paintings and other commodities with a stable price, is a good way of laundering money. The buyers purchase with drug money, for example, then send back the artworks to their own country, where they are sold again for clean, untraceable money.

'We have good connections with the Italians, in fact there are three Italian police officers here at the moment. We will liaise with them, and on the back of that we will put together a job, if we can identify the people who are buying.'

The recovery of a stolen Brueghel painting was a recent

case handled by the Arts and Antiques Squad. The picture, dating from 1565, is entitled *Christ and the Woman Taken in Adultery*, and depicts Christ on his knees pleading with the elders for tolerance while a woman stands by, her head bowed. When the picture was stolen from the Courtauld Institute Galleries in London in 1982, a man simply walked in, unhooked it from the screen where it was hanging, put it under his coat and walked out. It remained untraced until 1990.

'We received information that a famous picture was being offered,' said Detective Sergeant Tony Russell. 'They thought it had come from Switzerland, and that it was currently being touted around in London for sale.'

The information reached the Arts and Antiques Squad from more than one source, and soon Christie's were in touch, too, saying they had been called by a man who did not identify himself, but who said he had a picture for sale. From the description he gave, a valuer at Christie's immediately recognised the picture as the Brueghel stolen from the Courtauld Galleries in 1982.

'The caller talked a lot of rubbish to Christie's,' Russell said. 'He said he was a property developer, he had invested in the painting and he wanted to sell it. As a result of the call to Christie's, we got in touch with Dr Dennis Farr, the Director of the Courtauld Institute Galleries, and asked him if he was contacted to give us a ring.'

After a few days Dr Farr called the Arts and Antiques Squad and reported that a man identifying himself as 'Mr Brewgal' – with the emphasis on the second syllable – had called and offered the painting back to him, for a price.

'I think it was two million pounds,' Russell said. 'The

initial payment was to be £880,000 in cash, and the rest telegraphically transferred. As a result of this, with Dr Farr's permission we began monitoring his phone, and calls continued to come in from Mr Brewgal. We then fed in an undercover officer purporting to work for the Getty Museum, and a meeting was arranged in the Savoy Hotel, which was attended by Dr Farr and the undercover officer.'

There was also a covert police presence inside the hotel – among them DS Tony Russell and DS Dick Ellis of the Arts and Antiques Squad – and surveillance was also mounted outside.

Four men showed up to meet Dr Farr and the bogus representative from the Getty Museum. Two of the men acted as surveillance – one in the corridor outside the room booked for the meeting, and one downstairs in the bar – and at that meeting a lot of time was spent trying to work out the means of transferring the money for the picture.

'It was pointed out to them that to carry £880,000 in cash was impossible,' Russell said, 'and that perhaps £250,000 would be a more acceptable sum, with the rest telegraphically transferred. In the end the meeting broke up with the promise that they would meet again the next day in the Savoy. But the suspects failed to appear next day or to make any arrangements, and it then went quiet for several weeks.'

In the meantime several Regional Crime Squads in London had also had word of the Brueghel being on offer, and they were all running their separate operations to get the picture back. A meeting was held at Scotland Yard where it was decided that whoever first saw the painting would follow through and get it back; the fine details of arrests and charges could be worked out later.

Eventually Brewgal established contact again and arrangements were made for a second meeting.

'But the day before the meeting was due to go down,' Russell said, 'the painting was recovered by one of the Regional Crime Squads from an address in South London. They had a search warrant for the address, and the search revealed the painting on top of a wardrobe.'

A man was arrested and charged, but he was subsequently acquitted when a court accepted his story that he was simply holding the picture for someone else, and he had no idea what he was looking after.

'Funnily enough,' Russell said, 'Mr Brewgal and his associates, despite the fact that the painting had already been recovered, continued to negotiate with Dr Farr, and another meeting was arranged.'

Mr Brewgal again failed to turn up for the meeting that had been arranged, but measures had already been taken to find out who he really was. Following the meeting at the Savoy he was followed down the A3 in the Mini he was driving; the surveillance was a shade too discreet and they lost him, but they did have the car's number and checked the ownership through the Police National Computer. The car was registered to a property development company in Hampshire.

A watch was put on the Hampshire offices and the addresses of people working at the property developers were obtained.

'We decided to get search warrants and go and check those addresses,' said Russell. 'In the early morning of the day we were to make the raids, we met in a Portakabin police station in the middle of the New Forest. About fifteen Scotland Yard officers were there to check on the various addresses, with the help of several local officers. During the briefing, I said that when I was listening to one of the tapes from Dr Farr's telephone, I had heard Brewgal refer to himself by his real name. Whereupon a Detective Constable from Hampshire, just sitting in on the briefing, put up his hand and said, "I know him." I ignored the remark, thinking, no, that's impossible.'

The briefing continued and the Detective Constable eventually put up his hand again and said, 'I definitely know the man.' So he was asked who he thought Brewgal really was, and he gave the name. This was a man who did not work for the company which had been under surveillance; he did not live in the area, either, he came from Sussex. But the Detective Constable insisted he was right, and when he was given a description of Brewgal – five foot ten, blond hair – he said, 'Yeah, that's him.'

'We still didn't believe him,' Russell said. 'The odds of one Detective Constable, in the middle of the New Forest, just happening to know a suspect for a major art theft in the middle of London – a suspect who is from Sussex and we're in Hampshire – well, it's hardly likely. However, the Detective Constable was adamant that he knew our man, so we obtained another search warrant, went with him to an address in Sussex, arrested a man and found all the relevant paperwork and bank accounts and everything that was necessary to link him with the crime.'

He had not stolen the picture. He was in on the operation because he had passed himself off as a highly connected commercial schemer with a working knowledge of the art world, and he had been brought in to market the Brueghel. In truth he was entirely out of his depth and had probably never sold a picture in his life.

In the end three more men were arrested. The man who stole the Brueghel was never found or even named, and no one ever discovered where the picture had been hidden for eight years. Three of the men were jailed for three years, the fourth for two and a half years.

'One of the things that came out of the case,' said Detective Sergeant Dick Ellis, 'and we've seen it in other operations, is this business of stolen works of art being offered for sale by more than one group of criminals simultaneously.' The signs are that criminals engaged in art and antique theft, in Britain anyway, are becoming uncomfortably businesslike. 'We've seen videotapes of storage houses and lock-ups where works of art stolen by one or more teams are kept, and they are held by very professional handlers of stolen goods.'

In the case of the Brueghel, it was just bad luck for the thief that the picture was not being held in a professionally organised warehouse; bad luck for the negotiators, too, that a fluke identification put their front man in the hands of the police.

Increasingly, the central-warehouse system means the police cannot intercept works of art during negotiations, and they can't trace them through the negotiators, since the objects are not there to be intercepted in the first place, and the negotiators have no traceable contact with the commodities they represent.

(3) EXTRADITION, IMMIGRATION AND PASSPORT SQUAD

The work of SO1(3) is divided into two parts, and Part One is subdivided into five units.

Section One – 1: Extradition

Detective Chief Inspector Wright explained, 'When a fugitive runs away after committing a crime, or from prison, and he's thought to be in the United Kingdom, his country asks us to make inquiries to try and establish that he's actually here. If we find he is, we then contact his country via Interpol or through diplomatic channels and ask if they want to have him extradited. If they say they do, we ask them to supply us with the appropriate details to get a warrant at Bow Street Court to arrest him.'

SO1(3) has a national responsibility which covers England, Wales, at certain times Scotland, Northern Ireland, the Isle of Man and the Channel Islands; all warrants towards extradition are issued at Bow Street Magistrates' Court in London. Of the fugitives sought every year by SO1(3), approximately 30 per cent are found and arrested, which means between seventy and ninety arrests every year. The police have noted that an increasing number of fugitives, learning from the mistakes of others, take the trouble to learn about local and international legal procedures and have developed ways of digging themselves into communities. Very often they provide themselves with passable credentials and simply maintain low social profiles.

'Once we've located our fugitive and we've proved by photographs or fingerprints that it's him, we then go into the legal process of getting the warrant. Once we've got the warrant we can make an arrest, and when we've arrested him we bring him back here. He's charged and he appears before the Bow Street Court. It's up to the magistrate whether he grants the man bail, but I'd say about 85 per cent of fugitives we get are wanted for serious crimes, so he is likely to be remanded in custody.'

Several areas of appeal are open to the fugitive. If his hearing takes place in a UK court and an extradition order is issued against him, he has fifteen days to appeal against the decision. If he does not appeal he must leave Britain within one calendar month. Police officers from the country requesting the extradition come to Scotland Yard and are then accompanied, with the prisoner, to the airport.

A straightforward extradition with no legal complications costs between ten and fifteen thousand pounds; a drawn-out procedure can amount to twice or three times that amount. The cost is a combination of the police time taken up and an estimation of court costs, and is usually met by the country requesting the extradition.

Britain has extradition treaties with approximately 150 countries, the terms varying from country to country. Member states of the EEC have a group arrangement, with a simplified extradition procedure that needs no exchange of detailed evidence: the country requesting extradition hands over a résumé of the case against the fugitive, together with copies of their warrants, and on that basis a magistrate considers the application. In the case of an extradition request from the USA, on the other hand, the American authorities have to produce copies of all their evidence against the fugitive before the British magistrate can make a determination.

Probably the most famous extradition case in recent years was that of Loraine Osman. 'He was arrested here at the request of the Hong Kong Government in May 1985 for a large fraud out in Hong Kong and Malaysia. He was arrested and ordered, after the court hearings, to go back to Hong Kong. He then started an appeal.'

Osman obtained a writ of habeas corpus, which in simple terms is a court order questioning the validity of his detention. By raising many arguments and legal doubts under the terms of no less than nine successive writs of habeas corpus, Osman was able to remain on remand until December 1992.

'So he was actually in custody in Brixton Prison as a remand prisoner for seven years,' said Wright. 'It made legal history. It was when he put in his tenth writ of habeas corpus that the House of Lords said, "No, you won't be granted leave to appeal." And it was only then that the Home Secretary said, "Yes, he can be removed from the United Kingdom." So he went back on the 15 December to Hong Kong.' Wright admitted that he moved fast on that extradition – certainly fast enough to prevent Osman using any new delaying tactics. 'You have to be quick. It's an old saying – when the window's open, you go through it.'

Following Osman's return to Hong Kong, all charges against him were dropped and he was set free.

Section One – 2: British Passport Offences

In certain foreign countries the going price for a British Passport is as high as £12,000. In Hong Kong, where anxieties about the Chinese takeover in 1997 have made foreign citizenship the ultimate in desirability, Scotland Yard investigators have uncovered a racket where UK passports were being sold for one million Hong Kong dollars, which is about £80,000. There are people who find this a reasonable price for a document which lets them travel the world freely for ten years without the need for visas.

'Kuwait's another example,' said Wright; 'a place of unrest, people want to get out. Taiwan, they're an industrialised society, very wealthy, but the people want to have the opportunity to travel freely.'

The demand for passports is so strong that Home Office employees have been offered large sums of money to steal them or have them printed. Drug runners are always in the market for passports, since a long career in that business relies on regular identity-changes and freedom to travel when they must.

'With a British passport,' said Wright, '90 per cent of the time you don't need a visa, so a drug-runner can just walk into a country – even America now, if he wanted. A British passport and you're in. The same if you want to go to Canada. Going back to Hong Kong, we're finding that the Triads are using them, which is a problem.'

A recent investigation by SO1(3) disclosed that an employee of the Passport Office at Petty France was accepting money from the Triads – between £1,000 and £1,500 a time – to print out complete British passports at a computer terminal. The man, who was eventually imprisoned, admitted that he had made twenty-nine irregular passports.

Further inquiries led SO1(3) detectives to Germany. They ran an operation in cooperation with the German police, who arrested fifty-three people. Among the passports seized were twenty-four which had been produced by the man in London. Several other British people are currently being held on charges of providing passports illegally.

'We don't look at the one-off false application,' said Wright. 'We look at the organisers, earning large sums of money getting passports for particular types of people.'

Applicants for passports are often caught using false or forged names of counter-signees of the application forms. The late John Stonehouse, a discredited MP and one-time Minister of Posts and Telecommunications in the Wilson Government, tried the same tactic in 1974, picking up the idea from the novel, *The Day of the Jackal*; he actually managed to get a passport under a false name. It is harder to use that tactic successfully now that regulations have been tightened, but new 'scams' are always being devised by specialists in this branch of crime, who regard restrictions as nothing more than small barricades around massive opportunities.

Wright talked about a case involving the use of fake credentials on a large scale. 'It was an extradition and passport investigation. A British captain, his first mate, and a crew half English and half Malaysian. They were importing ninety tons a time of cannabis into the United States, doing the runs on a regular basis. When they were caught, it was found that each of the Britons on board had five or six British passports in different names. They had huge assets – we've recovered about £800,000 and in the States they've seized about £5 million. British passports in different names are worth any price to these people. If it comes to the crunch, a drug importer or a terrorist can just drop one name and start using another.'

Section One – 3: Major Immigration Abuse

Wright is opposed to the much less stringent British immigration controls which came into operation in January 1993.

'It's purely a personal opinion, but I feel we shouldn't drop our controls. We're finding more and more people are applying for political asylum. Or you get the economic migrant. Now either of those still puts a burden on the United Kingdom. We're a small island and we're over-populated already.'

Determination can produce extreme measures, and to desperate people no move seems excessive if it produces freedom of movement

'We are getting false applications by immigration consultants, or people who set themselves up as immigration consultants, making false entry and exit stamps in passports, to show that the holders are frequent travellers in and out of Britain, so that the Immigration Officer at the airport assumes they have the right of abode in Britain, when they've never been here in their lives. So, with this kind of thing going on, we work very closely with the Immigration Services. They have the expertise under the Immigration Act, and we have the expertise on the investigation side. We work very closely as a joint operation.'

Much of the initial information on illegal immigration comes from the Immigration Services, whose substantial rights under the Immigration Act do not include rights of arrest, search or seizure. Officers of SO1(3) use their powers and the powers of the courts to get search warrants and to arrest suspects.

False applications are not the only method available to those with the money to buy immigrant status. Recently a Nigerian barrister practising in the UK paid Englishmen between £500 and £1,000 each to go through legal registry-office wedding ceremonies with Nigerian women. The women were paying up to £4,000 each for the privilege of obtaining a marriage certificate which would grant them right of abode in the United Kingdom. These particular marriage documents were invalid, however, because they were the product of a demonstrable fraud. The women's details on the marriage certificates were genuine, the men's were not; there was also provable conspiracy to defraud between the parties. The women were prosecuted and served short prison sentences, on completion of which they were deported.

Section One – 4: Irish Extraditions

Warrants issued in Ireland against a fugitive are sent to England; there is no need for the Irish authorities to send evidence. The warrants are certified valid by a magistrate in the area where the fugitive is believed to be living, then officers of SO1(3) execute the warrants. When the fugitive is eventually caught and brought before the court, he only has to acknowledge that he is the person named on the warrant or warrants, and he is extradited forthwith, even for relatively minor offences.

'If terrorism was involved in a case we were handling,' said Wright, 'we would contact the Anti-Terrorist Squad, and we would work in conjunction with them, giving our advice and attending to the practical aspects of extradition – but we do not extradite terrorists.'

Section One – 5: Criminal Justice, International Cooperation

In 1990 the Criminal Justice (International Cooperation) Act was passed. Its stated intention was to enable the United Kingdom to give a wider range of practical assistance to the judicial authorities of foreign states in the investigation and prosecution of crime. At the same time the Home Office created a Central Authority, a body to authorise all requests for assistance both to and from the UK. Urgent requests, again both ways, are dealt with by Interpol's London office.

In terms of international cooperation in law enforcement, Wright sees this new power as ground-breaking, allowing the police, for example, to search a house in the UK in connection with a crime committed abroad.

'We can go along to a court on the authority of the Home Secretary and swear a search warrant. It's got so many ramifications . . .'

Section Two: Alien Deportation Group

Until the death of Joy Gardner in August 1993, following an attempt to arrest her, this group of officers, working in plain clothes under the supervision of Detective Inspector Wright, provided escorts for people who had been ordered to leave the United Kingdom.

Mrs Gardner collapsed and subsequently died following a visit by officers to her home to enforce a deportation order. Her family claimed that she died as a result of suffocation, after having her mouth taped and her hands restrained by a belt fitted with handcuffs. The official cause of death was kidney failure. Scotland Yard confirmed that the equipment used to restrain Mrs Gardner is standard equipment.

Scotland Yard also confirmed that three officers were suspended from duty following the incident and pending a thorough investigation by Essex Police. The rest of the Deportation Group were 'grounded' from further deportations for the time being. Senior management at Scotland Yard will decide when the officers will resume their duties. Meanwhile, the immigration authorities are using private security firms for deportations.

The Commissioner's decision to act quickly to suspend officers was undoubtedly a sensible one, since it had a calming effect on the local community and probably defused a considerable amount of tension. Nevertheless, the suspensions caused resentment inside the

Deportation Group, where it was felt that the officers concerned had been treated unfairly, since they say they acted properly throughout the operation.

(4) OBSCENE PUBLICATIONS SQUAD

Because the Obscene Publications Squad's daily business is to deal with some of the darker manifestations of human sexuality, recruits are vetted for resilience and emotional stability before they are accepted. Once a person is working for the branch, his or her wellbeing remains a concern.

'I was conscious when I came here that we must take steps to look after our staff,' said Detective Superintendent Mike Hames, head of SO1(4). 'It's no good waiting until something happens.'

Police and civil staff have visited Harley Street and learned how to relax, using the system known as Autogenics. The aim of the method is to reduce the individual's 'fight or flight' response to nervous strain and substitute an automatic tendency to relax whenever stress is imminent, thereby cancelling the threat.

Hames has a staff of fourteen policemen and ten civilians, working from offices on the seventh floor at Scotland Yard. The employment of civil staff in the Squad originated, in part, as a safeguard against police officers mishandling or misappropriating the material passing through their hands. That worry, in its turn, was a hangover from a time in the 1970s when corruption was widespread at Scotland Yard.

On 27 February 1972, the *Sunday People* revealed that the head of the Flying Squad had recently spent a holiday in Cyprus as the guest of a Soho pornographer. Shortly afterwards it was confidently alleged that his host's commercial success as a vendor of all kinds of pornography could be attributed to the protection he received from officers of the Obscene Publications Squad and the Flying Squad.

Subsequent investigations revealed that the then head of the Obscene Publications Squad had been taking 'inducements' from the pornographer and others for a long time.

Internal police investigations revealed that weekly and monthly payments for various levels of concession were paid by Soho traders to other senior officers (and to a number of juniors) in the Obscene Publications Squad and the Flying Squad.

In the end, at a trial commencing in March 1977, six officers were formally accused on twenty-seven different counts of corruptly accepting bribes totalling £87,485. All were convicted and sentenced to a total of forty-eight years in prison.

'It was a very corrupt situation,' said Hames. 'The Commissioner, Robert Mark, dealt with it by taking this department from CID and making it the responsibility of the uniformed branch. Uniformed officers from vice backgrounds were brought in to take over the work. Since that time there has not been a whiff of scandal.' However, the Obscene Publications Squad only returned to Specialist Operations in 1993.

Hames explained that nowadays there are other reasons, besides a wariness of corruption, for civilians being on the Squad. Among them is the fact that civilians viewing the seized material leaves operational officers free to deal with police matters.

'The Squad is here to enforce the law in relation to obscene publications of all sorts,' Hames explained, 'and there are quite a number of Acts of Parliament that we concentrate on, but the principal one is the Obscene

Publications Act of 1959, supplemented by the Obscene
Publications Act 1964.'

Under the Act, an offence is committed when a
person

    a. publishes an obscene article, whether or not for
       gain.

    b. possesses an obscene article for publication for
       gain, whether for himself or someone else.

The mere possession of an obscene article (which can
take the form of the written word, a drawing, a photograph, movie film, videotape or even an audio cassette)
does not constitute an offence against the Act. If, however, obscene articles are distributed among other
people, for money or free of charge, they are then
deemed to have been published and a breach of the Act
has taken place.

Police concern about an increase in the traffic in
pornography, especially that depicting sexual violence,
has been reinforced by statements of convicted sex offenders who have claimed to use pornography to fuel
their criminal impulses.

American serial killer Ted Bundy, in an interview
filmed shortly before his execution for the killing of
twenty-eight women and children, said,

> My experience with pornography generally, and
> with pornography that deals on a violent level with
> sexuality, is once you become addicted to it – and I
> look at this as a kind of addiction like other kinds
> of addiction – I would keep looking for more potent,
> more explicit, more graphic kinds of material.

Appetite growing by what it feeds on is convincingly
evoked all the way from Shakespeare to the records of
criminal excess held by police authorities throughout the world. The obscene and the taboo exercise an

attraction which, for some, becomes irresistible and arguably dangerous. 'You reach a point where the pornography only goes so far,' Bundy concluded. 'You reach that jumping-off point where you begin to wonder if maybe actually doing it would give you that which is beyond just reading it or looking at it.'

A difficulty for the police is the test for obscenity which they have to apply to the material coming under their scrutiny. According to the convoluted and imprecise language of the Act, an article is obscene 'if its effect, or the effect of an item within it, taken as a whole, tends to deprave and corrupt persons who are likely, having regard to all relevant circumstances, to read, hear or see the matter contained in it'. That definition was framed by Lord Cockburn, the Lord Chief Justice, in 1868. No suitable alternative has yet been written, although the police are anxious that somebody should try.

Some of the seized material falls on the hazy borderline of classification between erotica and pornography, and some may try to transcend both in its claim to be high art, but a lot of it leaves no room for doubt. Civilian officers of the Obscene Publications Squad spend a considerable time viewing this kind of material. Morale is sustained by an instinctive regime of distancing. Officers resort to black humour and raucous banter to soften the impact of so much that is offensive and potentially disturbing.

'We try to keep our spirits up,' Hames said. 'The people on the Squad who watch this material have an ordinary television set above the monitors, and it's not unusual to go in there and see the cricket on, or horse racing or something like that which distracts people.' And the officers are trained to be objective. 'They're watching for particular actions for evidential purposes –

in fact they look on each tape as a piece of evidence they're examining for court. But we do keep an eye on each other, and we talk about things that upset or annoy us. If we're revolted we say so; we off-load the problem.'

The distribution of adult pornography in Britain, most of it nowadays on videotape (technology has to a large extent ousted books and magazines), is fairly easy because it can be advertised through a variety of media so wide that the police find it hard to keep up with the trade. It is a multi-million pound business, but Hames insists that on the organisational side it amounts to no more than a large cottage industry.

'You might have four or five people who have a business which actually copies and distributes the material. They don't produce it, very few of them do. There's no need, so much is produced abroad in the USA, Holland, Germany, Denmark.'

One commercial ploy is to advertise pornography as being available from an address in Amsterdam. A certain cachet attaches to Amsterdam as the source of the very hardest-core material; in reality the orders are often faxed back to Britain where the pornographer actually bases his operation.

An apparent oddity of the law is that the police have no power to arrest anyone for distributing pornography. The maximum penalty under the Obscene Publications Act is three years' imprisonment; an offence becomes arrestable only when it carries a penalty of five years imprisonment or more.

'So,' Hames said, 'we could say to a pornographer, "We want to interview you on tape at so-and-so police station," and he could say, "Bugger off, I'm not coming." There's nothing we can do about it.'

In the 1980s the officers of Obscene Publications

began to notice that they were handling more and more filmed pornography featuring children. Until that time there had been no specific understanding that such a specialised genre as child pornography existed, or that the material had a distinct market.

Paedophilia is defined as sexual desire directed towards children. It is largely a deviation of men, with only a few female cases reported. No official statistics for paedophiles in Britain have ever been produced, since paedophilia in itself is not an offence.

Hames estimates that nowadays 90 per cent of the Obscene Publications Squad's work is concerned with material involving the sexual abuse of children. It is a matter of policy and the percentage, he believes, is just as it should be. 'We're here principally to protect people who can't look after themselves, the vulnerable in society. Children fall squarely into that category.'

In practice, therefore, the prime emphasis of the Squad's work has shifted from the Obscene Publications Act towards the Protection of Children Act of 1978, as amended by Section 160 of the Criminal Justice Act of 1988, which makes it an offence to possess indecent pictures of people under the age of sixteen, in the form of still photographs or moving pictures, or to allow such pictures to be taken.

Paedophiles are avid collectors of pornography and it is exchanged among members of paedophile 'rings'. Apart from being used as a trigger and aid to sexual fantasies, it is used directly in the seduction of children, to lower their resistance to sexual acts by showing them graphic evidence that such things happen.

'It's used to sexualise them,' is how Hames puts it. 'It's used to show them that it's normal for children to have sex with each other and with adults.'

Pornographic outlets selling adult material do not as a

rule handle so-called 'kiddie-porn', since even among
the dealers in mainstream filth there is a stunted ethic
which puts such material beyond the pale. Distribution
of child pornography, in general, is carried out within
paedophile circles whose members communicate covertly, since they cannot openly advertise.

'Operation Cathedral' is a case which shows how
certain pornographers operate, and how dedicated detective work can sometimes disrupt their activities. The
investigation began as a result of a raid by Devon and
Cornwall Police on the home of a man called Williams.
Letters found during the raid prompted the police to
circulate names and addresses from the letters to several
police forces; there was a strong suspicion that the
people named were in possession of obscene pictures of
children.

Police in Canterbury raided the home of a school
teacher and eventually called the Obscene Publications
Squad at Scotland Yard to say they had found some
nasty child pornography. Later, DS Graham Passingham and DC Dave Flanagan of Obscene Publications
viewed the tape that became pivotal to the case known
as Operation Cathedral.

'It was various home-made clips of a boy of about
thirteen or fourteen being abused – masturbated,' said
Flanagan. 'He had a noose round his neck at one stage,
fellating the man in the tape.'

There was a shorter clip of another boy, a child of
about seven, lying on a bed, being wakened by a man.
He was kneeling over the boy, holding the video camera
in one hand as he masturbated into the boy's mouth.
The policemen, both experienced officers, were disturbed by the tape.

'The distress of the boy is evident,' said Flanagan;
'he's whimpering and saying, "Please, no more . . ."'

But in a way, the *Snowman* music in the background – the *Snowman* programme was on, the soundtrack was being played while the offence was taking place, and the two put together I found very powerful. My kids like the *Snowman* music, and you know, the *Snowman* is a story children are entranced by, and to have that in the background while this child was whimpering, "Please, not again . . ." or "You're crushing me . . . No, no more . . ." I don't like the music now . . .'

'I thought it was as unpleasant as anything we've seen,' said Passingham. 'It was as nasty as you could get. The way the boy was abused and the way he pleaded, it was pretty horrible, really. I don't think you could get much worse.'

On one video clip was a shot of the older boy sitting in a Jaguar car outside a block of flats; the police saw the car's registration number straight away – D879 FDU.

'Now there were two things going on in this video,' Passingham said. 'You have the very young boy who was being sexually abused, and you had an older boy who was being sexually abused in the car, but they weren't shot together. They were in separate incidents.'

On the video clips both boys were addressed by a man with a strong Geordie accent. This, in addition to the evidence of the car's registration plate was all the working evidence the police had at the beginning of the case.

'One of the first things we did was get a voice analysis done of the two clips,' said Flanagan. 'That came back saying that the Geordie in Clip "A", with the car, and the Geordie in Clip "B", kneeling on top of the boy, were almost certainly the same guy. So that was a step forward. We took a step backward when the voice analyst seemed to think one of the boys might be a Geordie as well.'

Up to that point, a DVLC history of the Jaguar car, from the date of manufacture – December 1987 – until the day the inquiry began, had pointed the police in the direction of Nottingham. But now they were not so sure. A painstaking strategy was set up. The police would research the car's ownership from the time it left the factory until the most recent time an owner was registered.

The car had first been bought by a leasing company in Wellingborough, who leased it almost immediately to a pharmaceutical company in Cambridge. Two years later, the lease having run its course, the car was returned to Wellingborough.

'Then we had to decide if we should go to the pharmaceutical company,' said Passingham. 'The danger was, if we went to the main man there, the one who was using the car, he might have been a suspect as well.'

The Jaguar company had meanwhile supplied information about places all over the UK where the car had been serviced. At that stage it was a wide inquiry

The standard drill after the Jaguar lease had expired was for the leasing company to sell it at auction. It was auctioned and sold to a car dealer from Mapperley, who sold it in his turn to the most recent owner, a man in Nottingham.

'Now the current registered owner wasn't a particular suspect,' said Passingham. 'I still wanted to eliminate everyone from the inquiry leading up to him. So we went to the car dealer's in Mapperley and spoke to the owner. He looked through his papers and discovered he had actually sold the car once and bought it back a few months later, before selling it to the most recent registered owner.'

'The person who had owned the Jaguar for those few months had been shrewd enough not to register it for the brief time he had it, but he wasn't clever enough to give the dealer a false name.'

And he was stupid enough to let the number plate be seen on the video. Flanagan went back to the Anti-Vice Squad Office in Nottingham, where they checked their records and found that a man with the same name as the man who owned the Jaguar was known to them – he had a record of indecent offences against children. The photographs of the man on the file showed a strong similarity to partial images of the man in the video clips.

'He was just the right kind of suspect with the right background of offences,' said Passingham.'The details of an earlier offence were typical. The subject enticed two youths into his home and forced them to strip at knife point, and fondled their private parts, then forced them to engage in oral sex acts. In 1981 he had been sentenced to two years' imprisonment at Newcastle Crown Court. Since that time, I don't think he had come to the notice of the police.'

Passingham and Flanagan were now convinced they were on to the right man. To tighten the certainty they made an effort to identify locations visible on the video; several were checked and were found to be near where the man lived. One place actually turned out to be one of his former addresses.

'We still didn't know where the offences had occurred,' said Passingham. 'We knew one of the addresses appeared in the film, and that seemed to indicate where they had occurred, but it still wasn't definite. I remember we had a lot of discussion about this, because where the case is eventually dealt with is quite important – you know, where the children are now. After various meetings it was decided, on the balance of probabilities, that the children lived in the Nottingham area and that the case should fall within the jurisdiction of the Child Protection Team there.'

The Nottingham Child Protection Team set up the operation for the arrest of the suspect. He lived in a house on the outskirts of Nottingham. On the morning that the police turned up to arrest him, PC Flanagan was with them.

'I was in the back garden when he came out of the back door,' Flanagan said. 'He tried to flee down the garden. I just grabbed hold of him and took him back into the house. It was like watching a pin stuck in a balloon. He deflated visibly – he didn't break down in tears but he looked shocked.'

The accused made no attempt to deny the charges presented to him. His daughter was too young to understand what was happening, but his wife was distraught. 'That's another part of this job that I don't like,' Flanagan said. 'It's all very well arresting the offenders, but then you've got the offenders' families, and I mean, they're not guilty of anything, are they?'

In October 1992, at Nottingham Crown Court, the accused pleaded guilty to various indictments of indecency against children. He was sentenced to six years' imprisonment. Both Passingham and Flanagan were surprised that the sentence was so substantial. They believe sentences for offences against minors are generally too light.

Both officers believed the visible evidence of the young boy's pain and fright, in bizarre contrast with the lyrical music in the background, must have demonstrated to the judge, better than any verbal description, the hideous nature of the offence.

The children in the video clips were identified. The older boy, who had been fourteen at the time the tape was made, was able to identify the younger boy for the police. By the time the suspect was arrested, the older boy was twenty-one, and already had a child of his own.

In considering the developing situation with pornography transmitted by television, Hames foresees confusion.

'The Government has signed a European Community Directive allowing programmes that are legal in the country of origin to be beamed anywhere else in the Community. In effect, they are saying these programmes are legal, but if British customers were to copy the material on to their videos and distribute it, they would be liable for prosecution under the Obscene Publications Act. That is clearly a nonsense and I think we've got ourselves into rather a difficult situation. Pornographers will say, with every justification, "Look, how can I possibly be guilty of producing obscene material when you can get it on your television screen, and the Government says it's OK, it's legal?" That's what I'd say if I were in the dock.'

Hames sees encouraging signs of a global crackdown on child pornography. On the other hand, he has no illusions about the future spread of adult pornography.

'A market will determine the future of pornography in this country,' he says. 'Information technology and mass-marketing methods will railroad any feeble attempts at resistance from the police or customs service.'

(5) CENTRAL CHEQUE SQUAD

So-called 'plastic' fraud, using stolen or forged credit cards and cashcards, is the fastest-growing area of fraud

Obscene Publications Squad: Record of Operations During a Recent Year

Search Warrants Executed

Obscene Publications Act 1959	39
Protection of Children Act 1978	83
Section 8, PACE 1984	2

Material Seized

Obscene video cassettes	22,801
Obscene/indecent photographs	6,995
Obscene/indecent magazines	43,452

in the U.K. Detective Superintendent Chris Newman, Head of the Central Cheque Squad, talked about the two distinct areas.

'The bigger bulk of cases are with stolen cards. The people who steal them are usually street muggers and burglars, and they sell them to a person in their area who is a general handler – he will pay the thief £100 or £200 per card. The cards then go on to someone else who's a major handler at another stage in the fraud, and then they go out to a team that will actually spend the cards. So in the middle range, between the thief and the people who actually cash them, are a group of quite sophisticated criminals. They would be our targets.'

In 1988 major British banks lost £69.3 million through frauds committed with cheque cards, the various cash-point cards, Visa and MasterCard; they also included 'non-plastic' fraud, which accounted for £21.7 million of the total. In 1990 the figure rose to £150.3 million, with non-plastic fraud accounting for £29.5 million. Latest estimates suggest the total *for plastic fraud alone* is now well over £200 million.

'And that's only the banks,' said Newman. 'The

figures don't take account of the stores who produce their own cards. They lose a lot of money as well.'

Great Britain has the highest card-fraud figures in Europe. We also have the highest number of cards – eighty-three million. In this country 0.3 per cent of all card transactions are dishonest, whereas in the rest of Europe the figure is closer to 0.1 per cent. More card crime is committed in the UK than in the rest of Europe and Africa combined, and half the national problem is in London.

In view of the figures, the Central Cheque Squad is surprisingly modest in size. There are seventeen investigating officers, none of them with special fraud training before they joined the Squad. An officer should also be able to take the initiative in an investigation and control its progress.

'The police side is purely the proactive side of collecting the evidence, following the people, catching them with the goods, catching them spending, that's the idea. So we're not investigating fraud in the way that a company-fraud officer would. We're dealing with different criminals, too.'

The volume of crime in cards and cheques is so high that SOI(5) has to draw a minimum line, based on the scale of the offence, below which a case will be passed for handling to the local divisional police station. But, although the scale of a crime governs its importance, the scale and the amount of money involved are not always the same thing. In a cheque crime, for example, Newman's squad would get involved if the number of transactions amounted to four or five hundred.

'We've dealt with them where there's been more than a thousand offences taken into consideration,' Newman said, but he added that cases involving high-value single transactions, such as the cashing of counterfeit bankers' drafts, would also be taken on by the Central Cheque Squad.

The ways of committing fraud with cards seem to multiply with the number of cards issued. The commonest methods, in ascending order, are obtaining cards by false applications, stealing cards in transit, misuse by the genuine cardholders, and the reprocessing of lost and stolen cards through criminal networks. There has also been an increase in the number of counterfeit cards used in fraud.

Criminal end-users of stolen cards will often run teams, frequently groups of prostitutes, who will go out equipped with stolen cards and each bring in, on average, cash and goods to a value varying from £300 to £1,000. On gold cards the amounts obtainable are much higher.

This is the only area of crime where women have equality. Women's involvement in crime is comparatively slight, but when it comes to cheque and card frauds they are responsible for roughly 50 per cent. Newman sees a number of possible reasons. For a start, half the cards in existence are owned by women. Women, too, raise less suspicion at cash tills and sales points, and to a large extent they can easily be manipulated by men: a lot of those caught up in fraud are mothers in underprivileged areas. And if the women are prostitutes they are often being controlled by their pimps, who can make a lot more from stolen cards than they can from selling the women's services.

It is not uncommon for people arrested for card fraud to tell Cheque Squad officers about similar crimes being committed elsewhere. Usually they do this in the hope of landing a light sentence.

'The most difficult people to get at are the ones in the middle,' said Chris Newman. 'But because they are so successful, as well as causing fear, they also occasionally cause jealousy, and jealousy is a reason for informing in a number of cases.'

Hard cash plays a large part too. SO1(5) pay for information, as well as recommending lenient sentencing for people who have been particularly cooperative with the police.

'We get information usually about teams that are encashing cards, that's a typical tip-off. We're not bothered too much about the girls using the cards, we're more bothered about the guy who's taking them out in a car and dropping them off. Sometimes he'll be taking three or four girls, dropping them off at different shops, then picking them up along the road and dropping them off again at other shops. Now, *he'll* be the one with control of the cards. Then we're looking for who he got them from. We back-track from him.'

Another type of card misuse is called 'merchant collusive fraud'. A lot of losses by cheque and card fraud happen in shops and other retail outlets, where a proportion of the fraud results from traders taking payment by cards which they know are stolen. Another method is for a dishonest trader to emboss blank cards with the details from genuine cards and print this data on credit card vouchers. In one recent case eight businessmen made more than £1.5 million from blank plastic cards embossed with genuine information.

Counterfeiting of cheques and cards has increased dramatically. Three years ago it would have accounted for 1 per cent of the overall cheque-and-card-fraud problem; now it is nearer 15 per cent.

'In gold cards it's probably 50 per cent of the problem,' said Chris Newman, 'because they have credit limits of ten thousand, and the platinum ones are even higher.'

Two Chinese arrested in London were carrying a briefcase with £27,000 and over fifty counterfeit gold cards inside. The source of the counterfeiting was traced to a hotel in Hong Kong. Details of customers' gold cards were copied at the same time they paid their bills; the details were later added to false gold cards with Chinese holders' names on the front.

The extensive resources of the Triads have helped Hong Kong become the world's major source of counterfeit credit cards. However, advances in colour copying have made it relatively easy to produce authentic-looking replica cards anywhere in the world, including Britain. Encoding the replicas is easy, too – machines are available, for a few hundred pounds each, which can read the magnetic information on a card, store it in electronic memory, then copy it on to another card. Blank plastic cards with void magnetic stripes can be bought in Britain for £50 a thousand.

In the summer of 1992 an ambitious card swindle made tens of thousands of pounds for a gang of criminals in the space of only a few weeks. The fraud took place at travelling auctions in about forty different locations around England. A genuine auction company, selling off bankrupt stock, for instance, would unknowingly sub-contract a firm of crooked security checkers who asked potential bidders to tap their personal card numbers into portable machines, so that their cheque and credit cards could be validated. In reality the machines copied the encoding from the cards and recorded the personal numbers as they were keyed in. Fake cards were manufactured from the stored data and then used to milk the victims' accounts at hole-in-the-wall cashpoints.

'Security devices on the cards are being improved,' Newman said, 'but really the criminals are keeping up with the game. Recently we got information that a parcel was coming from Hong Kong to a London hotel. We followed it all the way from Heathrow to the hotel, where it was delivered to three Chinese occupying a room there. So we've given them time, and then when we've gone in there's thirty-one cards in two Chinese names, and two counterfeit passports in those same Chinese names. All those cards were gold cards, each one with a face value of ten thousand, certainly.'

A disturbing feature of the case was that the holograms on the cards, assumed by banks and card manufacturers to be a powerful anti-counterfeiting feature, were so good that officials from Visa believed the cards were genuine, until the police pointed out there were more than two dozen cards with only two bearers' names between them.

Detecting the frauds and tracking down the perpetrators is rarely simple, especially now that this area of crime is so organised, but in cheque fraud the old methods of detection can still be successful.

'Fingerprints on cheques can be very valuable to us,' said Chris Newman. 'You can't stop being nervous, so the chances are that you're going to sweat and leave your fingerprints on cheques particularly. And a bank teller will be suspicious straight away if you try and write cheques with gloves on.'

Cheques are far easier to forge than plastic cards, and the best forgeries are usually for very large amounts, quite often drawn on foreign banks.

In 1991 the Home Office Crime Prevention Unit issued a report on the way the police and the banks work to prevent all areas of card and cheque fraud. The report was fairly critical of the banks and said they should introduce more security devices. Chris Newman favours having photographs of cardholders on the cards, but when he discussed it with bank officials they raised a curious objection: a picture, they said, can be removed from a card and another one put in its place, thus invalidating the security of the scheme. It appeared not to have dawned on them that few criminals would risk having their faces on cards that might be kept by cashpoint machines or retained by suspicious bank tellers.

'Pictures on cards is the one area that we can't seem to get agreement on,' Chris Newman said. 'In the longer term I think biometrics is the answer . . .'

Biometric features incorporated into cards – retina and fingerprint recognition, for instance – are not much liked by the card manufacturers or the banks, largely because of imperfect performance, the cost, and the assertion that the public would object.

'There's going to have to be a big increase in time and effort put into these problems by police throughout the UK,' Chris Newman said, 'because now it's being recognised as a way of solving other major crime. If you don't investigate the plastic fraud, how are you ever going to find the guy who mugged the person in the first place? And in murders we're asked to find out if anything stolen from victims is cashed.'

He also believes a sound relationship with the banks is crucial in the unending campaign against fraud.

'We've criticised the banks, but to be fair, they really are getting their act together much, much better than ever before, and they're involving us, and we're having to try and keep pace and get our act together as well.'

(6) MOTOR VEHICLE SQUAD

As careers in crime go, car theft is relatively attractive. It is a non-violent crime so the penalties for getting

Fraud on Plastic Cards During a Recent One-Year Period

CATEGORY	PROPORTION	AMOUNT
Counterfeit	2%	£3 million
Fraudulent Application	6%	£7.4 million
Card not Received	25%	£30 million
Lost/Stolen	67%	£82.1 million

caught are low, and in London, where 95 per cent of stolen cars are taken on a steal-to-order basis, returns are high and turn-round is swift.

To combat the metropolitan car-theft industry, SO1(6) has forty-eight CID officers and approximately fifteen civilian staff, divided into four squads – East, West, South and Central. Central Squad is the mainstay of the department – the information and intelligence unit.

The squad's overall purpose is to investigate the organised theft of domestic and commercial vehicles, and industrial plant, in the London area. They operate from unmarked – though not particularly secret – premises at Chalk Farm in north-west London, where they have a centre of operations and a six-floor garage for storing recovered vehicles. The garage looks like an upmarket NCP operation, with Rolls Royces, Land Rovers, Porsches, BMWs, Jaguars and other prestige marques lined up on every floor. Elsewhere, in a disused aircraft hangar, SO1(6) have recently been holding thirty-eight JCB diggers as evidence in a case of large-scale industrial-plant theft.

Detective Chief Inspector Neil Giles spoke about the categories of car thieves. 'A certain number of them work in tightly-knit groups to run the organised theft of vehicles for a variety of purposes. There are those who ship abroad and make large profits. Others will literally steal ten cars to ring two – which means they will produce from the component parts of those ten cars just two for sale in this country, and they will scrap the rest.'

Other teams operate on a medium-scale, steady-turnover basis. 'I've been on operations where we searched premises with literally a garage full of spares, where they've broken the stolen motor cars down into their parts, racked them up, then offered them for sale through what the officers of the Squad call the comics.'

'Comics' are publications such as *Exchange and Mart* and a variety of dedicated weekly and monthly magazines offering spare car parts for sale through their classified pages. A lot of profit can be made that way, and efficient car thieves often work as contractors for teams dismantling cars and either selling them as spares, or ringing them so that they lose their original identities.

Giles explained a standard procedure in car theft.

'It would typically begin with an organisation having a market for either a whole vehicle, which would mean they had an identity for it already from a scrap yard, or a team who had a market for spares, or for parts of vehicles. In those circumstances, if someone in the organisation had the necessary skills, they would go and steal the car to order. If they hadn't the skills, and many don't, they would go to one of a number of young, excellent-quality car thieves who would, for a price, go out and steal a particular sort of car.'

It is surprisingly easy to move stolen vehicles abroad. Many are just driven on to roll-on, roll-off ferries, a number of which travel between Europe and Japan; prestige British cars are popular in Japan. 'Among the commonest ports for this sort of export are Southampton, Felixstowe and Liverpool,' said Giles. 'Tilbury and

Harwich get used a lot, too, because they're massive container ports.'

Operation Erasure was an inquiry conducted by SO1(6) in the summer of 1990. Through a contact in Customs and Excise they had reason to investigate both the source and destination of a Mercedes 500 sports car being shipped out to the West Indies. Investigations in Britain and in the West Indies established that a team of criminals had been visiting West Indian Islands, introducing themselves to wealthy people from the island communities, and offering to sell them high-quality motor cars from the UK market.

'They were duping these people because they were saying they could get the cars very cheaply,' said Giles, 'because they were repossessions. They could get them shipped out to the West Indies and the purchaser would end up with a prestige motor car at a very good price.'

The thieves were offering Mercedes, Jaguars, BMWs and other top marques. Prospective customers could stipulate make, model and even colour, and on their return to the UK the vendors would carry out the thefts through an organised team. The cars would be exported with a simple change of registration plates. No attempt was made to alter or disguise engine numbers or other fine details of identity. There are no systems at British sea ports to make exhaustive checks on every car being exported; provided the registration numbers show up on the computer as belonging to a car of the same general description which is not listed as stolen, the thieves have no trouble shipping the goods.

'The only reason we picked up this inquiry,' Giles said, 'was because a Customs officer looked at a car and didn't believe it was as old as the number plate suggested – he has an interest in that sort of car. He talked to a friend in the local police who went along and examined the secret numbers on the car, discovered it was a stolen one, and because it was stolen from London, he informed us.'

The Motor Vehicle Squad tracked the car back to the freight handler, who happened to have an extraordinary memory and could recall three or four other cars shipped by the same men, though under different names. He made a thorough search of his paperwork and came up with several possible identities for his clients.

'And while we were checking, and also getting to the bills of lading for the ships,' Giles said, 'we came up with another team who were doing exactly the same thing, and had been for many years. This ended up with us recovering about thirty vehicles in the West Indies, all high-quality cars.'

The police kept a watch on the shipping office in London, waiting for someone to collect the bill of lading for the car intercepted at the port; without the bill, which is a document of ownership, no one at the other end could collect the car.

'We struck lucky,' Giles said. 'The exporter didn't ask for the bill to be sent to the West Indies. He called to say he would collect it in person. So we just had to wait. We kept a watch for three or four days before the man turned up. He was a native of Montserrat, a guy who had lived in Britain for many years. He collected the document, then was arrested when he went outside with it.'

It then became necessary for SO1(6) to make follow-up inquiries in the West Indies. Giles and a colleague went to Antigua and to Montserrat. They found a number of people, mostly from the from top end of West Indian society, who had bought vehicles from the arrested man and his team. They reacted badly to the news that they were driving around in stolen cars.

'They were determined they were going to keep those cars. They went to court to try to fight in that corner. In Montserrat they failed, but the battle continues in Antigua – in fact the magistrate there has let the people have the cars back pending a decision.'

In the end, even after strenuous and lengthy detective work, only one associate of the man from Montserrat could be arrested, and the police could not hold him past the committal stage, because of the poor quality of the evidence against him. At the time the associate was arrested he was on his way, with his family, to live permanently in the West Indies, and he was in possession of a very large sum of cash. The court returned the money to him when he was released.

'The man we arrested was the fall guy, I suspect,' said Giles, 'but he was in the higher echelons of the organisation. I would have put him at number two. The organisation made a great deal of money, certainly over half a million pounds, but we only managed to convict one of them in the end. He got two years.'

A number of officers in the Motor Vehicle Squad are Vehicle Examiners. Their particular talent is to identify cars, plant machinery and other vehicles, even after they have been extensively altered to disguise their identity.

'They are extremely adept at identifying machines,' Giles said, 'but you can only identify a machine if the information is available, and sometimes the information that's been in our databases hasn't been accurate, so occasionally identification could take a great deal of work.'

One man who was good at disguising cars was known to the local community in Rainham, Essex, as Sierra Sid. 'He would buy a car that had been badly damaged in an accident or a fire, one that had been taken to a salvage yard at the end of its insurance claim and left to be scrapped. You can buy a badly damaged Ford Sierra for a few hundred pounds. It's a way for insurance companies to get a small amount of money back.'

Sierra Sid, having bought a wreck allegedly for spares, would take it back to his premises and chisel out its stamped-in numbers, take the index mark and the log book, and thereby have a ready-made identity for another car. If the scrap vehicle was a red Sierra, for example, Sid would obtain a stolen red Sierra of a similar age and model, and give it the identity lifted from the 'dead' car: he would do that by cutting out the stolen vehicle's identity marks, welding in the substitutes, changing the number plates and adding the dead car's log book. The result would be a saleable vehicle.

A bonus factor in vehicle-theft investigations is that the crime itself is a comparatively small field. Intelligence databases tend to show the same names over and over.

Giles does not believe that vehicle thieves are fundamentally different from armed robbers. A lot of armed robbers are violent lunatics, he says, but most of them see themselves as professional criminals. So do car thieves.

'Most of them start off by being the young car thief, the young *good* car thief, who grows out of the kick of stealing the car and driving it very quickly, and gets into the side where there's money to be made. It's all about money.'

(8) WAR CRIMES UNIT

In 1989 the War Crimes Inquiry, headed by Sir Thomas Hetherington and William Chalmers, considered 301 allegations and concluded that there was enough evidence to support criminal proceedings for murder against alleged war criminals living in the United Kingdom. A recommendation of the Inquiry was that legislation should be introduced, as quickly as possible, to give British courts the power to prosecute such individuals.

The Government endorsed the Inquiry's report and took steps to make its recommendations law. With the introduction of the Police War Crimes Act of 1991, the police were granted powers to investigate allegations of murder and manslaughter against individuals – now British Nationals, or resident in the United Kingdom – accused of committing these crimes in Germany or German-occupied territory during the Second World War. Scotland Yard's War Crimes Unit, headed by Detective Chief Superintendent Eddie Bathgate, was set up just nineteen days after the Bill became law.

The War Crimes Unit, operating on an annual budget of approximately £1.4m – provided by the Home Office – comprises a team of nine detectives, reinforced by five civil staff and two police Constables who manage the computer system. Two professional historians, working on a contract basis, carry out research work with the Unit.

Bathgate, going on record here for the first time to talk about the work of the War Crimes Unit, explained that, from the start, he favoured a pragmatic approach.

'I was happy to take this on with a view to, first of all, seeing if we could get at the truth of the allegations after forty-five or fifty years, and secondly, seeing if in doing so we could gather evidence that could be adduced in a British court of law to support a case and a prosecution.'

'The underlying theme to the whole thing is the Jewish people and the Jewish religion,' he went on. 'We are looking at the ghettoisation of Jewish groups, and then their subsequent elimination in different ways. We are talking about the murder of nine million children in the civil population.'

Although Jews were murdered in their millions, the investigations do not exclusively encompass Jewish persecution.

'There were whole villages razed to the ground – men, women, children. The material we've been looking at tends to indicate that this wasn't partisan warfare, this was retribution. When the German Army advanced and captured a swathe of land the battle-fronts progressed beyond that. Other groups were sent to take control of the civil administration in the occupied territory, under the command of a senior German officer. Often they employed the local civil servants, who collaborated with the occupying forces – some were members of the existing police force or fire brigades.'

Groups known as Auxiliary Police Battalions were recruited from indigenous populations. They were murder squads, created specifically to eliminate whole sections of the population. Bathgate said that historians and researchers have unearthed evidence that individuals who asked to leave the extermination squads were permitted to do so. 'On the whole,' he says, 'the people who were doing this work were volunteers. It was the 1940s form of ethnic cleansing.'

The detectives recruited to work on Bathgate's team are seasoned investigators who had no difficulty motivating themselves towards the specialised work of the Unit. Detective Inspector Dave Drinkald is one of them.

'When you speak to an elderly survivor who was a child in a concentration camp or in a ghetto,' he said, 'and they relate stories of taking half a raw potato from the hand of a dying man so they themselves could survive, and tell you they have lived with that memory every day since, you can't help being moved.'

Drinkald recalled an account of a woman surviving a mass shooting because she was holding her daughter and the bullets entered the child. There was so much blood the woman was thought to be dead and she was thrown into a pit with the other victims. After six or seven hours she put aside the dead body of her child and crawled naked from the pit, made her way into the woods and was given clothes by local peasants. She survived the war.

It was a visit to Auschwitz on a bleak November day that crystallised the inhumanity of the Holocaust for Drinkald. There he was, he said, well-dressed and over-nourished, yet feeling very cold indeed: 'And to think that people had been there in thin cotton pyjama-type garments, surviving on something like 600 calories a day if they were lucky – that brings things home.'

The war criminals, Bathgate says, have lived forty or fifty years longer than their victims, and that fact is motivation enough to do the right thing. 'I think a secondary motivation came from the arguments in Parliament – people who lived that way and did those terrible things, there should be no hiding place for them, and, if there is a hiding place, it ought not to be in our country.'

At present Bathgate's workload is forty-two active inquiries. Of those, seven are of the highest priority and reports on them have been sent to the Crown Prosecution Service to be assessed for possible prosecution. Three of the seven are moving towards being viable prospects for prosecution. Bathgate has no doubt that these people were members of Nazi killer squads.

The suspects are kept firmly under observation. 'We know where they are, we know where they're living. If anybody disappears then we need to find out quickly whether they've died or whether they've moved on. We keep tabs on them.'

Finding a suspect can turn into a protracted investigation. Records held by the Immigration and Nationality Department (IND) of the Home Office can be valuable in pinpointing identity, but their scope is not exhaustive. Between October 1950 and September 1952 over 200,000 people from Europe (and certain other countries) then living in the United Kingdom were interviewed. This undertaking was undermined during later years as files were destroyed and records went astray. As a result many searches related to war crimes have been hindered while others have been made impossible.

Drinkald said that the responses of Polish suspects has varied widely. Some do not want to be interviewed, some pretend they cannot speak English, some genuinely cannot speak English. Others, either directly or through interpreters, reveal everything, often in startling detail.

'Not surprisingly,' Drinkald said, 'quite a few of the wives had thought the men spent their entire military service in the Polish forces, and they are surprised to learn that they wore German uniforms.'

Sources of allegations are widespread. Apart from claims lodged by members of the public, the War Crimes Unit have dealt with information from the authorities of the former USSR, from other war crimes units in America, Canada and Australia, and from the Simon Wiesenthal Centre. (Wiesenthal, a Jew born in Austria-Hungary in 1908, is a longtime Nazi hunter and the founder and head of the Jewish Documentation Centre in Vienna.)

Even when the investigating officers are satisfied a suspect is the person they are looking for, it still has to be proved that he is the man his accusers believe he is.

In this respect the case in Israel of John Demjanjuk is relevant. Demjanjuk was brought to trial as a war criminal known as Ivan the Terrible, but subsequent evidence showed that, in spite of seemingly conclusive testimony, Demjanjuk and Ivan the Terrible were different men. The case has cast grave doubts on the viability of war crimes investigations conducted at such a distance from the events.

Time makes room for the faking of records and the wiping-out of trails. Evidence, therefore, has to be drawn from as many reliable sources as possible. Allegations have to be backed with solid evidence before there is even a chance of making a case. To this end, so-called cohort-witnesses can be valuable.

'It's the guy who says, "Yes, I shot these Jews, and so did he. But I've now done fifteen, twenty years in a Soviet jail, and he's been living in England, or America, or Canada." But *cohort-witness* evidence has its difficulties. I mean, we're effectively testing the word of a self-confessed murderer.'

No one is more aware than Eddie Bathgate that time is a crucial element in the investigations of crimes committed nearly half a century ago. Some procedures, however, simply cannot be rushed. But, in spite of endless problems and occasional setbacks, Bathgate does not believe that he and his people are wasting their time.

'Each one of these cases is quite a complicated murder inquiry in itself, and trying to conduct the investigations at a distance, using local people in foreign lands to assist us, is a steady process.'

It is paradoxical, in the light of their dedication, that soon the Unit will dwindle into redundancy. The suspects are mostly old or elderly people, and some who were under investigation are already dead. No one has publicly estimated how many cases will eventually come to court, or what percentage of the accused might be found guilty. Bathgate hopes that arrests and charges will be made during 1994.

'The Home Office has made no provision to fund the unit beyond the 31 March 1994,' he added. 'The senior officers at Scotland Yard are in the process of approaching them to review that decision.'

SO2

Department Support Group

The Department Support Group is a backroom outfit forming a part of Scotland Yard's efforts to streamline its structures and modernise management techniques. SO2 acts as an aid organisation to the whole of Specialist Operations, which consists, in present-day terminology, of five business groups: Crime, Security, Protection, Fingerprints and Laboratory.

'The term "business groups" is used throughout SO,' said Eddie Ellison, the Detective Chief Superintendent in charge. 'A couple of years ago we put our strategic cap on and tried to work out the most efficient way to deliver the service. The intention is to devolve responsibility, authority, and budgetary control down as far as possible towards the delivery of service. It is now accepted that Specialist Operations is five totally disparate groups gathered under the SO heading.'

Ellison regards the idea of competition between the departments as entirely healthy. There is a distinct business-school tone to his summation. 'In commercial terms, what we've tried to create is a holding company called Specialist Operations, and within the holding company the five business groups get as much autonomy as possible.'

He acknowledges the artificiality of the 'business' terminology. 'It's totally artificial,' he said, 'but on the other hand I can think of nothing better. At least it presents a picture. It may not fit in with the chain of command or the designated authorities at the different levels, but at least it presents a picture of a holding company, a group, a loose association with the holding company having certain responsibilities and no other titles. So, yes, we're stealing these terms.'

Operating alongside SO2 as an administrative half of the holding company is the Assistant Commissioner Specialist Operations (ACSO), whose major function is to coordinate the output of the five businesses, and to be a spokesman and general champion for Specialist Operations. It is ACSO who engages in debate about resources with policy and finance committees, and he is a member of the Association of Chief Police Officers (ACPO) Crime Committee. His job is demanding; to perform his role effectively he needs a team to organise and support the business groups. That is the function of SO2.

One regular item they organise is the monthly meeting of the Board of Directors. The Board consists of the three DACs from Crime, Security, and Protection, the Head of SO3 (fingerprint and photographic conglomerate), the Director of SO7 (Metropolitan Police Forensic Science Laboratory), the ACSO, and Detective Chief Superintendent Eddie Ellison.

'Plus whoever from SO2 has been doing work in connection with the topic that's on the agenda that day,' Ellison added.

Seventeen officers operate the Department Support Group. Apart from administering Specialist Operations, they have an internal administrative team to take responsibility for the 'paper flow' associated with all the activities at departmental level. Usually, that means handling the documentation from the Directors' Board Meetings, and the paperwork arising from the ACSO's work on the ACPO Crime Committee.

One of the services provided by SO2 is the Force Language Service, operated by three civilian officers. Their job is to determine the languages and specific dialects police officers may need to interpret in the course of their duty, and to recruit the appropriate interpreters. The recruits, who work on a part-time call-out basis, are trained in police procedures and interrogation protocol. After training they perform a two-way role, putting police questions to members of specific linguistic groups with whom the police have business, and passing back to the police any complaints or questions that the interviewees or their relatives may want to put in their turn.

The operations and responsibilities of SO2 are neatly divided into two main headings, Human and Material Resources and Performance and Management Information.

For most of his working life Eddie Ellison has been a serving detective. Now he has a department about as far from the work of crime detection as it could be. Nevertheless, he sees his years of practical policing as a useful backdrop to his involvement in economics and business strategy. He agrees his job of helping push the Met into the twenty-first century is slow, painful work, but he points out it was harder at the beginning.

'It was an effort, persuading people to put on paper first their moans, then their needs, in order to get the job done. But when we started delivering because of that, it was a sea change. When you see you can put kit where it'll do most good, then you've got motivation for getting the planning side and the paperwork done as efficiently and as quickly as possible.'

Ellison's job may nowadays resemble a company director's, but once a policeman, as they say, always a policeman. One day about a year after taking his office job at

Scotland Yard, he saw something odd at a railway station near his home in Surrey.

'Two young lads, nineteen or twenty years old, sitting in a car, and, well, the only expression is "getting the eyeball", I mean the way they were looking at me . . . when people are looking at you and they hold the eye contact they're either policemen or criminals. I went forward and did a lot of chatting, showing the warrant card. I took the key out of their ignition, I didn't want to get bounced off a bonnet as they drove away. I could see the car was full of gear – ladies' handbags, fishing rods, all sorts of bits and pieces. I got them out of the car and persuaded them they were going to walk back to the railway station with me, when the cavalry from Surrey arrived, three or four panda cars. The lads had been screwing cars all over the place that afternoon. Just before I arrived, it seemed, they had broken into a car right alongside the station, and the taxi service in the station had seen them do it and rung the police, who arrived in time to prevent the lads doing anything other than surrender to me. There's a buzz of adrenaline when you do something like that,' he concluded. 'No desk job and no budget-balancing can match it.'

SO3
Scenes of Crime Branch

Among the investigations recorded at the offices of SO3 is a memoir of a murder case in 1905 when two brothers, identified by their fingerprints, were convicted and hanged. It was the first case in England where fingerprint evidence had achieved a conviction for a capital offence. Nearly ninety years later, fingerprinting is still the most reliable method of identification available to investigators.

SO3, the Scenes of Crime Branch, employs approximately 550 staff, all civilians, most of them in Identification, Fingerprint and Scenes of Crime Officer grades. The remainder, about 200 people, are split roughly two to one between photographic and administrative grades.

Formerly, Scenes of Crime Officers (often called SOCOs) were either police or civilian personnel with basic training in fingerprints, photography and crime-scene examination. Dissatisfaction with their performance led, in 1988, to the scheme being discontinued. Since then, whenever a SOCO retires or resigns, he or she is replaced by an Identification Officer, a fingerprint expert who has also taken the old-style SOCO's forensic retrieval qualifications.

As well as fingerprints, Identification Officers look for shoe or boot prints, blood and other stains, fragments of solid material such as glass or brick, flakes of paint, fibres and hairs – all capable of yielding valuable evidence at the Forensic Science Laboratory.

A fingerprint is a deposit made from the combined oils and sweat of the skin, so it stands slightly proud on a smooth, non-porous surface; once it has been made visible with a dusting of powder, it can be lifted with a strip of adhesive tape. Prints obtained this way are called 'lifts'.

Fingerprint Officers and Identification Officers hand over the prints they find to SO3's Photographic Unit at Amelia Street, close to the main New Scotland Yard building. There, each 'lift' on its transparent support is converted to a photograph which can be examined in detail. The print is sent to SO3's searching teams, who try to match it to those on file.

Also at Amelia Street is a specialist fingerprint laboratory where they use chemical tests to find marks on materials – some plastics and various types of paper – that do not normally respond to powdering.

A total of ninety photographers work for the branch. A number are permanently attached to police surveillance squads and allied units, others are in a pool from which they can be called to a variety of jobs. SO3's photographers have to respond to circumstances exactly as if they were active police personnel. They will sometimes spend hours and even days in one observation position, and they must produce serviceable pictures under circumstances that are rarely ideal. To be of any use, the final shots must show a subject which is lit, scaled and printed to conform with the rules governing photographs used as evidence in courts of law, or in the assembling of scientific evidence.

Large numbers of people at crime scenes can be a hindrance to officers trying to preserve evidence and keep the scene just as it was found. To minimise that problem SO3 photographers make video records at the scenes of major crimes. The footage is used by senior officers at briefings, recreating the scene vividly and in detail, cutting out the need for subordinate officers to go to the crime venue.

Photography is an asset at all levels of police work. SO3, which is on call twenty-four hours a day, handles everything from photographs at post-mortem examinations to publicity stills at award ceremonies. Large-scale automatic processing equipment is available for fast results, developing and printing roll films in minutes if necessary. All work is now standardised on 6×6cm colour stock, the larger negative giving much higher quality than 35mm used under the same circumstances.

'Scenes Of Crime Identification Services is the area where we receive the fingermarks that have been retrieved from crime scenes,' said Newson. 'We try to identify those marks against a database of known criminals.'

Marks 'lifted' at the scene of a crime are returned to SO3's internal processing service where they are converted to photographic images, which are then examined by search teams.

At serious crime scenes care is taken to eliminate irrelevant fingermarks – these can be, for instance, marks left by the family who live at an address where a murder has been committed. Of the searchable prints that remain after elimination, Newson estimated that, on average, one in four or one in five will be identified.

All hand or finger marks recovered at scenes of crime are passed along for searching against the criminal database to an Area Search Team. Unlike the fingerprint records held by SO4, the marks which come to the Area Search Teams have been made inadvertently and therefore erratically. Searching them is far from being straightforward.

'If you'd retrieved ten fingermarks from a crime scene

it would be very easy to do a search,' Newson said, 'and that occasionally happens. But it is rare.'

In the case of the Knightsbridge Safe Deposit Robbery of July 1987, SO3 were able to identify only one mark within the premises, but it pinpointed an individual, Valerio Viccei, who was thereafter watched carefully by the police. His pattern of contacts eventually led to his being arrested, along with several others, and he was ultimately convicted. By identifying the lead player, Newson said, SO3 were able to give the police the key they needed to pursue the correct lines of enquiry and bring the case to a successful conclusion.

Because fingerprints can be classified by specific types, the process of searching is correspondingly narrowed. Instead of looking at 4.3 million prints held by SO4, the expert may only have to search two or three thousand marks on the database. Some patterns, though, confer more individuality than others.

'If you have ten ulnar loops on your fingers,' said Newson, 'from a criminal's point of view it's the best thing to have, because that's the most common pattern people have on their hands.'

An unusual case is recorded at SO3 as the Potter's Bar Golf Club Murder. It happened in April 1955, and the victim was a Mrs Elizabeth Curell. The only evidence the police had to work on was a smudged, bloody palm print from a golf tee marker.

'A palm is very difficult to search, if it isn't classified in any form,' Newson explained. 'You can only check it by going through from start to finish with every set of palms that you have. We have very few palm prints, they're not taken as a matter of course. We appealed to the people of Potter's Bar to have their palm prints taken, under a guarantee that the prints would be destroyed at the end of the search. We received a total of

8,989 sets, and on checking the 4,605th set, we identified the palm of a particular individual.'

The palm print belonged to eighteen-year-old Michael Quẹripel, who was subsequently proved to be the killer.

SO4
National Identification Bureau – Records

The records of nearly five million people are on file at the National Identification Bureau, which means that one adult in ten in Britain has been convicted of a serious offence. At present, the figures include only people convicted of offences which carry the possibility of imprisonment.

SO4 has two components, the Fingerprint Office and the Record Office. Between them they make up the centralised national fingerprint and record collection, containing prints and records gathered from all the police forces in the British Isles.

The main task of the records office is to sort and file criminal records and to transfer the information to microfiche sheets. The record office is run by Acting Detective Chief Superintendent Brian Harwood whose staff of 650, forty-eight of them police officers, deal with over two and a half thousand arrests every day.

A criminal's microfiche record has details of court appearances, convictions and custodial sentences. There are facts important to operational officers, such as whether the subject is known to have carried weapons, or if he is dangerous in any other way. The records are detailed but don't contain so much data that reading them becomes a time-intensive task.

'A record begins at the police station when a person has been arrested,' Harwood said. 'The arresting officer will take down such details as the accused's name, address, age, description, aliases, the MO of the particular crime, and so on. All that information comes here, usually accompanied by fingerprints. If the details are of someone who is already on record then the fresh details are added to the existing file, otherwise a new record is opened. Eventually the accused will appear in court and the result of the hearing will be sent here. It will be attached to the file and also added to the information on the computer, so that any operational officers searching the computer data will be able to find those details.'

The Method Index is a separate computerised file of 47,000 serious offenders who are clearly recognisable by their identity or method of working. Offences included in this category are typically murder, kidnap, fraud and other serious crimes where a distinct criminal method is likely to show.

Although the term 'criminal record' is still used to describe information held at SO4, the name is no longer accurate, since many of the records held by the department do not concern convicted criminals. If someone is arrested under the Prevention of Terrorism Act, for instance, and no subsequent charges are laid, the provisions of the Act permit a record of the arrest to be kept at SO4.

'If a person has a previous conviction record we can add to it,' Harwood said. 'Where they haven't got any previous record, and the current case results in an acquittal, the file has to be destroyed.'

There is what Harwood calls a 'weeding policy' with files. Generally if no additional offence is added to a record for twenty years, then the file is destroyed.

Criminal records are confidential and their contents, or parts of their contents, would be disclosed outside the legal system only in clearly specified circumstances.

Disclosures may be made for three main reasons: on grounds of national security; probity (some would prefer the word 'uprightness') in the administration of justice; and with a view to protecting vulnerable members of the public – for example children, or older people suffering from mental disability. Beyond those three reasons, chief officers of police have the right at their discretion to disclose records, or parts of records, in the public interest – although no such disclosures would be made in the cases of, say, hopeful scout masters or bank tellers. Home Office guidelines do exist, however, to help make decisions in borderline or otherwise difficult cases.

'Disclosure may be allowed in cases of crime prevention if it can clearly be shown to be in the public interest,' said Commander David Stockley, who is in command of SO4. 'In those cases disclosure facilities are granted by the ACPO Disclosure Committee.' ACPO is the Association of Chief Police Officers.

Harwood clarified the position of the individual who wants to know what information the police have about him on file.

'Under the Data Protection Act it is our responsibility to release information we hold on computer about an individual. A person can go into a police station, ask for a copy of his record on the Police National Computer (PNC), and, for a payment of ten pounds, he will be provided with a printout of it. The copy of the record is sent directly to him by post.'

In 1981 the Criminal Record Office, which until then was administered and funded by the Metropolitan Police, became the National Identification Bureau (NIB) which is, as its title suggests, a national resource, funded through the Home Office. The NIB's broad scope requires regular reviews and refinements of the system, which in turn call for special skills. One of these is the ability to get all of the NIB files on to a computer database. That responsibility lies with Detective Superintendent Bob Hamilton, who is the NIB officer working in liaison with the Police National Computer (PNC), in which the records are being stored.

'I am paid, basically, to get rid of the microfiche system,' he says.

Hamilton's goal is a completely computerised system of record keeping. 'That's the principle – to do away with NIB and the staff who process the information manually. Rather than send us data for filming, police forces will key the new information directly into the PNC from their local terminals.'

During the 1970s, when the staff of the Criminal Records Office were converting files to microfiche, they destroyed many millions of paper records, but when they found any of historical interest they held them back. The archive of classic cases now fills three metal filing cabinets in Hamilton's office, and includes such names as Ian Brady, Ronald Biggs, Timothy Evans and John Reginald Halliday Christie.

The contents of the records add an occasionally touching human dimension to the dispassionate work of filing and classification. There is, for example, the record of John Lee, once known widely as 'the man they couldn't hang'.

Lee was convicted in Devon in the late nineteenth century of killing an old woman, his employer. He was tried and sentenced to death. When he came to be hanged in an open part of Exeter prison the trap door refused to work, even though the hangman tried repeatedly to free it. Lee was taken away, the gallows was reconstructed and at a later date he was brought back to be executed. Again, the trap refused to budge. After a

third attempt failed, John Lee was set free, the first
murderer in Britain ever to be paroled. The surviving
record contains a letter from the Home Secretary of the
time to the Chief Constable of Devon, instructing him
to release Lee, but not to tell anyone about the parole,
presumably because it set an uncomfortable precedent:

> Please see that Lee is released and his whereabouts
> are not made known to anyone besides those of the
> police immediately concerned . . . Secrecy must be
> impressed.

The case of the Fox brothers is particularly significant.
Their details are on a file dated 1896 but their first
offence was in 1875. Albert Ebenezer and Ebenezer
Albert Fox were identical twins and frequent petty
offenders in the Hertfordshire area. On the occasions
when they were individually arrested they had a habit of
giving each other's details, which, apart from confusing
the authorities, also gave them opportunities for convincing alibis. Bailiffs, policemen and magistrates were often
baffled and couldn't ever tell them apart, until somebody
had the bright idea of trying the relatively new process
of fingerprinting. The separate and quite distinct prints
at last imposed a firm identity on the brothers.

'Evidence such as this,' said Hamilton, 'was no doubt
given to the Balfour Committee in 1901, which resulted
in the setting up of the Fingerprint Bureau at Scotland
Yard.'

(F) NATIONAL FINGERPRINT OFFICE

Every day of the week the fingerprints of approximately
2,600 people are received at the National Fingerprint
Office. Each set of prints is checked to see if its owner

has a criminal record. To do this, an expert compares the prints with those already in the National Collection of Fingerprints, which contains 4.3 million sets.

'If we don't have someone on file,' said Chris Coombes, Head of the National Fingerprint Office, 'we will create a new file. The actual identification of the prints takes only minutes; however, the volume of work means that from reception of a set of prints until the time we have finished with it, is usually five working days.'

Coombes has a staff of 163 fingerprint officers and thirty-seven clerical support officers – all civilians, like himself. Their real work is completed, he emphasised, once they have established an identification. The part of the record which is used to tell the investigating officer just who he has arrested, and what the previous convictions are, is dealt with by the Criminal Records Office.

'We have a much wider remit than just working for the police,' Coombes said. 'As a National Identification Bureau, our information is available to certain other players within the criminal justice system.'

The work flow is intensive. Prints are received from provincial forces by mail, and a dedicated van service brings in prints from charging centres within the Metropolitan Police District. An enhanced identification service is provided for the Metropolitan Police because the London courts very often deal with people within hours of arrest. For provincial forces speed is not so important, since people brought before provincial courts are usually remanded, giving investigators time to put their paperwork together.

Any ridged area of the hand or foot can be used for identification, but fingerprints are used because they can be taken with the least effort, and the ridges from finger impressions can be quickly sorted into groups for filing. The Henry system of fingerprint classification was first introduced at Scotland Yard in 1901; Sir Edward Henry, the originator, was a former Commissioner of the Metropolitan Police. His system was soon adopted by scores of other law enforcement agencies worldwide and, although there have been variations, the Henry system is now the most widely used method of print classification.

Prints are classified by a three-part process: by shape and contour, by the finger positions of the pattern types, and by counting the ridges in loops and tracing the ridges in whorls. All classification work is done with the naked eye, aided by a magnifying glass, just as it was in 1901. The accumulated information is incorporated into a short formula, which is known as the fingerprint classification.

'The other side of fingerprints,' Coombes said, referring to Scenes of Crime Branch (SO3), 'which most people think is the glamorous side, is the examination of crime scenes and the discovery of fingermarks. Each police force in this country has its own fingerprint bureau which is set up to deal with that sort of work. They will take marks from crime scenes, and compare them with prints from their local active criminals. That's a separate side of fingerprints which the National Identification Bureau does not get involved in.'

People can be identified from fingerprints long after they have died – it could be months or years after, depending on atmospheric conditions in the vicinity of the decaying body. The outer skin of the hand can sometimes be removed (it is called a dermal glove) and slipped over the protected hand of a fingerprint officer so that a proper set of prints can be obtained.

Identifications are measurably subjective. 'What has to be realised is that we are dealing with the *opinion* of a person who has great expertise in these matters,' said Coombes. 'The training programme for a fingerprint expert in this country is five years. Over that time he or she will have made thousands and thousands of comparisons, and that, together with the knowledge gained from intensive training programmes, is what makes them able to give an expert opinion. The defendant is safeguarded by the fact that sixteen points of similarity must be found – sixteen is considered to be more than sufficient to ensure that identity has been conclusively established.'

The work of fingerprint people is highly specialised and to a large extent intuitive; Coombes describes fingerprint experts as a brotherhood. Their expertise, it appears, comes from innate talent rather than acquired qualification. Coombes says he has employed people with degrees who could not cope with the work, and others with no more than one GCSE who are excellent. It is a personal thing, he concludes, but the training is important. Accuracy is important, too.

'Three experts will check an identification before it leaves this building,' Coombes said. 'If people make a mistake it's a disciplinary matter. I liken it to the Queen's Award to Industry, where if a company dealing with seventy-five thousand pieces of work made two mistakes a year, then I think they would probably be a very successful company. Here, if we make two mistakes a year we're a disaster. So, we need to have a rigorous discipline. We cannot afford to make mistakes.'

SO5

Miscellaneous Force Indexes

Four distinct operations are grouped under the heading
Miscellaneous Force Indexes. They are the Juvenile
Index, Central Index of Prostitutes and Adult Cautions,
Missing Persons Bureau, and the Character Inquiry
Section. The Senior Executive Officer in charge is
Roger Tiedeman, a civilian with a staff of seventy-two
people, also civilians.

The Juvenile Index is a card index of information
about incidents which have brought young people to the
attention of the police. It gives details of juvenile cautions, records of missing juveniles, and summaries of
welfare reports.

In the Index, a person is a juvenile until he or she is
eighteen. After that a record is destroyed, unless it has
details of a caution issued during the preceding three
years, in which case the record is kept until the caution
has expired. Cautions records are kept for three years.

'Cautions can be given to juveniles for any type of
offence,' said Tiedeman, and he added that a caution
would merit a full entry of the juvenile's details on the
Index. 'We would keep the name, date of birth, nature
of the offence, where they were cautioned, and the
date.' In 1992 the Index recorded 12,352 cautions of
juveniles.

Records of missing children are kept on the Juvenile
Index, as well as in the Missing Persons Bureau. 'An
officer on division might want to find out what is

known about a particular juvenile,' Tiedeman explained.
'He might ring in on a welfare matter, maybe he's found
the child wandering on the street, and he asks us if
anything is known and we say, yes, he's missing, or he's
prone to go missing.' Between 1 April 1992 and 31
March 1993, 10,527 missing boys and 11,363 missing
girls were reported to the Metropolitan Police.

The Central Index is an index of prostitutes, and of
cautions issued to adults. Tiedeman explained why SO5
keeps an index for prostitutes but none for burglars or
other categories of felons.

'A person who has been soliciting for prostitution can
only be charged with the offence if it is shown that they
have been cautioned twice within the previous twelve
months, or convicted once during that period. The
caution would be given under the terms of the Street
Offences Act. A charge made against a burglar, which
comes under the Attorney General's guidelines, needn't
take any account of the number of previous cautions or
when they took place, and that record would be kept in
the Adult Caution Index.'

Police need to know quickly if a woman has been
cautioned twice in the previous twelve months, and
SO5 provides a twenty-four-hour service to deal with
queries. Figures show that 2,885 prostitute cautions
were recorded in 1992.

The number of adult-caution records created in
London in 1992 was 31,313. A caution record does not
count as a criminal record and is not, therefore, recorded at the National Identification Bureau (SO4).
Each record is kept for three years, then it is
destroyed.

The Missing Persons Bureau mainly serves the Metropolitan Police, although roughly 5 per cent of the input
is from other forces. Its main purpose is to try to match

the descriptions of missing persons with those of dead bodies which have been found.

Most corpses are eventually identified, though in some cases a long time passes before a link is established between a description and an actual body. The longest time it ever took, in the experience of SO5 staff, was in a case where a woman wrote to the Bureau from Canada, trying to trace a son she had not heard from in thirteen years. The description she sent was very thorough, and it matched the record of a body found thirteen years earlier in Eastbourne.

A current mystery on the records is an old man found dead in the street in Eltham in 1990. He was between seventy and eighty years old and was wearing only pyjamas and a dressing gown; the body was clean, so were the clothes, and the man was clearly not a vagrant, yet, in spite of extensive circulation of his description, he has never been identified.

A piece in *The Times* in March 1992 revealed that, according to an internal report submitted by detectives, Scotland Yard's Missing Persons Index was so inaccurate it should be restarted from scratch with a check on every name still listed as missing. The article went on to claim that only five from a sample list of ninety-nine young people listed were still missing and that forty-five people, some of them listed as missing for up to ten years, had since been arrested, or come to the notice of the police, or were in custody, without anyone having updated the index.

Tiedeman said *The Times* article magnified the problems. 'What we have to bear in mind,' he said, 'is that the Index here is only as good as the information that's given to it. But now we do check to make sure that people haven't come to the notice of the police by way of conviction since they went missing.'

Between 1 April 1992 and 31 March 1993, 30,475 missing persons were reported to the Metropolitan Police.

In 1986 arrangements were introduced which allowed authorities to check with the police on people being appointed to jobs giving them substantial access to children. Guidance given by the Home Office specifically covered appointees in local authority education and social services departments, and the Probation Service. Since that time the scheme has been extended to include independent schools, the National Health Service, some voluntary organisations and the proprietors and managers of residential care homes and nursing homes. The inquiries are made through SO5's Character Enquiry Section, where thirty-two people are employed full-time carrying out checks.

'In relation to child-access inquiries we do a check with Criminal Records,' said Tiedeman, 'a check with Adult Cautions, a check with the local police in all the areas where the individual has lived during the previous five years, and another with the Aliens Registration Office if the applicant was born abroad. However, action in connection with the proprietors and managers of residential care homes is limited to a criminal record check.'

Since the checks are made specifically on persons in line to be employed by particular organisations or authorities, they are not made on everyone likely to come into contact with large numbers of children – the legislation does not cover the Boy Scout Movement, for instance. There are no provisions for church authorities to make inquiries, either.

'Lines have to be drawn,' Tiedeman said. His staff are already having to struggle to keep up with the huge intake of inquiries. 'We're receiving anything up to two thousand of them a week now, on average.'

He confirmed that persons checked by his department are first of all asked to give their permission. And if they refuse? 'I would think the authority is likely not to employ them,' he said.

SO6

Fraud Squad

The case of the self-styled 'Lady' Rosemary Aberdour, who defrauded a charity of £3 million, was handled by the Fraud Squad, but certain other prominent fraud cases such as Guinness, Blue Arrow, the Maxwell affair and Barlow Clowes were dealt with by the Serious Fraud Office (SFO). The distinction between the two bodies needs to be clarified.

The SFO was set up in 1987 to investigate and prosecute serious or complex frauds. If a case does not closely fit the specification for an SFO investigation – intricate financial scheming, the implication of prominent people, and a minimum of £5 million at risk or stolen – then in London it will be handled by the Scotland Yard Fraud Squad for investigation.

'We do have cases with more than five million at risk, but they're not terribly complex,' said Detective Chief Superintendent Tony McStravick, until recently the acting head of the Metropolitan Police Fraud Squad. 'They don't need SFO's powers. SFO deal with the most serious, complex fraud cases in the country.'

The new head of the Metropolitan Police Fraud Squad is Commander George Churchill-Coleman, a figure well known through the news media in his role as head of the Anti-Terrorist Branch (SO13), which he left at the end of November 1992, after seven-and-a-half years. He refers to himself as the new boy at SO6, but in fact he has worked on the Fraud Squad twice before, as a Detective Constable and a Sergeant, and later as an Inspector and a Chief Inspector.

'I don't think the issues have changed very much over the years,' he said. 'Fraud, I regret to say, is sometimes regarded as a less urgent crime than others, and yet, if you examine the impact on the community, and on the business community in particular, you will see that major fraud involves a great deal of money and a great deal of agony and anxiety. It affects the economy of the country, too, as we've seen in recent cases.'

The difference between dealing with fanatical, murderous IRA terrorism and the subtle deceit of those who commit fraud is not so wide, he suggests, as it might appear.

'You're dealing with a different type of individual,' he said, 'but you're dealing with a criminal, a man who's going to be devious in his dealings, who's going to produce false documentation, who's going to dispose of assets if he possibly can – all of these things apply for the whole of the criminal fraternity, and in all aspects of crime.'

The Fraud Squad is based in offices above Holborn Police Station at High Holborn. There are a total of 155 officers, of which four are women, all of them trained detectives; they are headed by a Commander, assisted by two Detective Chief Superintendents and four Detective Superintendents. Two operational Squads, 'A' and 'B', actively investigate frauds, while a third group, SO6 Support, deals mainly with Intelligence Gathering, Financial Investigation and Computer Crime. Four Detective Chief Inspectors, each with his own particular job at High Holborn, serve additionally as liaison officers between SO6 and the eight Metropolitan Police Areas.

Challenge is a large part of the job satisfaction in SO6. 'You're pitting your wits against them,' said Mc-Stravick. 'Most men who commit fraud are prepared to sit and answer questions. When I sit down and have an interview with a fraud man, it's an intellectual wrestling match.'

Apart from day-to-day case work, officers joining SO6 take a course in fraud detection, and there are in-house courses in specialist investigations such as public-sector corruption, computer fraud and multiple-share applications fraud.

The general fraud course lasts two weeks. It aims to give officers a grounding in accountancy, asset-tracing, methods of acquiring special warrants and the procedures governing the conduct of Fraud Squad personnel in civil court actions.

Although the course doesn't last long, and officers may expect to find themselves pitted against professionals with years of experience in financial dealing, Mc-Stravick does not think the preparation is inadequate. The essential element of the job, he points out, is detective work.

The daily work of Fraud Squad officers brings them into contact with experts from the commercial sphere and most of the specialist fields of finance. McStravick believes a certain amount of market-place sharpness rubs off on the officers, and feels it does their efficiency no harm.

Questions have been raised about the value of juries in complex fraud trials. It is argued that a jury of average people simply cannot understand the intricacies of large-scale fraud. But McStravick believes it is defence lawyers' tactics that need to be changed, not the jury system. It is in the interests of the prosecution to present a case in as simple and straightforward a way as possible. The trial policy of the defence, he says, is to create a smokescreen.

McStravick points out that the incentives to commit fraud are high, especially to anyone weighing the advantages against those of armed robbery. A lot more can be gained from a successful fraud than from walking into a building society wearing a balaclava and waving a shotgun – and the penalties for fraud are much less severe.

'The sentence for armed robbery can be twelve, fifteen, eighteen years,' said McStravick, 'whereas the most that I know a man has got for fraud is eight years. He was accused of stealing fifteen million pounds, and I think in the end the prosecution case was that he had had eight or nine million.'

More annoying to Fraud Squad officers is to see someone get a short sentence and to know he or she will come out of prison with the proceeds of their fraud intact.

'We very rarely get money back. The Robbery Squad, they occasionally get some. So do Drug Squads. But not us. The money's gone.'

In spite of the frustrations, McStravick considers the Fraud Squad to be the finishing ground for detectives.

'You will find that when the officer leaves here after four or five years and goes to division, he's invaluable, because he fears nothing in terms of paperwork and complexity. He's acquired the confidence to be able to sort out a case, to sit down and work out his investigative plan progressively.'

'A' Squad

'At the moment we're investigating just under two thousand cases of multiple-share applications,' said Detective

Chief Superintendent Howard Jones. 'They've been made by all sorts of people from right across the board.'

When certain public industries were privatised and issues of their shares were launched, the application brochures warned that only a limited number of shares were available to each applicant, and applicants could only apply for shares for themselves. At first, not many people appeared to notice the opportunities for fraud, then a few cases hit the headlines.

'If you bought shares at the time of privatisation,' said Detective Chief Superintendent Jones, 'very shortly afterwards they were worth considerably more, because only so many were floated. So there were some quick killings to be made.'

It is not illegal for an individual to make separate applications in the names of various members of a family, so long as those people receive their shares; it is illegal, though, for somebody to make multiple applications in the names of others and then keep the shares for himself.

'Some people have made a hell of a lot of money out of it,' Jones said. 'The scale is mind blowing. In some cases people made hundreds of applications across a whole range of flotations. We have a computer that goes back over most of the privatisations and it can put together names, addresses and multiple-shares applicants from the past. So if somebody does a multiple-share application tomorrow, say for Telecom 2, we could search back and find out whether they did it on gas, electricity, water, British Steel, British Airports Authority, right the way through. That way we find a pattern, and it shows propensity. We look at those ones more seriously than one-offs, even if the one-off person might have done a lot.'

Lawyers and police officers have been among the

1. Policy Committee, the senior management group. Anti-clockwise from the Commissioner, Paul Condon; John Smith, Deputy Commissioner; Graham Angel, Receiver; John Metcalf, Deputy Assistant Commissioner (Inspectorate); Sarah Cullum, Director of Public Affairs; Bill Taylor, Assistant Commissioner Specialist Operations; Roger Gregory, Deputy Receiver; Bob Hunt, Assistant Commissioner Territorial Operations. (Inset) Peter Winship, Assistant Commissioner Inspection and Review.

2. No 4 Whitehall Place, chosen by Sir Robert Peel as the original headquarters of the Metropolitan Police in 1829. The servants quarters at the back of the house were converted into a police station for A Division. In 1884, the Fenians planted a bomb which blew in a wall.

3. In 1890, the headquarters of the Met transferred to a new building on the Victoria Embankment. Designed by Norman Shaw, it was described by A. P. Herbert as 'a very constabulary kind of castle'. The pecking order was rigidly maintained. Senior officers had their offices on the lower floors; for others, the lower the rank, the higher they had to climb. The building is now used as offices by Members of Parliament.

4. In 1967, New Scotland Yard moved to its present home in Victoria, with the famous revolving sign. A classic product of bland 1960s architecture, the high-rise block is too small to house the headquarters of the Metropolitan Police. There are Scotland Yard departments all over London.

5. David Veness, Deputy Assistant Commissioner, (Special Operations), a product of the accelerated promotion scheme who has risen to the top. Sent to Cambridge University by the Met, his office is easy to find; there is often a Mozart symphony playing at full blast.

6. Superintendent Mike Hames, Head of the Obscene Publications Squad (SO1[4]). His detectives visited Harley Street to learn relaxation techniques, necessary when working with 'the darker side of human nature'.

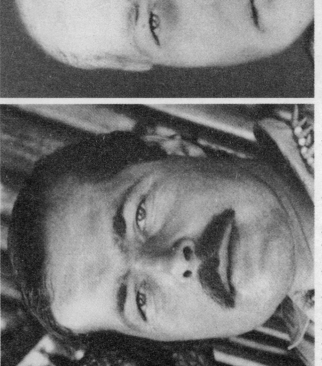

7. Richard John Bingham, the Earl of Lucan, known as Lucky Lucan, who is wanted by Scotland Yard for murdering his children's nanny Sandra Rivet, in 1974. The file is still open. 8. An artist's impression of how Lord Lucan may look today if, as Detective Superintendent Alec Edwards (SO1), who is in charge of the case, believes, he is still alive.

9. The National Fingerprint Office (SO4) receives 2,600 new cases a day from police forces in England and Wales. There are 4.3 million sets of fingerprints on file.

10. The Fire Investigation Unit, part of the Forensic Laboratories (SO7). Based in Lambeth, the laboratories are some of the largest and most modern in the world.

11. Commander John Grieve and Detective Superintendent Roy Clark, the two senior officers of Criminal Intelligence, SO11, one of the most covert squads in Scotland Yard.

12. John Howley, Deputy Assistant Commissioner (Security), who is in charge of Special Branch (SO12) and Anti Terrorist Branch (SO13), and Detective Chief Superintendent Eileen Eggington, in charge of protection (A Squad).

offenders, and, although fraudulent share applications
come from most sectors of society, people with inside
information or special knowledge of financial dealing
are the first to be investigated when SO6 checks the
legality of applications.

In the main, pointers like similarity of names and
addresses, or details of bank accounts, are what help 'A'
Squad put together strong cases in multiple-share
frauds. To get a look at a bank account, the police have
to obtain a warrant from a High Court Judge and not,
as is usually the case, from a magistrate. The warrant
can only be granted if the police demonstrate that a
serious arrestable offence has taken place, and that there
has been serious loss or harm to any person under the
terms of the Police and Criminal Evidence Act (PACE).
Granting the warrant is entirely at the discretion of the
Judge.

Talking about the traits of people who commit fraud
professionally, Jones cited greed, cunning, and effron-
tery. He added that they are often inclined to cheat their
own families.

'The common denominator, of course, is greed,' he
said. 'The person who makes the multiple-share application is greedy. The person who is the advanced-fee
fraudsman is greedy, and sometimes so is his victim.'

Another type of fraud investigated by 'A' Squad is
known as a 'commodities fraud'. Detective Sergeant
Peter Maxted elaborated.

'A company, Roadex Securities SA, was run and
owned by a Ugandan Asian. The business, which he
had been running for about two years, dealt in the
minor metals – tungsten, cobalt – metals for which there
is no terminal exchange . . .' There is a London Metals
Exchange which deals in non-ferrous metals, but not in

minor metals. 'They are just sold over the phone. Anyway, he was offering private investors the chance to participate in what he called cash-and-carry metal deals.'

He claimed to be buying metal at a particular price, then selling it on for a higher price, using his knowledge of the market to make the maximum profit in the least possible time.

The operation was highly plausible. He operated from opulently furnished offices – finest leather upholstery, teak furniture and fittings in the board room – and travelled around town in a chauffeur-driven Mercedes. It was later discovered that neither the well-appointed offices nor their furnishings had been paid for, and the car and driver had been loaned by a friend. But appearances were what mattered, and he appeared to be reliably prosperous.

'The investors put their money in,' Maxted said. 'They got their post-dated cheques. Then he would contact them again and say he had another deal coming up and did they want to participate? He'd say, for example, "This time it's going to cost you £65,000, but the return is going to be upwards of 10 per cent." So they put in the money, got their post-dated cheques, and before the settlement date on the second contract, a third contract would come up, and there would be the situation of the capital being rolled on from one contract to another, and just the interest coming out in cash on each transaction.'

That went on for nearly fourteen months, then the post-dated cheques began to bounce. At about the same time the man and his family left England and went to Switzerland. The first Maxted and his colleagues knew of the business was when forty placard-waving investors marched on Scotland Yard.

'This chap's office was in Buckingham Palace Road,

just down the road from the Yard. So a DI and I went down there to see what was what. We spoke to a few irate investors who had headed up syndicates worth something in the region of two and a half to three million pounds each. All that money had been raised by word of mouth, through friends of friends. There had been no advertising at all. A total of ten million pounds was involved. One guy was so taken in that he gave up his business and more or less worked full time with the entrepreneur, managing his syndicates and bringing in more money, and more money, and more money . . .'

The Asian's office had been left intact, so the Fraud Squad were able to begin examining the paperwork. Shortly after the investigation began, the inspection department of the Banco Exterior in Covent Garden complained to Bow Street CID that one of their accounts had been granted an unauthorised overdraft of a million pounds; the inspectors suspected the bank manager and his assistant were involved in a fraud.

'The bank account that was overdrawn was Roadex Securities SA,' said Maxted. 'So we had two frauds to investigate – first, the fraud on the bank and, second, the fraud on the investors of Roadex. It turned out that the sub-manager at the bank was massaging the Roadex account to make it look healthy. Following our inquiries, we arrested the manager and the sub-manager of Banco Exterior. We also arrested the second-lieutenant in the Roadex office.'

Eventually SO6 learned that the entrepreneur was in hospital in Brussels, having a sinus operation. SO6 asked the Belgian Police to identify him and detain him, as his extradition would be sought. He was eventually extradited back to Britain a year later, in October 1989. At trial he was charged with a number of criminal offences; he pleaded guilty on every count and was finally sentenced to six years in prison.

'The trial on the bank fraud involved the bank manager and a sub-manager,' said Maxted, who was sentenced to four years' imprisonment. The bank manager was acquitted. At a subsequent trial the bank manager got three years. An accomplice, was convicted of procuring the execution of a valuable security.

Maxted said the major part of the operation was taken up in identifying the investors, taking statements from them and studying the masses of paper related to their involvement with Roadex Securities SA.

'But the crux of the case,' he said, 'was that we had to prove none of these so-called metal contracts ever existed.'

Maxted consulted the chairman of the Minor Metals Trading Association. Between them they circulated all the Association's members, asking them if they knew Roadex Securities SA, and if they had ever traded with them.

'As a result,' Maxted said, 'we were able to show that in the space of twelve months only one metal contract had ever gone through.'

The ten million pounds obtained fraudulently by the accused was not recovered. It is reasonable to assume that it would be waiting for him, somewhere, when he left prison.

'B' Squad

Detective Chief Superintendent Rod Bellis explained and illustrated the time-proven 'long firm' fraud, in which, essentially, a villain obtains goods on credit, then sells them again without paying for them.

'You register a company, you probably buy it off the

shelf, and you register two, three, or four fictitious directors. You start to trade, and what you do is buy goods wholesale on credit from five or six different companies. To begin with, you might have to be financed to pay cash on delivery, because if they don't know you they'll run a credit check, and if you're a new company that will probably come back as "no trace". So it's cash on delivery, and as time passes and they learn to trust you, they extend payment over a period.'

The next step is for the new company to try to get credit from several companies they haven't dealt with before. As referees, the villain gives the names of the five or six companies he has recently been dealing with. These firms, of course, will give favourable credit references.

'And the people you then approach, they will give you credit, because you have good references. And then you hit the new companies. You gradually increase the size of the orders, you probably do pay some of these companies as well, and you extend the credit period. And then all of a sudden you order quite massively, dispose of the goods and decamp. That's long firm fraud, very basically.'

Another method of committing long firm fraud is to buy up a company which has traded respectably for many years and already has a credit rating. The purchaser keeps the original staff and the directors; few people know the business has been taken over. As with the fictitious company, the new owner goes through the same process of placing a massive order with the established suppliers, disposing of the goods, and decamping.

Another type of fraud investigated by 'B' Squad is charity fraud. Detective Chief Inspector Paul Brown of 'B' Squad described a recent case.

'Even in a recession, people are very generous when it comes to the emotive subjects – orphans, the starving – and you can obtain huge amounts of money just by wearing a forged identification badge and rattling a tin or a box or a bucket in the high street. That's a fraud which is very hard to detect initially. Easy to prove if we discover it, because the guy's just not an authorised collector.'

Some of the more subtle charity swindles revolve around the activities of fund-managers and fund-raisers, as distinct from the charities themselves. Fund-raisers will often approach administrators of a charity and tell them they are going to have a charity drive, and that their charity will be the beneficiary; usually the administrators will be grateful and thank the fund-raisers, and they might express their gratitude in a brief letter, which can often be represented as a form of consent.

'We investigated one like that,' DCI Brown said, 'where the people involved set themselves up as fund-raisers. The named beneficiary was a local charity that assisted with mobility for disabled people. The fund-raisers set up lotteries and various other money-raising events. On a lot of their documents they used the charity's name, and very close underneath it they put a number, which we believe most people assumed was the charity number. In fact it was these people's limited company number. They were collecting on behalf of the charity, but they were a *business* collecting, the charity wasn't collecting. And as a business they can take from the money raised reasonable costs, expenses and such like.'

From almost half a million pounds collected, the charity was given £88,000. The fund-raisers' way of life changed almost at once. Among other outward signs, they moved into a pleasant detached property and began driving Mercedes cars.

'It came to our notice through the charity thinking something was awry. The case went to the Charity Commissioners, who have powers to draw in accounts. They were extremely concerned and referred it to us. We searched offices and home addresses and found the real evidence. The fund-raisers' mortgage, for example, was being paid out of an account which purported to be for the lease payment on computer equipment to run the business. The outgoing so-called business expenses were paying for the home and cars and other luxury items, including a world trip.'

On closer examination of the paperwork, 'B' Squad officers found an added little 'scam': the family involved in the fraud, and their relatives, were frequent and substantial winners of the lotteries they had set up on behalf of the charity.

The case went to the Crown Court and the accused were convicted of false accounting – the jury rejected a charge of theft.

SO6 Support

A large area of this group's work comes under the heading of Intelligence Gathering and Development, and that in turn is divided mainly into the Commercial Crime Intelligence Bureau (CCIB), Disclosures, Target Surveillance Operations, and the Enquiry and Research Section.

Commercial Crime Intelligence Bureau (CCIB) This is a collection point for computerised information from inside and outside the Fraud Squad, which is organised on a database.

'The information comes from jobs that are already being investigated,' said Detective Superintendent Ken MacPherson, head of SO6 Support, 'and there's intelligence from contacts within the financial world in the City. All these, and contacts from registered informants, are fed to the database, along with any snippets picked up from the newspapers.'

All crimes investigated by SO6 go on the database. Available details of individuals currently or formerly known to commit fraud are registered there, too, although, under the terms of the Data Protection Act, files are reviewed every three years, and names that have not been active since the last search are removed. Although the contents of the database are used by police forces nationally, this remains a Metropolitan Police facility.

'It's come to be looked upon as a national crime intelligence unit,' MacPherson said, 'although other Fraud Squads have their own intelligence databases. There's talk of us having an index where every fraud that's reported in the country would be logged, along with the type of fraud and the officer dealing with it, so that when a fraud comes in you could check with the index to make sure there's nobody dealing with something similar, or even the same fraud.'

CCIB also keeps an extensive library of books and journals for guidance on the complexities of finance and the relevant institutions, as well as biographical and background data on prominent business people. 'The books are a source of reference,' MacPherson said. 'They are always available for officers throughout the Met.'

Disclosures Detective Superintendent MacPherson explained Disclosure by giving an example. A hypothetical bank manager has an account in his branch with an average balance of £800, and every month a salary cheque of £1,000 is paid in. This pattern is more or less steady, certainly to within a few hundred pounds, until the manager suddenly finds that somebody has paid £7,000 into the account in cash; the following month there is another cash payment of £6,000. Under new legislation, the manager would be obliged to report any suspicion of illegal financial transactions.

'Through his Head Office, under the Disclosure system, he will report the details of the suspect activity, which will then be reported direct to the NCIS (National Criminal Intelligence Service). We are the dissemination point of that information to the Metropolitan Police – we send particular information out to one of the Areas who have an asset confiscation desk. An officer will be appointed to the case and he will speak to the bank manager and do some background checks on the person whose account it is. There is no power to interview the bank's client at this stage.'

In the area of Disclosures, SO6 Support are effectively a post office between NCIS and Area. It is an onerous side of their work and one they are keen to be rid of. When the legislation first appeared there were approximately five hundred disclosures annually, but the figure now is closer to twelve thousand a year. Also, with new legislation coming along, bank managers are likely to react to the smallest irregularities.

'The problem for a bank manager,' MacPherson said, 'is that, under the new Drugs Trafficking Act legislation that's coming in, if he fails to disclose what proves to be a drug-money laundering operation, then he is subject to criminal proceedings himself. Under the Criminal Justice Act, on the other hand, if a bank robber puts stolen money through the bank, reporting it is only discretionary. If the bank manager doesn't disclose it, nothing will happen to him.'

The legislation is in fact being broadened to include penalties on bank managers for failing to report suspected proceeds from armed robberies. Any kind of exceptional money transaction, across the counter or by electronic transfer, will be subject to scrutiny if the manager or his staff become suspicious. The new legislation puts pressure not only on bank managers, but on chartered accountants, insurers and any other institutions dealing directly with money.

'In most cases of disclosure,' MacPherson said, 'nothing is done about it. But if you don't have an all-embracing policy like this, then the important ones will slip through the net.'

Target Surveillance Operations SO6 has its own surveillance team used by 'A' or 'B' Squad when they need information on people and/or transactions related to active inquiries. Detective Superintendent MacPherson gave an example of the squad's work.

'There was an insurance scam not long ago where eleven people were arrested. The surveillance team were able to trace where the various suspects lived, they followed them and actually saw one of them damage a car, the subject of a false claim, with a sledge-hammer. They were able to give evidence of illegal doings – although that's not part of their function, their job is purely intelligence-gathering.'

The insurance case involved a group of people who had been successfully making claims for accidents involving high-value cars, until it was noticed at the insurance office that the offending owner of a car in one claim would be the victim in another claim. All the accidents on the claims were fictitious and the claimants made hundreds of thousands of pounds from the fraud.

Once suspicions had been aroused, the SO6 surveillance squad began tailing people from a business address in Harrow, and the net spread so wide that, on the morning arrests were finally made, over 100 officers were involved. Without the back-up of diligent surveillance, the Fraud Squad would only have been able to home in on two or three of the suspects.

'The surveillance squad do not select their own targets,' said MacPherson. 'Most are selected for them. But in the course of their work they are developing their own intelligence, which can go on computerised databases for possible future use. That's an important part of surveillance, the developing and recording.'

Surveillance officers are chosen for various qualities, patience being an important one, since they often have to sit in cars for six, seven or eight hours at a stretch without moving. They have to blend into their surroundings; outstanding features would obviously be a drawback to their work.

'One of the secrets of good surveillance officers,' MacPherson said, 'is that they dress up to dress down. They put on clothes that they take off, because that's a quick way of changing your appearance.'

Enquiry and Research Section A Detective Sergeant and a Detective Constable run this unit, nicknamed EARS, which is described by Detective Superintendent MacPherson as the Station Office of the Fraud Squad.

'They deal with any telephone calls that come in, any allegations of fraud, any callers. Members of the public are entitled to come directly here with allegations of fraud. If they do they'll be seen by one of these officers who will take all the details. If he feels it's a matter that we should deal with, it'll be retained here. If not, it will be dealt with on division.'

Computer Crime Unit

Detective Inspector John Austen heads SO6 Support's Computer Crime Unit, manned by five police officers assisted by three technicians. Their job is to investigate all allegations of computer misuse in the Metropolitan Police District, and to deal with complaints from foreign countries of computer crime originating from unknown sources inside the United Kingdom.

'We're the only computer crime unit in the country,' said Austen, 'and one of the few in the world. We were the first. The FBI have only had a unit since late 1990. I started this unit in 1984. The only other countries that have them are Australia, Germany, and Holland.'

Their first prominent case involved two hackers called Gold and Schifrren. Hackers are technically sophisticated computer enthusiasts; the name is now almost exclusively applied to people who use personal computers to break into the computer systems of banks and businesses to obtain information, to alter vital operating procedures, or simply to do harm. Gold and Schifrren were able to open and peruse a number of bank-account files, including the Duke of Edinburgh's.

'With the help of British Telecom I charged them with fraud and forgery,' said Austen. 'They were convicted at Crown Court, then they appealed to the Court of Appeal, which threw the case out. So we appealed to the House of Lords on a point of law that they committed forgery, and we lost. But in losing I knew that we'd won, because there was so much publicity about it.

There was a lacuna in the law – everybody knew it. That's why we've now got the Computer Misuse Act.'

The first major hacking case to be brought under the Computer Misuse Act involved nineteen-year-old Paul Bedworth of Ilkley, West Yorkshire. Using a £200 BBC microcomputer, Bedworth hacked into networks at Lloyds Bank, the EC headquarters in Luxembourg, the *Financial Times*, various universities, and organisations engaged in medical research. Bedworth had two collaborators who admitted offences under the Act and were dealt with separately.

'Bedworth was very much the third man,' Austen said. 'What they were doing over a period of two or three years was breaking into computer systems all over the world to gain what we call system-manager status. That is, control of the computer, quite often to modify its contents, so it would be unworkable, or just to get into it and see what was there and come out again.'

M. Piedboeuf, a systems consultant from Luxembourg, explained to the court how Bedworth's intrusion into the computer of the European Organisation for Cancer Research meant that, for a time, consultant surgeons could not research the database because the system had crashed. Evidence was also brought to show that Bedworth had tapped into his mother's telephone line – because his own had been disconnected – and, through using his computer to 'trawl' various networks, had run up a telephone bill that ran to thirty-four pages.

'It took us two years to get them,' said Austen. 'At first we just had odd reports. I remember the first one. It was from the European Commission in Brussels; somebody had crashed their system – made it stop. They had traced the origin to the United Kingdom, but they didn't know where. There were no clues. We had to start tracing back through all these different network gateways, and most of the time, of course, there was nothing there.'

A network, in computing terminology, is simply a number of individual computers which share their information. Normally they are linked by telephone lines and they therefore go in and out of telephone exchanges. Datalines, which often connect large computer systems, go through points called gateways, reserved for computer data only, which do not carry speech traffic. On any network there are a large number of gateways.

'Trying to trace back through all that was an absolute nightmare. We eventually had hundreds of reports and we were pretty sure the intrusions were all by the same group of people, because we began finding messages that said "*You have been hacked by 8LGM.*" We found out eventually it stood for the 8-Legged Groove Machine.'

The group even began taunting the police with messages challenging them to find out what would happen next, and where. The big mistake the group made was to begin an electronic dialogue with organisations in the United States; in one of these exchanges a hacker revealed he had been a student at the University of Liverpool.

'That was our first break,' said Austen. 'Eventually these guys were on the computer systems eight to ten hours a night, and from the same person we eventually found out his first name. From finding that out, we eventually identified him. The difficulty now was, we knew who he was, but we could not prove what he was doing. The Secretary of State can grant a Warrant for Interception, but that wouldn't have been very effective in our scenario, because it cannot be used as evidence. So we decided to play a waiting game. We knew there was more than one person involved.'

Paul Bedworth, the hacker who went on trial, joined the group late into their activities, using the codename Wandii. Although as a team they caused widespread chaos, they never knew each other's real names, and only met for the first time in a police station after they were arrested.

'It took a lot of dogged detective work,' said Austen, 'and putting monitors on some routes they were using – we are allowed to put monitors on victims' machines. We found that one of Bedworth's victims was Leeds Polytechnic, and so we managed to get the people there to put on a monitor, and we were able to watch the traffic Bedworth was moving through, then we found some telephone numbers and eventually managed to trace where the people were.'

Austen outlined the consequences of their actions. They virtually wrecked the logic centre of the computer at the Polytechnic of Central London, doing damage that cost £200,000 to put right. Even after the computer had been fixed, huge amounts of information remained irretrievable. At the *Financial Times* there was serious confusion because they knew someone had taken temporary control of their computer, so they could not be sure if certain figures they published were accurate. Alterations had been made to some accounts on the EC Commission's computer in Brussels.

Austen and his team hoped that Bedworth's case would attract a penalty severe enough to deter any but the most rabid hackers, but after a fifteen-day trial at Southwark Crown Court in South London, Bedworth, who claimed that he was helplessly addicted to hacking, was acquitted of all charges.

Detective Sergeant Andrew Laptew, who headed part of the inquiry, said he was devastated by the verdict. He believed the prosecution of computer crime would be very difficult in the future, and that many prosecutions might be dropped if the accused claimed to be addicted.

The existence of computer viruses, and the increase in their numbers and varieties, is even more worrying than the activities of hackers. A computer virus is a program, designed as a joke or as sabotage, which can self-replicate, just like a real virus, by attaching to other programs and thereby moving from machine to machine, sometimes causing massive damage.

'The detrimental effect can be a very simple thing,' said Austen, 'such as putting words on the screen. There's one virus called Joshi, and all that happens is Joshi comes up on the screen, and to get rid of it you type J-O-S-H-I. And the Italian Virus is a ping-pong ball virus that bounces around the screen. It doesn't actually damage the data, but it's a damned nuisance. At the other extreme are viruses like Michelangelo and the Dark Avenger – they will destroy your data completely.'

Michelangelo is a variation of an early computer virus which, when activated, would scramble all the data in a computer's memory and render the machine's hard disc useless. Since the hard disc is often the storage medium for vast quantities of information, Michelangelo was invariably disastrous for machines which 'caught' it, though at present it seems to be dormant.

Nobody was ever arrested for creating and distributing Michelangelo, or the Dark Avenger, or Jerusalem, or the Maltese Amœba. 'There are now about two thousand of these viruses,' said Austen. 'They are distributed worldwide. We did make some arrests recently – six people, no charges yet. They called themselves the Association of Really Cruel Viruses. They have written new viruses and have been distributing them. There's no money in it. It's just vandalism.'

A widely publicised case handled by SO6 concerned the AIDS diskette. A diskette is a small computer disk used with personal computers. The function of a diskette (sometimes referred to as a floppy disk) is to carry electronic data which can be read by the computer.

In December 1989, approximately twenty thousand diskettes were sent from London to medical establishments and banks around the world, though not to America, claiming to contain information about the disease AIDS. Thousands of doctors and research scientists put the diskettes into their computers straight away. Immediately a message came up on their screens, telling them that if they did not send money to a specified company in Panama all their computer data would be destroyed. The discs were Trojan horses, and most people who received them fell for the trick.

'And they couldn't get out of the program,' said Austen. 'It was locked in. What the diskettes actually contained was a long program which fed certain instructions to the computers, so that, after they had been restarted ninety times, all the data stored in their memories would be encrypted and rendered useless.

'So we had people all around the world complaining to us – they knew we were handling it – that their computers didn't work. And these were important machines, most of them were to do with medical research into AIDS. So we had people like the University of Turin, who had lost about twelve months' data. We had the Coventry and West Midlands Haematology Department who had lost a lot of research data into AIDS. It was happening all over. The deal was that if they didn't send money to Panama, they wouldn't be sent the cure for their computers.'

SO6 advertised throughout the world, on television and in newspapers, telling people who had received the diskettes not to pay the money. Paying-up would have done no one any good, because at approximately that time the American Army invaded Panama. There was widespread civil disruption.

'And the computers, in the end, weren't ruined,' said Austen. 'We got one of the consultants that we use, a virus researcher, to write a program to counteract the one on the diskettes, and we distributed the antidote free of charge.'

Eventually SO6 found the man responsible for creating the AIDS diskette and distributing it. He was Doctor Joseph Lewis Popp, a consultant to the World Health Organisation. In need of a way to make money, Popp had flown to London and had his original diskette commercially copied. He mailed the copies from London, then left for Kenya to take up an appointment teaching people how to use computers in medical practice.

'He had a mental breakdown after about four weeks there,' said Austen, 'and they shipped him back to the States. He actually flew from Nairobi to Amsterdam. He was picked up by the police in Amsterdam because he was still in an abnormal condition. In hospital he asked for the protection of the American Consulate and they eventually got him back to Cleveland in the United States.'

Some time later an officer of the Intelligence Service in Holland saw a police report of a hospitalised American behaving strangely and talking incoherently about disks; the officer immediately remembered a memo from Austen asking police officers to be alert for someone who might know about computers. Austen received a call from Holland as he was wrapping his children's presents on Christmas Eve.

'We did a search for Dr Popp,' he said. 'The World

Health Organisation said he had been teaching in Kenya. We contacted the Nairobi police, who confirmed the doctor had flown from there on a particular date. Then we found out that the Customs in Nairobi had seized a package from him that they thought was suspect, and in that package was the seal of this company in Panama. So we knew we had the right guy. The trouble was, he was in Cleveland, and he had not committed any crime in America, which under the extradition treaty gets difficult. Anyway, we made an application and we eventually got him back.'

In due course a case was made for presentation in court, but the judge decided that Dr Popp was psychologically unfit to stand trial.

'So we shipped him back to America,' Austen said.

SO7

Forensic Science Laboratory

In March 1991, the Court of Appeal set free six Irishmen (the 'Birmingham Six') convicted and imprisoned on life sentences for the murder of twenty-one people in two Birmingham pubs in 1974. At the trial, crucial forensic evidence included chemical tests showing that two of the accused had been handling explosives near the time of the bomb blasts. The appeal which set the men free rested on forensic evidence showing that residues of soap or cigarette smoke could have produced the same test results.

The release of the Birmingham Six was the most sensational in a series of reversals dating from 1989. The decision gave rise to the appointment of a Royal Commission to evaluate the capability of the British criminal justice system. The findings of the Select Committee were released in March 1993. They commented that in only three of the seven recent *causes célèbres* (the Birmingham Six, the Maguire Seven and Judith Ward cases) forensic science was at fault. The mistakes, moreover, occurred between fifteen and twenty years ago, and were made by only two of the fourteen forensic science laboratories in the UK.

Although the findings exonerated forensic science from general claims of inadequacy, and none of the cases in question involved the Metropolitan Police Forensic Laboratory (MPFSL), the Director, Dr Brian Sheard, admitted that the appeals and the garish publicity had made it a difficult time ·for him and his colleagues.

Today, with forensic science offering a comprehensive array of skills and technologies in the service of justice, no other establishment has such a wide capability under one roof as the MPFSL at Lambeth Road, south-east London. However, there are people who believe that impartiality is impossible as long as the laboratory is under the control of the police.

Sheard has his own views on the question of independence, but they arise from concerns about practical management.

'It isn't clear that senior police officers have got anything to offer a laboratory,' he said, 'so that should make you wonder whether there should be a management link. They are asked to do far too many things that are not at the core of policing, and they shouldn't have to. You can argue that forensic science is one of those things. One way to simplify matters would be to have forensic science outside.'

Sheard added that his judgements and opinions on the siting of the laboratory are based on the optimum conditions for the forensic personnel to do their work. 'They are not based on considerations of integrity in any way. But I can well understand that if people on the outside think we should be moved because they feel that justice is more clearly seen to be done, fine.'

Turning to the MPFSL's national role, Sheard said it was limited: 'The Anti-Terrorist Branch (SO13) has a national role. Where they become involved in cases they call on their laboratory, which is us. So to that extent we've got a national role. Otherwise none, really. We're here to serve the Metropolitan Police and the City of London Police, but by a large margin, we work for the Metropolitan Police.'

The biggest operational headache that besets the MPFSL is the time it takes to get results. They are demand-led and resource-limited, Sheard said, pointing out that, although senior police ranks recognise there is a need to put levels of priority on the work being passed to the laboratory, police officers at operational level simply are not interested.

'They don't want to, they think it's wrong, and they expect to have a demand-led service. That problem has been solved by executive agencies using a mechanism which the police do not like, but it has been solved. They pay for services, they're a separate organisation.'

Eleven Detective Sergeants known as Lab Sergeants provide assistance at the scenes of major crimes, typically murder or very serious assault.

'Even quite senior Detective Officers can go through an entire working career and see very few murders, which means that if a senior Detective Officer has to deal with a very serious case then he may feel a little exposed, and they find it very reassuring indeed to have one of our Detective Sergeants with them.'

Physical Science Division

The Physical Sciences Division is the largest division in the laboratory, staffed by eight-five scientists and nine photographers and handling casework in a broad range of specialist fields. The term 'Physical Sciences' was explained by Mike Loveland, Deputy Director in charge of the division.

'We have a saying in forensic science, which is that every contact leaves a trace, and that's a basic principle that goes back to the days of Sherlock Holmes. In fact it was coined in the last century by a chap called Edward Lockard . . . These traces contribute to the possibility of connecting a person with a crime scene. Or, indeed, the traces may help to eliminate another person from the inquiry.'

The Physical Sciences Division incorporates the Criminalistic Department. 'I guess "criminalistic" is a word coined within forensic science to mean the science of looking for particular contact traces,' said Loveland. 'We narrow it down a little. In our laboratory it refers to things like glass, paint and soil, to things like putty, occasionally to noxious liquids used to stun a person during an aggravated burglary – ammonia is an example.

'We do quite a lot of work with vehicle paint, too. In the case of a non-stop accident we may have a person who's been killed or seriously injured, lying in the road with no vehicle in sight. Now, in the impact of the accident, the victim may have come into sharp contact with the bonnet of the car, picking up traces of paint and maybe even glass from a headlamp. At the same time traces of the victim's clothing will be transferred to the car.

'It is great to get a bit that fits a jigsaw puzzle,' said Loveland, 'and that is the sort of thing they do in Criminalistics. The burden of proof rests with them, the evidence must stand up to scrutiny in a court of law, so it has to be beyond reasonable doubt. That's a demanding responsibility for any scientist.'

Success is usually based on dogged comparison work and meticulous, detailed examination, aided by an understanding of 'latent' marks and the many ways of making them show.

'We use specialised lighting, like lasers and ultraviolet, sometimes chemical treatments, and often we manage to visualise a mark on a floor that would otherwise be invisible. This is valuable in establishing the route of entry to premises. Did they come in through the front door? Were they welcomed in almost? Did they come in through a back door? What we can do there is use various electrostatic lifting devices to reveal latent shoe marks and thus establish a probable mode of entry. Then the marks are recovered, again electrostatically; we bring them back to the laboratory, photograph them, and compare them with shoes from a suspect.'

The Serious Crimes Unit combines the skills of scientists, photographers and fingerprint experts to derive maximum value from contact-trace evidence found at the scenes of serious crimes.

'This was set up in the early 1980s,' said Loveland. 'What was happening at a lot of our major crime scenes was that there was poor communication – lots of specialists but none of them sharing their findings. And there was the worry of contamination, with so many experts in various disciplines moving around at the scene. So we decided to rationalise. First we decided that fingerprints could benefit from modern technology, both from the standpoint of light sources and chemical treatments. So, among others, we got Ken Creer, our chief photographer, interested with his lasers.'

Creer, recently awarded the MBE, is an expert in the visualisation of latent marks using lasers and other light sources. He is regarded as one of the world's leading authorities in his field. The work of his Photographic Unit ranges from the routine photography of exhibits to recording latent evidence with the aid of special light sources. The unit has the facilities and expertise to look at evidence on security films from bank raids; they carry out comparison checks on cameras and films featuring as evidence in criminal cases. For example, in certain cases they can match a set of negatives to the camera that took them.

'Photography, as we understand it in the laboratory,' said Loveland, 'is mainly a service unit. We capture on film a great deal that people want to present in court. So much of the work is in support.'

The day-to-day services of the Photographic Unit are provided mainly to scientific sections within the MPFSL and, on occasions, directly to police officers.

'There are something like ten thousand fires a year in London,' Loveland said. 'That's everything from setting fire to a wastepaper bin to burning very large premises, causing millions of pounds' worth of damage and probable loss of life. Our Fire Investigation Unit goes to all fatal fires unless there's a very good reason not to go. They're automatically treated as suspicious.'

'Roger Beret and his colleagues in the Fire Investigation Unit have spent a lot of time looking at hundreds of different types of fires. They go with a very open mind. They listen to what the Fire Brigade have got to say, because they may well have been there just after the fire started. They will look for the possibility of electrical faults, because a lot of fires are not criminal.'

Depending on the degree of damage, the investigators from the unit can deduce whether there was a short circuit in the wiring, leading to a fire, or if the wire melted as a *result* of the fire. A lot can be learned from the state of junction boxes and fuses. If a flammable liquid was used to start a fire, the heat rises but the liquid drops, so traces of the liquid may be found under floorboards and in basements. If the substance can be recovered it will be prima-facie evidence. If it is petrol, it may even be possible to specify the type. Even if there are no visible traces of a flammable liquid, the Fire Investigation Unit has a device which can detect the components of petrols and other substances by a process similar to smell.

'It's got a highly discriminatory sensory pattern,' Loveland said. 'Better than the human nose.' The device does not positively identify a substance, it indicates the presence of a component. 'What it would really say to us is, look, this particular area is worthy of further investigation. It tells us it may be worth taking debris from that area to bring back to the laboratory for further examination and chemical testing, so we can get unequivocal confirmation, or not.'

The speciality of the section known as Instrument Support is the analysis and comparison of specimens – petrol, tear gas, white spirit, oils, greases, paint – often in minute quantities. Methods used to analyse and compare include gas chromatography, infra-red spectroscopy and microspectrophotometry. All of these, in their separate ways, break down a substance into its components, revealing a pattern which lends itself to detailed comparison with others.

Traffic Accident Investigation is a section which applies specialist techniques in physics, metallurgy and engineering to a range of traffic cases. Accident reconstruction is a part of the unit's work, the main objective being to establish the speed of vehicles involved in collisions.

'Put simply,' Loveland said, 'you look at the skid patterns on the road, carry out measurements and from those you can determine the speed of a vehicle. Also from the skid patterns, and from damage to vehicles and other features, we can actually start to put together a picture of the sequence of an accident.'

'The section called Questioned Documents covers everything, really, from major fraud, demand notes across the counters of banks and building societies,' Loveland said, 'to threatening letters, forgeries and documents related to terrorist activity. Anything you can think of where a person might use a piece of paper and some means of writing on it.'

The work calls for experts with advanced skills in handwriting analysis and an understanding of the print characteristics from output devices like typewriters and computer printers. Some cases call for updated versions of long-established techniques, such as impression-reading.

'If you write on a note pad and you whip off the top sheet,' Loveland said, 'you can see on the second sheet the impression of what you wrote. But if you're very light handed, or if it's the fourth or fifth page down, the impression is too faint to see. That is where ESDA comes in.'

ESDA, Electro-Static Deposition Apparatus, has come to the fore in recent years as a result of evidence in police officers' notebooks being questioned, and in cases where investigators suspected that pages of 'testimony' had been added to statements after prisoners had verified and signed them. The process is straightforward: suspect sheets of paper are evenly charged with static electricity; powdered graphite is then poured in a stream across the surface of the paper and produces an image of any impressions, however faint.

'In a famous case we had,' Loveland said, 'the process actually showed up the pre-impressed home address of a man who had passed a demand note across the counter of a bank. We gave the information to the police and they went round to the house and waited for the individual to come back.'

The police rely heavily on the Questioned Documents section to verify handwriting, particularly signatures.

Given a large enough number of specimens, a competent document handler can establish a profile of a person's style, because, although handwriting varies widely even in the course of a single day, all the strokes made by one person conform to a broad but constant pattern.

'I think it's fair to say that in about 40 per cent of cases we say the person definitely wrote it, and in about another 20 or 30 per cent of cases we say they almost certainly didn't write it, and then there's that grey area in between, about 30 per cent, where, like a lot of other instances in forensic science, we have to say we cannot rule out the possibility it was written by somebody else, but it's in the scale of probable to highly probable that he did, but we can't get any stronger than that.'

In the Firearms Section guns are identified and fundamental checks, such as whether they can be fired, are carried out. Weapons like airguns, crossbows and electric stun guns are examined to see if they fall within the terms of the Firearms Act of 1968. Matching a bullet to the weapon that fired it is a major part of the section's work, and so is the study of spread patterns from shotguns, which can reveal details of weapons and the ranges at which they were fired.

Biology Division

Sixty scientists work in the Biology Division; ten others work in Research and Development. An additional ten personnel, laboratory assistants and clerical staff, make up a joint support group.

Most of the work handled by the division comes under three main headings – Fibres, Blood Grouping and DNA – and concerns offences against the person,

such as murder, sexual assault, serious assault and aggravated robbery.

'That involves extraction and identification of body
fluids like blood, saliva and semen,' said Peter Martin,
Deputy Director in charge of the Biology Division. 'We
look at most things that are zoological or botanical, but
our work also involves a lot of work with textile fibres.'

Martin explained the procedures adopted for fibre
examination in a case of armed robbery.

'Typically, an armed robbery involves more than one
man, and usually it involves more than one getaway car.
What the police would want us to do would be to
discover any links between their suspects and vehicles
used in the crime, and of course any discarded clothing,
including masks. Scenes of Crime Officers (SOCOs)
would take fibre tapings from the vehicles, using
Sellotape.'

Chromatography is a method of separating two or
more chemical compounds in solution by passing them
over a substance (filter paper, for instance) that absorbs
them at different speeds. The result is called a chromato-
gram, a pattern of coloured bands which can easily be
compared with others to establish or eliminate similari-
ties. The Biological Division keeps databases of fibres
and dyes for reference.

Martin outlined the Biological Division's standard
procedure at the scene of a serious crime.

'We type the suspect's blood, we type the victim's
blood, and we type the blood we find at the scene. If
there is a match there somewhere, we report it. But we
don't set out to look for a match. We set out objectively
to determine what is there, and then make an estimate
of what it actually means at the end. We might get an
exclusion. Let us say there is a fight and one person has
died. There is blood on a suspect, and in a simple case

the suspect is Group "O", the victim is Group "A"; we type the blood from the suspect's clothes, and if it is not Group "A", then we can say categorically it didn't come from the victim.'

The forensic study of blood groups and other constituents of blood are the basis of a new speciality, Forensic Serology. Any explanation of the importance of human blood in forensic work has to make two facts clear: one, there are many blood-group systems; two, a given blood sample can never be said to have come from a particular person (although it can be said *not* to have come from a certain person).

Blood also has what are known as 'secretor' characteristics; in other words, about 75 per cent of people secrete their Group substances in other body fluids, such as saliva, semen, sweat, urine and vaginal secretions. This is important in forensic work, as seminal and salivary stains can indicate blood group, as well as providing another dimension to identification by being 'secretor' or 'non-secretor'.

Martin provided another example of blood grouping being used to implicate or eliminate an individual from an investigation of a crime, in this case rape.

'A vaginal swab would be taken, and we would be looking for the spermatozoa, the sperm, to determine the attacker's blood group. But any semen on the swab would be contaminated by vaginal secretion, so we would find the blood group of both the man and the woman. Let us say the police have a suspect, we might do a straightforward grouping on him, to determine whether he could be responsible for the rape or not. If he's eliminated, we don't have to do anything else with him. We will go on and do a DNA grouping and hold that on record, so it can be checked against other suspects the police may have at a later date.'

DNA profiling is much more subtle and revealing than blood grouping. DNA stands for Deoxyribonucleic Acid, which is a fundamental component of living tissue: it is a constituent of the chromosomes, which carry the genetic information, the 'blueprint', that makes each human being unique.

'We can use substances like semen,' Martin said, 'because sperms are just a packet of DNA being carried around to perform a particular function. Cells from inside the mouth are another rich source of DNA, so are pieces of skin, pieces of muscle, pieces of liver.' DNA testing permits the scientist to be much more positive than usual in summarising his results. 'It enables us to say, with much greater certainty, that this blood came from this person, or this semen came from this person, this saliva came from so-and-so.'

Recently some doubt was cast on the reliability of DNA profiling. Martin, in common with many scientists, dismisses the doubters. 'I don't think any serious scientist in the subject would dispute the technique. The controversy surrounds the calculation of the frequency of profiles within a population. There is also dispute about how populations differ, and how we should actually carry out the calculations. The people who are the objectors to the mainstream way of doing this are very few in number, and are becoming very much marginalised.'

A key case in the early history of DNA profiling was the investigation into the murder of a twenty-two-year-old portrait photographer, Lorraine Benson, in London in 1988. Her body, naked except for a jumper and socks, was found in Cotenham Park Road, south-west London, hidden in brambles beside a footpath. The rest of her clothing and her handbag were scattered near the body.

In an alley behind shops in nearby Coombe Lane, police found Benson's earring and her carrier bag containing a change of clothes. Also in the alley was a Vauxhall car that appeared to be abandoned; it was thickly covered with dust except for an area on the lower part of the driver's door, where the dust had been disturbed in a way that suggested a struggle. A man's handkerchief found by the car was submitted to the MPFSL for examination, together with other objects from the two scenes.

The police were already investigating a series of rapes and attempted rapes in the area. They had all happened within three miles of the Benson murder, so there was the possibility of a link. Members of the public put forward a number of descriptions of the murderer, but none of them tallied with the Photofit description given for the 'Kingston Rapist'.

The post-mortem examination of Benson's body revealed that ligature strangulation was the cause of death; a patterned line around her neck corresponded with a length of rope found near the body. In the course of a probable struggle the victim had been punched on the chin, the nose and the skull, and there were bite marks on her left hand and arm.

No semen was found on the vaginal and anal swabs taken from the body and none was found on the clothing. Traces of saliva were found on swabs taken from the breasts and from the bite on the arm. Attempts to blood-group the saliva using the ABO system (the commonest grouping system) and one other were not successful, so the swabs were submitted to the MPFSL's newly established DNA unit for testing. The unit was already under heavy pressure, screening large numbers of suspects for a match with semen found in one case of the 'Kingston Rapist' series. The police were not convinced of a link in the cases, but the DNA profile of the semen, plus the DNA profiles of all the suspects' blood samples, were to be compared with any DNA profile found in the Benson case.

The man's handkerchief found by the car in the alley provided the evidence which solved the crime. The handkerchief was lightly bloodstained and some of the stains were mixed with saliva. Also stuck to the fabric was a yellow crusty material. Microscopic examination revealed this to be probably nasal, since mucus and large clumps of leukocytes (white blood cells) were present. The stain could not be grouped by conventional techniques, but, because of the amount of cell material it contained, it was perfect for DNA profiling.

The saliva from the breast and bite-mark swabs failed to produce any test results. The profile obtained from the nasal mucus was different from that found in one of the Kingston rapes, so, if this was the murderer's handkerchief, he could not also be the rapist. There was, of course, the possibility that the handkerchief had been dropped by someone unconnected with the murder. However, when Lorraine Benson's own DNA profile was finally established, the results showed that the mucus on the handkerchief was not hers, but the blood was.

A few weeks after the murder a known sexual offender, a nineteen-year-old, was arrested and charged with the attempted rape of a computer operator on 2 February 1989.

He offered no objections when asked for intimate body specimens. Samples of his nasal mucus and blood were despatched to the laboratory, together with his dental impressions. It was then a matter of waiting for results. In the meantime he was questioned intensively but denied knowing anything about Lorraine Benson's death.

DNA testing of the man's body samples and the others from the murder scene produced startlingly unequivocal results. The mucus on the handkerchief indicated a frequency of 1,497,000, which meant only forty people in the white population could show such a profile, and of that forty, half would be women. In other words, the evidence said that out of all the white men in Britain only twenty could have produced that mucus. The clincher was that the mucus sample freely given by the suspect matched perfectly that on the handkerchief, and odontology tests showed that his dental impression matched the bite mark on Lorraine Benson's arm.

The man was convicted of Lorraine's murder at the Old Bailey in October 1989.

The Research and Development team based in the Biology Division have the task of examining trends and developments in science, and finding ways of adapting appropriate applications to forensic work.

'They're a multi-disciplinary group,' said Martin. 'The major group at the moment are looking at the new generation of DNA profiling. Because the present techniques are not very sensitive, we need fairly large amounts of DNA. To the average person the amounts might look minuscule, but we want to work with even smaller amounts.'

Over the years, the MPFSL has been responsible for truly major developments in the fields of scientific crime investigation and detection.

'We've developed chromatographic methods of separating different types of evidence, particularly in drugs work,' Martin said. 'Many of the blood-group systems that are used in forensic science were developed in this laboratory. Methods for examining glass, for examining documents, particularly methods for examining shoe prints and recovering of them from scenes of crime – those are methods that are used worldwide, and they were all developed in this laboratory.'

Chemistry Division

Seventy-one people run the MPFSL Chemistry Division. Of those, sixty-four are scientists, the rest are support staff. There are three sections: Drugs, Toxicology, and Analytical Services.

The main work of the Drugs Section is to examine materials submitted by the police to determine if they contain substances specified in the Misuse of Drugs Act, 1971.

'To sustain a charge under any part of that legislation,' said Dr Bill Wilson, Deputy Director in charge of the Chemistry Division, 'it is necessary to prove that the material is in fact what it is alleged to be. Last year we had seven-and-a-half thousand drugs cases submitted, involving the examination of about 15,000 items.'

The Drugs Section is one of the largest in the world. 'It has grown over the years in keeping with the growth of drug misuse in society as a whole,' Wilson said. 'When I joined the laboratory twenty-two years ago, the section covered both drugs and toxicology. There was only a handful of staff in those days, about a dozen people in all. Now there are a dozen in Toxicology and thirty-seven in Drugs.'

Large-quantity drug seizures reported in the press are usually the outcome of work by Customs and Excise, intercepting cargoes at the ports. Smaller consignments, but many, many more of them, are regularly seized by the police. The Chemistry Division at the MPFSL analyses samples from both sources, so the test batches tend to vary widely in size – anything from the dust on a scale pan used to weigh individual 'deals', to shipments of cannabis resin weighing a ton or more. The methods used to test substances to prove whether or not they are drugs are precise, and they usually produce unambiguous results. But interpretation of the laboratory results, Wilson said, needs great care.

'It could be taken by a court that if a person has a tenth of a milligram of a drug in his pocket, then in terms of the person being in knowing possession of a drug, that is perhaps stretching credibility. On the other hand, if the police alleged that the person had drugs in his possession but had disposed of them when he was seen by the officers, then the small trace found in the pocket could be good evidence of the fact that something illegal had definitely been there.'

The major anxiety in the Drug section, as in others within the MPFSL, is not the level of accuracy of their procedures, but the time it takes to produce results. 'At the present moment,' Wilson said, 'we are taking something like seven, eight, nine weeks to produce 90 per cent of our cases, and the courts would like them very much quicker than that.'

The challenge is to get back to a system of doing the work quickly and efficiently, without making a single mistake in the 8,000 or 9,000 analyses carried out by the section every year. On the matter of fallibility in the testing procedures, Wilson says that counsel in court will often broach the point and ask an expert such as himself if he is infallible.

'And the answer is, of course, I'm not infallible. I'm a human being and I know I have made mistakes. But, as a scientist, I have checks and balances in my work, I work with validated methods within a quality management system which gives me the certainty, at the end of the day, that when I have produced a report, it is right.'

Some drugs are very easy to detect chemically, others are problematic. Crack, an almost pure form of cocaine, is produced from a solution of cocaine hydrochloride to which ammonia has been added (sometimes together with baking soda) to produce a solid which can be smoked. The presence of the cocaine is easy to prove by analysis. On the other hand, LSD (sometimes called lygerside, which is short for lysergic acid diethylamide) is harder to pinpoint, because of the tiny amounts in which it is sold and used. A typical dose will be a droplet in a piece of absorbent material like cardboard or blotting paper roughly five millimetres square; the dose usually amounts to no more than one tenth of a milligram. In addition, that tiny drop can be damaged by light, so if it is left in solution even in a moderately bright room it will decompose.

'Most of our case work encompasses only about half a dozen drugs,' said Wilson. 'They are heroin, cocaine, cannabis and amphetamines. The amphetamines form a group of three drugs usually known collectively as Ecstasy.'

'But in our job,' Wilson said, 'we're not interested in convictions. Catching criminals and putting them in prison is the whole aim of the police, but not the purpose of the forensic scientist. Our impartiality can only come from scientific objectivity, backed by an unbiased approach. The buzz we get is in the scientific achievement, not in the conviction.'

Toxicology, by definition, is the division of medical and biological science concerned with poisonous substances, detecting them and studying their chemistry.

'The toxicologists get involved in a much wider range of crime than their colleagues in the drug sections,' said

Wilson. 'There are a number of substances in our environment – alcohol, drugs, other materials – which from time to time may have an effect on a crime, or are part of the circumstances surrounding it. At the time of a sexual assault, for example, it is important to know if the accused had been drinking. Then again, from time to time people claim they have adulterated foodstuffs for the purposes of extortion. These are circumstances where the toxicology section would get involved.'

Poisoning as a method of murder is relatively rare, in spite of its prevalence in fiction. The likelihood of a potential murderer putting a seriously toxic substance into a colourless drink and getting someone to swallow it without (a) seeing something is wrong with the drink, or (b) tasting the poison, is remote. Some highly toxic substances do exist and a few of them are almost tasteless, but they are notably hard to obtain, and none of them would act instantaneously. Commoner substances, such as paracetamol and other pain killers, have to be administered in suspiciously large doses before they have any toxic effect.

In the section called Analytical Services a range of materials is analysed on behalf of other sections in the laboratory. The section has scanning electron microscopes, mass spectrometers and a range of other specialist instruments. In particular, they are expert at analysing gunshot residues.

'Gunshot-residue analysis is one of several areas in which this laboratory really has quite a lead on the world stage,' Wilson said. He outlined the procedure. 'When a gun is fired, metallic compounds will come out of the weapon as vapour. Some will be consumed in the action of the explosion, but their residues won't be. Most of the vapour comes out of the muzzle of the weapon, but some might come out of the breech, it might leak out of the cylinder, and when it has been blasted out it condenses. People expert in detecting and analysing gunshot residues can detect condensed particles on clothing, on swabs from hands and face, from the hair, and indeed from nose blowing.'

Minute traces of evidence can now be found by the scanning electron microscope, using a technique called dispersive X-ray spectrometry. This means tiny particles can not only be found, they can be analysed to show which metallic elements are present; this in turn will give the particles a specific identity – e.g. a primer from a particular kind of bullet.

The department recently bought a high-resolution nuclear magnetic spectrophotometer. Wilson hopes it will increase productivity a little, but he does not expect a saving in labour. If anything, they will probably have to work harder.

'When you're good at something,' he said, 'there's a law of diminishing returns. Every next step is that little bit more effort.'

SO8

Flying Squad

The name alone invites speculation. The history, distorted by hearsay and TV drama, gives us an image of hard-nosed cops tearing after the nastiest criminals in London, brandishing firearms and ready, always, to shoot first, then interrogate survivors.

The truth is a tightened-up version of the legend. The Flying Squad's job is to deal with the armed robbery of banks and building societies, security vehicles, post offices, cash in transit and jewellery shops. The work certainly calls for sharp wits and a lot of nerve, but it also needs intelligence, patience and a sense of proportion. Whatever appearances sometimes suggest to the contrary, Flying Squad are a thoroughly disciplined and efficient body of officers.

The Head of Flying Squad is Detective Chief Superintendent Bill Griffiths, who recently returned after an absence of nearly ten years. In the short time he has been back, he says he does not have the impression that armed robbers are any more professional than they used to be.

'This squad goes back to the sixties when a high degree of sophistication was deployed by some very clever gangs. I just think we probably have more people having access to that kind of knowledge. Perhaps younger, perhaps more inclined to violence than the more mature robber.'

Over 170 officers, five of them women, are based in

Flying Squad branch offices at Tower Bridge Police Station, Barnes Police Station, at Finchley and at an office known as the Rig Approach, at Leyton. At each office there are three squads of approximately twelve officers; each squad is a mix of Detective Sergeants and Detective Constables, with a Detective Inspector in charge. Approximately half the officers in Flying Squad are authorised to carry firearms. Flying Squad cars, often referred to within the service as gunships, are driven by PCs, who have detective status within the Flying Squad.

'The drivers are absolutely brilliant,' said Detective Superintendent Jeff Rees. 'When attack cars are coming into an armed robbery situation, the person at most risk is the driver. It's his job to put our armed men on the pavement, in the right place at the right time. If any shots are going to be fired, they're going to be fired at the driver.'

Flying Squad operations are broadly divided into what they call 'reactive' and 'proactive' operations, reactive being in direct response to a robbery, proactive meaning as a result of the squad taking the initiative in a particular case. Rees described the Flying Squad's involvement in a reactive operation.

'Somebody dials 999, the call will normally come into the information room at Scotland Yard and a fast-response vehicle will be sent to the premises. That will be a uniformed officer from the local division. At the same time we will be informed by radio and a Flying Squad car will go to the bank or whatever premises have been robbed.'

From that point various steps can be taken, depending on the nature and seriousness of the crime. Special Branch have their own Scenes of Crime Officers (SOCOs) who will come and deal with the collection of forensic evidence, including fingerprints. Many premises now have security cameras and any available photographs of the intruders are collected and taken away for detailed scrutiny.

'A routine piece of detective work that Flying Squad does more than any other branch is to try, very quickly, to link an offence to any other offences that might be related. Basically, we identify a series of offences. It may be that a robber will be attacking a bank one minute and a building society the next, but a really detailed description of suspect and method – for example, what hand he held the gun in – will show us the connection. The ultimate aim is that when an offender is arrested, perhaps for an offence at a post office, a list of every other armed robbery offence he has committed will quickly be sent to the officers handling the case.'

Approximately 60 per cent of major armed robberies in the United Kingdom take place in London. They are therefore handled by the Flying Squad. Rees says their success-rate figures are the envy of other police forces. One offence in every three is being successfully prosecuted. According to Rees that is a good figure, bearing in mind that the criminals involved resort to every means to avoid prosecution. It is also worth remembering that the Flying Squad do not get many convictions for offences which are 'taken into consideration': realistically, criminals have to be arrested and tried for specific crimes. In view of these difficulties and others, Rees says, Flying Squad's clear-up rate is high. He acknowledges that the murder clear-up rate is much higher, over 80 per cent, and agrees that his figures indicate an armed robber has two chances in three of getting away with his crime.

'We put a stop to series. Now very often we will know that a robber has committed, for example, twenty offences. We may only be able to charge him with one offence, so only one job is cleared up. But the significant thing, as far as we're concerned, is that the series has stopped.'

Rees said that the kind of people who commit armed robberies are not, in the main, opportunist criminals, although they do represent a wide spectrum of types. Some are amateurs, mature in years, who have been forced into armed crime by financial pressures. Most of them, however, are people approaching the pinnacle of criminal achievement; they are professionals who have done a lot and are prepared to do more. 'You don't get an amateur or an opportunist carrying out an attack on a security van crew,' Rees said. 'Perhaps, at the bottom of the pile, things like betting-shop robberies – some of those will be done by less professional criminals. But any man or woman who goes out, carrying a gun, to commit an armed robbery, at whatever level, is instantly dangerous.'

Professional armed robbers have two main ways of robbing security vans. One way is to threaten the guards when they are making deliveries, and steal the bags. The other way is to hijack the whole van. Rees described the second method.

'A gun is pointed at the head of a guard who is outside the van. The driver is told to open up the van or his mate is going to be shot. The security personnel will then be thrown out on to the pavement, or they will be locked in the back of the van while it is driven off. It will be taken to a place where the money will be taken from it – in the language of the trade, it will be slaughtered.'

A 'kidnap robbery' is dealt with specifically by the Flying Squad, in particular by Rees and a fellow Superintendent. An example was a case towards the end of

1991, when the family of a security guard were kidnapped. The kidnappers told him to go to work as if nothing had happened, and then drive his van to a particular spot, where he was to tell his colleagues what had happened, then drop the money out of the van.

'In that case the guard was courageous enough to come forward and tell the police what had happened,' Rees said. 'On Flying Squad we are geared to respond very quickly to major offences. We mobilised quickly, watched the bandits pick up the money, then followed them until we knew that the guard's family were safe. Then we intervened, recovered all the money and arrested all the people involved.'

In another case, Flying Squad knew that a particular gang intended to carry out a kidnap robbery, but they had no idea where. The only thing to do was keep them under surveillance.

'One particular night we followed them out of London and finished up in Devon. There, they put down a false-plated van beside an isolated farmhouse, then returned to London. The following week they went back to Devon, this time in a false-plated car. The following morning the three of them went out with the intention of kidnapping a bank manager's wife. We intervened and arrested them in possession of the usual robbery paraphernalia – masks, loaded sawn-off shotgun, noosed and knotted clothes line which we'd watched them buy, a flick knife and coshes. Also, ideal for our purposes, they were in possession of a tape recording of instructions to be given to the bank manager.'

The police intercepted the robbers before the man in question, the manager of the National Westminster Bank in Newton Abbot, ever heard the tape. The message, recorded in a disguised voice by one of the robbers, was sinister in the extreme, and would have had an appalling effect on any man hearing it, realising that the life of his wife was being threatened. This is a transcript:

> We have got your wife. If you do exactly what we say she will remain unharmed. If you alert the police we will know immediately and you will never see her alive again. We want you to get three hundred and fifty thousand pounds in large notes, used notes, and hide them in the boot of your car within the next twenty-five minutes. You will then drive your car along to your home and wait for further instructions.

In the event, the robbers had to abort the job because men were working in the vicinity of the bank manager's house. Nevertheless, the Flying Squad were ready and poised to intervene, since they never knowingly let a hostage be taken.

'Nothing puts us under more pressure than this kind of crime,' said Rees. 'Everything else becomes secondary and we put every resource we have into it, because a kidnap is a murder waiting to happen.'

In relation to tip-offs about bank robberies, Rees said that the information is never passed on to the bank staff. This is for two reasons: one, members of staff, knowing a raid was imminent, might begin to behave oddly; and, two, members of the gang might be working in the bank.

Rees spoke briefly of another important area of Flying Squad work, the proactive or targeting operation.

'We will receive information from some source or another that a man or particular men are planning an armed robbery, or that they're actively involved in committing robberies. Having carried out our preliminary work, we will then mount a major surveillance operation, with all that entails, in the hope of catching them during the course of an offence, or just before they commit one – that is the real aim. In Flying Squad terms, the ultimate achievement is to catch a team on the pavement, guns drawn.'

Superficially it might seem odd to arrest a gang on a lesser charge of conspiracy than to wait and charge them with full-blown armed robbery. But Rees pointed out that the penalty for conspiracy is exactly the same as that for armed robbery.

'Our difficulty,' Rees said, 'is to prove precisely what they were going to do. Timing is vital. You have to get them when you've got the evidence but before members of the public are put at risk.'

Pavement arrests do not often result in shoot-outs. In a two-year period, 1991 and 1992, Flying Squad officers fired shots on only two occasions. In one case the shots missed, in the other a man was wounded in the leg.

On the topic of informants, Rees said there can be many reasons why an individual will decide to give the police important information about other people. If the informant has been involved in a crime he or she could be co-operating in the hope of getting a reduced sentence. Some people inform out of jealousy, others out of spite. There is no predominant reason.

'Informants are our life blood,' Rees said. 'We need them, and we will move heaven and earth to protect them.'

A lot of informants have previously been armed robbers themselves; others, Rees admits, are motivated by the oddest reasons. In the drug world a man could be actively engaged in trafficking but would become an informant because he is morally opposed to the drug culture. 'Sometimes a man will take exception to a particular robbery team because, for example, when they're in a bank they put guns to the heads of customers.'

Variations of ethnic behaviour and social conditioning appear to apply to crime, certainly to armed robbery. General police experience has shown that teams of black robbers are much more spontaneous in their approach to crime. They will go out to rob a post office, for example, then change their minds because there are a lot of customers, then they see a quiet-looking building society and on the spur of the moment they go in and rob the place. That pattern can be compared to the behaviour of an experienced white team. Characteristically, they would look at the same building society premises, study them carefully at a distance, then go round the streets beforehand, sometimes over a number of weeks, resisting any impulse to act until they felt sure there were no police in the vicinity before they actually committed the robbery.

Professionalism in crime now extends to the use of sophisticated radio scanners. They are easily available, relatively cheap and unequalled for providing access to police activity in the immediate area.

A great deal can happen between the time when a case is put before a court and a jury pronounces its verdict. Men accused of armed robbery frequently use the same solicitors and barristers, and often the lawyers and their tactics will wreck a prosecution case.

Rees said that the lawyers' tactics make his life more difficult than it might be. 'We go through different fashions,' he said. 'One counsel will come up with a successful defence, and suddenly, because barristers talk to each other, surprise, surprise, they all start using the same defence until we find a way of countering it.' Flying Squad officers have frequently been very angry because they have known that major villains have just been acquitted in court. 'Acquitted not through their own cleverness,' Rees added, 'but through the cleverness and deviousness of their legal representatives.'

Another source of profound irritation to Flying Squad is the high number of escapes by criminals sent to prison on serious armed-robbery charges. These are not principally men who have climbed over the wall or forced their way out; they are prisoners in the early stages of their sentences who have been allowed out on home leave – a naive move on the part of the authorities, Rees believes – and have decided not to go back to prison.

'During 1992,' Rees said, 'eighty-three prisoners put away by the Flying Squad and serving long terms for armed robbery, failed to return from home leave. Of those, twenty-two have been re-arrested by the Flying Squad after committing further armed robberies while they were on home leave. I've got to say, that figure represents the ones we *know* have failed to return from home leave, there may be others we haven't even been told about.'

For years the Flying Squad suffered from the image created by the television series *The Sweeney*. The fictional officers were belligerent characters with powerful maverick tendencies; they worked hard, broke most of the rules to get their results and drank endlessly. That was no way to behave, Detective Chief Superintendent Griffiths agrees, and besides, it's just unprofessional. An élite can be an élite without making a song about it.

Nevertheless the Flying Squad does have a reputation for robust behaviour.

'There are some marvellous characters and they are tremendous fun,' Griffiths said. 'They know how to enjoy themselves, but they're more organised now than they might have been a few years ago. I would never

SO8 Offences Recorded 1 January to 31 December 1992

	OFFENCES	% VARIATION on prev. year	ARRESTS	DETEN-TIONS	% DETENTIONS (based on total offences)
Security					
Vehicle	154	−33.1	32	17	11
Bank	433	32.4	84	206	47.6
Post					
Office	165	31	26	39	23.6
Building					
Society	325	−38.6	53	147	45.2
Betting					
Office	447	41	31	103	23.1
Jeweller	54	−39.3	21	14	25.9
TOTAL	1578	−2.5	247	526	33.3

want to suppress that character, because we can build on it, that's what makes it so enjoyable being part of this particular team.'

SO10

Crime Operations Group

Until now, SO10 (Crime Operations Group) has probably been the most secret and unexplored group in Scotland Yard. Even within the Metropolitan Police, a lot of people have only the vaguest idea of what the officers of SO10 do. Their duties cover four of the most covert areas of policing: undercover operations, hostage negotiation, witness and jury protection, and the organisation of informants. Here, for the first time, officers of SO10 speak openly about their work.

Undercover Officers

John is an undercover policeman. His professional life alternates between the everyday work of a CID detective and a shadowy, hazardous undercover existence where he has pretended to be, among other things, a robber and a contract killer. Other SO10 work has meant officers impersonating consultants on arts and antiques, and getaway drivers for robberies.

A police cadet in 1963 and a full member of the Metropolitan Police since 1966, John is forty-seven and married, with two children. He joined CID in 1967 and is still a detective. He began undercover work in 1971, drawn to it by the opportunity to infiltrate organised crime in London, and to have a covert influence on the progress of major crimes.

Detective Chief Superintendent Roy Ramm explained

that undercover officers are chosen from serving police
officers in both uniform and CID departments for their
natural attributes and their skills.

'By natural attributes I mean their size, shape, colour,
gender. Nobody too physically outstanding is selected,
and we expect them to have some special skills that we
think might be useful in their undercover role, such as
speaking a foreign language. We then take them on a
training course for two weeks, which gives them a lot of
basics about the law, making sure that they know how
to avoid overstepping the mark.'

Undercover officers are not a group apart, Ramm
said, and the administration are keen to make sure they
remember they are Metropolitan Police officers who
will be called on to do ordinary duty. The majority of
them, in any case, perform routine duty for most of the
time.

John says he does not get particularly nervous doing
undercover work, and, although he admits he gets 'but-
terflies' from time to time, he is not especially prone to
worry. He does, however, take precautions almost as a
matter of habit. Everything he does is calculated, and
whereas, operationally speaking, he would never take a
chance, he would take a calculated risk: for instance, he
insisted that the recordings of these interviews be erased
after they were transcribed, so that his voice could not
be accidentally heard and, perhaps, recognised. He has
been involved in a lot of undercover operations (for
which he receives no extra pay) and has learned that
control, particularly of the emotions, is an asset.

John discussed a number of cases he has been involved
with, the first arising from a contact in the *News of the
World*, who approached Scotland Yard with information
that a man was looking for someone to murder his
wife for a fee. Through the special machinations of

undercover operation, John, in the guise of a contract killer, was eventually introduced to the man who wanted the job done.

'We went for a walk at a golf club. As we walked around the perimeter he unfolded the story to me. He was an ex-businessman, about fifty years of age, with no police convictions of any kind. He had financial difficulties. He also had an insurance on his wife for many, many thousands of pounds, and what he wanted was an accident on her, a car accident. During the course of that conversation I did say to him, "do you want to terminate her?" and he said, "I don't want her in hospital." He wanted a zappo job, a termination, a finalisation.'

The man said he would be able to arrange for his wife to park her car some distance from a pub in a small village on a Saturday around lunch time. He said she would walk from her car to the pub, and he wanted John to be driving a lorry along the road at that time, and to fake an accident in which the wife would die. He drove John around the route in question, and at a second meeting he produced the insurance policy as proof of the money he stood to gain. He also showed John a photograph of his wife.

'And then he did the most callous thing,' John said. 'He arranged to take her to see *Miss Saigon* in the West End of London the following weekend. This was so that I could be there, identify her; so that I wouldn't kill the wrong woman. So I went up to *Miss Saigon*, at a theatre off Bow Street, and I stood outside the theatre, and I saw him walking up hand-in-hand with his missus. We had arranged that he would cross the road to the pub opposite, then come straight back so I could get a full-facial of her. What happened was, as she walked towards me she looked straight through me, and was about three feet away. So then I could see clearly the woman I was to kill. It looked all right. They were on a night out, and she looked like a normal, nice middle-aged lady.'

The killing was planned for the following Saturday. The man did not have much money but he gave John a little in advance. The full fee for the job was to be £10,000.

'He had worked out his alibi. He was to go out and play golf on the Saturday, but he had told his missus he was going to meet someone in the pub and wanted her to join them. But he didn't want that person to see the car she had, so, if she parked it at a certain spot, then walked back to the pub, the car would be out of sight.'

John hired a lorry, big and old, and parked it up a side turning near the village pub on the day appointed for the killing. At two o'clock the man's wife arrived and parked her car at a distance from the pub, just as she had been told.

'She then went up to the top of the hill, turned left,' John said. 'I started the motor, drove up to the top of the hill, then I photographed her. She was walking down towards the pub with an umbrella up, because it was raining. She was walking quite quickly, and I photographed her as I drove towards her, driving this lorry on that little lane. And as I drove by I could actually see her move aside a little. That was the time when I was supposed to just turn the wheel half an inch. I'd have hit her with the lorry, which I think was a four-ton, which would have killed her stone-dead. I drove by her, she went into the pub, the police followed her in, took her out, explained everything. She did find it strange that her husband had asked her to do what she did.'

John knew nothing of the state of the relationship between the man and his wife. He is detached in his work and never wants to know more than is necessary to get the job done.

'All I know is that she was very shocked that her husband could have done that. Her husband was arrested on the golf course. Later, at the Old Bailey, he pleaded guilty to incitement to murder. In August 1992 he was sentenced to nine years' imprisonment.'

The undercover side of John's job, which accounts for 40 per cent of his work, is obviously a source of worry to his wife, although she is entirely supportive. 'She knows that I enjoy doing it,' he said. 'What she's always said to me is, "Provided you remain happy doing it, then I'll always back you, but the day you become unhappy doing it is the day you pack up."'

As for the effect of John's work on his own personality, he admits that people sometimes say it is difficult to get close to him, but he does not regard himself as being cold or withdrawn in any way. The problem is probably a transient one, connected with the job he is doing at a particular time. 'I have to portray what I am not – a contract killer, for instance.' Sustaining such a role is bound to mean that his everyday personality is modified to some extent, albeit temporarily.

Of all the hazards of this branch of police work, corruption is one of the more serious. 'I wouldn't pretend it's easy for anyone,' Ramm said, 'but undercover officers do see the money, they do see the fast cars, they see all the attractions. What they also see is the enormous downside of it, because the kind of operations they're in are resulting in people getting very long prison sentences, and if that's not a factor to dissuade, I don't know what is.

'It is compelling to see people you've been with, who you have regarded as attractive personalities, seeing them stripped of the Mercedes, seeing them stripped of the Armani suits and the gold Rolexes and all the trappings of wealth, seeing it all go and seeing that guy standing in the dock at the Old Bailey and maybe shedding a few tears as he gets a prison sentence in double figures. That's an enormous deterrent.'

Fortunately, Ramm added, London is a big place and the Met is a big police force. 'We are keen to make sure that the officers keep their feet on the ground, that they don't think they are part of Miami Vice, that they don't start to live their undercover role.'

John described a case with an organised crime connection involving a plan to rob a warehouse at Heathrow Airport.

'An informant received information that a number of people were planning a kidnapping and blackmail in relation to employees of the KLM Dutch Airlines at Heathrow Airport,' he said. 'At the same time, the informant received information that the same people were stealing lorry loads of goods from in and around Heathrow. I was briefed to meet a certain man.'

John, presenting himself as a professional robber, duly met the man, who explained that he had a number of criminal enterprises under-way. One, on a moderately large scale, involved the theft of lorry-loads of goods, and another, more important, involved a kidnapping.

He was employed at Heathrow Airport in a KLM warehouse, where he had made friends with a young woman who gave him information on the keyholders of the KLM warehouse vault. The vault contained gold bars, currency and diamonds worth very large amounts of money, certainly comparable with the haul in the Brink's-Mat robbery.

'He then introduced me to a man' John said, 'who went into great detail on the plan he had set up with a number of other people to kidnap the keyholder. Having kidnapped him, we would torture his wife and daughter, burning them with cigarette ends, slapping them, using general torture techniques, which would lead the key-holder to agree to go to the warehouse. I would look after the family and he would drive the van up to the back of the warehouse, and the contents of the strong room would then be loaded into the van.'

The torture of the wife and daughter was to be a joint effort, following which the women would be taken to the van and tied to stays specially installed for the purpose. They were to be kept in the van until the goods from the strong room were loaded, then they would be released. If the plan went wrong for any reason, the keyholder, his wife and his daughter were to be killed. John has no doubt at all that the family would have died if the criminals had thought it advisable.

The keyholder was then put under surveillance by the conspirators. He was followed and every detail of his routine was recorded and timed with a stopwatch. This went on for a number of weeks, until it was decided the operation could safely begin.

'We had firearms and stolen vehicles,' John said, 'and very early on a Sunday morning we met up at Scratch-wood Service Station, finished off our planning and agreed to go ahead. We had been supplied with every-thing, the details of the inside of the warehouse and everything that was there.

'We drove towards the keyholder's address. When we arrived we were balaclava'd up. He had a very good imitation firearm with him and CS gas. We had ties, stays, everything. We positioned ourselves opposite the house, underneath a vehicle. We saw the light come on in the premises. Unbeknown to the conspirators, the police had removed the family from the house the night before. We then came across the road, down the side, and we were arrested by armed police. Both of us. We were taken away.'

The whole of the operation was recorded. Eventually the men appeared at the Central Criminal Court where, after a lengthy legal battle, the police evidence was accepted by the court, and they were imprisoned for twenty and sixteen years respectively.

'They know who shopped them,' John said. 'I don't know what their thoughts are on that, that's up to them, I'm not a mind reader. They're not very happy, that's for sure.'

The KLM operation lasted five months. Throughout that time John and the other two men came together two or three times a week. 'For instance, on the day that we went to do the robbery we all had changes of clothing, and we came together to do the bit of work, which is the professional way of doing it. Every time I wasn't with them I would go back to my normal duties.'

During any prolonged operation there are bound to be bad moments for the undercover officer. Once, during the KLM job, John was in the van with the criminals, being followed by a surveillance team; at a traffic junction, the surveillance car jumped a red light and one of the criminals in the van noticed it. 'It blew the car the surveillance team were driving,' John said. 'I felt that if the car had been seen again that would have caused a major problem.'

The essence of passing himself off as a villain, John explained, is adaptability. 'I learn the background of the other person and I live that during the course of the operation.' The first fifteen minutes, he added, are the worst time. Once he is into his role and playing the part, the anxiety disappears.

He changes, psychologically, from being a police officer to being a criminal, and at the end of it he changes back, painlessly, to where reality is the life of a police officer and unreality is the criminal life. He does not find the transition difficult, to or from, and likened it to being a chameleon, changing colour to suit the surroundings. His sanity, he said, is underpinned by the realities and responsibilities of his job and his home life.

'The difficult part, really, is the length of time spent being the other person, and trying to remember what you said on the first meeting, or the second, or the twenty-eighth.'

And if at any time in the future, after abandoning a persona, the undercover police officer is suddenly confronted on the street by someone who knew him under the other identity, the answer, John said, is to front it up; 'You just say, "You're mistaken," and walk away.'

Undercover work is an extremely dangerous and stressful area of policing. To alleviate stress and other problems, an 'uncle' system is in operation where an undercover officer has somebody within the branch, another experienced undercover officer, to whom he or she can relate and talk over problems without management barriers or paperwork. Ramm says the officers, some of them young in service terms, are enormously courageous. None has ever been killed in the line of duty, but a few have been injured. In 1992 there was a covert ceremony where seventeen Commissioner's commendations were presented to undercover officers. Details of the awards could not be reported, not even in internal police notices.

Ramm was reluctant to talk about the finer details of day-to-day undercover policing; secrets are, after all, vital to safety and efficiency. 'We want an undercover officer to be able to work safely and to withstand scrutiny by the opposition.'

He was prepared to say, however, that undercover

officers get all the support SO10 can give, short of prejudicing the success of an operation. That includes shadowing by officers of SO11 (Criminal Intelligence Branch) whenever necessary. As for using hidden electronic communications equipment, Ramm said they have to be very careful about that.

'Officers will get a rubdown,' he said. 'They will be rubbed down, they will be searched for hidden transmitters and tape recorders regularly, so we need to be very careful how we deal with that aspect.'

In court, undercover officers stand behind screens when they give their evidence. They can be seen by the judge, by the jury and by both counsel, but they cannot be seen from the public gallery. Even though it would be dangerous as well as counter-productive to the police effort to reveal the identity of undercover officers, Ramm knows there are lawyers who would nevertheless try to discover officers' identities and use the knowledge against them.

John described a third case.

'An Asian man called Mohammed had been arrested in connection with an attack on a prostitute where, during the course of the attack, he had tried to bury her alive in the garden. As a result he was arrested and remanded in custody. While he was in custody he approached his cell mate and stated that he wanted the following carried out. He wanted the police officer in the case, a Detective Inspector, kidnapped and tortured to reveal the whereabouts of the witness he had tried to bury in the garden. When she had been found, and when it was certain she was the right woman, the police officer was to be killed.'

The cell mate was so horrified he got in touch with the police. As a result, an undercover officer – not John at this stage – went to the prison. He posed as a visitor, someone who had a connection with Sikhs on the outside who would be prepared to carry out the kidnap of the police officer and the prostitute, and subsequently murder the officer. He met Mohammed, talked to him, and went away. Later another undercover officer, a genuine Asian Sikh, visited Mohammed and discussed with him the details of the kidnappings and the murder.

'During the course of that,' John went on, 'the under-cover officer asked for some sign of good faith. Mohammed said that a kilo of heroin would be given as good faith. He explained that there was a man on remand in prison in connection with the importation of four kilos of heroin. Some cotton bobbins belonging to this man were in the possession of the Customs and Excise, who were not aware that hidden inside them was a kilo of heroin. The heroin, Mohammed explained, would be handed over as a sign of good faith, as soon as the bobbins were returned. Discreet inquiries were made of the Customs and Excise, the bobbins were opened and a kilo of heroin was found, which would be worth, at street value, £80,000. That was given to us as a sign of good faith.'

When that transaction was completed, John, in the guise of a professional robber, was introduced as the man who was to carry out the two kidnappings and the murder specified by Mohammed. John went to the prison where Mohammed was being held, accompanied by the two undercover officers who had set up the deal.

'You can imagine what the feeling was when we got to the prison, the three of us, police officers, purporting to be criminals. And I met this man, who had staring eyes – he would never let you break away from his stare. He explained to me that he had been arrested in connection with the assault, the burying of the woman, and that he had made a lot of inquiries to find her.

'I then established that he was a very rich man, a *very* rich man, and that he had the wherewithal to finance this type of operation, which he explained to me, down to the details of how he wanted the Detective Inspector tortured, so that he would reveal the necessary information. He also wanted clothing stolen from the police officer's home and from the woman's address, and said the defence would make it look as if the pair had eloped together. I said I was quite happy to do that, and he said he would introduce me to another person, who would be the person on the outside who would pay me the agreed fee of £100,000 for the kidnap, torture, further kidnap and then the murder of the police officer.'

The person on the outside turned out to be the man's mother, who was, John said, one of the most evil women he has ever come across. He met her at the prison, and on that first night arrangements were made to do preparatory work on the job: the work involved in a contract to kill usually entails following the proposed victim, getting to know their movements, finding out when they are at their most vulnerable with no witnesses around. At that first meeting the woman gave John £1,000 to begin his reconnaissance work. John subsequently photographed the targeted police officer coming out of the back door of a police station. He took the pictures to the prison. When Mohammed saw them he became very excited and said yes, definitely, that was the man he wanted tortured and killed.

At that point, John explained, the Detective Inspector was being given discreet police protection, because, although Mohammed had said no other contract was involved, he was such a vicious individual that it would have been unwise to rule out the possibility of him recruiting a second man to attack and possibly kill the officer.

'He was so pleased with the photographs,' John said, 'that he authorised his mother to release another £1,500 to me. Another meeting was arranged, and at that time the operation was planned in graphic detail. We then decided we had to take this matter further to show the intent, and to show that it wasn't just talk.'

The woman Mohammed wanted to track down was in fact a protected witness, already badly frightened by the ordeal of having been almost buried alive. With her full cooperation, she was taken by the police to a flat where she was tied up, gagged, and had a copy of the *News of the World* placed in front of her to corroborate the date; she was then photographed. The fact that she had apparently been kidnapped would imply, of course, that the Detective Inspector had already been kidnapped and tortured.

'We smuggled the photographs into the prison, showed them to Mohammed and his mother, and he was elated. But the mother said she wanted to see, she had to see we had the girl. She trusted the photographs but she wanted to be sure. So we took her to the flat, and she was recorded on video coming into the room, and she saw the woman tied and gagged, with a gun held at her head.'

She was convinced. On the way out of the room she said that the police officer must now be killed, and the flesh should be cut up and boiled, and it should be done carefully to avoid spilling on to the hot rings, which would give off a very bad smell. After a time John reported back to the woman and told her the police officer was now dead and the body disposed of.

'So what happened then was, we got a phone call from her, and I went out that night and I think I picked up £15,000 as part payment. Mohammed was coming up for trial the following Monday. And then she gave me a note that said I had to go and see him, and in the note it said I was to hold his piece of merchandise, which was the girl, I was to rape her, bugger her, make her shit in a bin, I could do anything. Then they wanted two other girls, witnesses in his trial, kidnapped, because we'd been so successful with the other two people.'

John went to the prison and Mohammed said he had another job for him: he was to spring a man by the name of Khan from prison. Mohammed had drawn a plan of the inside of the prison which was, John said, probably the best plan he had ever seen.

'Khan was inside in connection with the importation of a large amount of heroin, and I was to receive another vast sum of money for the job.'

The plan, which involved a hijacked helicopter entering the prison and lifting Khan out, was later checked carefully by experts and found to be entirely feasible. As a result, certain precautions were taken at the prison which now make such an escape impossible.

'We had enough evidence by now,' John said, 'and, as we were making up our minds to arrest everybody concerned the next day, Mohammed's mother got in touch with me again; she wanted to see me. When I turned up to see her I was wearing equipment which would corroborate what was said. She said that she had changed her mind about the woman that we had kidnapped, and I was now to murder her, shoot her, and tell Mohammed that she had tried to escape and I'd had to shoot her.'

Next day all the principals in the conspiracy were arrested. A number of trials followed in due course. 'The mother pleaded guilty to conspiracy to murder and various other offences and she was sentenced to seven years in prison. Mohammed pleaded guilty to conspiracy to murder, conspiracy to kidnap, conspiracy to supply drugs. He received a total of twenty years in prison. Khan got three years added to the sixteen he had already been serving.'

The toughest part of the operation for John had been making the visits to the Asian in prison. He has, after all, been a police officer for twenty-five years, so his face is known to a lot of criminals. 'When you go into the prison,' he said, 'there may be sixty people there, and only about three or four prison officers. If they suss you're a police officer then they won't be too happy. Going in was a calculated risk – I could check who the remand prisoners were inside, but I couldn't know who was going to visit them on any given day, because a lot of visitors don't give their true names. We did have a contingency plan, though, which I won't go into.'

John emphasised that he never analyses criminals' motives. That is someone else's job, and besides, the knowledge would not help him in his work. He will play along with a scenario as it unfolds, keeping his objectives as a police officer strictly to the fore.

'What I will never do,' he said, 'is talk them into it.' Apart from the moral considerations, such an action would make him an *agent provocateur*. 'But I don't talk them out of it, either,' he added, 'because I worry that if I talk them out of it, a week later they'll go and ask somebody else.'

Hostage Negotiators

'The bleep goes, or you're phoned at home,' Ramm said. 'OK, we've got a siege. What kind of siege? It's a man, it's two o'clock on a Saturday morning, the man's gone crazy. He's come home drunk, found his girlfriend in bed with another guy, he's produced a knife, he's threatening to kill everybody in sight.'

The second area of SO10's activity covers hostage negotiations and the training of negotiators. There are approximately eighty hostage negotiators in the Met, all of them, with the exception of a couple of Sergeants, serving officers with the rank of Inspector and above. They are spread across the Metropolitan Police District, and SO10 tries to ensure that there is a small nucleus of negotiators in every Area.

'There is, in addition, a team of ten coordinators,' Ramm said. 'They've all got other jobs, except for myself and my deputy, who are also coordinators.'

During a two-week stint the coordinator is on twenty-four-hour call.

'When the bleep goes it could be anything – the Turkish Tourist Board offices in Cork Street or wherever, a load of Kurds have gone in there and taken the place hostage, calling for a free Kurdistan. Or, a bank robbery's gone wrong and the robbers are trapped in the bank. Whatever. So we listen to what the scenario is. We give instant advice over the telephone . . .'

Advice can be called up on the screen at the Central Communications Complex (TO25): for example, in suicide intervention, the advice includes such imperatives as, 'Be non-confrontational; listen, don't argue; try to encourage the person to understand that you are there to help, that you are not interventionist.'

'We then identify negotiators who we think would be appropriate to attend the scene,' said Ramm. 'As coordinator, in 99 per cent of cases you go to the scene yourself, and you act as the nexus between the negotiators and the Incident Commander – the negotiators are there to negotiate, not to take over the incident, and that's very important to us. We see the negotiators as another tool in the Incident Commander's armoury. We are there to talk. If he feels our talking and our negotiations are going wrong, if he feels that a tactical option, an assault on the premises is the way forward, then that's his decision. We are there to give him professional advice on what we think the outcome might be, if we continue to talk. But it's up to him at the end of the day. So that's the role of the coordinator, to make sure that the Incident Commander understands what the negotiators are there for, to act as a go-between between the negotiators and the Incident Commander.'

All coordinators have experience of being negotiators, most of them for four or five years. In the London area, negotiators and coordinators are called out, on average, twice a week. Ramm described an incident he had recently attended.

Two children, girls of seven and eleven years old, had been knocking doors at Hallowe'en, doing trick-or-treat, when at one house a woman brandished a knife, grabbed the girls and held one of them hostage. The other managed to escape and raise the alarm.

'We got there and we negotiated through the letter-box,' Ramm said. 'After a while I decided that I couldn't be sure that the negotiations were getting close to a safe release of this little girl . . . I came to the conclusion that the hostage-taker was volatile, mentally unbalanced, dangerous. The situation was deteriorating and I couldn't offer a realistic chance of success. So we made the decision to negotiate in a certain way, which gave us the best tactical option, and we stormed the house. We managed to get the little girl out and the woman was arrested. She was battered and bruised and taken off, I think, to a mental hospital.'

Ramm has never been in a situation where he has lost a potential suicide, or a hostage.

'But since I've been doing this job, I have been responsible for speaking to officers who have been involved in cases which have proved fatal, and have proved fatal because we, the police, have had to open fire. The officers are deeply, deeply shocked. There is no doubt in my mind that the negotiators have given absolutely everything, they've drained themselves emotionally to try to resolve a situation which has deteriorated, and just gone beyond anything that they could have hoped to resolve. And they have been deeply hurt and moved by it.'

Some negotiators are so traumatised that they decide they cannot do the job any more. Ramm has found it beneficial to talk to these officers, to reassure them and to go over what they did, in close detail, pointing out that, although they feel they could have done more, the reality is that they could not, nor could anyone else. They are assured that they did their best, and in most cases are eventually prepared to negotiate again.

'We have the services of consultant psychiatrists, and we refer officers to them when we need to. In major sieges lasting more than twenty-four hours we can always call on psychiatrists. We can call on them at any time, but then in particular.'

Any place where a hostage-taker and hostages are located is known to SO10 as a stronghold, and there are two main types – a known location and an unknown location (usually the place where a kidnapper keeps the victim). In addition there are three main types of hostage-takers, known in police parlance as the mad, the bad, and the offenders for a cause.

'There are no hard lines around the edges,' Ramm said. 'The mad are people who are unbalanced, and they include some of the potential suicides. The bad are criminals but some of them are also slightly crazy, and some of the offenders for a cause, in my view, are absolute criminals, *unequivocally* criminals. But the difference lies in what they are demanding. The bad very rarely take hostages, there is no mileage in a criminal taking a hostage in a stronghold. Therefore, nearly all sieges involving criminals happen by accident, when a crime goes wrong. You're robbing a High Street bank and the cops turn up; you're in there, and suddenly you're wondering what you do when you've got a hostage.'

In unplanned incidents of that kind the negotiators want to offer the criminals another way out. They do not want to compound what has already happened.

'We can say to them, "What is the point of you making it worse for yourself? You've robbed a bank, you may have a gun, why add unlawful imprisonment and kidnapping to the agenda? What do you want to achieve? Get some mileage out of this by acting in an adult, sensible way, which will mean mitigation for you. You're not going to run away. That's not going to happen."'

The most difficult kind of siege negotiation to deal with is one involving a disturbed person as hostage-taker.

'Mentally unbalanced people present an enormous problem,' Ramm said. 'They are unpredictable. If an unbalanced person is threatening to kill somebody because he loves that person and wants to take that person with him, that's a very difficult situation.'

With terrorists, who form the bulk in the 'offenders for a cause' category, the police need to find out what their agenda is, assuming one exists. Usually they will be quick to declare it, and the police will then have an idea, often an extensive understanding, of who they are dealing with. It is important with such people, Ramm said, that they understand the agenda the police have, i.e. they will not give in to terrorism.

Then rapport must be established, and that calls for the skill and instincts of seasoned negotiators. Usually three negotiators are sent to a siege, and how they are used will be decided by the coordinator. Often it is a case of selecting the negotiator with the most appropriate accent: 'If you've got a really cor-blimey villain on the other end of the phone, he doesn't really want to be talking to a BBC newsreader's accent on the other end.'

From there on, the situation will deteriorate or stabilise in direct proportion to the talent of the negotiator.

'Really, it's about the verbal and interpersonal skills which we try to encourage the officers to develop for our cause. It's about actively listening, it's about trying to identify and understand what motivates, and not sympathising, not saying, "Oh, yeah, perhaps you're right, maybe we should have the troops out of Northern Ireland," or whatever. It's about understanding their point without being patronising, without being supercilious, not argumentative, or combative. The whole job is a strange combination of skills, but mostly it's about listening rather than talking.'

SO10 provides the training facilities for all hostage negotiators in England, Wales and Northern Ireland, and, although a separate course is run in Scotland, SO10 do have a lecturing role there. Four courses a year cater to a total of eighty students.

'We have four or five foreign students on each of the courses,' Ramm said, 'so there are fifteen Brits, loosely, including the RUC, and up to five overseas students, always including an FBI agent, another American cop from somewhere, and European students – we've a good liaison with the Dutch in particular.'

Witness and jury Protection

SO10 provides protection for witnesses whose evidence puts their safety, possibly even their lives, at risk. There is a menu of resources, Ramm said, balanced against the severity of the threat.

'If someone's given evidence against armed, dangerous criminals and we believe there is a continuing threat against him or her, then we will advise the witnesses to take advantage of everything we can offer. That might be an international re-location, it might be full re-identification for the whole family and close relatives, with all that entails. We have a number of arrangements with other countries which allow us to relocate people. Often they find it difficult to cope with, of course, and sometimes come back to their old areas and are prepared to bluff it out, and to use their own wit and guile. Others disappear completely. After initial contact with them while they're bedding-in, we lose touch with them.'

In Ramm's experience, a hardened criminal will nurture his grudges. Any person appearing for the prosecution in serious cases could be in grave danger.

'In illegal drugs transactions the amount of money involved can be astronomical,' Ramm said. 'So when we are looking at a drugs trial these days we are expecting the jury to be nobbled, for a start.'

Intelligence sources have found there are people who specialise in identifying and intimidating members of juries. They have been known to sit in seats close to jurors in otherwise empty trains or buses, then appear as spectators in court, right in the line of vision of the juror they are trying to frighten, staring, doing no more than being there. That kind of pressure, Ramm said, is very intimidating to honest, innocent people.

'And because police evidence is not readily believed in courts now, we do have very well put together cases, with independent witnesses and sound evidence, so we expect the witnesses to be got at, too. When we have a witness with something really serious and damaging against the defendants, evidence perhaps on which a case hinges, then we will relocate, re-identify, re-house and provide all the back-up we would for a supergrass in the old days.'

Informants

'We will pay an informant anything from £50 to £100 at the bottom to several thousand pounds of public money for the recovery of large quantities of drugs,' Ramm said, 'and I wouldn't want to put a ceiling on it, because, as far as we're concerned, there is no ceiling. We don't say we pay up to a maximum, it depends on the work.'

Informants are precious to the police. There can be no doubt that, increasingly, they are the life blood of major crime investigations. SOIO does not handle informants directly, but provides the structure for officers to deal with them. The department makes an effort to use informants innovatively within the law, and provides the money to pay them. Ramm explained how informants are registered and regulated.

'The officer finds his informant, registers him locally and with us. Once he's registered and he's into the force informant scheme, he has to be handled in a certain way. If he works well and is thought to deserve a reward, we determine what the information was worth and he is paid by us. The DAC makes the reward after checking how much an informant in West Ham, say, is being paid for what he does, or an informant in Hounslow, so we are getting the money about right. We also set the boundaries for the informers' participation in crime. They are allowed, by law, to participate in crime only to a certain degree, and it has to be a crime that is already planned.'

If an informant is told there is going to be a bank robbery, and reports the planned robbery to the police, he can provide the car for the robbers' getaway without paying a penalty under law. He cannot, however, be involved in the planning of the robbery. Although informants' behaviour in this respect is carefully monitored by SO10, the more sensible ones are likely to play to the rules anyway, in view of the substantial payments.

In addition to drawing on their own resources, SO10 send out what they refer to as 'begging letters', seeking rewards from banks and building societies, insurance companies and loss adjusters, and any other sizeable organisation whose losses have been minimised by the actions of an informer. If the donor of a reward wants to remain anonymous, SO10 will act as an iron curtain between them and the informant, making sure that no clue is given as to the source of the money.

'Very often informers want something other than money,' Ramm said. 'Very often informers are criminals who are in trouble, and they want their "worthy actions" discreetly brought to notice. So there is a system where the Deputy Assistant Commissioner can write a factual letter, without embellishments, dealing with the value of the information given by the informer. Sometimes it will play a part in the sentencing if the offender pleads guilty to the offence he's charged with. Similarly, we can write to the Home Secretary and bring the same facts to his attention.'

If someone has committed a serious offence and has provided only minor help to the police, a letter on his behalf will have no significant mitigating effect on the severity of his sentence. It works best in a criminal's favour if he has helped the police before he finds himself in trouble; a person on a serious charge who is suddenly inspired to assist the law has less chance of being rewarded with a lighter sentence.

Malice is another reason for some people becoming informers. Clearing the field for themselves is another. One tactic is for an informant to tell the police about someone dealing in drugs in a particular area; then, when the dealer is arrested, the informant moves in and starts dealing there himself, having simultaneously ingratiated himself with the police. Ramm said his department needs to be alert to a lot of abuses perpetrated by informants, but he insists they are nevertheless an important element in countering organised and serious crime.

Disclosure, the recent change in legal procedure requiring the police to disclose identities of informants and others who would previously have remained anonymous, has had a profound impact on SO10.

'It's affected us dreadfully,' Ramm said, 'absolutely dreadfully. We are concerned that on simple fishing exercises without any probative value, we are asked to disclose, just to try and make us throw in the towel. It jeopardises informers particularly, and, whereas maybe a year ago Disclosure was not an issue which I needed to concern myself with, I suppose I now spend something like 30 to 40 per cent of my time on Disclosure issues, giving evidence about the system, about officers, attending meetings with counsel, with the CPS, trying to protect the officers in the system. The way I see it, we have nothing to hide, but a lot to protect.'

SO11

Criminal Intelligence Branch

'In policing terms, we're the silent service,' said Detective Chief Superintendent Roy Clark. 'There's hardly been a major job in the past twenty years where SO11 hasn't played a fairly significant part. But never, to my knowledge, has anybody stood up and said, "That was an SO11 job," or "SO11 would have been in on that."'

Although it is vital that the officers of SO11 work clandestinely, and that their achievements should attract a minimum of publicity, Clark believes there is a need for his department to demonstrate, in some way, the part they play in policing the metropolis.

'We're in the age of the performance indicator,' he said. 'We're in the age of the senior police officers taking personal contracts on performance. Now when you actually take that into account, no longer can the Commander SO11, or the Detective Chief Superintendent SO11, afford not to say, listen, if there's credit due there, we want some of that, because we're required to show that we're performing. We're in that game now.'

The Criminal Intelligence Branch is a service department for the other specialist squads. This is the first time a member of SO11 has spoken publicly about the department's work.

'We gather intelligence,' said Clark. 'Here at the top level, at SO11, we ensure the purity of the system, in theory. We control the system of intelligence right down through Area to division, and ensure it flows upwards and out to the team that can best act upon any intelligence that's forthcoming.

'We've now got NCIS (National Criminal Intelligence Service), which puts a national perspective on intelligence gathering and intelligence flow. So we are no longer the top intelligence gatherers in the country, NCIS exist above us. But we're certainly the top one in the Metropolitan Police, and we're the conduit between NCIS and the Met.'

There are 180 officers in SO11, headed by Commander John Grieve. Many of the officers are engaged on what are described as miscellaneous functions, including liaison with prisons, Photofit, and witness albums – better known as mug shots.

Much of the information collected about an individual can be obtained in the public domain – the simple fact that a person subscribes to a telephone network usually means his address is available from the Phone Book. But there is no Freedom of Information Act in Great Britain, and many Government departments will not share their information with others.

'The tax people do not freely give up information about people's tax returns. So it's not always easy to draw up financial information. But we certainly get to know where people live, we know what car they drive, we can report sightings of that car. We set up points, watch him go past, and see which way he's going and try to work out who he could be visiting or what he could be doing in that area. And you can actually put observation points at his associates' places, and see who he's mixing with at any one time.'

Clark said that SO11 do not often follow cars. The whole practice of following is becoming so devalued, he said, that nowadays it is the last resort. 'It's the surest way ever of letting a criminal know that he's subject to police operations.' It is nevertheless true that SO11 do still follow suspects, and on lengthy pursuits they use a variety of cars. They will also use 'lumps', or electronic tracking devices, on cars they want to pursue at a safe distance. But Clark was unhappy about discussing any of the details of mobile surveillance. 'Even talking about it means that people will be looking in their mirrors, and that makes our job all the harder.'

Major criminal targets tend to be hypersensitive about surveillance. Many of them are aware that the criminal activity they are currently engaged in could net them fifteen or twenty years in prison next time, so their level of caution is often on a par with clinical paranoia.

'One villain learns a part of how to avoid police,' Clark said, 'and he'll pass that on to his colleagues, and maybe in return he gets some information in an area he wasn't too sure about. I think there's probably as much conversation goes on among villains about how to avoid police activity as there is among police officers about how to bring them to justice.'

Efforts are constantly being made to devise new techniques of surveillance and intelligence gathering. Civilian analysts help SO11 by preparing graphical representations of crime and criminals which throw into relief many aspects and traits of criminal behaviour that are not apparent from reams of written reports. 'You can actually start to build up pictures of activity that point to a certain criminal,' Clark said. 'Our analysts are very good at presenting on one sheet of paper pictures you could never have dreamed of.'

Clark would not be drawn on the numbers of officers employed on major surveillance work; he would only say that a job gets the resources it needs. Most jobs, he added, don't need many officers at all. And none of them would stand out even in a small crowd.

'They are average people, there's nothing exceptional about them at all. People are not accepted if they have bright red hair. If I walked past a villain's house every day to see what car he was using, and I had bright red hair, he would probably remember me quite distinctly. If I was just a bland person of average height, average weight, average greyness of hair – average appearance, I'd probably blend into the grey background. So that is a consideration. Police officers tend to look like police officers, but in an organisation of 28,000, we've got an awful lot that don't look like policemen.'

SO11 has been central to a number of major cases, among them a prosecution for importation of drugs brought against a particularly well-known criminal. 'He was a very active criminal in London, a major criminal in virtually every form of crime for many, many years,' Clark said, 'believed to be untouchable, and everybody else had tried and not succeeded. But now he's serving a fairly long term of imprisonment, because the activities of this branch make us able to develop a collection plan. And when he was right for it, he was arrested.'

Being selectively enigmatic, Clark was reluctant to enlarge upon the meaning of *collection plan*, but he did reveal that SO11 were tasked by the Regional Crime Squad to watch the man. In explaining what happened then, Clark reverted to the phrase *lawfully audacious*, which he favours when fine detail is out of the question: 'It so aptly sums up what we do without actually saying how we do it. So we were lawfully audacious in our pursuit of what our criminal and his people were up to, and when the package was there, when we had some idea that the time was right to move in, he was moved upon.'

He went on to say that SO11 watched the man for months, though not continuously, because it was not necessary. 'We put him down at times and took up other jobs, then picked him up again. Gradually the picture of activity built up.

'Prison Liaison Officers keep tabs on known criminals, who will continue to be criminals both inside and when they come out of prison. And when a criminal's coming out of prison the officers will let us know that he's out, that he's back into the game so to speak. And of course there is information forthcoming from prisoners themselves.'

Collators, the divisional officers who gather and classify all the information available on active and persistent criminals in their region, work to a discipline that is overseen by SO11, who write the collators' manuals. In spite of firm guidelines, it is a flexible system, allowing for local emphases in crime and the setting up of subsidiary indexes.

Clark would say nothing about telephone tapping, which is, nevertheless, an important part of surveillance work. Mail is also intercepted whenever that is deemed to be necessary. The Home Secretary has imposed a strict ceiling on the number of active warrants which the police may hold at any one time, but it is true nevertheless that the numbers granted in England and Wales in 1992 (756 telephone taps, 118 mail intercepts) were the highest since the Interception of Communications Act came into force in 1985. They were, however, substantially lower than some newspaper reports have claimed.

The application procedure for a warrant to tap a telephone, or to intercept mail, must be strictly observed: from SO11 it goes through two further stages before it is passed to the Home Secretary, who must authorise every single telephone tap as well as every individual mail intercept.

The principal SO11 teams combine their intelligence to develop long-term operations against criminals. Often these are operations which other groups within the Met have found impossible or too difficult, and they are invariably long-term.

'It sometimes may take a year to eighteen months to bring a job to fruition,' Clark said. 'And those operations are lawfully audacious in their pursuit of intelligence, and in the gathering of it, and in forming a collection, and in determining what area of criminality a team are active in, and in virtually delivering them on a plate to whatever specialist team is most suitable to deal with them.'

Clark touched on the matter of Disclosure, which is the name commonly applied to a new procedure where any fact or any matter which may have a bearing on a criminal case must be revealed by the police to the CPS, who will then decide whether or not to disclose it to the defence.

'It means that we are required or requested to discuss in infinite detail, in the public forum of a court, in front of the accused who quite frequently are criminals, and their criminal associates, and the media, the techniques and the tools of the trade that we use. Now that cannot be productive. We are finding our ability to be effective is damaged by having to discuss publicly the way we go about our job.'

Clark agrees that in enlightened times it is right that the public should know more about the structure of the police and the various ways they work. 'There is a need for us to acknowledge that people know the police use surveillance and criminal intelligence analysis to bring criminals to boot. So let's actually acknowledge it, but let's not give away the tools of the trade.'

On the topic of informants Clark is not reticent. The

best sources are live sources, he said, and SO11 use informants a lot. Deduction, observation and evaluation are fine, but if someone who is reliable says 'It's going to happen next Tuesday,' then that is prime information. There would seem to be a difficulty in recruiting informants, since officers of SO11 work with so many other departments and are never obviously in one place for any length of time. But Clark said that a change of custom has eradicated that problem.

'Gone is the ownership of informants,' he said. 'They are now seen as the property, if I may use that word, of the Service as a whole. In my young days on the Flying Squad, if I or one of my colleagues had an informant, we jealously guarded who that person was. Now we've got our officers being involved in a Robbery Squad job, say, and being introduced to Robbery Squad informants because they need that inside knowledge to help interpret what they see. So gone is the parochialism. There's a far more open atmosphere among detectives.'

An eighteen-month study of the workings of SO11 resulted in a report, issued in June 1993, which proposed greater use of computers, added resources and a new network of intelligence officers to produce a directorate of intelligence which would be operationally similar to Military Intelligence.

'Outside consultants looked at all our intelligence structures,' said Commander John Grieve. 'That meant everything from intelligence offices at divisional police stations right up to what we were doing in SO11 here at the Yard. Among their conclusions, they said that if we wanted to catch more criminals in the act, we should raise the status of intelligence and do more targeting.'

The findings of the study tied in with the Commissioner's view that better intelligence is the way forward in improving figures for serious crimes solved. Catching criminals in the act means there is a much stronger chance of convictions, and much less likelihood that criminals will put forward imaginative and often bizarre defences which can cast doubt on prosecution cases.

The ultimate purpose of the proposed directorate of intelligence would not be simply to coordinate the intelligence effort more effectively, Grieve said, but to do something positive with the intelligence.

'It's the analysis that's important. There's stacks of data out there. I'm inundated with informers and information. It's turning that information into something we can use, that's what the intelligence function is, while keeping our sources of information secret.'

The analysts will have a greater role, he said, and so will the field intelligence officers. A major responsibility of the directorate would be to deploy people accurately and give them precise, unequivocal information about criminals and the crimes they are going to commit. Grieve said this will get results, and it will also get convictions in court. 'The big issue for us,' he added, 'is how to do these things without showing all our secret toys.'

The terminology used to discuss and describe criminals often has a fictional, almost glamorising imagery which Grieve does not find helpful.

'It's very attractive to impose a hierarchy on these things – and the Mafia, the Triads, they do have a hierarchy and they *are* here. But most of what goes on here under the heading of organised crime is loosely organised. Yes, it's project crime; yes, it nets them vast profits. But it is not hierarchical like people want it to be.' Nor is it immune from attack and penetration, he pointed out. 'It's very well penetrated by us. The only difficulty we have is in turning the information we have into evidence. Catching them in the act is very, very hard work, because we've had to disclose the tricks that we have.'

Matters are not made easier by television, especially in programmes which expose the investigative process in major criminal cases. Some TV exposés, he said, have provided criminals with blueprints on how to commit specific types of crime.

'I'm well aware it makes good television, but it doesn't make the intelligence officer's task any easier. Yes, of course, we want to publicise our successes, we want to be shown to be successful, but every time it's done, it makes the job that much harder.'

In spite of the fact that various kinds of street crime are on the increase and are generally poorly controlled, Grieve believes that major organised crime in London is being contained.

'I think we are keeping the lid on much more effectively than is done in some cities of the world,' he said. 'But we are not doing as well as we could do. The work is very resource-intensive, and the Commissioner has to balance up what he wants to do across a range of issues, and Disclosure – I don't want to keep harping on about it, but Disclosure is a major issue. We had some really good successes in the seventies, but since then we have had to declare our hand over and over again, and explain precisely what we are doing.'

There is also a persuasive argument for innovation in intelligence work: 'Criminals that we target do not repeat mistakes. They are very, very conscious of the tricks we can deploy, so we must constantly be thinking of something new.'

SO 12
Special Branch – Introduction

Now that Special Branch have decided to go on record, John Howley, DAC Security, sees no reason why they should not have done it sooner. A Yorkshireman who joined the Met in 1958, he believes Special Branch has kept its talents hidden for too long.

'There is nothing very secret about the way we work,' he said. 'The secrets are the content of the information that is obtained, and some of the techniques that are used to obtain it. Broadly speaking Special Branch is a part of the police service and is as open as other departments, though some of the things that it does need to be dealt with sensitively.'

In December 1984, the Fourth Report of the Home Affairs Committee, entitled *Special Branches of the Police Force*, aired a widely held view:

> There is little doubt that the Special Branches of the police forces have been in danger of acquiring a sinister reputation of a force which persecutes harmless citizens for political reasons, acts in nefarious ways to assist the security services, is accountable to no one, and represents a threat to civil liberties.

'Part of the process of coming more out into the open,' Howley said, 'is the specific intention to demolish some of those attitudes and old beliefs. Special Branch is a part of the police force that has a job to do, but it's also a part of the police force which is accountable.'

Although the Home Affairs Committee Report went on to give Special Branch an almost clean bill of health, there are still worries.

In February 1992 the Labour Party's offices in London were broken into, and on a TV news interview John Prescott, the Shadow Minister of Transport, said, 'We know from experience the role of Special Branch and these intelligence organisations. They have been pretty active against the Labour Party over a long, long time, and often you can't prove it.'

Howley says it is worrying for everyone in Special Branch that someone in a responsible public position should make such a sweeping assertion with, he presumed, no collateral whatsoever. Howley said that if Mr Prescott had had any real suspicions, it would not have been long before he wrote to the Commissioner about them.

A front-page story in *Today* on 13 May 1993 had the banner headline ANNE WAS BUGGED BY SCOTLAND YARD, above a story which claimed that telephones in the home of the Princess Royal at Gatcombe Park had been secretly bugged, and calls had been recorded by Special Branch. Howley was asked bluntly if his branch had been bugging the Royal Family.

'Definitely not,' he said. 'And if anybody was intercepting the communications of the Royal Family, I would suggest that it's got to be some private enterprise outfit using fairly sophisticated technical equipment which can be obtained today, commercially. It's very unlikely that even the Security Service [MI5] would become involved in that.'

Within the British system of policing, each Special Branch is responsible to its own Chief Constable. In most other European countries, however, every Special Branch equivalent is connected to a national structure, of which counter-terrorism is usually a component. Howley sees advantages in such a system.

'It achieves better coordination, and I think, if the funding for such a unit for counter-terrorist work was central, it would make the provision of resources somewhat easier. But the notion of that goes against the ethos of the British police service, which tends to be fragmentary, associated to local level. Local policing for local purposes suits the British way of life. But some police problems have ramifications beyond the local, and terrorism is one of them. In that respect a need for cooperation and coordination is very high.'

Howley believes – and it is a strictly personal view – that Britain should have a national counter-terrorist body without delay. 'But the Government is not inclined to move in that direction; they do not, at this stage, want to contemplate giving somebody national powers to undertake police work in various police force areas.'

An effective national counter-terrorist unit, in Howley's view, would need the skills of police officers and those of the Security Service.

'But a national effort to draw those two sets of skills together would probably need help from other sources as well,' he said. 'HM Customs, for instance, have an important role on borders. And there would need to be people with Fraud Squad backgrounds, to attack terrorism where it gathers its finance. There's a Terrorist Finance Unit in Northern Ireland. It draws together Customs, Northern Ireland Office, Royal Ulster Constabulary and the VAT people, and they all work together to head off as many of the terrorists' fund-raising activities as they can. Something on those lines should also be considered as part of a national counter-terrorist body here.'

He said there is nothing special at all about Special

Branch personnel. 'I have in that part of my command 530 police officers, thirty-eight of them women, and 150 civil staff. With those numbers you need to have somebody with specific responsibilities in terms of personnel policy and career development, and we have a Personnel Officer the same as any other department would.'

The Personnel Officer looks for recruits who are comparatively mature, experienced, reliable and recommended by their existing line management. In London, because of the large numbers of people involved, and because the hierarchical structure goes right up to the level of Commander, the career pattern can have a considerable degree of variety; that fact, coupled to the particularly absorbing nature of work in Special Branch, means that most officers, once there, tend to stay for the rest of their careers.

Academic attainment is not essential in recruits, but it is nevertheless valued by the administration. 'We look for a fairly high level – it's another of the characteristics,' said Howley. 'Special Branch has a higher proportion of people with university degrees before joining than any other part of the Metropolitan Police, and by a long way.' The proportion of graduates in Special Branch is nearly five times the average for the rest of the police service.

The recruitment rate over the past few years has been approximately thirty officers a year, drawn from an average of 200 applicants. Consequently Special Branch are able to cream off the best, the one applicant in every six who comes closest to their requirements.

'Six or seven per cent of our personnel are women,' Howley said, 'which is higher than you find in the CID generally, but not as high as you find in the police service as a whole.'

In October 1992 the Security Service and Special Branch entered a partnership. The Security Service is now responsible for intelligence-gathering on IRT (Irish Republican Terrorism) on a national basis, a task formerly the province of Special Branch 'B' Squad.

'It was a blow to a lot of people who had had a great deal of involvement, particularly over the last twenty years, in the Irish Republican Terrorist field,' Howley said. 'They felt that their efforts were being to some extent undermined. However, the Government decided to go in a particular direction and we've made every effort, and so have the Security Service, to make sure that the arrangements are now working in the very best way possible.'

Howley admits that the Security Service are better at gathering and analysing intelligence, and better at presenting the product of their analysis. What they lack, he believes, is the police officer's understanding of the psychology of criminals. The police are better, too, at understanding the rigorous requirements of the law, particularly the requirements in terms of evidence in criminal cases being brought to court.

On a specific point of terrorist control, Howley said it is vitally important to retain the right to keep a suspect in custody for seven days.

'Something to bear in mind,' he said, 'is that the police can only detain someone for forty-eight hours under the Prevention of Terrorism Act, and for thirty-six hours under the Police and Criminal Evidence Act.'

When a person suspected of committing a terrorist act is arrested, the police are under great pressure to carry out all the necessary procedures – fingerprints, photographs, forensic tests, confirmation of identity – in only a couple of days.

'Another thing that's important is holding people

incommunicado,' Howley said. 'When you've arrested somebody you think is a significant player in a terrorist crime, if there are other players still being sought, you don't want that individual alerting them.'

There was, for a time, a long-running debate about whether VIPs being protected by Special Branch 'A' Squad should in future receive their personal security from Royalty and Diplomatic Protection. The matter was finally resolved between the Commissioner and representatives of the Home Office, and the VIPs remained with Special Branch.

For a time, the loss of primacy in Irish affairs, and the possibility of losing the protection function to Royalty and Diplomatic Protection, combined to put a severe dent in morale within Special Branch.

'Both of those matters were practically running in tandem,' Howley said. 'The fact was, everybody here knew that two very important areas of activity, traditionally important for more than 100 years in both cases, were being re-examined and the possibility had been put forward of a change. I'm fairly happy now that things are back on to a level course, and we seem to be going in a direction where we can see some of the future clearly. That's got to be a good thing.'

For the future, Howley has the feeling that the present good balance within Special Branch will persist, that the current operational arrangements will certainly suffice, with minor adjustments, unless there are unforeseen shifts in political or terrorist activity.

'As for the other police forces in Britain,' he said, 'I don't think there's any need for Chief Officers to look in a different direction, to consider either increasing or reducing the size of their Special Branches.'

'A' SQUAD

The job of Special Branch 'A' Squad is to provide personal protection, in the form of plain clothes officers working closely with the protected person (the 'Principal') anywhere in the UK or, if the case merits it, throughout the world.

'A' Squad is run by Detective Chief Superintendent Eileen Eggington, one of the most senior women in the Metropolitan Police.

'Very little of our work takes place abroad,' she said. 'We only leave the country with the Prime Minister, the Foreign Secretary and the Home Secretary. We would only accompany somebody else abroad if the threat was assessed to be high in whatever country they were visiting. So as of right it's the three top people who get protection throughout the world, otherwise it's dependent solely on the assessed threat – the assessment comes from the Security Services.'

Protection is specifically against the threat of terrorism. Once a high threat assessment has been made by the Security Services, the Principal concerned is approached by Eggington, who will talk over the position and offer the appropriate kind of protection.

'They don't have to accept it,' she said, 'but in my experience nobody has ever rejected the offer.'

Threat levels are graded from One to Six:

> Level 1:   Specific information says the subject will be the target of an attack.
>
> Level 2:   Information and events indicate a high threat to the subject.
>
> Level 3:   Intelligence, circumstances and recent events indicate a threat.
>
> Level 4:   A threat exists, based on the subject's

position, nationality, background, or
political status.

Level 5: Low level of threat.

Level 6: No evidence of a particular threat.

'Level One is very rare,' said Eggington. 'It means
there's a hit team about to strike. I suppose the nearest
we've come to that is with Salman Rushdie. Level Two
is the high threat – Margaret Thatcher, for instance.
She is still at Level Two and will probably remain at
that level for some time.'

Another person at Level Two is Lord Mason, who
stays at high-threat level because during his term as
Northern Ireland Secretary in the seventies he introduced internment; the IRA, Eggington pointed out,
have long memories. In all, eighteen people in the UK
are currently assessed as being at high-level risk. Fourteen of those people are at Level Two. The Protection
Officers guarding high-risk people are responsible solely
for the protection of the Principal, not for his or her
family.

'Technical' protection is laid on at the homes of
people assessed as Level Three. The Commissioner
comes into this group. 'I can't detail the package that's
provided, because that would be too sensitive,' Eggington said, 'but at Government expense the Home Office
install lighting and alarms which hopefully would counter any attack on the Principal's address. No protection
officers are provided.'

. Level Four includes people who are at general threat
from terrorism because of their work or their position.
Eggington has not been assessed, but she believes she
might be at Level Four. Other Special Branch officers
might also be at Level Four, and certainly some Army
officers. As for Levels Five and Six, they do not really

come into the reckoning. 'A' Squad is concerned principally with Levels One to Three, '... and Four just a little bit,' said Eggington, 'with security advice, and guidance from a Home Office booklet.'

Foreign nationals visiting the United Kingdom, or working here, do not bring their own protection, as is sometimes believed. Their protection during their stay in Britain is entirely in the hands of Special Branch 'A' Squad.

The duration of protection is governed by the threat assessment. 'We regularly review it,' said Eggington. 'Once it goes down to Level Three, we start to negotiate taking it off. That's not always straightforward. Once somebody has been used to having personal protection it's a fairly traumatic thing for it to be taken off, because not only have they had Special Branch officers with them all the time, they've also had an official car and driver.'

People living in the province of Northern Ireland who are at risk are protected by the RUC. When they come to the mainland Special Branch takes over the role. People like the GOC Northern Ireland, and the Revd Ian Paisley – 'PIRA [Provisional IRA] would love to have a pop at him if they had the opportunity,' said Eggington – come into this category.

'Where you get individual VIP visitors who have had a problem with indigenous terrorist groups, then they are far more concerned about the level of protection to be provided. The Americans have had a great number of problems – not just attempts but assassinations – and therefore they are very edgy and a lot of Secret Service agents come with them. The agents sometimes come over on recce visits weeks, certainly days in advance.'

Only two foreign ambassadors in Britain – the

American and the Israeli – have Special Branch protection at present. The others have protection by uniformed officers (from SO16, Diplomatic Protection Group) on duty outside and, sometimes, inside their offices and residences, but no plain-clothes officers to accompany them on their daily business.

Discussing the reconnaissance work done by 'A' Squad officers, Eggington acknowledged that a huge problem at any gathering attended by a high-risk Principal is knowing who to trust.

'The important thing in providing protection is making sure the risk is reduced, and also that the Principal's vulnerability is reduced. By going to a place in advance you know exactly where the exits and the entrances are. It could be there are demonstrators there, or people who are merely going to cheer – it's important that the local police are aware and that they will provide adequate uniformed coverage to make sure the public are kept at bay. And, obviously, in the advance visit the hosts have to be spoken to and all arrangements made for the safety and protection of the Principal. Part of the decision, too, would be whether to put in what we call explosives dogs.'

When a person being protected by 'A' Squad makes a speech in a large public room or hall, there are usually a number of armed officers at strategic points throughout the audience. Officers of 'A' Squad on protective duty are always armed. Increasingly the weapon they carry is an Austrian Glock, a lightweight semi-automatic pistol made largely from plastic. Smith and Wesson revolvers are also used.

The last time an attempt was made on the life of a Principal being protected by 'A' Squad was in 1982: the Israeli ambassador, Shlomo Argov, was shot in the head as he came out of the Dorchester Hotel. The gunman was a member of the Palestinian terrorist group Abu Nidal. Argov was accompanied at the time by only one Protection Officer, who chased and shot the gunman – who had turned on him – who was then arrested. Argov survived the attempt, but he is now permanently bedridden and is barely capable of speech.

Ten years ago Special Branch was not as well set up as it is today. It would nevertheless be an impossible task to guarantee someone's safety if the IRA or some other terrorist group set out to murder them, and was prepared to die or be arrested.

The Salman Rushdie case is a nightmare because Rushdie has to be protected from Islamic fundamentalists, to whom dying in the execution of a *fatwa* would be the precise opposite of a tragedy. Since attacks by suicidal assassins cannot be ruled out, the danger to the Protection Officers as well as Rushdie is potentially enormous. Eggington would be much happier if Rushdie simply stayed at his safe house and did not go out at all.

'That would be easy as far as we're concerned, but clearly from a human rights point of view it wouldn't be acceptable. But the more he moves about the more vulnerable he is, and we have to increase resources to protect him.'

Special Branch Protection Officers are trained by SO19, the Force Firearms Unit, who have both an operational and a training role. There is a three-week bodyguard course and unarmed combat training. Special emphasis is placed on disarming techniques. Positional tactics enter the training picture, too – Protection Officers have to know how to place themselves in a variety of situations.

'They have different formations in different circumstances,' said Eggington. 'It's important how they position themselves near or around the Principal, and when drawing up in a car there's the question of where to position the car, where to get out, where to let the Principal out. They dictate to the Principal which side he gets out of the car, and they know what side that will be because they've already made an advance visit to the place.'

'If you've got an absolutely determined terrorist attack,' Eggington said, 'then, unless you have a real ring of steel around the Principal, I don't think you could prevent it. I think we are fortunate that the Irish terrorist does not like to be captured, and they certainly don't like to be killed. This is something in our favour. Our biggest fear is from the Islamic fanatic who doesn't have any such fear, who considers death as just a step nearer to heaven. That's our biggest fear, but the majority of our Principals are at threat from Irish terrorism.'

Of 120 officers in 'A' Squad, only one other besides Detective Chief Superintendent Eggington is a woman. 'The last two women I've had on the Squad have not passed the bodyguard course, and it's mainly in the handling of the weapon. I think it's probably because a woman's hand is smaller. It's a physical problem. In these days of equal opportunity it could be that something will have to be done about that, because it clearly puts women at a disadvantage when it comes to qualifying.'

'It's not such an attractive job for a woman,' Eggington said. 'Speaking personally, I would find it very difficult to be a full-time Protection Officer, because a lot of the time is spent alone, staying in a hotel. What do you do? Go to the bar of an evening? I'm being practical now – for a woman, being alone in a bar can be a bit difficult. Also, what does a woman wear? During the time that a Protection Officer is out with his Principal he might have an evening function that requires him to wear a DJ, and he will have his DJ ready. He can wear it every evening for a week and nobody would think about it. But for a woman, well, I would feel embarrassed turning out in the same old garb every evening. So the problem becomes a real practical one – of changing as well, for there aren't the facilities for a woman to change, whereas a man can slip into the gents.'

Eggington was among the first six female Special Branch Officers to be trained as an authorised shot. 'I was then being employed on protective duties, unarmed. Then it was decided women should be trained to carry firearms. And I enjoyed it, I have to say. I found there were practical difficulties to carrying the firearm, because it had to be kept in a handbag and therefore the drawing of the weapon was more difficult. Our one female Protection Officer uses an under-arm holster, so she has to be careful about buying her clothes. They have to be loose to fit over it, otherwise it's a matter of carrying the gun in the handbag.'

Protection Officer to Margaret Thatcher must be one of the most stressful jobs in the UK. Detective Chief Inspector Barry Strevens was Mrs Thatcher's Protection Officer from 1978 to 1982, and again from 1985 to 1988. He took up the duty again when she resigned as Prime Minister in 1990, and he is still with her.

Lady Thatcher is a considerable security risk, being one of the IRA's top targets. 'The death of the hunger strikers,' Strevens said, 'they remember to, "It took forty years to get Klaus Barbie; if it takes us that long to get Thatcher, we will." So, yes, she is one of the top targets, and we have to adjust our security accordingly.'

Lady Thatcher has the final decision on where she goes and what she does. Her Protection Officers can only advise her. Nevertheless, she pays attention to advice. Barry Strevens recalled a recent occasion when he was unhappy about her attending a particular event, so he took his concerns to her privately. She listened, and she cancelled her attendance at the event. Strevens says she has never yet gone against his wishes.

While the principal threat to Lady Thatcher remains the IRA, she is still forthright and opinionated on domestic and foreign affairs, so she might easily become a target of other terrorist outfits.

'She's very open in her ideas about the Serbs in Bosnia,' Strevens said. 'She says what she thinks about them, which is a worry in certain quarters. You can't be indifferent to Lady Thatcher. They either like her or they hate her, and that always creates problems for me.'

Awareness of existing threats and being alert to possible new sources are priorities for Strevens. 'I'm not just looking at terrorists, I'm looking at the crank, because you've got to remember that people who attract public attention also attract cranks that want to move in on their publicity.'

In October 1984, IRA terrorist Patrick Magee planted a bomb in the Grand Hotel, Brighton, which nearly succeeded in killing most of the Thatcher administration.

'It changed everything, really,' said Barry Strevens. 'All sorts of security arrangements and procedures had been undertaken before that incident occurred, but here was a device that was laid down well ahead of time.'

Nowadays sophisticated electronic equipment used by POLSA (Police Search Advisers – SO13) would detect the hidden device, but at the time of Brighton the instruments did not exist.

'We use more technical equipment now than we did in the past,' Strevens confirmed. 'And in '84 we just put the dogs round Mrs Thatcher's room. But you certainly wouldn't have thought of going a couple of rooms up. Now it's different. We check everyone going into the hotels well in advance of the time when the Principal's going to be there. Searches are taking place three or four months, even six months before an event is going to occur – like the party conferences at Brighton and Blackpool.'

The Brighton bomb was the most serious attack ever mounted against Margaret Thatcher; all others have been comparatively mild. 'We've never had a gun attack,' said Strevens, 'we've never had a knife attack or an acid attack. We've mainly just had bricks, eggs, wood, people trying to hit us with placards – even daffodils.'

When Lady Thatcher appears at official luncheons or dinners, Strevens is usually on the next table, or the one next to that. It is customary on such occasions for the Protection Officers to be arranged in a pattern around the Principal. 'We can have a triangular formation with one on one side looking at her, one on the other side, and one at the back. And so the one at the back's got both of us in view, we're watching different aspects. The one at the back is the link with our people outside. They may be uniformed officers, or the local plain clothes people. They are a link, so that if anything's happening they inform that man at the back and he gets straight to me, and similarly with us through him.'

When Lady Thatcher makes a speech at one of these functions, she either speaks from her table, or more usually from a podium. 'So she will walk to the podium,' Strevens explained, 'and I will have already decided, on an advance recce, the position I will take up, which will be to the side of the podium and slightly back, with a view of the exit door, or the door where the catering staff come and go. So I've got that controlled, I'm controlling that door and I'm looking at the audience and watching the doors at the back, watching people come in, and my colleague will be on the other side, and the third man will be standing well back. So we are all standing, and we are all covering her.'

If someone were to stand up in the middle of the speech and produce a weapon, Strevens would either step in front of Lady Thatcher to shield her, or one of his colleagues would get in front of her and Strevens would lead her away to a safe room. Every venue has a safe room, always accessible to where Lady Thatcher will be making her speech.

'We would take her there until we had cleared up. Similarly we would take her to a safe room if a device went off. There would be a phone there, we would want to know what was going on before we moved out into a hostile environment.'

In the event of time being too short, with a gunman fifteen yards from Lady Thatcher, ready to shoot, there would be only one course of action.

'I'd have to try and take him out,' said Strevens. 'I'd either have to take him out or I'd take her out of the way. My job would be to come between her and the bullet.'

A female officer, a Detective Sergeant, is now on Lady Thatcher's protection team. The arrangement means that it is entirely possible to keep a protection officer by the Principal's side at all times. In the case of such a prominent target, that is a highly desirable state of affairs.

'The art of being a good protection officer,' Strevens said, 'is that you always remember you are there for one purpose and one purpose only, and that's to protect that individual. If you start to forget that, if you start to think you're part of this magic circle, and think you're accepted by everyone because they treat you wonderfully, you'll soon learn differently, because you're only wonderful whilst that person is wonderful.'

'B' SQUAD

Chief Superintendent Malcolm MacLeod believes in giving credit where it is due. Talking about the Provisional IRA – or PIRA, as they are commonly called within the Met – he said that in recent times they have become much more professional than they were back in the seventies. 'Call it respect, call it what you like, you've got to accept and acknowledge they are a capable organisation.

'If we take the Provisional campaign from 1973 onwards, and look at the way it's been conducted, I think it's true to say that in those days there was less coordination than there is today. The type of campaign that was being conducted in those days was reckless, it was indiscriminate, and in many ways the ASU (Active Service Unit) was probably out of control. They've got better at it in terms of discipline and control, and in their handling and manufacture of devices.'

'B' Squad is where Special Branch began, and it began because of Irish terrorism, which has occupied the Squad's attention and energies right up to the present day.

The trouble started in 1883 with the Fenians, an Irish nationalist secret society who ran a bombing campaign in London aimed at disrupting the British Government as a step towards gaining independence for Ireland. Special Branch – which began life as the Special Irish Squad, later became the Special Irish Branch and was finally re-named Special Branch early in this century –

was established initially to counter the threat from the Fenians.

The Irish-based wing of the Fenians was sometimes called the Irish Republican Brotherhood, and the name was still used after Fenianism died out. A member of the Brotherhood, Arthur Griffith, founded the Irish nationalist party Sinn Féin (meaning 'We Ourselves') in 1905. Links existed between Sinn Féin and a militant nationalist group called the Irish Volunteers, formed in 1913; this was the forerunner of the Irish Republican Army (IRA), founded in 1919.

From the start, the IRA's leading objective was to undermine British rule in Ireland by the use of armed force. In 1969 the organisation split into two wings, the 'Official' IRA and the 'Provisional' wing, the so-called 'Provos' – young, fiercely patriotic militants who favoured terror tactics.

'In February 1972,' MacLeod said, 'a bomb went off at Aldershot barracks, killing seven people. That was the first and last attack of the present mainland campaign by the so-called Official IRA. The campaign proper by the Provisionals didn't get under way here until March 1973.'

Since October 1992 the Security Service and 'B' Squad have been in partnership. The Security Service is now responsible for intelligence-gathering on IRT (Irish Republican Terrorism) on a national basis, a task which was formerly the province of 'B' Squad.

'We still have a role to play in a national context,' MacLeod said. 'We provide operational support and surveillance to other police forces, and we make our inquiry officers and operation officers available to assist local police if there is an IRT incident on their patch. So, although the Security Service has the intelligence lead, police will still talk to police on operational matters.'

OPERATIONS

'B' Squad has three operational teams headed overall by a Superintendent, with a Detective Inspector in charge of each eight-man team. These are the front-line troops and much of their work is traditional policing.

'They carry out the day-to-day inquiries,' said Mac-Leod, 'they follow intelligence leads to try to identify PIRA suspects who may be here on the mainland, and they try to identify safe addresses. These are the officers who will go out of London if necessary and help the constabularies with any operations that might be running in their areas.'

Operational officers rarely make arrests. During the course of an operation there will usually be an anti-terrorist team 'piggy-backing' the 'B' Squad team, and if arrests have to be made they will be made by anti-terrorist officers, who will be responsible for assembling the evidence and taking the cases to court.

RESEARCH UNIT

Highly sensitive intelligence comes to Special Branch from a number of sources, and the Research Unit is a clearing house for the material. There is regular liaison with the Security Service through this office, which also prepares IRT status reports, based on its officers' analysis of incoming intelligence.

INTELLIGENCE: Source Unit

The biggest change since October 1992 has been in the area of intelligence gathering. The national role of 'B' Squad was taken over by the Security Service, but intelligence gathering in the London area remains the responsibility of Special Branch. 'We've got more manpower devoted to this particular task than we had previously,' MacLeod said. 'Within this unit we have a section dedicated to the recruitment and cultivation of agents in the London area.'

SUPPORT: National Joint Unit (NJU)

This section is headed by a Metropolitan Chief Inspector and two Metropolitan Inspectors, with about fifteen provincial officers who join on attachment for periods up to three or four months. The role of the NJU is to act as a conduit for intelligence and on records searches at seaports and airports around Britain, and to monitor the implementation of the Prevention of Terrorism Act (POT). In connection with POT the Unit works to the Home Office and reports all arrests, detentions and other significant developments. Additionally, the NJU prepares applications to the Home Secretary for extensions to detention orders and, on occasions, exclusion orders. More than 300 exclusion orders have been served under the Prevention of Terrorism Act since 1974; approximately eighty are still in force. The Unit has also been responsible for coordinating an operation called Octavian, mounted after an IRA car bomb killed Conservative MP Ian Gow in July 1990.

'The object, first, was to identify the most likely public figures to be targeted by PIRA,' MacLeod explained. 'We went through the line-up of politicians, senior military people, people in public life. We drew up a list and did assessments on these individuals. The consequent list of vulnerable VIPs was sent to all the constabularies. We then actually carried out surveillance on the addresses of the VIPs. That was the object of Operation Octavian, to monitor suspicious sightings, anywhere in the country, in the vicinity of the homes of

VIPs. It was one such patrol, at Sir Charles Tisbury's house in Hampshire, that led to the arrest at Stonehenge of McAuley and Quinliven, two fugitive IRA terrorists.'

MacLeod added that Octavian has now been changed; its operation is left to the discretion of local police forces and it now has a different name, which he was not prepared to reveal.

SUPPORT: Liaison with Metropolitan Police District

When a sizeable measure of 'B' Squad's function was passed to the Security Service in October 1992, it meant that 'B' Squad could devote extra resources to the capital, and they now spend more time in liaison with divisional police. 'Officers of "B" Squad travel around the Metropolitan District and speak to the various local intelligence officers,' MacLeod said, 'or the local information officers, the collators, who may well just stumble across somebody who is of interest to us.'

SUPPORT: 90 Security Section

This is the Royal Military Police unit, responsible for the protective security arrangements at military establishments in the London area. Special Branch 'B' Squad give advice and support to 90 Security Section in any relevant way they can.

SUPPORT: Public Order Support Group

A section which monitors IRA support groups such as the Wolfe Tone Society and various other bodies sympathetic to the Republican cause. It is essential to monitor these groups, MacLeod said, in view of the serious public order issues that could arise from their activities.

'If there is a major demonstration coming off in London, for example the anniversary of Bloody Sunday, our people would prepare a public order assessment dealing with the numbers likely to turn up, the likely mood and volatility of the demonstrators, whether any opposing groups are likely to turn up and, potentially, what this means for policing on the day.'

Regional Desk Officers These are 'B' Squad officers who work directly with Special Branches in the constabularies, offering advice, going out on visits and giving joint presentations with the Security Service.

Civilian Support To run efficiently, an outfit like 'B' Squad depends on civilian personnel to handle the day-to-day administration.

Security Service Attachments (Threat Assessment) A number of 'B' Squad officers are on attachment to the Security Service. 'The threat assessment on public figures, for which we were responsible until last October,' said MacLeod, 'is being taught by our officers to the Security Service officers. They're teaching them the ropes in terms of preparation, research, and analysis of the threat.'

INTELLIGENCE: SO13 Cell

A Detective Inspector and several other officers of 'B' Squad are attached to SO13 (Anti-Terrorist Branch). They feed Special Branch intelligence to where it will do most good in anti-terrorist investigations; they also send back information to 'B' Squad, keeping them updated on anti-terrorist investigations.

INTELLIGENCE: Prison Liaison

There are approximately sixty IRA terrorists currently serving sentences in Britain, and the prisons are a useful source of information.

'It's important that we maintain good liaison with the prison authorities to find out what the latest situation is, and who the visitors are,' MacLeod said. He declined to say whether IRA terrorists in the prisons provide information to Special Branch. 'Every prison has a security officer, and it is the security officers our people speak to.'

SECURITY SERVICE CELL IN SS AND SB

Following the changes made in 1992, a group of Security Service officers is now attached to Special Branch. 'They carry out searches of our database,' said MacLeod, 'and they act as an interface between us and the Security Service whenever day-to-day problems arise.'

Looking at important successes of recent years, MacLeod was reluctant to give 'B' Squad the whole credit for any of them.

'No one agency or department has the monopoly,' he said. 'If there's any kudos going, it's got to go to the police officer who happens to stumble across a member of an ASU. It is sometimes overlooked, but it's basic coppering that's as effective in countering PIRA as pre-emptive intelligence. Take the instance at Wanstead a couple of years back. An off-duty PC saw a man acting suspiciously; he stopped him and spoke to him, introducing himself, and the man ran off. Shortly afterwards it was discovered the man had a lock-up garage with an arms cache inside.'

Much credit does belong with 'B' Squad, notably the capture of the Brighton Bomber, Patrick McGee. In 1993 James Canning was jailed for thirty years for conspiring to cause explosions, also for possessing forty kilos of Semtex explosive, a loaded revolver and six Kalashnikov assault rifles; his mistress was sentenced to three years for possessing rifles and for making money and property available to Canning, knowing it could be used for terrorism.

As a sideline on the Canning case, MacLeod pointed out that it is unwise for police officers to think in stereotypes when they are hunting terrorists. 'There's a tendency to imagine the individual involved in this kind of activity being young and well disciplined, as some of them are,' he said, 'but in the case of Canning the IRA used somebody who had been living over here for a very long time, a middle-aged man who had adopted a normal lifestyle, who played golf and drank in the local pubs.'

MacLeod could not go into the details of some noteworthy cases simply because they fall within the area of official secrecy. Facts and figures, too, have their security aspects. 'I wouldn't wish to indicate the amount of resources and effort that we're putting into this counter-terrorist drive, but it's quite considerable.'

As for the 'secret police force' image of Special Branch, MacLeod dismisses it as nonsense, pointing out there is a difference between 'secret' and 'sensitive'.

'If anybody's interested to know what we're all about, they can go to HMSO and get a copy of the Home Office guidelines on Special Branches. There's nothing terribly secret about it.'

ACTIVE SERVICE UNITS – PROVISIONAL IRA
– UK MAINLAND
An Abridged List

1971. Tooting Bomb Factory

MAGILL, Brendan   Arrested 25.3.71, sentenced to 2
                       years – Excluded 1973

McGARRIGLE,   Arrested 25.3.71, sentenced to 3
  Joseph P.   years – Excluded 1973

22.2.72 Aldershot Car Bombs

JENKINSON, Noel   Convicted 14.11.72, sentenced
                       to life imprisonment

KISSANE, Francis   as above

DUIGAN, Michael H. as above

March 1973

This group was known as the 'Winchester Ten' and
were responsible for the four large car bombs in March
1973.

PRICE, Marion   Arrested 8.3.72, sentenced to life

PRICE, Dolores   as above

HOLMES, Paul   as above

FEENEY, Hugh   as above

KELLY, Gerrard   as above

BRADY, Martin F.   as above

WALSH, Robert M.   as above

ARMSTRONG,   as above
  William J.

McLARNON,   Sentenced to 15 years
  William   imprisonment

February/March 1974 Conspiracy

4.2.74   M62 coach bombing and 10.9.73 King's Cross
Railway Station.

26.3.74   Claro Barracks, Rippon. 12.2.74 Defence College, Latimer

WARD, Judith	Arrested 18.2.74, sentenced on 4.11.74 to life imprisonment. Released 1992
McMULLEN, Peter	Arrested USA

Coventry Four

RUSH, Thomas Gerald	Arrested 13.4.73, sentenced to 8 years
FELL, Father Patrick	Sentenced to 12 years
STAGG, Francis	Sentenced to 10 years, deceased
LYNCH, Anthony Roland	Sentenced to 10 years

Birmingham – Wolverhampton Group

This group was responsible for a series of bombings in Birmingham and Wolverhampton during the period 1.8.73 to 3.8.74.

YOUNG, Gerald Peter	Arrested in August 1974
BLAKE, Stephen Adrian	Sentenced to between 10 and 18 years
ASHE, James Joseph	see above
SMALL, Gerald	see above
MADIGAN, James	see above
GUILFOYLE, Patrick	see above
DUFFY, Joseph	see above
MURRAY, Michael Joseph	Arrested November 1974, 12 years
REILLY, Michael Patrick	Arrested December 1975, 10 years
CHRISTIE, Patrick Arthur	Arrested November 1975, 10 years

Birmingham Six

CALLAGHAN, Hugh	Arrested 21.11.74, sentenced 15.8.75
HILL, Patrick	Sentenced life imprisonment
HUNTER, Robert	as above
McILKENNY, Noel R.	as above
POWER, William	as above
WALKER, John	as above
KELLY, James	as above
	(later released on appeal 1991)
SHEEHAN, Michael G.	Arrested 3.12.74, sentenced 15.8.75 9 years imprisonment

Guildford Four

ARMSTRONG, Patrick	Arrested 1.12.74–7.12.74, sentenced 22.10.75 life imprisonment
HILL, Paul	sentenced 22.10.75 life imprisonment
CONLON, Gerard P.	as above
RICHARDSON, Carol M.	as above
	(All later released on appeal 1990)

Maguire Seven

MAGUIRE, Anne Rita	Arrested 7.12.74 and 24.2.75
MAGUIRE, Vincent	sentenced to 14 years,
MAGUIRE, Patrick	5 years, 4 years, 12 years, 12 years, 14 years, and 12 years imprisonment
CONLON, Patrick J.	see above
O'NEIL, Patrick J.	see above (later released on appeal)

MAGUIRE, Patrick   see above
SMYTHE, William J.   see above

The Balcome Street ASU
The first four became known as the Balcome Street
ASU following the siege. The team was responsible for
the 1975 bombing campaign.

DUGGAN, Harry	⎫
DOCHERTY, Hugh	Arrested 12.12.75, sentenced
BUTLER, Edward	10.2.77 life imprisonment
O'CONNELL, Martin	⎭
CUNNINGHAM, Anthony	Sentenced 28.2.77, 10 years imprisonment
MURPHY, James G.	as above
KEENAN, Brian Pascal	Sentenced 25.6.80, 18 years imprisonment
QUINN, William J.	Arrested 21.10.86, sentenced to life

Firearms Dealers
This team attempted to supply PIRA with a large con-
signment of weapons and radios.

HIGGINS, John Joseph	⎧ Arrested 17.5.76, sentenced
SMILEY, Gerald	6.4.77, 5 years,
DAVIDSON, James M.	4 years, 2 years imprisonment
CAUGHIE, Eddie	Found not guilty

Operaton OTIS
This ASU was also known as the Tuite ASU; Tuite was
intimately involved in the bombing campaign of 1978–
1979; their bomb factory was found in Trafalgar Road,
Greenwich.

TUITE, Gerard	Arrested 4.3.82, sentenced 13.7.82 to 10 years imprisonment; Tuite later escaped from Brixton Prison
GLENHOLMES, Richard	Sentenced to 10 years imprisonment
CAMPBELL, Robert	as above
STOREY, Robert	Acquitted
KEENAN, Christine	Acquitted
PARRATT, Margaret	13.3.81 suspended sentence
O'MALLEY, Jacqueline	as above
McCOMB, Gabriel	Arrested 25.1.82, sentenced to 17 years imprisonment
CASSIDY, Lillian	Bound over
CASSIDY, Bernard	as above
CANNON, Brian	Sentenced to 6 months imprisonment for supply of false documents

Hyde Park 1982
Responsible for the Hyde Park bomb of 20.7.82

McNAMEE, Gilbert	Charged 18.8.86, sentenced to life

Operation Find
This team was responsible for the bombings in 1981 and the find of bomb making equipment and weapons at Pangbourne 26.10.83.

KAVANAGH, Paul	Arrested 17.3.84, sentenced to life
McVEIGH, James	In custody Dublin 21.1.83
QUIGLEY, Thomas	Arrested 3.12.83, sentenced 7.3.85 to life imprisonment

McNAMEE, Gilbert   Charged 18.8.86, sentenced to life imprisonment

ELLIS, Desmond   Acquitted

The Harrods Bombing Campaign

The campaign started with a bomb at Woolwich on 10.12.83 and ended with the bomb at Harrods, 17.12.83 when 6 people were killed. Bomb making equipment and weapons were found at Nottingham and Northamptonshire in January 1984.

KAVANAGH, Paul   Charged 22.3.84, convicted 7.3.85

VELLA, Natalino   Arrested 23.6.84, sentenced to 15 years

McNAMEE, Gilbert   Charged 18.8.86, sentenced to life

Brighton and the Glasgow ASU

Magee was responsible for the bomb at the Grand Hotel in Brighton on 12.10.84. This team aimed to place a number of long-delay time bombs all over the country but were arrested in Glasgow 22.6.85 where a cache of weapons and bomb making equipment was found.

MAGEE, Patrick   Charged 29.6.85, sentenced 24.6.86 to life imprisonment

McDONNELL, Gerard   as above

SHERRY, Peter   as above

O'DWYER, Ella   as above

ANDERSON, Martina   as above

CRAIG, Donal   Sentenced to 10 years imprisonment

McKENNY, Michael   Charged 8.5.86, sentenced 14.4.87 to 16 years imprisonment

Operation Denmark
Group associated with a find of bomb making equipment in Cheshire, February 1987.

McLAUGHLIN, Patrick J.	Arrested 19.2.87, sentenced to 20 years imprisonment on 17.6.88
McCOTTER, Liam	As above, sentenced to 17 years

Operation Thames
Team arrested following the discovery of the Clapham bomb factory in December 1988.

MULLEN, Nick	Arrested 7.2.89, sentenced to 30 years imprisonment on 8.6.90
WADLEY, Eamon	Arrested 21.12.88, acquitted
SHEEHY, Patrick	Deceased

Operation Shuttle
A find of explosives was made at Hampstead Heath on 10.10.89.

McBREARTY, David	Excluded from UK.

Operation Pebble
Finds of bomb making equipment and firearms in Wales and Luton in December 1989.

O'DWYER, Liam	Sentenced to 30 years imprisonment on 6.12.90
McCOMB, Damien	as above

Operation Venus
Arrested after a car chase in Wood Green and discovery of firearms on back seat of car 22.5.90.

O'DONNELL, Kevin B.	Sentenced 15.3.91 for firearms offences to 9 months imprisonment. Later shot dead by Sec. Forces in NI (1992)

Operation Rebound

On 11.11.90 in Hanover Road, Willesden, explosive items and firearms were found in a Lada motor vehicle; the following were arrested in connection with the find.

McCAULEY, Pearse   Escaped whilst on remand in Brixton Prison (now i/c in R of I)

QUINNLIVAN, Neeson   see above

McKANE, William   Acquitted

McKANE, Siobhan   Charges dropped by CPS

DOCHERTY, Martin   Excluded.

'CE' SQUAD

'The Security Service studies subversion as it affects the state,' said Detective Chief Superintendent Bob Potter, Head of CE Squad. 'We tend to view it as it affects public order on the streets of the capital.'

CE Squad (the name comes from an amalgamation of two former squads) has a strength of approximately 140 officers, plus civilian staff. The Squad's function is to keep the peace on the streets of London. Their responsibilities cover three main areas: International Terrorism, Public Order and Investigation.

When the Security Service took primacy over Irish affairs in October 1992, their relationship with CE Squad was unaffected. 'The new arrangement only affects "B" Squad,' Potter said, 'and eventually we feel that in their relationship they will use us as a model of how they should continue.'

On any investigation involving the Security Service and CE Squad, there is no sharp demarcation between the contribution of one or the other. Strictly speaking, intelligence gathering is the responsibility of the Security Service, while executive action – e.g., making arrests or breaking up illegal or disorderly gatherings – is police work and is therefore the responsibility of CE Squad.

Right-Wing Groups

'You only have to mention right wing in certain circles,' Potter said, 'and people look at what's happened in Germany and they imagine it happening here. That's not the case in this country. Here, the right wing's history has been one of factionalising – whenever they get together, they break up, usually over leadership and personality problems. They are a very small part of society and their main threat comes from physical confrontation with the left wing on the streets.'

The largest of the right-wing groups in Britain is the British National Party (BNP). At one time the National Front was the largest but their membership has waned, mainly because of divisions in the leadership, and many of their old supporters have moved over to the BNP. They claim to have fifty branches, with a total membership of 4,000, although it is believed that 2,500 would be more realistic. Potter confirmed that they claim a far larger membership than they have, and the terminology is misleading: a branch could consist of as few as two people.

'They go in two camps,' he said. 'There's the old, more intellectual side, the people who actually plot and produce the literature. Then there's the street thugs. The person who's quite happy to go along to a football match to kick someone is the sort of person who's attracted to the British National Party. Typical members have short haircuts and wear big boots. They want the hard look.' Taken overall, Potter says, the BNP have no power base in Britain. 'If we can put that myth to bed forever I'd be very grateful.'

Membership of the BNP tends to be a mix of mindless thugs and people committed to a right-wing ideology. 'There are certain among the leaders,' Potter said, 'who are anti-Semitic, anti-black, whatever, and they use it to play on the fears of people.'

Often the mere presence of someone is provocative enough to cause trouble. In July 1992 the right-wing historian David Irving held a peaceful meeting inside a students' hostel in the West End of London. Left-wing opposition turned up and mounted a noisy protest. 'So, although he wasn't out to cause trouble,' Potter said, 'the fact that he was there created trouble.'

On these occasions police impartiality will always be misread by one side or the other. Potter remembers when, as a uniformed Inspector, he protected the National Front from the left wing on a Saturday, and on Sunday he shielded the left wing from the National Front. He was called a fascist pig on the first occasion and a communist pig on the second.

The group calling itself Blood and Honour is a growing movement of neo-Nazi skinheads. 'They're part of this new wave of punk rock,' Potter said. 'They like to play very heavy-metal music, and the words are often racist-motivated. The problems occur, again, when the left wing try to break up the concerts.'

A group called Combat 18 typify a right-wing trend towards a survivalist philosophy, adopted usually by splinter factions, who dress in army fatigues and engage in military exercises. Combat 18 is very small, Potter says, and they cause no problems.

Before a demonstration in London by the political

right or left, CE Squad produce a written assessment for the uniformed officers; this is usually a projection of the likely course of events. The evaluation is based, in part, on the Squad's accumulated knowledge of the groups and how they are known to behave. At the briefing before the demonstration an officer from CE Squad will be present to pass on the latest available intelligence.

'Some people call it crystal-balling,' said Potter, 'and often I suppose it is, but we try to give our uniformed colleagues, who have to deal with these people physically, some idea of what the group's intention is. The more information and intelligence we can give them, obviously the better they can police the event. They can get the right number of officers on duty, because nowadays cancelling leaves and doing weekend work is very, very expensive.'

On the day of the event, CE Squad officers watch out for known troublemakers and identify them to the uniformed officers.

'But you have to remember,' Potter said, 'we can only arrest people for criminal offences. We don't have political offences. So, to be arrested, a person must have committed a criminal offence.'

Even with the European borders coming down, Potter does not foresee an increase in racial tensions in Britain. 'The Government has said we are still going to have some sort of immigration control. As long as that remains, the catalyst for unrest doesn't exist. And we don't have the problem of long land borders with other countries – like the German–French experience of a huge border that is uncontrollable. What we have are specific points of entry around the country which we can control.'

CE Squad keep intelligence files on the various right-wing groups. The main purpose of the files is to monitor the action of people with a history of violence. Files are closed only when Special Branch feel that the individual's propensity for violence has gone. Files are never closed without consultation with the Security Service, who may have quite separate reasons for wishing a file to remain open.

Left-Wing Groups

Five prominent groups in this category are Anti-Fascist Action, Red Action, Direct Action Movement, Workers' Power and the largest of all, the Socialist Workers' Party (SWP).

'The most violent of them,' said Potter, 'are Direct Action Movement. They are the ones with head-cases in their ranks who will, for no reason, just go and kick someone who they feel is a right-winger. These groups call themselves anti-fascist, but that's a peg to hang their hat on at the moment. Right now the left wing lacks a *cause célèbre*. They had it way back with CND, then the Vietnam Solidarity campaign. The Poll Tax for a while gave them an issue that combined the whole spectrum of left-wing alternatives. The one they've all latched on to, currently, is anti-racism.'

Many of the people on the left wing, like their opposite numbers on the right, are committed ideologists who genuinely believe in the ultimate goodness of their cause. The trouble starts, Potter says, when ideology becomes action on the streets, which can result in some level of violence: 'That's where we really become involved.'

Although Special Branch deals with both sides in exactly the same way, the political left wing in Britain is much larger than the right wing.

'I think on the left-wing side they're usually more committed,' Potter said. 'They're more politically aware, and there is some genuine feeling behind it. They're not the same people as you see on the right. They've got two O levels instead of one.'

The degree of violence on the left is relatively low, but CE Squad have to remain alert to groups being infiltrated by subversives who want to hijack the organisation for their own ends. Even when a danger spot has been identified, there is always the risk that inadvertently heavy-handed policing will be seen as state oppression rather than reasonable intervention.

'It's a very difficult judgement call,' said Potter. 'We have to shift priorities all the time. A few years back some strikes were being hijacked, there were subversive elements in the unions getting themselves elected to positions where they could do considerable damage. That doesn't happen now.'

The Socialist Workers' Party were blamed for the high levels of violence in the Poll Tax riot in Trafalgar Square in March 1990, but Potter says that was unfair. 'There was an element of the underclass taking part who weren't affiliated to anyone, they just saw some sort of violent demonstration going on and thought they'd have some of that. I think alcohol also played a part in it.'

It was equally unfair, he said, to blame the SWP for starting the Poll Tax riot. All they did, in his view, was seize upon the Tax as a vehicle for promoting political unrest, which they did mainly with leaflets and by holding public meetings.

Animal Rights National Index This department collects, organises and disseminates information about animal rights activists and activities throughout Britain, but there is also an operational side to ARNI, and it falls within the CE Squad's public order responsibilities.

The index consists mainly of several thousand names and addresses. 'Animal rights isn't a simplified structured organisation with a top, a middle and a bottom,' said the spokesman. 'It is not easily identifiable. We put people into two main classifications, general and more positive, and with the more positive ones we're talking in hundreds and the general ones we're talking in thousands.' Other data held on the index relate to acts of violence and criminal damage, and to terrorist activity.

Analysis being an important part of the department's function, regular assessments are made of current targets, and of probable sites of aggression in the future.

'To say that somebody comes from Yorkshire doesn't mean that next week he won't be involved in an incident in Bristol, or even further south at Exeter, say. Boundaries are not a predominant consideration in the work we do.'

'ARNI is looking at extremism all round the country,' Potter said. 'The operational side, as it involves us, is concerned with animal rights matters in London. We're looking at individuals involved with hunt saboteuring, contamination of products, things like that, in London alone.'

He gave an example.

'Just about every other Sunday there's been a demonstration at the chicken slaughterhouse at Leyden Street, in the East End. It's a protest about the methods they use to slaughter chickens, and we get involved helping our uniformed colleagues there. There have been break-ins at research laboratories and at hospitals, and of course there's all the criminal damage done to butchers' shops and pet shops. It's our job really to bring it all together and give the local police a picture of what's going on.' Identifications are made by consulting ARNI and, when necessary, more localised records. 'We would try to look at the main organisers and any of the troublemakers and help identify them to the uniform side.'

There are very few fox hunts in the London area, but the Brixton Hunt Saboteurs Association make forays into Surrey and Kent to cause problems for the hunting fraternities, so CE Squad try to help the police in those areas, too. Potter says Special Branch try to be proactive in these matters, but when animal rights issues are measured against political terrorism, they scarcely feature on the list of priorities.

'The average cell is two people. You see them in a pub, they have a few drinks, and then they decide to go and take some sort of action. That's on the one hand. On the other hand you get these groups of, say, forty or fifty of them who will break into premises – and they will have taken legal advice and will know that if they don't take anything they're only trespassing, which isn't a criminal offence, but deliberately causing damage to property is.'

For Special Branch, the worrying factor with protest and sabotage groups is the tendency to escalation, the need in certain individuals to intensify their protests until a point is reached when a person is no longer protesting, he is committing criminal damage, and shows no sign of drawing the line there. 'Criminal damage isn't terrorism,' said Potter, 'but sticking a bomb under someone's car is.'

Arni Statistics

1990   *Crimes as reported: 573*
                    Estimated cost of damage: £551,350

Main Targets   Vehicles, farms, breeders, butchers,
                        other shops.
                    Devices used at 43 locations.
                    Estimated cost of damage: £63,000
                    Hoaxes: 63
                    Arrests: 438

1991   *Crimes as reported: 1,811*
                    Estimated cost of damage: £8,584,000

Main Targets   Vehicles, abattoirs, furriers, butchers,
                        other shops.
                    Devices used at 45 locations.
                    Estimated cost of damage: £5,300,000
                    Hoaxes: 98
                    Arrests: 648

1992   *Crimes as reported: 689*
                    Estimated cost of damage: £1,957,000

Main Targets   Vehicles, labs, farms, butchers, abattoirs.
                    Devices used at 26 locations.
                    Estimated cost of damage: £1,000,000 +
                    Hoaxes: 54
                    Arrests: 385

International Terrorism

Stated simply, CE Squad's role in the sphere of international terrorism is to monitor events around the world
and estimate how they will affect London, if at all.

This, again, is an area where Special Branch work closely with the Security Service.

'They've got the national role,' Potter said, 'looking at international terrorism that affects the United Kingdom. Our remit is London, bearing in mind that the majority of the embassies, the high commissions and other diplomatic premises are in London, and so are the national airline offices. The major targets for international terrorists are right here.'

International terrorism in Britain is not aimed at the British, Potter added. 'It's aimed at targets like Iranian dissidents. A lot of Iranian effort is against their own people over here, so the effect on UK interests isn't great.'

Potter says there is no shortage of plots to kill people. 'There was a job last year where two South Africans, a policeman and a policewoman, came over to London and met up with three members of the UDA, with a view to killing a dissident South African policeman who had gone over to the ANC. Now the evidence wasn't there, but the two were arrested and held for a while, and they were eventually deported.'

Since the threat from Russia has diminished, numbers on the international terrorism teams have been reduced. 'People have been moved to the Irish squad,' Potter said, 'to Heathrow and to support and to protection, because protection is an ever-growing empire.'

There have been no overt international terrorist acts in London since 1989. Salman Rushdie remains the primary worry.

'We know the Iranians remain very dedicated to killing him. It is constantly being announced that the *fatwa* is still on. They've upped the reward to nearly three million dollars now.'

No particular group can be singled out as targeting

Rushdie. 'That was the whole idea of the reward from the *fatwa*,' Potter said, 'it was to encourage any old nutter to try and get to him. But certainly the Iranian Intelligence Service is working very hard to find out where he is.' Potter knows who the Iranian Intelligence agents in London are. 'A lot of these people are accredited diplomats and, you know, they just have to step over that line . . .'

Unrest in India, Pakistan and Bangladesh invariably has its repercussions throughout the corresponding ethnic communities in Britain. 'There was a disruption at a Sikh temple in India not so long ago,' Potter said, 'which manifested itself over here in attacks on various Hindu and Muslim temples. People try to exact some sort of revenge and a lot of criminal damage is caused. Part of what we try to do is look at potential flashpoints and see what's going to happen over here.'

'In some countries politics is more important than football,' Potter said, 'and people get very committed. If a particular group doesn't fulfil certain people's needs, then they'll start up their own group. It's very difficult keeping track of the organisations, they come and go. There was a lovely case the other day, it involved the Shining Path of Peru. I was surprised to learn we had a big Peruvian problem in London, and then I found out it was Turks who were involved and causing all the trouble. Four hundred Turks demonstrating in sympathy with Peruvian affairs. Don't ask me why. You've just got to go with the flow. The South Orkneys Liberation Front, that's the future. We've identified both penguins already.'

Potter paints a restrained, peaceful picture of the streets of London at present, certainly as far as international terrorism is concerned. A fair measure of the peace can probably be ascribed to neatly-timed disruptive work by CE Squad and the Security Service.

Potter finds plenty of reason to be wary. 'South Africa has been a problem over here. You don't think of them as creating real problems, but when they come over and try to kill people, that's a problem for us – and there have been other problems with them. And there's Zaire – there's a lot of unrest over there, so is that going to be reflected over here? We have to look at that. We have to keep a watching brief and try to identify trouble spots.'

Every year thousands of people from foreign countries apply to become naturalised British subjects. At the request of the Government, officers from CE Squad's Naturalisation Squad interview selected cases and recommend whether or not naturalisation should be granted.

'We'll go along and interview them,' Potter said; 'we'll examine their financial records and so forth. We look at a very, very small percentage of these people. I think they're the difficult cases. Occasionally there are things that are glaringly not right, so before a decision is taken by Home Office they ask us to look into it.'

Another 'desk' within CE Squad is the Terrorism Research Unit. Their role is to act as a central repository of information, so that when an assessment is needed on a particular place or faction or situation, they can quickly bring together the components and produce what is needed.

There is also a European Liaison Section, set up in 1977 to get round the unwieldy mechanism of Interpol, which is so enmeshed by its own networks that finding, for example, the name of the registered owner of a car in London with Swiss number plates could take weeks.

'Because of the network that's been built up within

Europe on the terrorism side,' said Potter, 'you can lift
a phone, ring up your counterpart in Switzerland and
he will have that detail. It's a very good system, dedicated purely to terrorism, whereas Interpol is general
crime. We now have terrorist liaison officers in Holland,
in Germany and in France, and we've got French,
German, Spanish and Swedish officers attached to
their embassies here, who take part in this terrorist
liaison.'

He believes that the days of the Special Branch being
an ominous, ill-defined presence, forever shadowing
society, are giving way to an era of openness. Within
reason.

'MI6 are going to get a charter,' he said; 'they're
going to become real, because up till now they've never
officially existed. It's like the CIA in Langley, they've
got signs up now. When MI5's number gets in the
Phone Book, that's when we'll really be out in the open.'
(Subsequent to the interview with Potter, the Security
Service has published a glossy brochure and a box
number.)

'P' SQUAD

A number of agencies, including the Security Service,
the Foreign Office and the National General Intelligence's Drug and Football Intelligence Sections, rely
on 'P' Squad to keep track of travellers in and out of
London's airports.

'We operate now at Heathrow, Biggin Hill and
London City Airport,' said Chief Superintendent Eric
Docker, head of 'P' Squad. 'We have roving commissions at some of the smaller airfields, too, like Denham,
and we watch the ships at the Port of London.'

Terrorist Incidents Since 1983

YEAR	INCIDENT	RESPONSIBLE
1982	Attempted murder of Israeli ambassador	Abu Nidal (Palestinian)
1984	Bomb plot	Libya
1984	Murder of WPC Yvonne Fletcher	Libya
1984	Murder of dissident El Giahour	Libya
1985	Murder of Horeau	Seychelles
1986	Bombing of dissident Fazeli's bookshop in Kensington	Iran
1987	Car bomb attack on dissident Parviz	Iran
1987	Murder of political cartoonist Naj El Ali	PLO/Force 17
1987	Murder of dissidents Tavakolis (father and son)	Iran
1987	Murder	Sikhs
1988	Murder by poisoning	Iraq
1989	Incendiary attacks on bookshops selling *The Satanic Verses*	Iran

'We will look at people as they walk towards us, look at their body language. We note the way they answer questions, how generally cooperative they are,' said Docker. 'Under the Prevention of Terrorism Act we have an absolute right to stop people and question them. We do not need reasonable suspicion. And we can hold them if necessary for up to forty-eight hours. Any detention beyond that requires the Home Secretary's authorisation.'

Limitations on manpower mean that in some areas the Special Branch presence is little more than a token, although events have shown that any police presence can be better than none. For example, only one 'P' Squad officer is stationed at Biggin Hill, but he and the airport's single Customs officer recently made a random check on a newly-landed aircraft and found sixty pounds of cannabis in the cockpit.

'We're very much demand led,' Docker explained. 'Other Special Branch Squads have active inquiries on the people they're interested in. "P" Squad has none of that. We rely on other agencies to tell us who *they* are interested in.'

Intelligence gathering falls into two groups – International travellers and duties under the Prevention of Terrorism Act.

'Where international travellers are concerned,' Docker said, 'there is a scheme, very much a non-precise targeting method for the benefit of the officers working at airports, which indicates categories of travellers of interest to the Immigration Service, or the Security Service, or the Home Office. The foreign people in these categories may be of interest, not because they are potentially subversive, but because some of our agencies may be looking to recruit people.'

The circuitous language meant that recruitment could be for purposes of counter-espionage. The nationality of targeted persons would change from month to month in line with the developing political scene in, say, the Middle East.

'Sometimes we get requests to back-check on people to see if they've entered the country,' Docker said. 'It means going back through immigration records, sometimes airline ticket stubs, things like that.'

Manpower problems, coupled with the sheer volume

of travellers using the larger airports, can make the work of 'P' Squad arduous, especially when they are looking for a specific traveller, very often one suspected of involvement in terrorism. In Heathrow's Terminal 3, at 6.00 a.m. on a weekday, thirty Immigration officers might be working on the desks and the immigration hall can be packed with people from recently landed long-haul flights. In that situation there might be a maximum of two Special Branch officers on duty. Usually they are positioned behind one-way glass at one end of the row of immigration desks. When more officers are on duty, a number of them will often mingle with the crowds.

'They will try and identify their targets, using what information they have, and also the "policeman's nose",' said Docker. 'And they will perhaps have a look at a person, chat with him, maybe do a couple of searches through our own records at Special Branch to see if anything is known. And if they do find something of interest, then they will develop it a bit further.'

On the face of it, finding a needle in a haystack would be easier than isolating one person from the hordes passing through Terminal 3 Arrivals, given that a single jumbo jet can bring in a passenger load of more than 400 people. If a target's name is available then it is given to all the Immigration Officers on duty; a name *and* a flight number will narrow the search dramatically.

'You have to wait for the person to come forward to the desks,' said Docker. 'You can't possibly pick him or her out.' Often 'P' Squad officers are not looking for any specific person, but are interested in an individual flight – 'because we know that particular flight normally has something of interest on it somewhere. Immigration know what sort of things we're looking for, and we go from desk to desk to desk, watching the officers, listening to the questions they're asking people, looking at passports over the officers' shoulders. Then, if necessary, once an Immigration officer is finished with someone, we have a chat with him. Sometimes, the Immigration officer will come to us and say, "I'm not happy about this person. He or she has given me what appears to be a strange address, they don't seem to have any money, can you do a few checks on them?" A lot of our success comes from good liaison with Immigration.'

Taking a hypothetical case, an outbreak of civil disorder right across India, Docker explained the reactive procedure in 'P' Squad.

'We would be given a list of people who were thought to be a threat either to the Indian High Commissioner, or the Commission itself. Immigration would be notified and if these people turned up they would be examined. Immigration would decide whether they wanted to land them or not, and if they did, then we would talk to them. We might report their movements and send them on their way.'

The dropping of European immigration boundaries produced few significant changes in procedure at London's airports. Immigration have adopted a lighter touch with outbound controls, and with the selective way they examine British passports on the way in.

'As for Special Branch officers,' Docker said, 'well, we were asked to put a lighter touch on our controls, too. My attitude to that was, if our touch was any lighter, we wouldn't be there at all.'

The bulk of work for 'P' Squad's ninety officers at Heathrow is related to the Prevention of Terrorism Act. Docker estimated that two-fifths of 'port strength' Special Branch officers are engaged on these controls, largely because Customs and Immigration have no duties under the Act. Travellers from Northern Ireland and the Republic of Ireland do not pass through any immigration control, but they are scrutinised by Special Branch officers.

'There is a theoretical Customs control for those coming from the Republic of Ireland,' said Docker, 'but, since the first of January 1993, there's the phone – pick it up if you've got something to declare and a Customs officer will come and see you. They've got a very, very light touch on that. There's only a Special Branch control, and that's one we keep manned continually.'

Individuals coming in off Irish flights are checked against intelligence from Special Branch 'B' Squad, from the RUC and sometimes even from the Republican Garda; there is also a list of approximately eighty people who are subject to Exclusion Orders under the Prevention of Terrorism Act. In addition to all that, Docker said, the officers will use their professional instincts.

The scrutiny given to suspected Irish terrorists is much more thorough than that applied to travellers in Terminal 3, and Docker believes it is effective. Recently a man was stopped because a 'P' Squad officer simply did not trust the look of him; it transpired that the officer had singled out an IRA terrorist, who was eventually expelled from the country under an Exclusion Order. Docker admits he is surprised that IRA terrorists still use Heathrow Airport, 'But we know that they still do.'

On average, three hundred people are arrested every year at Heathrow. Special Branch officers are often involved in the arrests simply because they are the only police officers at the travellers' points of entry and exit. Crime arrests, Docker estimated, account for between 30 and 40 per cent of 'P' Squad's work.

The National Ports Office began in the 1970s. It served as a central agency distributing information to

Special Branch officers at the various ports. After the Metropolitan Police Special Branch were withdrawn from the ports in the provinces (in 1978), they retained responsibility for the National Ports Office, and nowadays it is run by a Detective Sergeant and a Detective Constable. Among other duties, they produce a monthly Port Circulation Sheet, listing what Docker euphemistically describes as 'people of interest', as well as specifically cancelling the names of those no longer of interest. The information is circulated to the 160-plus ports in Britain. Accompanying the names on the list is a graded system of recommended actions.

'It uses letters that mean different things,' Docker said. 'For instance, if it has *Action F* on it, it means arrest. If it has *Action E* it means don't arrest, but identify and report. If you get an *Action TF*, the *T* means Terrorist, so you're being told to arrest a terrorist.'

The National Ports Office also circulates information on child abduction cases, whether they concern wardship orders or legislation under the Children's Act.

Docker admitted that, if it really became necessary, he would have to use force to return a child to the jurisdiction of the High Court; 'But God forbid I should ever have to do it.'

Except in rare circumstances, Special Branch have no power to detain an aircraft on the ground; they usually have to rely on the pilot agreeing to a delay. Recently one of Docker's officers boarded a West Indian Airways plane at Heathrow to arrest a woman. After a certain amount of disturbance the woman was persuaded to leave the aircraft, but when the officer asked if her bags could be removed, the pilot refused. He said it had already cost too much money for him to stay past his take-off time; he would arrange for the bags to be sent back from the other end. So the plane took off without the woman, but with her bags on board.

'Forget your average man who's wanted for criminal damage, or theft or assault,' Docker said. 'It's not worth it, it's too expensive. I remember one case several years ago, we had a Libyan Airways plane brought back for some reason. The person we wanted was hauled off, there was a bit of an argument at the time, and the eventual bill for bringing the aircraft back, and the ground fees and everything else, was something in the region of sixty or seventy thousand pounds, which was presented to the Metropolitan Police. The Commissioner politely told them what they could do with it, and we never heard anything more.'

Although a majority of pilots would agree to return when they were asked, the expense of requesting the return of an outward-bound aircraft can be harrowing. If the plane in question were, say, a Boeing 747, just beginning its trip from Heathrow to Hong Kong, the present-day cost of having that one jumbo turned back would be in the region of a quarter of a million pounds.

The Channel Tunnel will bring its own difficulties. Docker said his main problem would be finding extra staff to carry out Special Branch duties. He had no concrete plans before him, but he believed that 'P' Squad would have facilities at Waterloo International Terminal, alongside Immigration, to monitor passengers exactly as they do at the airports.

'If you look at the projected maximum number of trains,' he said, 'I think it's something like thirty a day, each one capable of carrying up to eight hundred people. That makes individual examination of passengers nigh-on impossible. So, again, it will be a fairly light touch at Waterloo.'

There will be other problems, and unavoidable anomalies – for example, French police officers working at the English end of the Channel Tunnel will wear their guns, but British officers will be unarmed. The British Police, Docker pointed out, are much less liberal in their approach to firearms.

'At Heathrow,' he said, 'we have two guns which are kept in a locked safe in our Special Branch office. They are only used for what we would term transit protection. A good example is the Reverend Ian Paisley, who turns up at Heathrow now and again, totally unannounced, and says, "I've arrived." And he gets protection over here. So until 'A' Squad could get a Protection Officer over to the airport, one of my officers who is authorised for firearms would obtain a gun, and he would either stay with Reverend Paisley at the airport, or take him into town to meet up with the proper Protection Officer. That's why we have two weapons there. But we're not armed. We certainly wouldn't be armed for any other reason than that.'

SO13

Anti-Terrorist Branch

'We are the anti-terrorist executive arm,' said Commander David Tucker, head of SO13. 'If we know of terrorists operating in London or anywhere outside, we'll cooperate with the local force, we'll be there to effect the arrest. The distinction is between intelligence-gathering and operations. We are the anti-terrorist operations arm.' They are also one of the few Scotland Yard squads with a national responsibility.

'At present 95 per cent of the work here is PIRA related,' said Tucker. 'The other 5 per cent is the threads of international terrorism. The work tends to fall into three categories – Irish is the biggest, then there's Middle-Eastern terrorism, and the Indian subcontinent is still volatile, and, given the Indian population in Britain, there is still some terrorism, so the scope for an escalation is always there. And we have overhangs. One of the Superintendents here is dealing with a man serving a prison sentence in Austria, who will eventually be extradited to Britain to face charges of placing bombs in London in 1985.'

The Anti-Terrorist Branch has just under 100 officers, but extra manpower can be drawn from other SO branches. Their role is almost entirely reactive; they respond to terrorism once an offence has been committed. If, however, advance intelligence showed that terrorists were likely to come to the UK, surveillance and possible arrest prior to a crime would be the responsibility of SO13. 'The rough guideline,' Tucker said, 'is if people hit the UK mainland with an identified intention to commit a political crime, then it's our area of responsibility.'

In practice, 'B' Squad of Special Branch would receive the terrorist intelligence, they would pass on the identity of the individuals to SO13, and the surveillance operation would be run by Special Branch alongside SO13. At all times two Special Branch officers are stationed with SO13 to act as a conduit between the two departments.

The Anti-Terrorist Squad has an Appeals Team, a group of officers detailed to handle general information which, although not urgent or particularly significant at the time, may eventually be of use. 'We get a lot of it,' Tucker said. 'Somebody will report that last week he advertised his lorry for sale and two Irishmen turned up and paid for it in fifty pound notes and gave an obviously false address. That's general stuff we need to react to, but not within the hour, and it is not specific to any inquiry.'

The Bomb Data Centre is a collation system, an office where the details of every explosion and every incident are logged for comparison. The analysis of bombs is carried out at Woolwich, but the analysis of information about bombs – for example, the purchase chain of components – is kept in the Bomb Data Centre. It is an international resource and there are regular requests for help from abroad.

'The Americans have been in touch with us since the bomb in New York,' Tucker said. 'Because of the IRA activity here, and apart from the Spanish authorities and their troubles with the Basque Separatists, this seems to be the acknowledged centre of expertise. We have had discussions with the Italians as well, following the murders of the judges in Sicily.'

Tucker discussed the Anti-Terrorist Squad reaction to an IRA bomb blast at Camden Town on 27 February 1993.

'Shortly after noon, there was a call from someone claiming to be from the IRA, using a recognised codeword, saying there was a bomb outside the Kentucky Fried Chicken in Oxford Street. That area was evacuated but there was no explosion. A second call, ten minutes later, said there was a bomb outside the Kentucky Fried Chicken in Camden High Street. The area was evacuated and thirty or forty minutes later there was an explosion at almost the other end of the street, about four hundred yards from the Kentucky Fried Chicken. Well, of course the local police had evacuated the restaurant and people were standing as close as five yards from the explosion.'

The bomb was made from approximately one pound of high-explosive paste and was planted in a waste bin. The blast injured eighteen people, some of them seriously. Tucker was notified but not called out when the warnings were issued, because there are many hoax bomb warnings in London. Calls about genuine bomb threats are often made, in the first instance, to radio stations, or to the Samaritans. In this case the first call was made to the Samaritans. Tucker believes the Samaritans are used because they are an organisation where it can be guaranteed the telephone will be answered quickly by someone who is not likely to panic, who is used to crises and will react in a responsible manner.'

'The Samaritans relayed the call to Scotland Yard immediately,' Tucker said, 'and it came here as part of a computerised process . . . My people here were on stand by. Because of hoax calls we did not respond until there was an explosion.'

As soon as the bomb went off, Tucker's office called

him and the SO13 Duty Officer was despatched to the scene, where the first priority was to assemble witnesses and question them. The area was sealed off and officers from SO13 collected pieces of the bomb. They also looked for and collected parts of the box or bag originally containing the bomb, plus parts of the waste bin, with fragments of the bomb casing lodged in them.

'The explosives officer can tell you fairly accurately how much explosive was used, and quite often the container in which it was placed. It is surprising, when you think how an explosion appears to destroy everything, just how much can survive, and can be gathered up and compared. We are quite often able to identify a series of bombs from the usage of component parts.'

While evidence was being gathered at the scene, Tucker briefed a senior local police officer, who then made a statement to the media.

'The statement to the press is important,' Tucker said. 'The problem is that sometimes we have to give them the story very quickly and all we can issue is a general appeal, calling for witnesses who saw anything suspicious, and so on. It's only perhaps three or four days later, when we've gathered up the evidence, that we can be more specific in our appeal.'

Returning to the mechanics of a terrorist bomb investigation, Tucker confirmed that as many pieces as possible of the bomb are collected, and these are sent for evaluation to the Defence Research Agency (DRA) at Woolwich. Collection of bomb fragments, as well as other potentially important debris, is done with the help of a van equipped with sterile brooms and sterile dustbins.

From then onwards, extreme care is taken at every stage in the building of the case.

'Because we are dealing with people who will almost certainly not speak from the moment they are arrested, it's essential that my officers are experienced, and able, and expert at the gathering of evidence and preserving the integrity of exhibits. It's essential that they are completely at the front end of knowledge of the law. They need to be experts on PACE [Police and Criminal Evidence Act], and to know the procedures for making the tape recordings at interviews.'

Under the terms of the Prevention of Terrorism Act, the police now have more time to put together a case while keeping suspects in custody. 'We need more time because terrorists are quite often trained in anti-interrogation techniques, are told to say nothing and most of the time do just that. Also, although we have a tremendous increase in our ability to retrieve forensic evidence now, it still takes time – three or four days rather than a few hours. PACE effectively gives us twenty-four hours, the POT Act gives us up to seven days.'

Tucker is aware that peaks and troughs are a perpetual feature of IRA campaigns, and if there are times when the terrorists appear to be down and on the run, there will be others where they appear very much ahead and doing damage.

'At the moment we are successful,' Tucker said, 'but I'm not complacent and I know that this isn't the end to a campaign. Our hope and our prayer here is that the need for an anti-terrorist branch will disappear, but for the moment the indicators are that it won't happen in the immediate future.'

Tucker has the authority to investigate all terrorist activity within the Metropolitan Police District; he also has the authority to coordinate anti-terrorist investigations nationally, which in his own view means that he is able to get to a scene quickly, give advice to the senior officers and the investigating officers, and provide expertise in the shape of officers experienced at investigating terrorist crimes and gathering forensic evidence.

He does not find the notion of a National Anti-Terrorist Branch compelling. He points to the fact that officers from SO13 currently spend time with provincial forces, heightening their awareness of IRA tactics and increasing their ability to deal with terrorist incidents.

In spite of the IRA's ability to attack any time at any spot, and in spite of the certainty that they are ruthless and will put bombs in shopping centres a week before Christmas, Tucker believes that simple vigilance has damaged them. The notion has become a cliché, he said, but vigilance is the answer; it is largely the reason why it is now very dangerous for the IRA to operate on mainland Britain. Vigilance has meant that the IRA do not find a haven in the Irish community; 'The great majority of Irish people living on the mainland are as incensed about IRA activity as anyone else, and it's significant to me that we rarely find these people living in Kilburn or Camden Town or other recognised Irish areas.'

Tucker says anti-terrorist work is different from main-stream police work because, in his job, the criminal is part of a criminal organisation.

'If you're hunting a serial rapist or a serial murderer, you eventually arrest someone and the series ends. You've removed an evil and there's cause for satisfaction. This is different. We are not fatalistic, but we are realistic, we know that success can be short term. We can take out a particularly active cell, but we're up against an organisation, and these people will be back.'

EXPLOSIVES OFFICE

'The day you forget fear,' said Graham Lightfoot, 'is the day you should actually stop doing this job.' Mr Lightfoot is head of the Metropolitan Police Explosives Office. 'You've always got to have some degree of fear, although it doesn't tend to be there when you're doing the job.'

Lightfoot and his colleagues are unofficially known as bomb doctors. They are the individuals who approach unexploded bombs, sometimes handle them and, more often than not, make them safe. The precise numbers of these men are a secret they prefer to keep, but Lightfoot confirmed they provide a twenty-four-hour service from a Central-London base, using ordinary marked police vehicles. Each team consists of two people; the one in charge is an Explosives Officer, and he is a civilian.

'We're all ex-military,' Lightfoot said, 'members of the Royal Army Ordnance Corps, now the Royal Logistic Corps. Before joining the police we had experience in Northern Ireland and other parts of the world, dealing with bomb incidents.'

The team's vehicle is driven by a police officer. He helps the Explosives Officer to prepare equipment, assists with questioning and tackles any other matters that call for the attention of a police officer.

In 1992 the Explosives Office received 2,233 calls from the public. The vast majority of those were hoax calls or false alarms: the number of explosions, finds of explosives or items defused amounted to forty-seven. Lightfoot described their procedure when a suspicious object is found.

'Let's say a suspect item is reported to the police by a member of the public, or maybe a police officer finds it himself. Once he becomes suspicious, he will contact the duty officer at the local station, who will call the SO13 Anti-Terrorist Branch direct. They'll take brief details and pass them to us through a secure direct phone or, if we are out dealing with another incident, over the police radio network. Once we've got the basic details, an Explosives Officer is despatched to the area.'

At the scene, pedestrians and onlookers are cleared from the immediate vicinity of the suspicious find and a cordon is set up. The Explosives Officer will then question the duty officer and anybody else at the scene and try to determine what the object might be. It may be visible from a distance, in which case a drawing is often made, and recordings from any security cameras in the vicinity are checked to see if they have any significant pictures.

'Once that is done,' Lightfoot went on, 'the Explosives Officer will plan his procedure for making the device safe. Like all procedures in this category, you prepare for the worst and hope for the best. As it is a form of risk management, there are always things that can go wrong. If we are going to use a controlled explosion we make sure that people in the vicinity know something is happening, and when there is a bang they are prepared for it.'

Each Explosives Officer wears a helmet and a made-to-measure bomb suit of toughened protective fabric, tailored to provide maximum shielding without restricting movement when he works.

'The main protection the suit gives us is from fragments,' Lightfoot said. 'We are protected as we approach the suspect item, and as we walk away from it. When we're right on top of an explosive device, no matter how much protection we've got on, it's no good.'

To assist the work of moving or defusing bombs, the

Explosives Officer uses EOD (Explosive Ordnance Disposal) Remote Equipment – often referred to by the press as a robot, and known to Explosives Office personnel as a wheelbarrow – for carrying tools and other items right up to the suspect object. A television camera fitted to the wheelbarrow shows the object in close-up and helps the Explosives Officer to use his equipment accurately.

In the case of a suspect briefcase, the Explosives Officer would first open the case with a controlled explosion. 'We would place a disruptive device close to it, without touching it,' Lightfoot said. 'That will open it. If we decide to use the wheelbarrow, we can fire the disruption equipment from that, then we can use the camera on the wheelbarrow to see exactly what has happened.'

There are various types of disrupters, also known as pig sticks. They are explosive charges which constitute weapons in their own right, and they can be lethal if they are mishandled. They come in three sizes – small, medium, large – and ideally the one chosen for use on the briefcase should also disrupt whatever is inside, rendering it harmless. If the case had already been X-rayed, for instance at an airport, and the suspect device was spotted and the case was left inside the X-ray machine, then the X-ray picture would give the Explosives Officer a clear image of the type of device he was dealing with.

'Depending on the type, there are many options open,' Lightfoot said. 'We might even cut into the case if we consider that to be a safe option. We always go for the safest option, of course. We never cut or open anything without knowing exactly what we are doing. If we do not know what we have on our hands, we recall an adage we were given in our early days in the military, applicable especially when dealing with unexploded shells: *If you don't know it, you blow it.* The same applies to dealing with suspect items. If you cannot see exactly what is there you must not tamper with it in any way. Instead, you use remote explosive, opening it with a disrupter or something similar.'

The hardest job nowadays is locating the bombs; once they are found there is every chance the Explosives Officers can render them harmless. This situation is supported by a healthy flow of specialist intelligence between Northern Ireland and mainland Britain. The IRA tend to use Northern Ireland as a proving ground for their methods and devices; by the time they are used in mainland Britain they are expected, and measures for dealing with them have been implemented.

In de-activating a bomb, the object is to separate the different components so that they cannot function as a unit. 'We're trying to get the timer and the detonator and the battery and the main charge all separated,' Lightfoot said. 'So even if part of the bomb functions, we don't get a major explosion.'

The difficulty in defusing a bomb depends more on how it has been placed than on cunning intricacies in the circuits. A device under a car is not too hard to deal with, but one pushed into a girder several feet up in the air creates more problems.

'Going on from that,' Lightfoot said, 'our branch and others within the Met train officers on the beat to draw plans of areas where they have found suspect devices. Most of the places we're called to, we've never been to before in our lives. So we need some knowledge of what the building looks like if we have to go up to the fifth floor and into a certain room.'

Discussing the way terrorists have taken advantage of developments in explosive technology, Lightfoot said that in the early 1970s IRA bombs were made from combinations of home-made and commercial explosives – the latter being the kind generally referred to as dynamite, commercially available to coal mines, quarrying contractors and demolition firms. There was then a period when the majority of IRA bombs were made entirely from commercial explosive, the last one being detonated outside Chelsea Barracks in 1985.

'When Semtex was made available,' Lightfoot said, 'that was an ideal explosive for them to use. It is a plastic explosive, more powerful than any commercial explosive. Whereas before they were using, say, two pounds of commercial explosive, now they only needed to use ten ounces or a pound of Semtex to get the same results.'

Recent major bombings in London have not involved the use of Semtex, however. The explosive used was developed by the IRA and is, fundamentally, a mixture of chemical fertiliser and sugar. Lightfoot would not go into more detail than that, other than to add that the new material was found at the scenes of incidents in various locations, including Baltic Exchange, Staples Corner, Stoke Newington, Tottenham Court Road and Canary Wharf.

Whatever the structure of an explosive, he went on, it is inherently dangerous. 'All explosives, by their nature, are hazardous, though some are more sensitive than others. The worst explosive of all is what we call a low explosive, such as gun powder and other combinations which ignite and burn very easily. Even the movement of one crystal against another could cause ignition. Over the years in London and elsewhere in the United Kingdom, at least ten schoolchildren have been either seriously injured or killed making explosives like this. They have been mixing them, even banging them into metal tubes, and the device has functioned, killing them. One case I remember from my Army days: a boy of fifteen was manufacturing a very, very sensitive explosive in his shed in the back garden, and it functioned suddenly, blew both his hands off and he bled to death.'

He mentioned that twice a year, on average, they are called to apparent car-bomb incidents in London which do not involve bombs at all, but are in fact suicides where the victim has spread petrol around the inside of a car and ignited it, in some cases causing an explosion.

One of the most difficult disposal jobs Lightfoot ever attended was when he worked on CMD (Conventional Munitions Disposal). A live shell dredged out of the Thames was stuck fifty feet up in a gravel hopper in the Thames estuary. Lightfoot had to climb into the hopper, which was full of sand, remove the shell, then blow it up at a safe location nearby.

The hardest thing to do, Lightfoot believes, is to go where a suspect device has been found, and to prove there is no bomb. With a vehicle, an Explosives Officer can only be sure there is no bomb on board after he has reduced it to a heap of scrap. He always has to guard against a ready opinion of the case on hand. Experience helps; 'You develop a sixth sense. I certainly did in the early days in Ireland.' Even so, no chances are taken, the assumption is always that a bomb exists, until there is solid proof that it does not.

No other job is quite like that of an Explosives Officer. In the main they are middle-aged, and a number of them, like Lightfoot himself, could be taken for insurance agents or bank managers. The work calls for steadiness and, to an unusual extent, faith in personal judgement. Lightfoot quotes a former Royal Engineers bomb-disposal officer who said that the ideal men for this job are not perfectionists, but not shoddy in their work, either; they are methodical, logical people who do not crack under pressure.

'A lot of marriages have broken up over the years because the wives couldn't take the stress, though in most cases the Explosives Officers' wives have grown up with the gradual rate of increase, and obviously have faith in their husbands' judgement.'

Inevitably in such desperately dangerous work, officers are sometimes lost. Roger Goad died on 29 August 1975, hunched over a bomb in Kensington Church Street. On 26 October 1981, Ken Howorth died when a bomb exploded inside a Wimpy Bar in Oxford Street.

'We don't really know what happened,' Lightfoot said. 'There is always, no matter what anyone says, *always* an element of luck, and maybe, with those two men, their luck ran out. They may have been given wrong information, or they saw something incorrectly. You can never really tell.'

On a world-wide scale, it is a sombre truth that because of their vast experience, the Explosives Officers of the Metropolitan Police have become the leading authorities on explosives and the techniques for their disposal.

'We have the equipment and the knowledge and the expertise to deal with virtually anything that can be thrown at us,' Lightfoot said. 'But I don't believe in the term "expert". We're all on a learning curve, it's just that some are further up than others.'

COUNTER TERRORISM – CONTINGENCY PLANNING

The man in charge of Counter Terrorism, Chief Superintendent Barrie Henry, describes it as 'A department designed to coordinate all activity in security and counter-measures to terrorism.'

Although plans for dealing with terrorism in the metropolis existed before 1984, there was no coordinated policy of response until after the siege of the Libyan People's Bureau in April of that year, when WPC Yvonne Fletcher died in the gunfire from a pro-Gaddafi group inside the bureau. That event led directly to the development of a police unit with the dual function of coordinating security measures and anti-terrorist action, and countering terrorist activity.

To illustrate the work of Counter-Terrorism Contingency Planning (CTCP) in its anti-terrorist role, Henry described how this department – which he operates together with a Sergeant and a Constable – would have responded to an incident like the Iranian Embassy siege of 1980.

'Let's say the siege happened in Westminster,' said Henry. 'Eight Area (Central London) would take responsibility for handling it, and they would set up their usual police procedures – there would be somebody in a forward position close to the scene, and somebody back controlling the incident in slow time.'

'Slow time' decision-making requires a senior officer to make a careful, unhurried assessment of a situation so he can reach decisions aimed at tackling long-term contingencies; this is distinct from 'quick-time' decision-making, which deals with crisis developments needing immediate action.

'Our role would be to advise on the set-up, to advise on communications and particularly on what agencies should be called in, depending on developments, to help the DAC of Eight Area. We have responsibility for maintaining liaison with the security services and, when appropriate, with the Foreign and Commonwealth

Office, if particular foreign nationals are involved. We would also be in touch with the Cabinet Office Briefing Room (COBR) at the Home Office, which has responsibility for deciding, on behalf of the Government, when or whether the military can intervene.'

If a time came, as it did in the 1980 siege, when the negotiations and police containment were obviously not reaching a point where the terrorists might surrender, and if it seemed that the lives of hostages were increasingly in jeopardy, the option of storming the besieged building would have to be considered. Authority to use Special Forces, probably the SAS, could be granted only by the Home Secretary, through the COBR. Liaison between COBR, the Special Services and the police would be maintained by CTCP.

Overall, CTCP performs a swift hook-up job between the various bodies concerned in any serious incident caused by terrorist action. They also provide expert advice on procedure at every stage.

In countering terrorism, the department aims always to make it harder for extremists to carry out their attacks. This can be done, for example, by analysing bombing campaigns from the moment they start, determining whether a pattern (conscious or unconscious) is being followed by the terrorists, and making tactical projections to counter or cancel their next moves.

To some extent, SO13 uses the methods employed to hinder terrorists in Northern Ireland. Bombs still go off in Ireland, but nowadays, as a result of persistent intelligence-gathering by the police and security forces and action on all the important lessons learned, terrorism in Ireland is obstructed at practically every turn.

Effective counter-terrorist policies for London railway stations are a priority, and CTCP has studied the difficulties. When a bomb goes off in a busy station like

Victoria the disruption is aggravated by hoax callers, usually claiming that another bomb has been planted. For a time all rubbish bins were taken out of London's stations; this was a bad move, since rubbish soon accumulated to such an extent that plastic bin bags were brought in to cope with the problem. The bags were a worse potential hazard than the bins.

Henry said it would be easy to have the bins emptied once an hour to a strict rota. 'So they know when a call comes in telling them a bomb has been planted, that at one o'clock those bins were emptied, so if it's ten past they know they'll be fairly empty and can be examined quickly. And if one is full up then it stands out and gets immediate attention.'

POLICE SEARCH ADVISERS

The acronym POLSA stands for Police Search Adviser. Within the Metropolitan Police approximately 300 divisional officers are POLSA-trained, which means they are expert at making systematic searches using methods and equipment unique to this branch of police work.

Search teams vary in size, depending on need, and are made up from trained POLSAs called from ordinary police duties at divisional police stations. Their searches fall into offensive and defensive categories. Offensive searches are for stolen or illicit goods, drugs, firearms or explosives; defensive searching entails the securing of a venue or a route. In searching for drugs and explosives, POLSA teams will use 'sniffer' dogs whenever it is necessary. They also use categories of search equipment, most of it electronic, which no one is yet prepared to discuss openly.

Learning about human ingenuity is an unending

process for POLSAs. Drugs have been found tucked into hollows in the tops of window frames, inside telephone mouthpieces and door knobs, buried in corks, suspended in wine bottles and replacing the stuffing in cushions. Houses have had false inner walls built so that contraband could be concealed in the gap, and false or disused chimneys are regularly used to hide anything from drugs, tape-decks and pornography, to banknotes and stolen antiques.

Large houses can be searched quickly, since more officers can be used, whereas two officers working in cramped conditions might take as long as eight hours to search a loft. On average, it will take a POLSA team four hours to make a thorough search of a two-bedroom house. The head of POLSA, Chief Superintendent Barrie Henry, acknowledged that with such thorough searching there are times when damage to property is inevitable, and sometimes it can be extensive.

'Any damage we cause,' he said, 'even if the case in hand results in prosecution and conviction, we always repair.' Describing the process of defensive searching, he cited the example of a search along the proposed itinerary of a procession.

'The whole route is searched. We look at all the street furniture – we're aware of manhole covers, drain openings, things like that. We look in the sewers, then we have the entrances sealed, or electronically watched, to ensure they stay clear until the event has taken place. We look at all the opportunities there might be for sniper-fire, and, in liaison with SO19 (Force Firearms Unit), we work out anti-sniper positions.'

Personnel checks are part of a POLSA team's duties before major events in hotels, conference centres or public buildings where high-risk figures are scheduled to appear. The hardest kind of person to monitor is usually one who has slipped through the advance personnel vetting. In some cases the potential assassin is a 'sleeper', a terrorist or saboteur who stays inactive while he establishes a position of security and trust.

In September 1990, an explosive device was found in a lectern at the Royal Overseas League during a function being attended by the then Commissioner of Police, Sir Peter Imbert; the culprit in that case was a sleeper, a cook who had worked at the League for some time.

'This department grew from that,' said Henry. 'We were developed as a result of what happened at the Royal Overseas League.'

When POLSA teams check buildings where conferences are to be held, they give top priority to bomb searches. 'When a conference is taking place in a single room,' said Henry, 'then we'd be looking for things the size of matchboxes. If we are checking the foyer and it's a wide one with people walking back and forward along the middle, then we would be looking for something a bit larger.'

SECURITY OF POLICE BUILDINGS

The security of police stations, section houses, police-staff houses, safe houses and other buildings where the police have a controlling function is in the hands of civilian specialists. Usually they work in the department of the Receiver, but, whenever necessary, they operate on behalf of SO13, assessing a threat to a particular building and recommending protective measures. Chief Superintendent Barrie Henry gave an example.

'Maybe the Flying Squad want to use a house for certain activity against criminals, say as a safe house for a supergrass, and they want it protected. SO13 would move in and make sure it was safe. Then they would probably recommend that covert protection be mounted outside, in the form of officers watching the place.'

The kind of criminal to catch the attention of SO13 would be the man or woman trying to damage a building, rather than somebody breaking in with intent to hurt people inside. A case in point is New Scotland Yard itself, a nineteen-storey building with a public road running past the front doors. In October 1992 it was revealed that an IRA plot to detonate a 300-pound bomb outside the building was narrowly prevented, and senior officers, Chief Superintendent Henry among them, acknowledge that Scotland Yard must always be considered a prime target for groups hostile to the police. For that reason, substantial plans are in place to protect the building.

Henry clarified the distinction between the operatives of SO13 and crime prevention officers.

'The role of our people is to protect against a terrorist threat. Usually terrorism is all we deal with, in whatever form. But the security of police buildings does occasionally spread into the territory of ordinary crime. Even so, the criminals in question would be seriously violent types who intended to burn down Woolwich Police Station or shoot some detectives at Catford, something of that nature. When we know anything of that kind is likely to happen, then our people will provide specialist advice.'

BACK HALL

A woman approached the Constable on duty at the front desk at Scotland Yard and told him she had been infected with dysentery over the telephone; the person who did it, she insisted, must be arrested. Another time a frantic-looking man went to the desk and begged for help: he had put over £250,000 in a bank account, but he had forgotten which bank or building society he used. Several times people have rung up from America to ask to speak to Sherlock Holmes. It's all in a day's work for the staff of Back Hall, the perversely named front-entry hall at New Scotland Yard, the only legitimate way into the building.

The odd name dates from the early days of the Met when policemen entered and left by the back door at the first headquarters at 4 Whitehall Place, Westminster. The present-day duties of Back Hall are not vastly different from what they were in April of 1837, the first time it was mentioned in an official document.

In general terms Back Hall is responsible for security of the headquarters building, for dealing with the public, and for providing certain support services. In addition, the man in charge, the Back Hall Inspector, assumes the routine responsibilities of a 'duty officer' for Scotland Yard. Other security checks operate outside specific departments within the building.

A Back Hall Constable is on duty at Scotland Yard twenty-four hours a day. He answers inquiries, directs visitors and checks passes and warrant cards whenever necessary. Any caller who wants to lodge a complaint against a police officer is always seen by the Back Hall Inspector in person.

The front-line security of New Scotland Yard is the permanent responsibility of the Back Hall Inspector and his staff, and recently it has undergone a radical change. Since the building is a prime target for the IRA, it was decided that the old system of people coming and going unhindered, simply showing cards to security personnel as they passed, was inadequate. Now the front doors to the building give direct access to security pods. These are glass-walled units permitting the passage of one person at a time, and access is only granted after a scanner has validated the magnetic data on the visitor's security card.

In the past the Back Hall area was poorly served by security cameras; now there is a revised system, using more and better cameras, backed by a comprehensive monitor system manned from a control room, from which all emergency fire arrangements would also be handled. Increased numbers of officers are now on foot patrol outside the building, and all vehicles are identified by an electronic pass system before they are allowed into the precincts of Scotland Yard.

The old system of security was not at all lax, but, in spite of that, in 1991 a woman managed to slip past the security in Back Hall and wander around the building. She got to the seventh floor where she found a full set of riot gear – including helmet and body armour – and decided to take it away with her. She managed to leave the building unchallenged, even though she was weighed down by the heavy gear. Her family discovered the theft and returned the equipment to the police.

Standing slightly apart from the endless comings and goings of Back Hall, on a marble stand beside a perpetually burning flame, a Book of Remembrance lists the names of the members of civil staff who lost their lives while on active service, or as a result of enemy action in two World Wars. During that period 1,076 members of the Metropolitan Police Force and seventy-two members of civil staffs were lost. In the same hall is the Roll of Honour, commemorating the police officers who have died on duty. A page of this book is turned every morning. The entries are a poignant reminder of the dangers faced every day by police officers. Three of the most recent are:

WPC YVONNE FLETCHER: On the morning of Tuesday 17 April 1984, WPC Fletcher, of C District, was on duty with other officers policing a demonstration outside the Libyan People's Bureau at 5, St James's Square, London SW1, when shots fired from a window of the building fatally wounded her.

DETECTIVE CONSTABLE JOHN FORDHAM: On 26 January 1985, DC Fordham, of C11 Branch, was engaged on surveillance duty at West Kingsdown, in connection with a bullion robbery, during which he received multiple stab wounds from which he died.

PC KEITH BLAKELOCK: On Sunday 6 October 1985, PC Blakelock was engaged in policing serious disorder on the Broadwater Farm Estate, Tottenham, when he was attacked and killed.

MILITARY LIAISON (WAR)

In the event of war breaking out, the Commissioner of Police would take charge of measures which used to be gathered under the heading of Civil Defence. In that situation, this small department would work in liaison with the military on the Commissioner's behalf.

Military Liaison has no permanent staff. In time of war its work would be carried out by senior officers within SO13. Communications between the police and the Armed Services on numerous topics – the movement of injured personnel, threats of public disorder, information on terrorist activity or the passing of reassurances between the military and the public-information media

– would be handled by the department. Their sole function, at all times, would be a close and steady liaison with the military.

ROYALTY AND DIPLOMATIC
PROTECTION DEPARTMENT:
Introduction

In April 1993 three separate incidents involving intruders at Royal residences made the headlines in the British press. The danger may have been overstated in some cases, but breaches of security at that level are serious and they impact directly on Deputy Assistant Commissioner David Meynell, head of the Royalty and Diplomatic Protection Department (RDPD). It takes only one deranged or unbalanced individual to get over a Royal garden wall or through a set of embassy railings, and Meynell is held responsible.

'My second week in this seat, that actually happened,' he said. 'Not only did somebody get over the wall, but he managed to get into the Royal Palace before we were able to capture him. That same day I had an interview with Her Majesty and with the Home Secretary.'

On that occasion, even though the intruder got inside the Palace, contingency plans worked and any real danger was averted. Nevertheless, Meynell admits that the notorious incident in 1982, when an intruder called Michael Fagan managed to bypass Buckingham Palace security and enter the Queen's bedroom, is one of his professional nightmares.

Another pressure is the fact that, although RDPD is part of the Metropolitan Police, as much as 90 per cent of its time is taken up on national duties. Bearing in mind that the department's manpower and resources are taken directly from the Metropolitan Police, Meynell feels that in performing national duties RDPD should find ways to minimise its demands on the local service. Thinking along those lines, he believes a case could be made for a national agency, centrally funded, to carry out protection work.

The Home Office commits 1 per cent of the Commissioner's budget to financing national responsibilities, including the protection of the Royal Family, the Royal residences, the Ministers of State, their homes and their offices. The money comes from the Met (so half is from the London ratepayers), even though a major proportion of the work being financed can be described as national or international.

'At present, the 1 per cent of the budget they give us doesn't cover our costs,' Commander Bob Marsh said. 'The argument has always been, why should the ratepayers of London pay for what is essentially a service to the country and not just for London itself?'

There has been talk of certain Metropolitan Police functions being privatised. 'I wouldn't rule it out,' Marsh said, 'particularly with the Palace of Westminster Division, which is a policing function entirely within the House of Commons and House of Lords, which could be privatised. In fact, most of our staff there are civilians. I wouldn't rule it out for the Royal palaces, either, although, from a professional and personal point of view, I would hate to see it happen. I think we are a part of the Royal London scene and should remain so.'

Remaining a part of the Royal scene is inevitable for officers on protection work. 'Open any newspaper and there are Royal stories,' Marsh said, 'and of course every time a member of the Royal Family goes out, he or she has a Protection Officer, and they become as familiar figures to the press as do the members of the Royal Family. So the press take an interest in what's

13. Lady Thatcher, one of the highest security risks, receives twenty-four-hour protection from Scotland Yard. Her personal protection is provided by Special Branch (SO12). On the left of Lady Thatcher is Detective Constable Chris Strickland; on the right, Detective Chief Inspector Barry Stevens, who has been with Lady Thatcher, off and on, since 1978.

14. The Queen Mother and her protection officer, Detective Superintendent John Kirchin (SO14). Aged ninety-three and no longer able to move quickly, protection is more difficult for her than for a younger person. Kirchin refers to her as 'the lady'.

15. The motor bikes and vehicles of the Special Escort Group (SO14) provide armed mobile protection for the Royal Family and local and overseas VIPs as they drive around London. The SEG also escorts bullion lorries from the Bank of England and convoys of confiscated drugs and firearms on their way to be burnt.

16. Chief Superintendent Kevin Delaney in charge of traffic (TO14) keeps in touch with his work the hard way, by bicycling to and from his office.

17. The Public Order training centre (TO18) in Hounslow is known throughout the Met as Riot City. Tactics in controlling street disturbances changed significantly after the Notting Hill carnival in 1976 when police came under attack and had neither protective shields nor proper training to cope.

18. The Poll Tax Riot in Trafalgar Square, on 3 March 1990, was the last occasion that police lost control of the streets of London. Trouble broke out when violent elements in the largely peaceful crowd of 300,000 clashed with police; 341 arrests were made.

19. The Central Communications Complex. CCC is the nerve centre of the Metropolitan Police. In 1992 they received 1,274,511 emergency calls. Twenty-four hours a day they are able to summon assistance within minutes from any department of the Metropolitan Police.

20. The Air Support Unit (SO26) has three helicopters. They are used for locating suspects on the run and searching rooftops for sensitive public order occasions like Trooping the Colour.

21. A diver from the Thames Division Under Water Search Team (TO29) searches a pond on Wimbledon Common for the weapon used to murder Rachel Nickell.

22. Sue Merchant, one of the most senior and able women at Scotland Yard, is Director of PRAMS, Performance Review and Management Services.

23. A mocking letter, supposedly from Jack the Ripper, which is one of the exhibits in the Black Museum.

PLATINUM-IRIDIUM BEAD   G.MARKOV LONDON 1978
diameter 1.53mm

1839/16

24. Also displayed in the Black Museum is this 1.53mm platinum-iridium bead which was used to murder the Bulgarian dissident Georgi Markov in 1981.

25. In June 1993, the Department of Public Affairs decided that the success of the anti burglary campaign, Operation Bumblebee, should be used to improve the image of the police and arranged for the Commissioner to be photographed in front of an advertising poster. The newly appointed Home Secretary, Michael Howard, joined in.

happening to an officer, and they're likely to comment upon his behaviour and conduct.'

The pressure on younger officers attached to the Royal household is high, and they are subjected to severe tests of aptitude and character before they ever become Protection Officers.

'Fortunately it's a job so highly prized by police officers that we don't run short of recruits,' Marsh said. 'We always have people of the calibre and quality we want. The tests range over a period of about eighteen months. They are skill based – driving, shooting, social skills, knowledge of the world, there are lots more, lots I don't want to go into detail about. Over such a long period, under severe testing conditions, we can be sure we are getting the right material.'

The blending of embassies and high commissions into residential areas (as distinct from the practice in other countries of having them set apart) presents the Diplomatic Protection Group (SO16) with a number of problems.

'The diplomatic part of London is not delineated by compounds or large spaces surrounded by embassies,' Marsh said. 'They are buildings that can be next to schools, stores, or private homes. They have no gardens in front and usually none behind, so sometimes it's difficult to isolate them from threat the way they are in other countries. It's an accident of our history, this is a town with small streets and very close buildings. So we tackle diplomatic security in ways not readily visible to the public eye.'

Marsh realises that his job is not the most secure one in the Met. 'Unfortunately, as we all know to our cost from years ago, one break-in at the Palace reaches the international press and you get calls for resignation. That kind of responsibility rests with you all the while you are doing this sort of job, all the way from the top to the very bottom. All our officers are very much aware that they each have only one chance.'

SO14

Royalty Protection Branch

SO14 has a responsibility to the DAC, Royalty and Diplomatic Protection Department, for three separate jobs: personal protection for certain members of the Royal family when they are away from their residences; technical protection of all Royal residences and estates throughout Great Britain; support, administrative personnel and training for the Royalty and Diplomatic Protection Department.

There are eighty Personal and Close Protection Officers, two of them women. They are all uniformed officers who work in plain clothes. Personal Protection Officers are allocated to individual members of the Royal Family; they work in teams of two, three and sometimes four, all dedicated to the same person. At public functions and major events Personal Protection Officers are supported by Close Protection Officers, who work as a pooled resource; they provide what Chief Superintendent Hugh Kinloch describes as an envelope within which Personal Protection Officers work, and they form a link between the Personal Protection Officers and the local police.

All Protection Officers of SO14 carry handguns while they are on protection duty. They can use heavier weapons if they need to. In their vehicles they carry sophisticated medical equipment and supplies, including blood plasma. They are trained in emergency techniques that go some way beyond ordinary First Aid training, and they can use the medical equipment by themselves in an emergency.

There is a difference between bodyguard work and protection. Bodyguard work is the part of SO14 duty usually seen by the public – the officer staying close to the Principal in a crowd or in any public place. A Protection Officer's role is wider than that. 'They are part of the Household team,' said Kinloch. 'He or she is an adviser to and confidant of the Principal and other members of the Household. The Protection Officer undertakes reconnaissance visits at home and overseas, and will have the major responsibility for the security arrangements of such a visit.'

Sir James Waddell, in his review of Royal security after the attempted assassination of Princess Anne in 1974, said,

> The dangers to be guarded against are assassination, or assault short of assassination, and kidnapping. And the sources of the danger, broadly speaking, are madmen and exhibitionists on the one hand, and groups of criminals or political extremists on the other.

'That statement remains as true today as it was then,' said Mr Kinloch. The attempt on Princess Anne's life, he says, was a catalyst which changed Royalty protection significantly.

'Up until that date, with all due respect to our predecessors, Royalty Protection was very much a gentlemanly art, done by certain officers who were not terribly well trained. It was from '74 that the strength of Royalty Protection was first increased. We introduced the requirement of careful selection of officers, and for better training, and we introduced the first team of Close Protection Officers, who were then to support the Personal Protection Officers.' The killing of Earl Mountbatten in 1979 led to another review and another increase in the strength of the Branch.

It is always wise, of course, to maintain a sense of proportion. 'The threat to the Royal Family from terrorists and assassins,' Kinloch points out, 'is considered to be less than that in ministerial protection for politicians. We more often have to deal with what we describe as the lone adventurer, the person of unsound mind, or the pure exhibitionist.'

When Earl Mountbatten was murdered in Ireland by the IRA he was not accompanied by a Protection Officer. 'We tend to protect those in line of succession to the throne,' said Kinloch. 'If Earl Mountbatten were here now he would not be receiving Royalty protection under the present rules.'

Beyond the members of the Royal Family who are in line of succession, it is a matter of discretion for the Home Secretary and the Commissioner of Police of the Metropolis, with the consent of the Queen, to decide who else should be given protection, and at what level.

When a member of the Royal Family makes an appearance in public, SO14 rely very much on the intelligence gathered by the local police, and on the general goodwill of the public themselves. The innermost ring of security is the team of Protection Officers; next come the Close Protection Officers; beyond those are the local police supported by local intelligence and information.

'But if a determined assassin chose to attack a member of the Royal Family,' said Kinloch, 'it would be extremely difficult to counter that.'

Security is carefully checked in advance of a Royal visit. 'We carry out reconnaissance with local police or security services abroad. It may be that in certain circumstances the Protection Officer would say that there were unacceptable risks and consequently he might recommend that a part of the trip be adjusted accordingly.'

Royal visits abroad present special problems. Where local conditions are not up to the normal standard of those in the West, and safer travelling and health conditions for the visitors would be desirable, a great deal of help is given by the Foreign and Commonwealth Office.

It is not literally true that when Prince Charles goes skiing, his Protection Officer has to get on skis and follow him. 'A number of our Protection Officers are skiers,' Kinloch explained, 'so when a member of the Royal Family goes to Switzerland or Austria, we send skiing officers, who are invariably not their own personal Protection Officers.'

Prince Charles's Personal Protection Officer does not ski, but he doesn't mind being left out of trips to the slopes, since he claims to be allergic to snow.

During the Royal Family's recent troubles, protection officers were understandably affected by events – a person's low spirits are bound to affect the mood of those who live or work close to them.

There is nothing on record to say if retired officers of SO14 have ever been tempted to write their memoirs, replete with first-hand anecdotes about the Royal Family. Kinloch thinks the Official Secrets Act, which his officers sign when they join the police service, is an adequate deterrent to anyone tempted to cash-in.

'But I've got to say,' he added, 'Protection Officers do become very, very loyal to their Principal and to the Royal Family, and the notion of telling tales is anathema to them, they would see it as a great breach of trust.'

SO14's role of providing technical protection for all Royal residences in Britain is not to be confused with the work of the Royal Palaces Division, who are responsible for uniform protection. SO14 provide the technical protection – alarms, cameras, etc.

'It's a small group of officers who would be equal to Crime Prevention Officers on division. It's that sort of work. They carry out surveys of Royal premises and make recommendations for security features – cameras, lights, gates, glazing, alarms, that sort of thing.'

The work of installing is done by another department on the recommendations of SO14, who also obtain the co-operation and agreement of the Principals. 'All of this, of course, is worked through the DAC, who is ultimately responsible to Her Majesty.'

Superintendent John Kirchin has been the Queen Mother's Protection Officer for seven years. In his view, she regards the entire population of Britain as her extended family and feels no apprehension when she is out among them. She does not appear to be particularly aware of having armed protection, either.

'I would say that she's had the package of protection around her for so long that it's part of getting up in the morning,' Kirchin said. 'I would never wish to say that she is anything other than courteous at all times, but I'm not someone she needs to be aware of.'

Kirchin previously worked with Princess Alexandra. He acknowledged that there is a big difference in providing security for a young, fit person who can take swift avoiding measures, and a ninety-two-year-old woman who cannot be rushed or pushed about. Another problem is that the Queen Mother is an extraordinarily popular person, arguably the best-loved woman in Britain, so people instinctively move close and reach out to her during her public engagements. Among the well-wishers and admirers, there could easily be one person who meant her harm.

'One never knows for certain,' Kirchin agreed. 'The whole job we do is one of constant assessment, assessing every second of the time we are out there, particularly in walk-about situations. I just try to keep a firm finger on the pulse of events and remain aware, constantly aware.'

Repeat events, such as the Queen Mother's practice of going out on to the street outside her London home on her birthday, cause Kirchin most worry. 'Anything that repeats,' he said, 'anything that happens regularly and is predictable, that's the worst scenario for anybody protecting a VIP.'

In the years that he has worked as a Protection Officer he has learned to spot people who might cause trouble. He knows that none of his instincts is foolproof, but collectively they give him an important edge.

'There is often something in the way they dress,' he said. 'Then I notice if they don't seem to belong, or whether they are at ease – when a member of the Royal Family is doing a walk-about it's normally a happy occasion, so if there's somebody who doesn't look cheerful or at ease, he needs to be watched. We invariably position people at the back of crowds, because a person who is going to do something stupid will normally have planned the aftermath, the getaway, and he will almost certainly not be down at the front.' In many areas of modern police work the police officer's interpersonal instincts tend to be underdeveloped, but in protection work, Kirchin says, an officer soon develops a nose for somebody who is not right.

In his twenty-one years in RDPD, he has seen some officers removed from the job after only a short time. 'The reason they have gone,' he said, 'is because they forgot what they were here for.' It is easy, he believes, to be affected by the rarefied life surrounding Principals, and just as easy to believe that in some way they are involved in that life. 'I've never been a part of it,' Kirchin said flatly. 'I am a Superintendent of police. By the nature of the job I do, I am party to a way of life which is not mine by right.'

Over the years he has had his share of bad moments. He recalled one at a reception in a museum, when he was working with Princess Alexandra. A woman among the guests was drunk and becoming violent. Kirchin could see an ugly scene developing so he found the woman's husband and told him either to make sure his wife was going to behave herself, or to get her out of there. In the end it took the husband and a member of the museum staff to get the woman out to the accompaniment of language which, Kirchin said, was not pleasant.

'Then there was an occasion on a ship,' he said, recalling a launching he attended with Princess Alexandra. 'We had a lady who was the secretary to the chairman of the cable company who were launching the ship. She had been involved in the whole setting up of this visit and she had been under enormous strain; perhaps people hadn't necessarily appreciated that. Half-way through lunch I glanced across from where I was sitting and saw this woman talking to the person on her right. The trouble was, she was sitting at the end of the table so there was nobody on her right. She was chatting away vociferously, then she started talking to the person on her left, who was already talking to the person on her own left, so she didn't respond. Then the woman stood up and I had to act, because it was quite apparent that she had lost her marbles. She was having a complete and utter nervous breakdown.' Kirchin is always alert to possibilities of that kind, because he is aware of the degree of strain affecting people at top-level public events. 'On a different occasion I watched an old soldier make a speech of welcome alongside the Principal and, having finished the speech, he literally died as he sat down and slid underneath the table.'

It is important, Kirchin believes, to observe protocol in his dealings with those he protects, since it serves to keep the borderlines defined. 'When you meet your Principal for the first time on any particular day, the bow and the "good morning" with title, and the same again at night when you leave, regardless of how close you are to your Principal, is an absolute necessity, to my way of thinking. It reminds you of your situation, and it also reminds the younger element of the family, if they need reminding, that you are there to do a job, you are a professional, you are not staff, you are there quite specifically as the police officer. Any blurring of those lines, and you will start to lose your effectiveness.'

To match the variety of surroundings in which he finds himself, Kirchin has an extensive wardrobe. A lot of it was paid for by the Met when he first joined RDPD, and there is a monthly allowance for upkeep, but he feels it is inadequate.

'My white tie, my morning dress – I purchased them twenty years ago, and it's my good fortune that my figure's stayed the same all that time, otherwise the clothes would be useless to me now, and it is not cheap stuff to replace. I've been through about four sets of black tie in the last twenty-odd years, because you do wear it a great deal, you wear it out. Now the first one, the job provided that. The rest of them I've had to buy.'

On duty Kirchin always carries a Glock handgun. Although it is heavier than the Smith and Wesson, it has a larger load-capacity and greater fire power. 'Obviously, the firearm is a necessary part of the job, but I frankly don't think about it very much. I do all the training on it that I need to do, and I attend all the necessary courses, and I try to maintain a very high standard on the thing, but it's not something I'm in love with, it's not something I feel I need to have with me all the time.'

In twenty-one years of protection work Kirchin has never had to draw his gun. He is sure, nevertheless, that if he ever had to shoot to kill in the defence of his Principal, he would do it without hesitation.

'Otherwise I wouldn't have been here for twenty-one years,' he said. 'If I was not prepared to do that I would be drawing my money under false pretences. You've got to be prepared to go down that road, and it's also why you've got to be fairly hard. If you get too close to what you're looking after, then maybe you'll be thinking about the wrong things. You've got to judge the situation as it arises, with as few outside problems affecting that judgement as possible. You are there as a policeman, so you ask yourself, *is it justifiable in police terms*? And if it is, then you have to act.'

SPECIAL ESCORT GROUP

The Special Escort Group (SEG) is based at Barnes, South West London, and regularly provides motorised escorts for members of the Royal Family, certain Government Ministers, other VIPs and visiting heads of state and government.

Inspector John Gouldsmith, head of the SEG, recalled an occasion when two officers had to put themselves in jeopardy to protect the people they were escorting.

'Around the Reigate area there is a long island,' he said. 'It's one-way on either side. The group were escorting the President of Germany into Town, and they had reached this one-way system when the two motor cycle riders out in front were confronted with a car driving straight at them. They tried to wave him into the side of the road. But he didn't stop, he kept coming. The riders had to position their bikes to take the impact and protect the car behind them. They were both knocked off their bikes and injured, one of them severely. The Presidential escort carried on, because you don't stop or you might be falling into a trap. Someone at the back was detailed to attend to the injured officers and get them to hospital.'

The car that hit the motorcyclists was driven not by a terrorist, but by an eighty-year-old man who had become confused by the road signs.

'The German President was most concerned about the two officers' welfare,' Gouldsmith said. 'He visited them in hospital and so did his wife. Several months later, both SEG officers were awarded the Iron Cross 3rd Class, and every year they are invited to a dinner at the German Embassy.'

As a direct contrast to VIP work, the SEG escort certain prisoners to and from court and prison. They also provide an escort for cash and bullion movements, and other high-value cargo such as drugs or weapons scheduled for destruction.

The team consists of an Inspector, five Sergeants and thirty-five PCs. Their vehicles are Model K-100 BMW motorcycles, Rover 827 saloon cars, Range Rovers and a Sherpa bus. The group is armed, when appropriate, with revolvers and Heckler and Koch MP5 carbines.

The group uses motor cycles and/or motor cars depending on the type of escort. 'The vehicle travelling in front goes out ahead looking for potential problems,' explained Gouldsmith. 'It also takes command of junctions when we come to them, so that we have a non-stop run.'

On an escort job using three cars, use is made of Tri-Sound sirens, each giving off a different note, to alert other drivers that there are three distinct vehicles in the convoy. On each occasion only the driver of the lead car knows what route will be taken, and he makes it up as he goes along. Sometimes a helicopter provides back-up in order to give an early warning of problems ahead or any unusual activity behind the convoy.

Drugs confiscated by the police are regularly taken to special locations to be burned. When the Crown jewels are needed for a ceremonial occasion the SEG provide a four-wheel escort from the Tower of London to the particular venue. The Royal art treasures are similarly escorted and, throughout every escort run, all of the drivers maintain radio contact with each other.

'We use our own radio sets, and we've got ear pieces so we're hearing what is happening all the time. The lead car keeps giving directions, telling the others which way he's going and talking them through hazards, and at the same time, if we have the helicopter on an escort, he is listening in, and he is throwing down information, too.'

The Queen is normally escorted by four motor-cycles. 'We give her a Supervisor, which is a Sergeant or myself, and three PCs. All the other members of the Royal Family that we escort get three motor-cycles.'

There is a technique for making sure that the Queen gets to official engagements when she should – not early, but on time. The motorcyclist driving directly in front of the Royal car adjusts his speed throughout the journey to govern the time it takes to reach a given destination; he is unofficially called the 'easy rider', although Gouldsmith says it is the hardest job on escort duty.

Every member of the SEG is a Class One driver and Class One motorcyclist. 'Without wishing to appear big-headed,' said Gouldsmith, 'I can say we are the top drivers in the Metropolitan Police Force. On top of that we do all the necessary firearms courses, the bodyguard protection courses, and an anti-hijack course, which is a week at the Hendon Driving School, where they teach various high-speed turns, how to break through a road block if necessary, where to hit the vehicle that is trying to block you . . .'

Following a recent change in Metropolitan Police policy, officers are now appointed to the SEG for a five-year term. The group has two women members, both over 5 foot 8 inches tall. That, Gouldsmith explained, is because of the design and weight of the motorcycles. Anyone under the required height, woman or man, would have trouble straddling a BMW K-100.

SO15

Royal Palaces Division

Superintendent Peter Hamilton believes the policemen on security duty at London's Royal Palaces are the best untrained psychologists in the country.

'Every day of the week we'll get something somewhere,' he said. 'Someone unusual will turn up. We get people who believe they are the rightful heirs to the throne. Other ones want to come in and advise the Queen. They want to be marriage guidance counsellors, or they want to do harm to the Royal Family.'

The Royal Palaces Division is responsible for policing Buckingham Palace, Kensington Palace, St James's Palace, and the home of Princess Alexandra in Richmond Park. They also police Windsor Castle, even though it is not within the Greater London area and, when the Royal Court is at Edinburgh, the Division has responsibilities for security at the Palace of Holyrood and Balmoral.

Superintendent Hamilton is in command of 281 officers, ten of them women. He wishes more women would apply, but in the three intakes of new officers that have taken place since he has been in charge, there has been only one female applicant.

Approximately 75 per cent of the officers are authorised to carry and use firearms on duty, although the number of armed posts varies according to circumstances. Wherever the Queen happens to be in residence the police numbers are increased, and naturally the number of armed officers will be higher.

In July 1982 an intruder called Michael Fagan managed to bypass Buckingham Palace security with no apparent difficulty. He actually entered the Queen's bedroom and sat on the end of her bed as she slept. As a result of Fagan's intrusion the security at Buckingham Palace was completely transformed, and for a time there were actually more officers on duty than there are now. Six-month postings of officers from several divisions were arranged so that cover could be increased at all the Royal Palaces.

'And the system has evolved from that time to the one we have today,' said Hamilton. 'If things go correctly it will continue to evolve because we don't want to stand still, we want to meet the needs prevailing at any particular time.'

For ease of description, Hamilton and his staff refer to each of the Royal residences as a unit. Buckingham Palace is by far the largest unit, where they are responsible for protecting the Royal Family when they are inside the buildings.

'Buckingham Palace has many hundreds of people working in it each day,' said Hamilton. 'It also has large numbers of contractors and visitors, so we have a very sophisticated pass system which we are responsible for administering and enforcing. We also have the ever-present threat of terrorism, so we have a system of policing which has developed – well, I think the phrase is post-Fagan.'

Although finer details of the security measures at Buckingham Palace are classified information, the broader measures are known. There is a comprehensive system of cameras (infra-red included), beams, alarms, and Semtracks, which is an electronic 'tripwire' installation; the rigorous pass system applies to staff, contractors, visitors and people attending investitures and garden parties. There is also a sophisticated control room, filled with TV monitors, where a handful of officers permanently watch the screens and supervise the alarm systems. They are in touch with other officers at strategic positions throughout the Palace.

The greatest security concern is terrorism, specifically an attack by the IRA. So far they have made no known attempts to penetrate palace security or to plant bombs in the vicinity, but the police believe that the target of a car bomb in 1992 may have been a Royal residence.

'A mini-cab was hijacked in the Holloway area and the driver was forced at gunpoint to drive to Central London,' said Hamilton. 'There was a bomb in the vehicle and it detonated later in the West End, but what emerged was that the actual target may have been Buckingham Palace or St James's Palace. The driver was made to drive around the area before abandoning the car.'

The biggest security headaches during the year tend to be garden parties, investitures and diplomatic evenings. 'We also have things like the Garter Ceremony at Windsor which is our responsibility,' Hamilton said. 'A colossal amount of organisation goes into the garden parties. But the main line of defence is the policeman, as always, standing on his post, patrolling and being watchful.'

PC Tony Haines joined the Royal Palaces Division in 1963, when it was called 'A' Division, and he is the second longest serving officer in the division.

Tony Haines is 6'7" tall. When he is on duty in London he is usually to be seen on gate duty at Buckingham Palace. His face is known to thousands of people and probably features in snapshot albums in every civilised reach of the world. Of all the nationalities he has to deal with at the palace gates, he finds the Japanese the most difficult to handle.

'I think it's because they're here for a very short time, they don't understand the language so they don't do as they're asked. They are very keen to get their photographs, and the thing about the Japanese is they have to stand in the photograph, they must stand there with the policeman. So you have a whole coachload, you can have sixty or a hundred disgorge from a bus, and they all want their photograph taken. Well, obviously, you can't accommodate everybody.'

Like every other police officer on duty at the Palace, Haines has to be alert at all times. 'Most people I see are Royalists, of course. Not an hour ago, a guy came with a box of Dairy Milk chocolates for the Queen, because he was sympathetic about her recent problems. Other people who show up are just curious. But if there's somebody who doesn't seem to fall into those categories, I watch, and he can be somebody naughty . . .' There is a photographic index of cranks who have shown up at Buckingham Palace. 'Thousands of them,' Haines said. 'I wouldn't know most of them by sight – but a hell of a lot of them I would.'

Although present-day security at Buckingham Palace is very tight, intruders still occasionally get through. In a recent twelve-month period five men were arrested inside the Palace precincts. Hamilton believes that the point to bear in mind is that intruders are caught. He points out that it is relatively easy to get into the gardens of a large estate like the one surrounding Buckingham Palace, but it would be a lot harder to get inside the main building and do harm.

'Now this is where I've got to be just a little bit guarded,' he said, 'because what I won't do is describe the ultimate tactic we have to prevent these people, and the ultimate tactic *is* to prevent them. Sufficient to say, they get into the garden and we deal with them. They don't get into the building – or they very rarely get into the building.'

In July 1992 an intruder did get into the main building. He apparently walked through an open French window before being arrested in a passageway.

'I was very disappointed he got into the building,' said Hamilton. 'Having said that, I must also say a lot of my officers did an awful lot of good work that day which went unrecorded. One officer was commended for his actions.'

'You have to remember we've got the Army here inside the Palace,' Mr Hamilton said, referring to the soldiers who change the guard and look strikingly photogenic in red tunics. But they have more than a ceremonial role to fulfil. 'Half a company of troops. They're written into our response plans and they give us valuable help.'

Five policemen known as Corridor Officers are stationed inside the private quarters at Buckingham Palace. Their job is specifically to protect the Queen, and they travel with her when she visits Balmoral, Sandringham and Windsor, where they perform precisely the same duties as they do in London.

Lancaster House, which is owned by the Government, stands within the confines of St James's Palace. International conferences, meetings and general political and diplomatic gatherings are held there, attended by such people as the British Prime Minister and Northern Ireland politicians, all of them considered to be more highly at risk than the Royal Family. In addition there are the State Apartments where frequently a thousand people at a time attend functions. As if all that were not enough, there are the *paparazzi* to contend with.

'They live on their wits,' said Hamilton, explaining their persistence. 'They're only as good as the candid photographs they can get, so we have to do our damnedest to keep them out.'

In terms of security some threats are obviously much more serious than others. The worst situation Hamilton can imagine is a member of the Royal Household being taken hostage. Measures are on hand to prevent that happening, but the threat remains a prime concern, given the Royal Family's highly visible public role. Apart from his understandable concerns about the safety of individuals, however, Hamilton is sure that Buckingham Palace is now secure against any intruders.

SO16

Diplomatic Protection Group

On 12 July 1991 a large group of Kurdish demonstrators stormed the Turkish Embassy in London's Belgrave Square. Minutes later the building was surrounded by more than 100 shirt-sleeved, flack-jacketed police officers, training Smith and Wesson .38 Specials and Glock 9mm automatics on the embassy windows. The officers, members of the Diplomatic Protection Group (DPG), were backed by armed-response vehicles crewed by the Force Firearms Unit (SO19), carrying submachine guns, surveillance equipment and powerful Dragon searchlights. The square was sealed off by other units as the DPG team secured the area around the embassy. The demonstrators, outnumbered and outmanoeuvred, gave themselves up without a shot being fired.

There are over 130 embassies and high commissions in London, and the Diplomatic Protection Group (SO16) are responsible for protecting all of them. When an embassy telephones for help, the DPG are geared to arrive within two minutes.

'And we are responsible for the protection of certain politicians and VIPs,' said Chief Superintendent Alan Evershed, head of SO16. Emphasising the main difference between SO12 (Special Branch), SO14 (Royalty Protection) and the DPG, he said, 'We provide uniformed protection for foreign diplomats – foreign ministers in particular, sometimes heads of state. Special Branch are responsible for the personal protection of

VIPs, whether they are heads of state, diplomats or leading politicians. Personal protection is only provided by us to ease the strain on Special Branch, at times when abnormally large numbers of VIPs are visiting the country.'

The first responsibility of SO16 is the protection of ambassadors and high commissioners and their missions, including the official residences. Evershed, a large, jovial character, enjoys the work and appears to find the personalities agreeable.

'I police the diplomatic community. I find that they are, in the main, true representatives of their countries. They are fascinating people to deal with. All races, all colours, all religions, and to deal with them is a privilege.'

The DPG, approximately 450 strong, operates from four bases in Central London – Cannon Row (also their headquarters), Walton Street, Tottenham Court Road and Kensington. The group's control room at Cannon Row coordinates messages from the mobile units.

'They record what we call frequent visits, all the changing of posts,' Evershed said. 'They facilitate the checks our officers make on suspect vehicles or people, just like an ordinary police station control room. In addition they will monitor and evaluate the movements of VIPs in and out of the country. For instance, we will be informed of the movements of visiting heads of state, because, although they may not have personal protection, certainly we will know where they are, so, if a response is needed, we can respond. In the event of an ambassador from a sensitive country staying at Claridges, say, and if Special Branch were giving him protection, then we would a: be aware; b: make an armed response if there was an incident, and c: we would give him personal protection in the hotel at night.'

Apart from personal attack buttons installed in high-risk embassies, the DPG relies on twenty-four-hour 'response policing' to protect most embassies. This is backed by six red response cars, each carrying two officers with handguns, six armed motorcyclists (daylight hours only), and a personnel carrier known as Ranger 500, carrying a Sergeant and four Constables, armed with Heckler and Koch carbines.

'The DPG was formed in November 1974,' Evershed said. 'Until that time, ordinary uniformed divisional officers were given firearms courses and assigned to posts outside embassies, or at 10 Downing Street, or the homes of prominent politicians.'

The requirement to protect an embassy does not give the police automatic right of access. In all cases permission must be asked before they set foot in any foreign mission or embassy. Evershed was keen to point out that he did not know of any occasion when the police had been refused entry to an embassy, although he admitted that the Libyan People's Bureau was a hostile exception at the time when WPC Yvonne Fletcher was shot and killed. At the present time, he says he would be confident of gaining entry to any embassy in London.

Another major priority of the DPG, in addition to the protection of ambassadors, embassies, high commissioners and their missions, is the protection of the Prime Minister's office at 10 Downing Street, together with the homes of prominent politicians at high threat level within the DPG area. Evershed explained that in a little more detail.

'All of Downing Street is my responsibility, not just number ten, but number eleven and number twelve, the buildings and the people inside them. The Foreign Secretary and the Home Secretary both receive our protection.'

The degree of protection is determined by the degree of threat. The threat is assessed by Special Branch and SO16 respond accordingly: an individual could receive personal protection backed by SO16, or it may be SO16 alone. In recent years the Chancellor of the Exchequer has not been considered to be at a level of risk that would warrant personal protection, not even after unpopular budgets.

Fluctuations in international politics naturally affect the level of attention given to individual embassies by the DPG. Whereas one ambassador might be unlikely to need protection, others may merit regular visits from mobile patrols, or even an officer posted on the steps outside as a deterrent.

'Missions and Ambassadors' residences are sensitive places,' Evershed said, 'and they are sensitively alarmed, and for that reason the alarms will go off for various reasons, most of them having nothing to do with breaches of security. That nevertheless triggers a response from the information room. They will despatch a car and motorcyclists, and they will always despatch the Duty Inspector, within the maximum two-minute response time.'

The Inspector is sent to an embassy as a mark of the serious consideration given to the representative of a foreign country.

Crime prevention is an important feature of DPG work. A full-time Crime Prevention Officer visits embassies to examine existing security measures and to discuss possible improvements. If asked, he can give authoritative advice on special door locks, window bars, the use of 'delaying' elements in the design of embassy reception areas, internal alarm systems, safe rooms and escape routes. A brochure for the guidance of embassy staff, issued by the DPG Crime Prevention Services, provides detailed advice on the correct location of offices, the use of electronic aids to security, and proper control of the human element in security management.

The everyday world of community and business-sector crime is not entirely off-limits for the officers of SO16, but they are not encouraged to get involved. In the event of a DPG patrol encountering a serious crime taking place in their area, they would respond as ordinary police officers only in the primary stages.

'I don't want my officers to get drawn into criminal situations,' Evershed said, 'because their role is an anti-terrorist one. Of course if they stumble upon a crime then they will act as any other policemen who are the first officers on the scene. But I would expect them to withdraw as soon as other officers arrived.'

Evershed does not believe that any of his officers has ever fired a shot in the line of duty. 'I've been here on and off for four years, and I think the answer is no, we haven't. I know people think we live in a violent society, but if we go back 100 years it was almost certainly a lot more violent.'

All DPG officers are armed, and Evershed believes they should carry their guns openly. He does not believe the overt display of firearms would in any way damage the image of the London police officer. Apart from other considerations, it is inconvenient to carry guns covertly, as all except a few armed police officers do at present. Until recently women DPG officers had to carry guns in handbags, which are even more awkward than shoulder-holsters when it comes to drawing a weapon. Now the uniform skirt has been specially redesigned so that an automatic handgun can be carried out of sight in a holster within a customised pocket.

'We, as a department,' Evershed said, 'asked the previous Commissioner if he would reconsider his policy of covert carriage of firearms. He considered it with his policy committee and decided that the policy would continue, so we carry our guns covered.'

Of the approximately 450 members of the DPG, the curious figure of 1.6 per cent are women. A handful. Evershed says he finds no difference, in terms of general efficiency, between his male and female officers, and he is disappointed there are not more women in SO16. He thinks the reason, in part at least, is that the firearms-toting, male-club image of the DPG has overtones of machismo which deter women recruits. 'We're not like that at all,' he maintains. 'I would like to see us approach the Metropolitan Police average for female officers, which is about 13 to 14 per cent.'

In general, vigilance is the main function of the Diplomatic Protection Group. The stamina and patience of officers on fixed duty outside embassies and other buildings is central to that prime function, and the administration of SO16 does what it can to maintain the officers' drive and morale.

'We try to strike a balance between what is practical and what is logistically possible in relieving our officers,' Evershed said. 'We try not to leave them so long without a break that they get bored, or their alertness suffers and they aren't able to do the job properly. We rotate them as often as we practically can – they don't just do fixed-post duty, they will get postings to one of the Ranger cars, which are running all the time. And there are officers trained to do hotel protection at night, so there's variation there, too. It's designed to break up the sheer bloody monotony of standing on a fixed post. We mix and match their duties and keep them alert.'

SO17

Palace of Westminster Division

Since the November night in 1606 when a cellar door at Westminster was opened to reveal Guy Fawkes guarding twenty barrels of gunpowder, there has been a steady awareness in the minds of the public and the Palace authorities alike that Parliament is a clear focus for acts of individual and collective violence. SO17 is a response to that awareness.

Just as the police presence at Heathrow Airport is provided by the Metropolitan Police for a fee, so the services of the Palace of Westminster Division are sold to the Palace authorities. The policemen, policewomen and security officers are trained and equipped by the Metropolitan Police which then charges the Palace of Westminster for their services.

In the Houses of Parliament Alfred Longhurst is known as Head of Security, and to the police he is Chief Superintendent, Palace of Westminster Division. The position he holds originated in the aftermath of an IRA bomb explosion in Westminster Hall in 1974; the Deputy Commissioner of Police of the Metropolis at the time, James Starratt, conducted an inquiry into security, and his report the following year recommended that a Chief Superintendent be put in charge of security at the Palace of Westminster. SO17 itself has been in existence for a little over two years.

In effect Chief Superintendent Longhurst has three bosses – the Commissioner of Police, Black Rod (House of Lords), and the Sergeant at Arms (House of Commons). Surprisingly, he does not find that they pull him in different directions.

'No, it's not too bad at all,' he said, 'because they've all got the same interests at heart. There may be differences of emphasis and means, but generally speaking they're harmonious.'

Deputy Commissioner Starratt's report of 1975 laid down the purpose and function of the security presence at the Palace of Westminster:

1. To provide for the safety of Members of Parliament, staff and visitors.
2. To prevent unauthorised access to and within the Palace of Westminster.
3. To safeguard the buildings and their contents from damage.
4. To protect the contents of the buildings from theft.
5. To maintain good order within the precincts of the Palace.

Chief Superintendent Longhurst emphasised that SO17 is run as nearly as possible on the lines of an ordinary police division. Their major priority is to maintain vigilance against the threat of IRA terrorism at the Houses of Parliament; as Longhurst pointed out, it is not a theoretical danger. After the bomb of 1974, another in March 1979 blew up under the car of Airey Neave, the Conservative spokesman on Northern Ireland, killing him as he left the Commons car park.

The duty of SO17 to protect the Parliamentary buildings extends further than is generally realised.

'It includes the Norman Shaw buildings,' said Longhurst; 'that's the old Scotland Yard, and a number of outbuildings besides.'

The House of Commons presents an obviously greater security risk than the Lords. Longhurst sees the threat as twofold: there is the ever-present worry about Irish Republican terrorism, and the hazard built into a democratic process that allows broad individual freedoms, to the extent of the public being allowed to spectate from the gallery of the House of Commons.

'We're relying on the instincts of the highly experienced police officer,' said Longhurst. 'He has the benefits of long experience in conventional policing, the "coppering" instinct. It can't be guaranteed, but he can usually pick up the person who's maybe a little nervous, or not one of the usual types to be visiting the public gallery – that subtle kind of policing plays a part.'

In an emergency further support is available from an armed-response vehicle of the DPG which would be rapidly on the scene. In addition to general perimeter security, there are other electronic detection and alarm systems.

There have been occasional attempts to disrupt the running of the Lords and the House of Commons. While a heavily and overtly armed presence would clearly provide a strong deterrent, this would offend against the very nature of the Houses of Parliament. On one occasion a group of lesbians abseilled into the Lords, and another time flour bombs were thrown from the public gallery of the Commons. In April 1992, members of Greenpeace climbed on to scaffolding around the Victoria Tower.

'We have to look at the way British society runs itself,' said Longhurst. 'We don't want policemen armed, it's a very, very basic expectation of the British public, all the more so in regard to the Houses of Parliament. But given those sensitivities, I'd say that we can still match any potential threat with the host of measures that we take.'

Before SO17's own first line of security, the visitor entering the House of Commons by St Stephen's entrance has to go through a rigorous search – much tighter since the events mentioned above – including baggage X-ray. Beyond that point there are several internal security layers which vary in intensity according to the need in given areas.

An important arm of SO17 security is the Search Team, whose brief is to keep both chambers, the Lords and Commons, in a 'sterile' condition. They make thorough searches before the Houses sit, and perform searches on motor vehicles. Deep searches are also performed, with sniffer dogs brought in from outside to search for explosives prior to each day's sittings in the chambers.

'We should remember that the security for the Houses rests really with the Officers of the Houses,' said Longhurst, pointing out that SO17's responsibility for security reaches to the doors of the chambers, but not beyond. The police play no part in the policing of the chambers when Parliamentary business is being conducted. 'The responsibility exercised through Black Rod's office covers the Lords, and that from the office of the Sergeant at Arms takes in the Commons.'

People who behave improperly within the precincts of Parliament are simply asked to leave. Most arrests, and there are very few, are for theft, usually committed by staff or contractors. When someone is arrested a detention cell is available.

Surveillance around the Palace is aided by a host of closed-circuit television cameras, monitored from SO17's own control room, which is manned by police and civilian security officers. Like other control rooms it is a focal point for communications, providing a radio link to Scotland Yard and various means to summon emergency forces should they be needed.

In the event of disorder in one of the chambers, the restoration of order would of course be the responsibility of the appropriate House Officer – Black Rod or the Sergeant at Arms – and his staff. If their efforts failed, then theoretically SO17 would be required to intervene.

Nearly a million people visit the Houses of Parliament every year. Surprisingly, they do not create a particular headache for SO17. Longhurst finds that in general they become hushed and docile, as visitors do in churches, and he believes the atmosphere of the place is largely responsible. Even deputations tend to be orderly, whatever their agenda.

'The bottom line,' said Longhurst, 'is that we will protect Parliament, and if things are getting out of order and we feel there is too great a level of threat, then we'll start slamming doors. But,' he added, 'it generally doesn't work that way.'

SO18

Police National Computer Bureau

The new Police National Computer is called, not surprisingly, PNC2. It is the first step towards the development of a full computerised National Criminal Records System (NCRS), within which all forces will take responsibility for their own computerised national criminal records.

When NCRS appeared on the horizon it became clear to the Specialist Operations Executive that new working procedures would have to be devised. They decided to establish a new branch to manage all of the Metropolitan Police Service records on the Police National Computer. The new branch is SO18.

PNC2 came on stream in the autumn of 1991, carrying information in two main groups, Vehicles and Names. The target of a National Criminal Records System, in practical terms, is an extension of the Names facility. It will be a straightforward addition, but a huge one which will considerably enhance PNC2's benefits to police investigations and efficiency.

The computer already holds detailed information on millions of people who have criminal records; it also lists people the police want to interview in connection with a crime, people who are reported missing, and people disqualified from driving. It can describe a person's appearance, list his aliases, and give details of his criminal record. The entry also carries markers which can include a warning if the person is violent or whether he is likely to be armed.

'As far as vehicles are concerned,' said Detective Superintendent Peter Burnett, who heads SO18, 'the computer keeps records of vehicles that have been lost or stolen. It also gives details of registered owners of vehicles, in fact a copy of what is kept by DVLA, so that in most cases we can find out the details we want without having to make reference to DVLA. The computer's response comes within seconds.'

The main PNC2 computer is linked to over 2,600 terminals, two hundred printers and forty-one police computers in fifty-five police forces. Data passes along the network by the fastest available route for each transaction, using key switching points in the Midlands, the North of England, Scotland, and Wales. Using PNC2's broadcast system any police force can transmit important or urgent messages – for example, an officer chasing a suspect who might try to leave the country can alert ports and airports all over Britain.

A proportion of the sixty members of staff in SO18 work in the monitoring section. Here they check the quality of records which are submitted before putting them on to the computer, or before sending them on to the National Identification Bureau (NIB). Burnett explained this part of the process.

'When a person is arrested at the police station the fingerprints are taken and a form is completed with their personal details, plus the description and type of their offence. The fingerprints and the form are then submitted to NIB via SO18. Here, the documents are checked and validated before they are passed on to NIB.'

This procedure is a prelude to SO18 taking full responsibility under NCRS.

'We need to make sure all the information we put on the computer is as accurate as possible, as eventually we will be entirely responsible for it anyway. So part of this section's duty now is to make sure that errors in the past are put right, and that all data that will be copied over to the fully computerised system is completely accurate.'

There is a twenty-four-hour desk in SO18, handling urgent material that has to be processed and entered on the PNC2 network with a minimum of delay. 'The information that we want on the database very, very quickly is about people who are wanted for serious crime, such as murder,' said Burnett. 'That information has to be circulated as fast as possible. That's the job of the twenty-four-hour desk – as well as cancellation of wanted persons who have been arrested.'

As the main users of PNC2 – roughly 24 per cent of the work handled on the system is theirs – the Metropolitan Police need a computer tailored to do what they want at the speed they want. To that end SO18 has a voice in the ultimate design of the new database, with a representative team regularly meeting with the design group.

Summarising the function of SO18, Burnett said, 'The main reason was to build the Metropolitan Police's own unit for inputting information on criminal records, and taking from the National Identification Bureau any function that is seen as the responsibility of the Metropolitan Police.'

As time passes, the proportion of police officers operating SO18, at present more than a third of the total staff, will be steadily reduced. 'With a minimal number of police officers remaining as advisers,' Burnett said, 'I would think SO18 would be virtually totally civilianised in the future.'

And would this be done with a view to getting more officers back on the streets?

'Yes. Definitely.'

SO19

Force Firearms Unit

'No matter what anyone says, you always have fear,' said Inspector Andy Latto, echoing Graham Lightfoot of the Explosives Office. Latto is in charge of SO19 Black Squad. 'You never get to a point where you think "I'm not frightened."'

There are 27,000 officers in the Metropolitan Police and roughly 2,000 of them, including forty-five female officers, are authorised to carry firearms. 'They are split into two parts,' said Superintendent Mike Waldron, who is acknowledged to be one of the country's leading authorities on firearms. 'The majority, probably twelve hundred, are in protection departments, that is departments responsible for the protection of people or premises. The remainder also tend to be divided down – either they're in full-time units like robbery squads, or they're officers attached to a divisional station who can draw weapons if a need arises.'

All these people are called Authorised Firearms Officers (AFOs), and are mainly uniformed police. Few CID officers are AFOs.

The need for a specialised firearms unit within the Metropolitan Police was first seriously raised in 1966, when three police officers were shot and killed in Shepherd's Bush. 'It was such a traumatic thing,' said Waldron. 'It hadn't happened before, and all those who were in the service at that time could say precisely where they were when they first heard the news, just like most people can say where they were when they heard that Kennedy had been shot. Because the criminals involved were armed and had proved themselves to be highly dangerous, firearms were issued to police officers.'

The Commissioner at the time decided that proper firearms training should be set up for the police and a number of ex-military personnel were selected to be instructors. They took a few courses, visited training facilities abroad, and finally set up a training centre in London. Similar moves were made in police forces nationally at roughly the same time.

'And so there's been a gradual build-up over the last twenty-five years of all the knowledge, not only in London but countrywide and throughout the world,' said Waldron. 'It has all come together and is building all the time.'

SO19 has five teams of seven Constables, each team headed by a Sergeant. All team members are Specialist Firearms Officers (SFOs), which means they have undergone advanced training. They wear blue shirts, dark blue jumpers and dark blue berets. There are also five ARVs (Armed Response Vehicles) on twenty-four-hour patrol, crewed by three officers.

An ARV can be identified by a yellow spot painted on the roof, a mark used for identification by helicopters. The crew's primary job is initial response, backing up officers who call for help on the streets and supporting them until more substantial help arrives, if it is needed. The ARV crew perform ordinary police duty, although care is taken not to involve them in anything that would cause prolonged delay. During routine duty the crew is unarmed. Smith and Wesson handguns and two carbines, plus ammunition for the handguns, are carried in a locked safe on board the ARVs. Usually, permission has to be granted by a Commander before a crew can draw weapons and ammunition from the safe. However, if an officer of Commander rank or above cannot be reached, they can be given authority by the Chief Inspector in charge of Central Communications (TO25). If the crew find themselves in a situation where there is a visible threat to life, where delay in responding could have tragic results, then they can go ahead and draw their weapons without authority.

'All that keeps the police on the UK mainland from being a fully armed police service,' said Waldron, 'is the morale, the morale of the force. The police officers themselves are satisfied that the arrangements for their safety are adequate. If, on the other hand, they believe that they're being used like sacrificial lambs for the sake of a tradition, then there will be a build-up of resentment that will eventually catch fire, and you will end up with a fully armed police force.'

Chief Superintendent Rick Johnson, Head of SO19, believes that any discussion of an armed police force should address the need for a less than lethal means of using firearms to suppress crime or disorder. He was not sure that a baton round (or 'rubber bullet') would fit the bill, unless its velocity could be substantially reduced.

'It can be lethal at less than twenty metres,' he said, 'and it can be lethal at more than twenty metres if it hits someone on the head. What you're supposed to do with the baton round is aim for the torso at over twenty metres, and then fire, and the likelihood is that you won't kill the person. But there was one fatality in Northern Ireland a few years ago when the bullet did just that – it actually hit the person in the torso and killed him.'

Johnson believes the 'less than lethal' answer would

be something like CN gas, a variation on CS gas which overwhelms the target immediately. CN is not yet approved for use by any police service.

'The philosophy of this country,' Johnson said, 'is that you shouldn't do that sort of thing to people, you shouldn't spray them with these noxious things, it's distasteful. But it's not so distasteful as shooting somebody.'

On the main topic of whether to arm the rank and file police or not, Waldron believes there is little evidence to show that firearms make any difference to their personal safety. 'If you look at the situations where police officers have been shot, and on occasions killed,' he said, 'you would be hard pressed in a lot of cases to show that, had the officer carried a firearm, the firearm could have saved his life, or could have prevented serious injury.'

In June 1993, the Commissioner of Police, Paul Condon, was quoted in the *Independent on Sunday* as saying that, because of the rise of terrorism and crimes involving guns, the British police could be carrying guns as a matter of routine within ten years. Mr Condon's comment was made in the light of reports that detectives in the East End were dealing with one firearms incident a day, and that at least three million unregistered firearms are currently circulating in Great Britain. Condon added that, although he did not see the arming of the police as inevitable, he did believe it was probable.

In the meantime, as the debate on firearms dies in one quarter and flourishes in another, the Force Firearms Unit remains available for emergencies.

'We work with Flying Squad, Regional Crime Squad and TSG,' said Inspector Andy Latto, 'and we are committed to terrorist road-block searches, stops and so on. Then we get the on-the-spot jobs where something serious happens and we're called in. Most of the time it'll be a robbery or a domestic dispute – a husband's holding his wife hostage, he's holding himself hostage, that type of thing. If the armed robbery is one where the robber is entrenched inside, we then go and do what we call a dig-out – that is, contain the premises and call the robber out.'

If a hostage is being held and his life is being threatened, then SO19 may attack at once, but usually, containment and negotiation are enough. While the firearms teams wait, they cope with fluctuating nervousness and fear. The pressure on firearms officers is severe and often prolonged, and has inevitable reverberations; their families are conditioned to expect disturbances in their lives.

But it is not all stress. Latto believes his officers become deeply involved in their work and experience a strong sense of achievement when a difficult job turns out well. He gave an example.

'In the middle of 1992 we were with the Flying Squad, chasing an escapee from prison, a violent criminal known to have been involved in several robberies – in fact he had been involved in one five days before they began the operation to find him. We were providing firearms backup for the Flying Squad surveillance teams. One day the search took us to a Surrey town, where a Securicor van calling at a supermarket was thought to be a target for a robbery. Surveillance confirmed that four men, all of them probably armed, were in cars in the car park outside the supermarket. It was suggested by Flying Squad officers that we should arrest them there and then. But due to the safety aspect I wouldn't allow that. These men were dangerous.'

While the men were being watched the Securicor van arrived and left again without incident. The police decided that maybe the armed men were on reconnaissance. As the police continued to watch, the men left their cars and walked together into a fenced-off park where people exercised their dogs. The men sat on the ground and talked.

'We decided we would give them a certain amount of time,' Latto said, 'and when they were leaving we would arrest them. It was about six-thirty, a bright summer's evening. There were children playing near the spot so I sent officers to secure the area, to make sure no innocent bystanders would be caught up in whatever happened. The only way into the park area was through a gap in the fence wide enough to admit a car. The Flying Squad officers and the full Black Team were in five vehicles in all, guided in by a surveillance motorcyclist.'

As the vehicles entered the park the four armed men obviously knew what was happening. They got up and scattered. One drew a gun and pointed it at the lead vehicle. He then appeared to change his mind about shooting and instead turned around and ran for the fence. The other three were already over the fence and he was soon behind them. They ran across a busy dual carriageway, scrambled through a thick hedge on the central reservation, then ran out across another dual carriageway. On the other side was dense woodland, with a stream and open fields beyond.

'The escapee was eventually cornered in the stream by two police dogs,' Latto said. 'He was up to his waist in water, ditching a Smith and Wesson and a shoulder holster in the water. As we approached we warned him we were armed. I was carrying a Heckler and Koch carbine and a Glock handgun, my partner had a Glock and a shotgun. He looked up at us and said, "I've fallen in here and broken my leg." He looked at the gun, which was floating half-submerged a couple of feet away. He said, "I'm going to go for it . . ." We shouted at him, told him not to be stupid. We went on shouting but he insisted he was going to go for his gun. We shouted at him again, and suddenly he just put his hands on his head. He decided he didn't want to go for the gun. Probably once we had said to him "We'll shoot you," he realised that we would. It eventually turned out he hadn't broken his leg at all. He ran through the water and officers jumped on him right there in the stream. He was secured and handcuffed, and even then he went on trying to escape.'

Discussing the way his colleagues respond to fatalities in their work, Latto said they are always shocked, no matter how strenuously they deny it. 'If you injure someone else, you do suffer a high level of shock, and the more injury you cause, the higher the level. One of my roles as supervisor is to be aware that my officers will feel some stress immediately because as soon as they pull that trigger certain things happen and their bodies react in certain ways. It's either minimal, or the kind of shock where they switch off totally.

'Usually they go quiet, or they may start saying, "Is he all right? Is he dead?" Things like that. But usually they just go quiet. The other thing that is noticeable, and they all mention it afterwards, is the slowness after an incident. You had a job, you had a build-up, and then there was a shooting, and everything becomes very slow. All the follow-up procedures take a long time, and then that becomes annoying, and they feel let down.'

'In 1991,' said Mike Waldron, 'in London there were 1,520 armed operations carried out by all armed officers. Shots were fired once by police in London in 1991, and that was by one of our officers who, dressed in an ordinary uniform, was shot at by a mentally disturbed person who was armed with a shotgun; during the incident a woman officer was wounded. There were no fatalities, and out of the 561 operations carried out by our own firearms teams here, they didn't fire a single shot.'

Much of the criticism of the Force Firearms Unit stems from a wariness, among members of the public and the police hierarchy alike, of radical change in the traditional image of the British police officer.

'A police officer, when he's selected, is not selected to carry a gun,' said Chief Superintendent Rick Johnson. 'His whole uniform is designed not to carry anything but a truncheon. We still keep the image of the British policeman. I mean nobody's fooled that the Diplomatic Protection group aren't armed, but still the image is maintained.'

Weapons should only get into the hands of responsible people, Waldron says, and that is done through tighter legislation and much tougher control of firearms. That, in conjunction with a relatively small armed police unit, he believes, is a balanced reaction to the threat of sieges and shooting sprees.

'The advantage in having training reduced to a small number of people is that you can do a far better job. We can train two thousand a lot better than we can train twenty-seven thousand.'

Waldron admits that the selection of personnel for SO19 is not easy. Vacancies are limited, but there is a small, steady turnover of staff, so recruitment is constant. Between twenty and thirty new people join the unit each year and there are always many more applications than vacancies. Waldron recalled that the last time they had twelve vacancies to fill, over three hundred people applied.

'Training is at Lippett's Hill, where we're looking for

officers who are fit, and who can think. We put them through an exercise that requires them to see a situation and determine how they're going to deal with it. If they are already Authorised Firearms Officers we'll give them a shooting test, although the qualification isn't essential, because we can always provide a firearms course. Following that, they have to take a two-weeks' residential course, during which we'll put them through most of the situations we think they're likely to come across in the course of their normal duties.'

There are no women officers in the main SO19 teams, and only three in the ARVs. Waldron says he would very much like to attract women into the department, but efforts have not been very successful. He points to the small number of women AFOs in the entire Metropolitan Police as an indicator of their reluctance to get involved in firearms work.

There is a feeling in some quarters that SO19, ARVs apart, tend to be an élitist and inaccessible group of officers who keep themselves apart. Waldron believes there are a number of reasons for this. One is their concern to deflect media interest in their identities.

'There is a feeling that once the media have got a name and a face, if anything then happens involving that person and the name and the face are tied together, the face will be on the front pages of the newspapers, and it will be splashed across the news headlines from various libraries. It's quite a reasonable fear to have.'

While maintaining that his SO19 officers do not see themselves as a unit apart, he says that on the firearms teams there is a greater level of camaraderie and mutual protection than would be found on most teams. They have total trust in each other, he says, and he believes that means they will trust outsiders less. Having gone that far, Waldron admitted that his people tend to be defensive about themselves.

'Oh, yes, they are, because they often feel they're misrepresented. They feel there are those who would love to make their name in the firearms field who have never had anything to do with armed police, or the police use of firearms, yet nevertheless consider themselves, and are considered by others, to be experts. But those people are listened to far more than they should be, and my men have no way of saying, "Hang on a minute, that isn't right."'

While naming no specific offender, Waldron pointed to the way newspapers and other media responded to the shooting of a man in the north of England.

'Within a couple of days expert opinions were being produced as to what went wrong, why the police did it wrong. Now the unfair thing is that the officers who were involved in that can say absolutely nothing to contradict what's been said. There are security laws; there are rules of evidence that say that you cannot say anything which is likely to prejudice any future court hearing.

'Because the police service cannot answer back,' Waldron went on, 'there is a feeling that the police service *will not* answer back, or has got something to hide, or cannot answer back because the person criticising them is probably right.'

Extensive media coverage of many SO19 operations compounds the suffering of some officers from the condition called Post Traumatic Stress Disorder (PTSD), which sparks severe symptoms in some witnesses and participants following a psychologically traumatic event. Symptoms can include re-experiencing the event through dreams; emotional numbing to other life experiences and relationships; depression and cognitive difficulties (e.g., inability to concentrate).

'We sent officers up to help with the recovery of bodies from the plane crash at Lockerbie. When they arrived at the scene they couldn't see any bodies, and then slowly they began to recognise *bits* of bodies. One of the officers described seeing a section of body that was tangled up on a railing, but he had to stare hard to make himself believe it *was* part of a body. Then, when he realised it was, he looked around and began seeing other parts. If the officer is going to get over that, and not have it seriously affect him for the rest of his life, he needs some sort of counselling.'

Stress disorder affecting officers of the Force Firearms Unit is not helped by a barrage of criticism they cannot refute.

Waldron was eloquent on the sense of isolation that can engulf firearms officers after a heavily-reported case where someone has been shot.

'What you want is to be able to talk to somebody and say what you've done. In the middle of all that you know there's going to be a big investigation, supervised by the Police Complaints Authority; you know there's going to be a lot of very senior people spending a long time dissecting what you've spent a fraction of a second doing – and in the middle of all that you read somebody, for whom you've got no time whatsoever, giving his view on what you did. That adds to the frustration, and it starts to make you believe that you're on your own and that nobody's backing you up. That is a problem that every police firearms unit has got, and I don't exclude this one.'

When someone is shot dead by a policeman there is an automatic investigation, which will either be carried out internally by the Complaints Investigation Branch, or, at the request of the Police Complaints Authority, by an outside police force. The officer involved is taken off firearms operations, but is not suspended from training or from operations, since suspension is viewed as a presumption that he or she is to some extent culpable. It is considered important that no stigma is applied prior to an investigation; an officer is removed from firearms operation at this time, Waldron said, only to make sure there is no chance of the incident being repeated.

Asked how an officer is affected by killing someone, Waldron said there was no straightforward answer. Individual responses vary widely. 'Also, you get reactions that you see and reactions you don't see, and wouldn't know about unless you were aware they could exist. Going back ten or twelve years, it was not at all uncommon for an officer involved in a shooting fatality to ask to be taken off firearms entirely. He'd had enough. It wasn't very well managed. The idea that there could be some sort of need for counselling – and by counselling I mean talking it over, I don't mean some sort of psychiatric examination – had not caught on.'

Talking it over, Waldron is convinced, is crucially important, whatever the degree of reaction in the officer involved.

'Those who do talk about what has happened, and those who accept it, generally have no problem whatever with going back on armed operations. I think we are getting better at managing the post-incident procedure as far as the officer is concerned. We've a long way to go, though. We're forever talking about it, and we're forever learning new theories about it.'

The offshoots of PTSD can be alarming. Apart from the standard symptoms, distortions of remembered time and distance are not uncommon, and the memory of sounds can be obliterated. Waldron knows of cases where officers, chasing an armed criminal, have not heard themselves call out, 'Stop! Armed police!' even though they have called out more than once and so have other officers around them. Another disturbing feature, which tends to grow out of multiple stress, is described by psychiatrists as 'a sense of foreshortened future': depending on circumstances, sufferers do not expect to have stable careers, or marriages, or children. In many cases, they do not believe they will live much longer.

Turning from psychological pressures on firearms officers, Waldron described a situation – some say it is a psychological syndrome – known as Suicide by Cop, which arises from mental disturbance on the part of people facing police guns.

'Suicide by Cop is an American expression. It is used to describe situations where a criminal or a hostage-taker who doesn't have the courage to take his or her own life, decides to go out and challenge the police in such a way that they will be forced to shoot.'

In June 1992, a railway worker called Peter Swann, who was on bail for an armed robbery, died in Bromley Hospital six hours after being shot by an SFO team of SO19, following a two-hour siege at a block of flats in Penge. A woman who witnessed the shooting said that Swann brandished a gun and shouted at the police marksmen. She quoted him as saying, 'Shoot me or I will shoot you.' A spokeswoman from Scotland Yard said that Swann threatened to kill himself and two unarmed officers who were the first to confront him. Armed officers later challenged him twice. They too were threatened, and fired a number of shots, one of which killed Swann.

Officers joining SO19 will have already completed a

two-week firearms course, which teaches the basic skills of handling and using a revolver. They will begin their service in ARVs and will undergo a further two-week course on using the Heckler and Koch MP5. After that, ARV officers will spend twenty days a year in refresher training.

'They can then apply to come on to an SFO team,' Waldron said, 'and there is a selection for that which involves a job-related fitness test and a test of their shooting ability. Their general performance during the time they were on ARVs is assessed too. When they are accepted they will have to do a six-week course for the team. That involves more concentrated work, using building sections and room sections, covering everything up to and including hostage rescue.'

Rapid entry to premises is an important skill for SO19 officers, and new people spend time learning how it should be done. Waldron says there are two ways of dealing with an armed person in a building. The first is to knock on the door and ask him to come out; that usually works. However, the knock is a preliminary move, it precedes a pause for a response, and the person inside can use that space to destroy evidence like drugs or property that the police are hoping to find inside.

'We've had occasions,' Waldron said, 'when we've been sitting around the outside of a building and there's been a lot of smoke coming out, and when we get inside we find thousands and thousands of pounds worth of banknotes burnt in the sink. So what you have to weigh up is, how worthwhile is it to do a rapid entry? By a rapid entry I mean getting into the building, finding the person you're looking for, and stopping that person from destroying any evidence – while at the same time not allowing him to get hold of a firearm and start taking shots at you as you go in. That takes quite a lot of training and quite a lot of pace.'

A variety of hardware is used for rapid-entry work, ranging from sledgehammers to sophisticated hydraulic rams. As an aside on this topic, Waldron said that a fundamental rule when using a sledgehammer is never to use too much thrust, as it is likely to go clean through the door and either get stuck or fly out of reach, leaving the door substantially intact.

One of the most difficult types of SO19 operation is a siege.

As soon as SO19 arrive at the scene of a siege they take control of the area and cut off all escape routes. The second stage is to establish contact with someone inside the besieged premises. The third stage involves negotiating a settlement, while being ready to resolve the incident by force if necessary.

'The ARVs would establish the initial containment, and probably the first contact as well, before hostage negotiators arrive at the scene,' said Waldron. 'All ARV teams have training in the basics of negotiation so that they know what to do – there are things you can say and things you can't.'

A resolution by force would be carried out by officers of the main firearms teams; authority for such action would come from the Incident Commander, who would not necessarily be from SO19, but would have an officer of SO19 with him as an advisor. Almost from the start of the operation, plans would be made for handling a surrender, even if there was no indication from within the premises that the person or persons inside wanted to give themselves up.

Officers spread out in a cordon at the scene of a siege are contacted by a coded radio system of signals called

'Sitstat' – Situation Status – which uses five categories to relay information on the siege status, and to indicate whether or not officers should use their weapons, regardless of what they might be able to see. Waldron gave an example.

'If we have a situation where there are an unknown number of terrorists, but we know there *are* a number of them, and an unknown number of hostages, but again we know there are a number of them, the fact that an officer on the cordon maybe sees one terrorist inflicting severe injuries on one of the hostages, that would not necessarily mean we would want the terrorist shot. The reason for what he is doing, although unknown to the officer on the cordon, may be understood by the Incident Commander. The firing of one shot to stop the terrorist might mean the slaughter of fifteen, twenty, thirty hostages inside the building. Therefore the Incident Commander is prepared to have one hostage sacrificed in order to ensure the rescue or the safety of the others.'

Waldron says the easiest sieges to deal with, from a police point of view, are those involving terrorists. They tend to be the most straightforward because in most cases they follow a predictable course. There are, of course, exceptions.

'I was at the siege of the Iranian Embassy and the siege at the Libyan People's Bureau in St James's Square, where WPC Yvonne Fletcher was killed,' Waldron said. 'The one at the Libyan People's Bureau was different, and it was probably one of the most traumatic. The way of dealing with it was, in fact, comparatively easy. But there were lots of undercurrents. We didn't have a terrorist inside an embassy who had taken it over, we had the embassy people themselves, they were actually responsible. If there were hostages, they were several thousand miles away in another country. We had an unarmed police officer who had been shot, so there was obviously a certain amount of feeling on the police side, a determination that those responsible would be brought to justice and appear before a court. And yet you had the political ramifications of all that. Within two or three days there was a general feeling that whoever had done it was going to get away with it. Which they did.'

In the siege of the Iranian Embassy, SO19 had to hand over management of the situation to the military – specifically, to the SAS. 'They don't just turn up and assault a building,' Waldron said. 'It takes a lot of work to get to the point where they can do that, and the people they do that work with are the police officers who are there at the scene, the majority of whom will be from SO19. Like the police, the military can't work in isolation. They need back-up and support and assistance. Because they haven't the manpower to do the whole lot, there are lots of things they need which we can provide them with. So there's a very, very close link between the police services all over the country and the military, specifically to allow for this change-over between one responsibility and another. That does, of course, involve training together.'

While an ambush is not the same thing as a siege, it can often have enough points of similarity to make it the province of SO19. Chief Inspector Norman McKenzie described a Flying Squad job, an attempt at a combined ambush and armed robbery, which involved the active participation of SO19.

'Information came during the course of the night that a gang of robbers had broken into a bank in Islington. They were waiting in the bank for the manager to turn up in the morning, and as he came into the bank that would set off the alarm. He would switch it off, the robbers would then grab him and tie him up, then they would proceed to empty the safe.

'In fact they had broken into the bank at ten o'clock at night, and during the course of the night one of their people, for some reason we did not know, called the police and told them what was going on. So what our team did in the morning was, we contacted the bank manager and explained what was going on. When he got to the bank, a team followed him in through the door. The robbers were waiting in there with a gun, but our people were much quicker than them, and caught them.'

The most difficult sieges to deal with, in Superintendent Waldron's experience, are those which begin as domestic disputes; then someone in the family takes another member of the family hostage and the character of the situation undergoes a grave change. Inspector Latto recalled such a case.

'The subject was a man with a background of mental illness who was attending Alcoholics Anonymous and who had not been drinking for six months. Then suddenly he started again overnight. He came home, threw his wife out of the house and took his five-year-old son hostage with a breadknife. Local officers went to the scene, then we were called in because it was a hostage situation. When negotiators arrived we gave them cover with an ARV crew. We then had to get a Commander's authority to call out a specialist team, which took a long time.'

The negotiators had to talk to the hostage-taker through the letter box. Eventually he asked for a priest and one was brought. Before long, the priest managed to create another problem.

'He started to agree to demands, saying, "Yes, we can

do this for you, yes, we can do that for you," which creates the situation where the hostage-taker will say, "I want it done *now*. I need this *now*. If you don't do it I will kill the child." What had happened was, the man had two voices talking to him in his head, one telling him to kill the boy, the other telling him not to do that. All the time this was going on, he was carrying his son around with the knife at his throat.'

It was decided between Latto and a senior coordinator that if there was any increased danger to the child, Black Team would rush into the premises, using explosive devices to distract the man.

'And then he did turn violent, and I decided along with the chief negotiator that if we could resolve it quickly by having the door slightly open, then we would. He asked for his own doctor because he blamed a lot of this on the doctor. So it was agreed that the doctor would come. She eventually arrived, started talking to him and said, "If you come out I'll give you all the things you asked for.' And he opened the door. At that point we stormed in and rescued the child. No one was harmed.'

Superintendent Waldron related a similar, if more shocking, case from the mid-1980s. A man looking for his common-law wife had turned up at a flat in Northolt, where she was hiding, and confronted her. She managed to escape, leaving behind the woman who was the tenant of the flat and a young child, a girl of five. As the escaped woman ran to summon the police, the man stabbed her friend to death and took the child hostage. The siege began on Christmas Day and lasted into Boxing Day. The man's threats to harm the child kept the police at a distance from the flat.

'And while all this was going on,' Waldron said, 'he was barricading the flat. Bedding, chairs, wardrobes, you name it, were all pushed up against the front door. He blocked the kitchen window, too, which opened out on to the balcony, and even the balcony was blocked, making it more and more difficult to get in there.'

There was a serious worry at this point that the hostage-taker would be able to harm the child, perhaps even kill her, before the police could know what he was doing, let alone find a way into the flat. And then the man seemed to attempt an escape.

'He came out through the front door, which was his only way out, without the child. I watched him do that and I was sure he was going to try to escape. As soon as the other officers saw him they came out from the various places where they were hiding and tried to capture him. But he wasn't trying to escape at all. He was looking for more material to strengthen his barricades. When the officers ran at him he got hold of a riot shield and defended himself with it. He got back into the flat before they could stop him.'

Now the situation was critical. The hostage-taker was back in the flat and even more agitated than ever, screaming that he was going to kill the child. The police decided their best action was to break into the flat and stop him.

'They eventually managed to smash their way in through the bathroom and kitchen windows,' said Waldron. 'They had to get through broken glass, across a sink, through barricades and build-up – the officers going in through the bathroom had similar problems. And they found themselves in a totally dark flat, with the man somewhere in there with the child. The light was just enough for them to see him sitting on the settee, and he was in the process of stabbing the child in the neck. I think three shots were fired, and one of them hit him, and the child was grabbed out of his arms. As they were moving away from the couch the knife fell out of the child's neck. Fortunately she survived. He ended up getting convicted and he went to prison.'

Waldron repeated that terrorist sieges are far easier to manage, in the main, than the domestic kind. 'With the terrorist siege you know who the good guys are, you know who the bad guys are, and you know what you have to do. Everybody knows what their job is, and they just get on and do it. But when you've got a domestic situation you don't know how much damage the hostage-taker is prepared to do. If they don't mean it, but say they're going to do it anyway, do you then commit your resources to forcing an entry to stop it? If you do that and you end up having to shoot that person, and it turns out to have been unnecessary, then you were wrong. It's a very, very difficult situation to be in.'

Each siege adds a little more to a firearms officer's knowledge of how to deal with them, Waldron says. 'But anybody who says there's a right way of doing it, or claims to be an expert on the subject, is kidding himself.'

Weapons

The Hague Convention, just after the turn of the century, stated that, in war, soldiers should be killed cleanly and with as little suffering as possible. 'To get that sort of effect,' said Chief Superintendent Rick Johnson, 'they used what is known as "full metal jacket" or ball ammunition. Now this particular ammunition is used in war, but because its use is a convention between countries, the Home Office decided that that was the most appropriate ammunition for the police to use as well. It causes a clean wound and a minimum of suffering.'

The trouble is that such ammunition often passes

clean through its target, doing minimal damage on the way and perhaps hitting some innocent person in the vicinity.

'We've gone away from that to a certain extent,' Johnson said. 'We now use soft semi-jacketed or soft-nosed ammunition, which will stop over-penetration. But in a lot of circumstances it doesn't stop the person committing further acts or attempting to escape. The service will, at a later stage, have to reconsider: if a person is committing a criminal offence and he is endangering life, should we actually use a bullet that is going to incapacitate him to an extent where he doesn't want to play any more?'

The hollow-nosed dum-dum bullet, unlike a full-metal-jacket round, flattens on contact, carrying a quantity of soft tissue ahead of it and creating an exit wound many times larger than the hole it makes on entry. The dum-dum usually causes considerable internal damage. Johnson does not advocate anything so extreme as the dum-dum bullet – in any case, it is illegal in the United Kingdom.

'But we should look to another form of ammunition that operates efficiently, and doesn't allow the suspect to put anybody else in danger. If you've got a person who is intent on using a gun, then that person should be stopped, and you should stop him in a way that doesn't endanger anybody else. If that means using a round of ammunition that will stop him, even if it does cause a little bit more trauma or suffering, that's much better than the risk of over-penetration and risk to other people.'

The handgun carried in all Armed Response Vehicles is the Smith and Wesson Model 10, a six-shot, .38 calibre revolver which has been in continuous production since

1899. It was introduced to service with the Metropolitan Police in 1974 and is the standard weapon of forces throughout the United Kingdom.

'It's accurate up to about twenty-five yards, possibly,' said Waldron, 'fifty yards if you're a very, very good shot, but twenty-five yards is the average.'

Another handgun used by SO19 team members is the Glock Model 17, an Austrian self-loading pistol, with a seventeen-round magazine delivering 9mm bullets. It has been in service with SO19 for three years and was introduced initially as a possible replacement for their standard-issue handgun at that time, the Browning 9mm. The Glock proved very popular and has been taken up by other groups within the Met, notably Special Branch (SO12) and Royalty Protection (SO14).

The other gun carried in an ARV is a Heckler and Koch MP5 carbine which, as already noted, is intermediate between a handgun and a high-velocity rifle. Its thirty-round magazine delivers a 9mm bullet identical to that fired by the Glock self-loading pistol. The MP5 normally has settings for single-shot or automatic fire, with a facility on some models for a three-shot burst. SO19 officers use it in the single-shot setting only. The Heckler and Koch is good for distances up to about 100 yards, which takes it beyond handgun range.

SO19 also carry a pump-action shotgun which is gradually going out of favour in the police service, largely because of the superior performance of the Heckler and Koch carbine.

'But there are some uses for which we can't give up the shotguns,' said Waldron. 'One of them is for delivery of CS gas in a small cartridge called a ferret. You can also fire a round called a Hatton, which is made of compacted lead dust. As soon as it hits anything it breaks up. You would use a Hatton round to get through a door very, very quickly. You would fire it at the hinges, at an angle from one side of the door, and it would quite happily smash the hinges out. You couldn't use the Hatton round on people, but you can add it to the repertoire of ways to get through a door.'

The top-range weapon, used by the best shots in SO19, is the Steyr SSG Police, a .308 calibre counter-sniper rifle.

'There are some people,' Waldron said, 'who just have a natural way of shooting a rifle and making it look easy. I'm not one of those people. The officer using a Steyr has to guarantee a first-round operational hit on a target the size of a man's head at four hundred metres, and a first hit on a target the size of the top half of a person's body at eight hundred metres.'

Image intensifiers, often called night sights, are used on the Steyr and the Heckler and Koch. 'When you put them on top of a weapon,' Waldron said, 'you can see for 100 metres in total blackness. You can identify a person at that distance, and determine if it's necessary to use the weapon.'

Distraction devices, which Waldron describes as being no more than fireworks, are standard kit. 'I think the slang term for them is flashback. They're not designed to cause injury, although under certain circumstances they may do. They are designed to distract. If officers need to go through a door or a window in a very short space of time, it is possible somebody is waiting on the other side of the door or window to shoot them. So you want that person looking the other way, you want him distracted. A mechanical way of doing that is to use one of these distracting devices. I guarantee if one comes flying into a room you have to look at it, there's no way to stop yourself. I've seen them go off dozens and dozens of times over the years and I cannot stop myself from looking at them, because it's just natural, especially after hearing a bang.'

CS gas has been available to the police for twenty-five years. In that time it has only been used twice. CS is a lacrimator, a substance which attacks moist mucous membranes in the eyes and mouth, causing stinging, a copious production of tears, and constriction of the breathing passages.

'CS gas would be fired from a shotgun, although it can be fired straight from canisters,' Waldron said. 'I must emphasise, though, the only time we would use gas, distraction devices or the Hatton round would be in something like a hostage-rescue situation. There is the danger, in using any of them, that you could inflict an injury without being able to predict beforehand what that injury is likely to be, or who's going to receive it. Certainly as far as the Hatton round is concerned, you can get a hinge flying round the inside of a room, and if you're going to fire CS gas, there's a good chance the people inside are going to panic and start trying to fight their way out, and they could be injured as they're coming out through the doors and windows. So, the only time you use this stuff is when *not* using it would have far, far worse results. If you've got someone who has taken hostages, and you've got people who are about to be killed, then they will happily accept getting a few cuts and bruises, because it's an alternative to dying.'

And, always, firearms officers will shoot as a last resort. 'We only shoot if it's necessary,' said Inspector Andy Latto. 'We would rather talk and arrest them quietly than shoot. That's why in this country we have very few shootings and why we have very few in this department. We deal with many operations, but we only fire a small number of shots.'

The seriousness of taking a human life weighs as

heavily on Latto as on anyone. But it does not interfere with his capacity to do his job.

'I want to do this job. I applied to come into the department and perform this role. I have a family, and if my life's in danger and my family would suffer, then it's not something I should think about too deeply. I'm here to do a job, and if I have to shoot someone to do that job properly, then I will do it. After the shooting I may decide that I never want to do the job again; I'll never know until that occasion arises. If it's a justified incident, though, and I've taken action that is correct, then I'm sure I'd be able to live with it.'

SO20

Forensic Medical Examiners Branch

Approximately 110 doctors work for the Metropolitan Police as Forensic Medical Examiners (FMEs); they are better known to the public as police surgeons. SO20 was formed in March 1993 to administer the Forensic Medical Examiners Service when it was discovered that some FMEs were making huge sums of money from the police.

FMEs are organised into groups of between two and ten. Each group is at the service of a number of divisional police stations. A senior FME is paid a retainer of £2,030 a year, while the annual retainer for an ordinary FME is £400; once a diploma in jurisprudence has been obtained, an FME's retainer is increased by £690 a year.

'Then there is a fee for a call-out,' said Ken Pratley, SEO (Senior Executive Officer) of SO20. 'It does depend on what they do when they're called out, but the day rate is around £35, and the night rate is £53.70.'

'The name Forensic Medical Examiner was chosen so that they are shown *not* to be members of the police service,' said Pratley. 'They are independent medical people called in to do a job. They're not our employees – there's an ethical issue there.'

The work of FMEs is limited. They can be called to the scene of a death, and are required to certify that death has occurred. But that is all. After that the forensic scientific teams take over. In cases of assault, rape, or child abuse their work is also peripheral and amounts to little more than a certification of injuries: specialists (e.g. gynaecologists) would be brought in to examine the deeper forensic implications of such cases.

In the case of a person detained at a police station showing signs of injury or illness, an FME would be expected to administer whatever medical help was needed and generally to treat the prisoner as any GP would with a patient. The FME's medical advice is also sought and acted upon if a detained person needs, or says he needs medication.

'The Forensic Medical Examiners Service is not giving us the value for money that we and the public deserve. I think it cost us something like 5.2 million pounds in 1991/1992, which makes it a very expensive resource,' Pratley said.

'The current method of working has been in vogue since 1982, and we think it's time for change and improvement. We want to open the FME Service up to market forces through competitive tendering. The doctors don't like the idea of competitive tendering . . .'

At present an FME's contract runs until he is sixty, with two years' notice to be given of the termination of the contract.

'Now there are a number of proposals,' said Pratley. 'One is a short-term contract, another is sessionally-based fees, instead of a per-item-of-work fee, so you would have a doctor sign on for an eight-hour shift, and he or she would be with us for that period, and would do anything that's needed within their area during that period. They would do their paperwork, and their statements, and they would be at our beck and call.'

Pratley's job, stated broadly, is threefold: to identify problems within the existing FME Service, to decide what can be done to make improvements, and to organise the improvements. Resistance from doctors is inevitable. They have been used to certain patterns and procedures for many years.

'The earnings some of them make from us are extremely high,' Pratley said. 'There's the possibility that those earnings will be reduced. We're not looking to cut the cost of the service, we want to improve the value we get.'

He quoted an example of a doctor being called at 3.30 in the afternoon and not turning up until 8 o'clock at night.

'Now I find that unacceptable. The police won't call the doctor unless they think there is a need, and the doctor is contracted to provide us with a service.'

Fees paid to individual FMEs during the period 1991/1992 varied between £2,000 and £140,000.

'The doctors and the forensic side were a sacred cow that had never been looked at before,' said Pratley. 'But with the initiatives the last Commissioner introduced, that has all changed.'

TERRITORIAL OPERATIONS
Introduction

Territorial Operations (TO) is mainly concerned with support to the Areas, and the formulation of policy. Much of the support is physical: for example, TO are responsible for training horses, dogs, and dog handlers.

Terry Siggs is Deputy Assistant Commissioner, Territorial Operations. 'I've been all over,' he said. 'I was at Brixton as a Superintendent, in the East End as a Chief Superintendent, and I've dealt with National Front problems and industrial problems with the building of the Thames Barrier. I've been Commander in West London, I lived through the 1981 riots as a Commander in Southall. Later I was DAC of West London with the old One Area, which went from Chelsea up to Kingston and the airport.'

Referring to his present job, Siggs continued, 'Air Support, of course, that's got to be central because of the cost and obviously it would be impossible for each Area to have an Air Support Unit, so we've got that. We've got Thames Division which serves the majority of our Divisions and Areas. We've got many units like that where we're in support of Area and Division, but they're not big enough or don't lend themselves to go into Area totally, and they are the things which I'm sure will stay very much in the centre when restructuring is complete.'

In outlining the function of TO, Siggs cleared up a question which has puzzled many people – why does a uniformed Constable or Sergeant attached to Scotland Yard bear the letters CO on his shoulders? It stems from 'Commissioner's Office', Siggs explained; at one time, all branches working from headquarters were designated CO.

Siggs insists that, in spite of suggestions to the contrary, the relationship between the TO administration at Scotland Yard and the eight Areas is not particularly strained.

'It would be very foolish to say that any of us have had a smooth ride, in that we agree with everything that's going on,' he said. 'But over the years, what is done by TO headquarters is done virtually in agreement with Areas. Things are organised centrally, which would be very difficult on an Area without assistance. In public order, for example, it is very difficult to gauge the manpower requirements, the intelligence, the logistics. For someone like Eight Area, where they've got constant pressure on them for demonstrations and operations of various kinds, involving sometimes thousands of officers, they are quite able to get up and do it themselves. But others are not. Now centrally in TO20 they are involved in every operation, they know how to set up an operation, so Areas without the expertise can turn to TO20 for support.'

'Because of a very wide span of control and difficulty, obviously Bill Taylor, the Assistant Commissioner who now has responsibility for Territorial Operations, has got to rely greatly on the eight Area DACs and myself, because on top of TO concerns he has got some of the most difficult situations in SO, with anti-terrorism and Special Branch activity, firearms – I mean, there are so many difficult areas of policing that he's dealing with.'

That, however, will not always be the case.

'As devolvement takes place over the next couple of

years,' Siggs said, 'Mr Taylor's responsibilities will diminish. We will have the new Areas, probably five in number, with control being very much in the hands of the Area Assistant Commissioners, or whatever they might be called.'

TO1

General Department Services and HQ Support

Apart from organising the Police Stations and Married Quarters Gardens Competition, TO1 has several less charming responsibilities. They fall under the headings of Manpower Control, Divisional Office Functions for HQ staff, Rambling Letters and HQ Liaison. The person managing those categories and many others is Mrs Beryl Reeves, who is Director, Support and Administration, Territorial Operations.

'The job involves looking after all the administrative and support policy in the whole of Territorial Operations (TO) – that's headquarters, areas, and divisions. It means providing services and standard procedures the department requires, so that it can achieve its objectives.'

Mrs Reeves's responsibilities cover departments TO1 to TO7 and she has direct management of approximately 430 people. The fundamental purpose of TO1, she explained, is to lay on support services for TO headquarters, which includes jobs like organising the pay of headquarters officers. 'It's making sure that the police get paid the right amount, that if they're sick it gets notified to Personnel – that sort of admin function.'

As for administering the Police Gardens Competition, Mrs Reeves said it is not really a part of TO's strategic function, but the job is fitted in anyway, and has been since 1986. The annual competition is held under the auspices of the London Gardens Society and has the stated aim of 'stimulating pride in London, more especially by the cultivation of flowers and home gardens'. As an unsought bonus, the Queen Mother has been known to tour winning stations during the summer months.

They also take responsibility for correspondence reaching Scotland Yard that cannot immediately be assigned to any particular person or department. This is the category called Rambling Letters.

'Many are from people who are slightly nutty,' said Mrs Reeves. 'For example, people write in saying that they think they're being threatened by electricity directed at them by their next door neighbour, or by the Duke of Edinburgh.'

SO1 receive between six hundred and seven hundred of these letters every year. Those not of a specific nature are noted in the General Registry file and then disposed of in the confidential waste. Letters touching on local matters, e.g., traffic noise, vandalism, or perhaps containing useful information, are sent to the appropriate divisions or provincial constabularies.

Some letters contain money to 'help' the police. The donations are returned by recorded delivery or, if there is no return address, the money is accumulated until it reaches £5, and is then sent to F1 with a covering memo 'For credit to MPS Fund as miscellaneous receipts'.

'Tear-ups' are letters from people with a lot to say, but none of it of any use. Other mail falls within the boundaries of mischief, delusion, or serious mental disturbance, such as the letters from people who believe they are being followed by the Special Branch or MI5. Others report seeing aliens, and there have been complaints from men and women who suspect they are being turned into other people. One recent letter was

from a man convinced he was being victimised, and he
had a shrewd idea why:

> . . . I can only assume this is a concerted effort by
> certain traffic wardens to punish me, all because I
> refuse to have sex with them, male or female. Well,
> you won't get a sausage out of me, duckie, so
> there . . .

'It's not only letters,' said Mrs Reeves, 'it's all sorts of
strange things – parcels, packages, some of them containing very dubious items which I wouldn't like to go into.
We don't think we should have that function, but Registry think that it's not theirs, so we're stuck with it.'

At a more productive level, it is one of TOI's HQ-
support functions to compile and send forward the Territorial Operations section of the Commissioner's Annual
Report.

'In short,' said Mrs Reeves, trying for an overview of
TOI's purpose, 'the department deals with anything
that Territorial Operations headquarters needs to keep
functioning in terms of administration.'

Market testing is now being applied to the Metropolitan Police and the work has fallen to TOI. The concept
is that the police should analyse their functions and
decide which of them must continue to be performed by
the police, and which could be delegated elsewhere.

'Then we test the market,' said Mrs Reeves, 'and see
whether there is someone out there who could do it for
us, better and more cheaply.'

The second wing of TOI, the Planning Unit, provides
a service to the Assistant Commissioner Territorial Operations (ACTO). He often needs statistical data, or
progress reports, and it is the job of the TO Planning
Unit (TOPU) to provide what he needs. TOPU also
liaise with their counterparts on area – the Area Planning

Units – to ensure they are all working in the same strategic direction, and to make sure that the work of planning proceeds in a coordinated fashion right across TO. This involves TOPU in drawing up departmental guidelines on how planning should be managed, and on how to report performance every year as an annual appraisal exercise.

TO3
Area Support

An Area Deputy Assistant Commissioner (DAC) has a lot of power, certainly enough to allow him a flexible approach to his job. In the increasingly business-attuned structure of the Metropolitan Police, however, certain corporate duties give him less latitude. It is the function of TO3, Area Support, to help the DAC carry out these corporate duties. Mrs Beryl Reeves gave a typical example, first of all explaining the roles of the people involved.

'Every area has a DAC, and every DAC has a Senior Executive Officer (SEO) to help him with his administrative responsibilities – if you like, the SEO is the equivalent of me in TO headquarters, but at a lower level. So, whereas I'm responsible for all admin and support for the whole of TO, an SEO on an area is responsible for the admin and support on the whole of that area. As head of TO3 I meet regularly with the SEOs to advise them on the latest corporate policy and corporate directions, and I seek their views where there's discretion allowed to put forward a corporate case on any particular issue.'

She also provides SEOs with individual support. If, for example, they need a computer and they have difficulty getting the model they want through the Provisioning Department, they can approach TO3, who will try to help. TO3 will put forward finance bids for almost any essential resource.

'Every area needs vehicles,' said Mrs Reeves. 'Information technology, too, and communications to survive and do its job. I examine all their requirements, find out how urgent their need is, determine if it is absolutely essential. And then I put together the whole of TO's resource needs in the form of a bid for money.'

TO3 has an Inspectorate Department, which periodically inspects, either on a rolling programme or by request, a particular function of a division or of an area. After the inspection they produce a report. It is Mrs Reeves's job, especially on support proposals, to make sure the recommendations of the report are carried out. She is aware that there has been resentment at divisional level about the amount of authority wielded from the centre of the organisational structure.

'Resentment exists,' she said, 'but it's gradually diminishing and I believe the continuum we started of devolving power and authority will, as it progresses, dissipate any resentment.'

The continuum Mrs Reeves referred to began in 1985, with a reorganisation within the Metropolitan Police to devolve responsibility from the centre. 'That was the first push towards decentralising the power,' she added. 'Everything we're doing now is moving along that continuum. There are lots of culture changes and re-education required to achieve full effectiveness. There are people who can't accept that the centre still isn't in control.'

As the running of the Service takes on more of a business-orientated structure, personnel at all levels are having to confront new challenges. Powers of budgeting, cost control, resource control and resource management are being devolved to them.

'We are a business just the same as anywhere else,' said Mrs Reeves. 'Our rules might be different, we don't make a profit in the same sense that a commercial company does, but there is no doubt that we are now being governed much more by economic factors. We have to run ourselves on cost-effective lines. We have to ask ourselves, "if this was a company would we be out of business by now if we carried on working like this?" And if the answer to that is yes, then there's something wrong.'

She is committed to the belief that management skills, as developed in worldwide industry and commerce, have a powerful and defining role to play at all levels in the future of the Metropolitan Police.

'In future,' she said, 'the bobby on the beat will have to recognise that if he wants to be more than a police constable, he's got to acquire management skills.'

TO4

Public Carriage Office

The Deputy Assistant Commissioner Territorial Operations (DACTO) is the licensing authority for all taxi cabs and licensed taxi drivers in London. On his behalf the Public Carriage Office issues licences to both the cabs and their drivers.

The Public Carriage Office is in Penton Street in North London. Once a year a taxi owner must take his cab there for inspection and for renewal of the cab licence, which is the familiar 'Hackney Carriage' identifying plate on the back of the vehicle. The inspection is tough and if a cab fails, the licence is withheld until the shortcomings are put right and the cab is presented again for inspection. The 'knowledge of London' examination for prospective taxi drivers is also supervised by staff of the Public Carriage Office.

When a person applies to become a licensed taxi driver he has to submit to a series of tests, among them a thorough medical examination and a CRO (Computer [formerly Criminal] Records Office) check to make sure he is not a criminal.

Sometimes the granting or withholding of a licence is a matter of judgement: a person may have a criminal record but there can be certain mitigating circumstances. The sole criterion is how likely it seems, or not, that the person will be a danger to the public or to his passengers.

Assuming he is permitted, the applicant then embarks

on the time-honoured process of acquiring 'the knowledge'. He gets what is known as a book of runs, which is a compendium of standard point-to-point journeys across London, and from that – and from actual experience of travelling the routes – he has to learn by heart all the major routes and runs of London. During this time his progress will be checked periodically, and eventually he will move on to the full knowledge-of-London examination. Some applicants pass after only a year, others take as long as three years.

When he has passed the knowledge exam, the applicant is given a driving test to make sure he can actually drive a London taxi cab. After that, he is allowed to take to the road as a fully-fledged licensed driver.

The licence is renewable every three years. When it comes up for renewal another CRO check is carried out. If the driver's record is clean, and if there have been no complaints about him from the public – or not too many – the licence is renewed for a further three years.

Mrs Reeves conducts hearings on behalf of DACTO in cases where taxi drivers appeal against their licences being suspended or revoked.

'I conduct the hearings then give DACTO a report and make a recommendation, and then he makes a decision.'

A driver could have his licence revoked because of rudeness, but not for an isolated instance. At the Public Carriage Office a record is kept of all taxi drivers and any existing complaints or judgements against them, and if a pattern begins to develop it shows up clearly. There is a system of warnings before a decision is taken to suspend or revoke a licence, and if, after being warned, a driver continues to offend, the appropriate action is taken. On average, sixty drivers a year go before the personal hearing, and of those no more than a dozen will eventually appeal.

To some people it seems odd that the Metropolitan Police still administer the inspection and licensing of taxi drivers and their cabs. Mrs Reeves believes it is a traditional relationship which should continue, if the high standards of the London taxi service are to be maintained. She added that she believes the current system of licensing and general administration suits everyone concerned.

'Taxi drivers by nature always moan, but if asked if they would like to move away from the Metropolitan Police as the controlling body, I think the majority of them would say no, they would not.'

TO5

Central Ticket Office

After the police take away a car for illegal parking, or when it has been wheel-clamped, or after a parking ticket has been issued, the Central Ticket Office (CTO) attends to the enforcement of the penalty and any follow-up action.

The greater part of the work is done by computer. If a ticket remains unpaid, automatic fine-enforcement follows and automatic registration at a Magistrates' Court, at which point it becomes the responsibility of the court to follow through and collect payment. Mrs Reeves reeled off the consequences of letting a parking fine ride too long.

'Once a ticket reaches the stage of a fine enforcement, it doubles in penalty value. And if the court needs a bailiff to go out and serve a warrant, you also get bailiff costs on top. That's the straightforward issue of a parking ticket. The main function the staff of the CTO are involved in is dealing with exceptional stuff.'

People write in to say that the removal of a car or the issue of a ticket was unfair, or unjust, or illegal; they might on the other hand admit they have committed a breach which invited the issuing of a ticket, but there were mitigating circumstances. Others are highly imaginative – one man wrote admitting that his car was parked on a restricted bus stop, but there were extenuating circumstances:

I am a paranoid schizophrenic and currently under the impression that I am a bus. I am being treated for this disorder and would appreciate you looking sympathetically at my case. I would appreciate a prompt reply to my letter as I am running late. Please reply to the above address with a copy to the Inspector at Finchley Bus Depot.

Another man was annoyed that his obviously incapacitated car had been ticketed, and issued a plea from the heart:

With a name like Levy, you may correctly assume that I am of the Jewish persuasion, i.e. 'one of the chosen people.' Do you think it is possible, just for once, you could do me a favour and choose somebody else?

Around two million parking tickets are issued in the London area annually, and the number is growing. So are the complaints. CTO handles 340,000 letters a year.

'Ticketing, clamping and removal may seem very routine functions,' said Mrs Reeves, 'but they have the potential to generate more heat and anger in the general public than most other areas of police activity. The general reaction of a lot of people is, "Why are you doing this to me? Why aren't you spending your resources catching criminals?" The public generally, I think, feel that this routine traffic enforcement is not something the police ought to be involved in any more.'

The Road Traffic Act 1991 ushered in legislation which effects a transfer of responsibility from the police to the local authorities in London, covering the whole range of permitted parking, including parking meters and residence bays. In due course local authorities will be able to apply to the Department of Transport for permission to create what are known as special parking areas, SPAs for short. Within each of these, if agreed and accepted, a local authority can perform every enforcement function, including yellow-line regulations as well as those governing the parking place. When that legislation comes to full fruition, the only stationary-vehicle parking enforcement remaining to the police will be on Red Routes and certain other priority routes.

'So gradually the work of the CTO will diminish,' said Mrs Reeves. 'Also diminishing will be the number of removals and clampings we undertake, because part of the transfer of power for enforcement includes the power to clamp and remove vehicles, and that will also pass to the local authorities.'

The Road Traffic Act has in effect decriminalised most of the parking offences. Under the old system traffic offences were covered by criminal law, which is why cases were dealt with through the magistrates' courts.

'De-criminalisation not only means that local authorities can contract out certain of the functions and do it via agents,' Mrs Reeves said, 'they can also keep the money that accrues, which we could never do.'

TO6
Central Services

Anybody who wants to buy or otherwise obtain a gun covered by Section 1 of the Firearms Act must have a certificate granted by a chief officer of police. That is the law, and in London the Commissioner of Police decides whether a person is eligible to have a gun. The department at Scotland Yard called Central Services (TO6) acts on behalf of the Commissioner in deciding who should be granted a firearms certificate.

'It sounds a very simple process,' said Mrs Reeves, 'but it's very complicated. The troubles arise from the classifications of guns. They fall into categories and you have to know what these categories are. I mean, when is a shotgun not a shotgun? When is it a firearm? And when is it a prohibited firearm, the kind which a Home Office decree says no one can possess in this country? There is also a lot of politics attached to this, because there are many shooters' rights associations, who tend to have the perception that the police are oppressive towards their members. And of course there's the Hungerford affair, which changed the rules.'

In August 1987 Michael Ryan, a holder of a firearms certificate and member of a gun club, went on a shooting spree in Hungerford, Berkshire, killing sixteen people (including his mother) and wounding fourteen others before he shot and killed himself. Following the incident, checks on existing shotgun owners became much more stringent and the vetting process for prospective owners was tightened.

'What we have to ensure is that the weapons are, as far as we can be certain, not likely to become a danger to the public safety or the peace.'

Although the personnel of TO6 are civilians, the work of investigating applicants' backgrounds and evaluating the security of their premises is done by police officers at divisional station level. TO6 sets the policy and procedures, and the police work in accordance with that.

At present, the majority of applications for firearms certificates go through without any difficulty, but some applicants are clearly not suited to hold firearms certificates, like the man who was found to have an animal pen in his living room with a large dog inside; the rest of his home was rigged out like a fortress. Other certification problems concern young children because, surprisingly, there is no lower age limit for the possession of a firearm.

'We go through a certain process,' Mrs Reeves explained. 'We check with the boy himself whether he's responsible enough to handle a gun, that he will always be with one of his parents when he uses it, that his parents are giving him good guidance. We try to take every possible precaution and be absolutely sure that this is a sensible person.'

Applications have been received from people as young as nine. Below that age TO6 are not inclined to give an application serious consideration. In the event of anyone, child or adult, getting a firearms certificate then going out and doing something terrible with a gun, TO6 and the police would have to submit to an inquiry. The same would apply if guns were stolen from premises that had been declared safe for the storage of firearms.

Firearms and Shotgun Certificates: Statistics for a Recent Year

Firearms Certificates

New certificates granted	746
Refusals of new applications	11
Certificates renewed	2,432
Refusals to renew	16
Variations	1,895
Certificates revoked	17
Certificates cancelled	886

Shotgun Certificates

New certificates granted	3,572
Refusals of new applications	48
Certificates renewed	9,485
Refusals to renew	54
Certificates revoked	41
Certificates cancelled	1,612

'That's why we're careful about perimeter security and the security of the cabinets where guns have to be kept,' said Mrs Reeves. 'But there's a point beyond which you can't go. If at the time someone is asking for a certificate you visit his premises and things look OK, then fine. But you don't know after that. I mean, in some cases people leave their shotguns in the back of their cars overnight, and cars get stolen, or broken into. A police authority can't be held responsible for that. So then we have to ask the question – is he a fit person to continue holding a licence?'

ARMOURY

The armoury is a small room, roughly fourteen by fourteen feet, tucked away in the depths of Scotland Yard and protected by a high-security door. Hundreds of weapons of every kind are stacked around the room, together with cases of ammunition in an extensive range of calibres.

'This is the central armoury for all the handguns, shotguns, rifles and everything else in the firearms line, even air weapons, which are handed in, found, or confiscated within the Metropolitan Police District,' said Charles Bayer, the Force Armourer and Explosives Liaison Officer. Bayer is a weapons enthusiast, who in 1992 gave up his job in the National Westminster Bank so that he could indulge his love of firearms.

'These all come to me when they're finished with at police stations, when perhaps a case is over, or the owner has handed them in and has signed a disclaimer renouncing any rights to them. They come to me and I deal with them as part of my daily routine.'

A delivery of weapons awaits Bayer when he turns up for work at 8.30 every morning. He sorts through the weapons, making sure they are all unloaded, then he enters their details into a firearms register; there is a similar register for ammunition. 'Then I decide what to do with them.'

Of all the weapons received at the Armoury, 85 per cent will be destroyed. They will be either cheap current production air weapons, or blank-firing handguns, the two groups that form the bulk of the weapons received.

'The other 15 per cent is made up of what I call the good stuff,' said Bayer, who maintains a collection of approximately 300 weapons within the armoury. 'It may be historic firearms like single-action Army Colts, or any number of other fine firearms, or maybe not even so fine, but still worth holding because of their historical value.'

Good, usable firearms are often passed on to operational units such as SO19 (Force Firearms Unit), or one of the Metropolitan Police shooting sections. When weapons wear out, Bayer is often in a position to replace them.

'This room is one of the better kept secrets of Scotland Yard,' he said, 'and what I have here, I like to regard as an instructional selection; it contains one of almost every type of weapon, from air pistols up to hunting rifles, shotguns – full-length and sawn-off – semi-automatic handguns, revolvers, blank-firing pistols, a bit of everything. Firearms inquiry officers or firearms inspectors who are working with firearms out on Division can come up here and have a look around, see what it's all about, let me familiarise them with different types of weapons and dispel a lot of the old myths.'

The turnover in the little armoury is impressive. CS gas canisters, legal throughout Europe and in the USA but not in the UK, are regularly confiscated from passengers arriving at Heathrow Airport; Bayer receives them in bags of 300 at a time. During the first four months of 1993, excluding the CS canisters, he received approximately 1,000 weapons for processing.

Going back to the 15 per cent of weapons which are not destroyed, Bayer said that good target weapons, such as .22 target rifles, revolvers in .38, .357 and .22 calibre, and self-loading target pistols of .22 calibre, will be offered to one of the Metropolitan Police shooting clubs, but by far the largest proportion of the retained weapons will go to museums. In that category Bayer said, 'and to possess one you need to have a special condition written into your shotgun or firearms certificate, because they are classed as firearms disguised as other objects. Some date from the turn of the century, others are much more modern.'

A prized possession in the armoury's collection is a hunting rifle, made by one of the top European custom gunmakers, Auguste Francot of Liège, Belgium. It is worth between £4,000 and £5,000. It was constructed and engraved by hand, and is on a par with anything made by the top London gunmakers.

'We got it through Heathrow Airport,' Bayer said. 'Somebody was trying to bring it into the country without the correct documentation. It was seized by Customs and the owner subsequently never recovered it, so after three months it came to us. We will keep it here for a time, then it may well go to the Tower of London sporting gun collection.'

Late in 1992 a gun was brought to the armoury which Bayer identified as a Holland and Holland Royal, number one of a pair, and one of the finest English shotguns ever made. It was listed at Holland and Holland's as having been stolen. The ultimate possessor of the gun, before the police got hold of it, had chopped off the barrels and used the gun to hold up a building society, getting away with approximately £800. The irony was that, in order to get his modest haul from the building society, the thief had effectively ruined a weapon worth anywhere between £5,000 and £7,000.

TO7
Divisional Support

Any charity organisation wishing to collect money on the streets of London has to be vetted by TO7, Divisional Support. Similarly, when a pub landlord wants a special extension to the hours when he can sell alcohol, his application will be considered under criteria established by TO7. This branch has a duty to make sure that traffic processes and procedures are standard across the whole of the Metropolitan Police District.

'I do have staff in TO7, but only a very small number,' said Mrs Reeves. 'The way we control this process is by what's known as an operating manual. It's a Bible, if you like, on how to follow the procedures, and we make sure it's kept up to date and issued as guidance to staff in the police stations.'

TO7 regulates the number of public collections made in London by charities. An effort is made to keep the numbers of flag days and other collections within reasonable bounds, at the same time making sure the allocations remain fair to the organisations concerned.

'The number of people who want to collect for charities exceeds the number of days available in the year,' said Mrs Reeves. 'We have an annual list drawn up of all the people who have been granted approval to make public collections of whatever kind – that includes house-to-house collections. And it's statutory that we make sure of the *bona fides* of the people who want to

collect. We make criminal record checks to be sure –
again, that's all required by legislation.'

A check is also made on the charities' accounts, since
there are ground rules which say that only a certain
proportion of the money collected can be devoted to
running costs.

'We do like to see that most of the money collected
actually does go to the charity and isn't absorbed in so-
called administration.'

TO9
Crime and Divisional Policing Policy Branch

'We do not stick policy down the divisional officer's throat,' said Detective Chief Superintendent Chris Flint, Head of TO9. 'We formulate policy based on the Commissioner's corporate strategy.'

TO9 handle policy on jury vetting, on the organisation and staffing of Child Protection Teams, on staff levels in detective offices and on the procedures between coroners and police during murder investigations; they organise liaison with the Sexual Offences Steering Committee, and guidelines on asset confiscation. TO9 is a classic 'head office' department.

There are three desks: Support, Operations, and Criminal Justice. There is also a small section called Research, which examines new legislation going through Parliament and anticipates the resource implications if the legislation is put into effect.

Inspector Ken Forward runs the Support Desk. He looks into all policy on drink-drive legislation and is a member of a number of related committees. If there are changes to legislation, or additions, he will put them into notices for the information of the divisions, areas and headquarters units.

Under the heading of Police Buildings and Vehicles, Inspector Forward is a link between the Met's Property Services Department and groups (or individual officers) needing premises for anything ranging from section policing to accommodation for Child Protection Teams.

'It's like that with vehicles, too,' said Chris Flint. 'There is actually one agency, TO9, rather than all eight areas, dealing with matters arising between the people needing vehicles and our Transport Department.'

Detective Inspector Andy Claiden and Detective Sergeant Jamie Chaplin, also on the Support Desk, are responsible for a group of functions under the headings CSG, CRIS, CIPP, and Crime Administration.

CSG stands for Crime Support Group. Each division has one: they are made up entirely of civilians who process all case papers relating to crime arrests. CSGs work in accordance with a guidance manual, and it is the duty of Andy Claiden and Jamie Chaplin to keep the manual updated.

CRIS is the Crime Reporting Information System which at the time of its installation, several years ago, was seen as a breakthrough in the processing of criminal records.

'But there are computing problems,' Claiden said, 'and it might be another two or three years before it comes on line. Our function up here is to link in with the implementation team to see how we can progress this. But,' he added, 'there's a lot of doubt that we'll ever see it operating as it should.'

CIPP is the Criminal Investigation Priority Project, set up in the late 1980s to examine the way crime is investigated in the Metropolitan Police. The Project team, headed by Commander George Ness, produced roughly 170 recommendations which said, in summary, that crime investigations should be based on the model of detectives in small teams, operating under a Detective Sergeant, all with specific roles – 'Really,' Chris Flint said, 'to provide a more structured approach to young detectives in how they go about their work. That system is in place, and, to all intents and purposes, it has made a radical overhaul, for the better, of crime investigations.'

In the category called Crime Administration, Andy Claiden and Jamie Chaplin set up regular six-weekly meetings of senior Area Detective Chief Superintendents. The meetings provide an opportunity for the eight men – one from each area – to discuss points of policy and other operational topics in a central forum.

On the Operations Desk, Detective Inspector Eric Bowker and Detective Sergeant John Ashton take responsibility for Child Protection Teams. Each area has one of these teams and in some instances there are two. Each team consists of a group of police officers who, under the leadership of a Detective Inspector, deal with all allegations of child abuse in their area. All the officers – male and female, detectives and uniformed – are experienced in this field of work. Under the terms of the 'Working Together' scheme which was created following the Cleveland child-abuse cases, the Child Protection Teams maintain contact and cooperation with Social Services and other agencies involved in the cases they handle.

A Home Office initiative, echoing sections of the Mental Health Act, has intimated that mentally disordered offenders should not necessarily be treated as criminals. Two members of the Operations Desk team, Inspector Chris Smith and Sergeant Paul Etheridge (a former mental nurse), are looking at possible ways of directing mentally compromised offenders away from the criminal courts.

One effective measure is already working at Horseferry Road Magistrates' Court, where duty psychiatrists have been appointed. An accused person showing signs of disturbance or mental impairment can be interviewed by the court psychiatrist who will then make a recommendation as to disposal – that is, whether the case should go through the court as normal, or whether the court should be bypassed and the patient referred to care.

Major Crime Policy is an imposing category of Operations Desk work which is dealt with by Detective Inspector Steve James. 'Robbery, sexual offences, asset confiscation, the review of falling arrest rates, the compilation of arrest figures and the like, they would all come under his wing,' said Chris Flint.

A big concern of the Met, and the Operations Desk in particular, is the rise in Band Two robberies – the kind committed in off-licences, garage forecourts and the smaller shops. (Band Three robberies are street-level robberies, Band One are the highly-organised kind dealt with by Flying Squad.) Steve James's role is to examine operational tactics in relation to the robberies, to home-in on particular weaknesses and advise local officers.

Liaison with the Crown Prosecution Service (CPS) is a duty of TO9's Criminal Justice Desk. The liaison is actually with the chief Crown Prosecutors of London, and Detective Inspector Mike Rutter is the link between them and the Metropolitan Police. In recent times, relations between the Met and the CPS have not been good. 'I think we've acknowledged that,' said Chris Flint. 'You know, if they build up a rapport things go quite well. This doesn't always happen, but I think things are getting better.'

That is just as well, because operational officers will now be obliged to talk to the CPS a lot more than before, both at the early preparation stages of cases, and later to reveal what evidence they have. This is because of the troubled matter of Disclosure, the procedure whereby any fact or any matter which may have a bearing on a criminal case must be revealed by the police to the CPS, who will then decide whether or not to disclose it to the defence.

'I think we are going to be dropping out of a lot of cases where there is even the slightest risk of exposing our informants,' Chris Flint said. 'Until we get some leads from the Court of Appeal on how we are expected to work within these rules in respect of informants, then we will probably take the safe way out – maybe the better way out.'

PACE, originally introduced in 1984, required the Home Secretary to issue Parliament-approved codes of practice to give stronger safeguards to suspects and workable guidelines for the police. Several codes of practice were issued; a number of them were withdrawn, amended, and then reissued. PACE, by any determination, is difficult to understand.

'People are still getting muddled with it,' said Chris Flint. 'hence the helpline we operate.'

Inspector Brian Roberts has devised a computerised help service which permits an officer on division to tap in questions about particular aspects of PACE (e.g. if a prisoner has been in custody for three hours, should he then be given a meal?); the computer will either give him a direct answer, or it will interrogate him first until any ambiguity is eliminated from his question. There is also telephone help, and TO9 maintains and updates manuals aimed at clarifying the Act.

The Crack Unit came into existence in 1989. At that time the unit consisted of twelve or thirteen officers who, although not established as a main unit, had a specific role in gathering and evaluating intelligence about crack (officially called crack-cocaine, a purified and highly addictive form of cocaine). For a time the unit functioned extremely well.

'After about three years,' said Chris Flint, 'the question was raised, do we need to have the unit in its present form, or should it operate more in conjunction with area drug squads?'

Each of the eight areas has its own drug squad – one Detective Inspector and twelve Detective Constables. They deal with the whole spectrum of drug trafficking on their area, so the suggestion was made that the Crack Unit officers be involved with the drug squads and add their measure to the range of expertise already there. It was decided that the suggestion should be implemented, and on 1 April 1993 the eight officers who by then made up the Crack Unit were dispersed, one to each of the eight areas.

Crack seizures are on the increase, and DCS Flint is not sure that the police can answer the mounting need for assistance, especially in inner-city communities, now that the Crack Unit is gone.

Crimestoppers is a small group headed by a Detective Inspector, a Detective Sergeant and three Detective Constables, with a civilian support staff. Using a dialling code and telephone number which are the same from any part of Britain, they provide a service where people can call in with any information they have about crime, criminals or criminal activity; the callers' anonymity is preserved, and the telephone is answered by someone who knows precisely how to take information over the telephone.

The effectiveness of the scheme is illustrated by a case in Battersea. A young man walking home in the early evening was attacked and hit over the head with a baseball bat. He later died of his injuries. There were no apparent witnesses, and for a time it was thought the victim might have caused the injuries himself by falling over. An appeal for witnesses was broadcast and shortly afterwards a woman called the Crimestoppers number.

She said she had seen everything and described the people involved. They were identified, and in due course a man appeared at the Old Bailey and was convicted of the murder.

Finally, Flint talked of a strange anomaly in a police service that is trying hard to prepare for the twenty-first century.

'At present we are being asked by the CPS to supply a record of taped interviews with suspects, a very brief summary of the salient points. This is incredibly time consuming, and research has shown that it is not very efficient or effective. It takes ten minutes to write out one minute of interview time.'

Incredibly, in 1993, detectives are expected to transcribe interviews themselves, by hand.

'We could go for playing of the tape in the court,' said Chris Flint. 'But the judiciary say that's impractical because there will be statements by the accused which need to be edited out . . . Now there are people saying, look, far better if police officers do a full transcript of the tape-recorded interview – in other words, hand the tape over to a typist.'

That arrangement would certainly release officers to do the work they are trained for, but senior officers see a snag: the resource implications, they say, are considerable. In other words, it would cost a lot of money to hire enough extra typists to make the transcripts.

TO10
Courts Division

If a person living in London fails to pay a fine on time and someone turns up at his door demanding payment on pain of imprisonment, the visitor is probably an Enforcement Officer attached to TO10.

Every year the department's staff make approximately 50,000 arrests of citizens for non-payment of fines, and they collect about £2.5 million from those who do pay when pressed. Warrant enforcement is a secondary function for the police officers of TO10 and is increasingly being done by the 203 civil staff. The main job of the 368 Constables, 108 Sergeants and 203 civil staff of various grades attached to fifty Magistrates' Courts and eleven Crown Courts is to control and manage prisoners who have been arrested at police stations and have to make court appearances.

Court duty officers take charge of prisoners when they arrive, and remain in charge of them throughout the time they remain in court. The officers make sure prisoners go into the dock when they should and take all reasonable measures to make sure they don't escape. If the accused is remanded in custody, the duty officers take him to the cells.

Chief Superintendent Alan Moss, the immediate Head of TO10, believes that the courts themselves should do the work of warrant-enforcement. 'If we can civilianise the function then there's no reason why the courts themselves shouldn't civilianise it. They already employ bailiffs to recover money from outstanding fines anyway.'

Although the security of a Magistrates' Court is a responsibility regularly taken on by the police, it is only a secondary reason for their presence in the court buildings. 'Our role is the custody of prisoners,' said Moss. 'That's the main reason why we have officers in the court in such numbers. There is an additional function of keeping the peace at court, which is something we manage because we are there.'

As more emphasis has been laid on putting police officers on to the streets, the numbers of officers in courtrooms has steadily diminished. Nowadays the courts have the discretion to hire their security officers from private organisations, and the police encourage them to do that.

The most serious emergencies they usually have to deal with, in terms of danger to the public, are prisoners escaping or trying to escape.

'There's about a dozen or so escapes each year,' said Mr Moss. 'Methods vary. Some prisoners vault over the dock, and occasionally it's a breakout from custody or the cells, or during the transfer of prisoners to and from prison vans.'

Extra manpower to deal with an average of twelve escapes a year would be seriously counter-productive. Instead of increasing the guard TO10 encourage good design in procedures for transferring prisoners from prison vans to courts. The newer courts have enclosed van bays which considerably improve security.

Police officers attached to TO10 are specially trained in the care and handling of prisoners, as well as being given a working knowledge of the technicalities of warrants, particularly fine-enforcement warrants. There is no specific training for unarmed combat, even though the officers will be expected to escort and supervise violent criminals. TO10 officers are never armed, although on occasions when potentially dangerous prisoners are being supervised security is tightened up, and officers of SO19 (Force Firearms Unit) may even be brought in.

No one is summarily assigned to court duty, all officers are volunteers. Typically the uniformed men and women of TO10 are approaching the end of their police careers, although there are some younger officers.

'There are advantages,' said Mr Moss. 'There's no night duty. The hours are settled. The courts rarely sit on a Sunday – and not too long on a Saturday, either.'

Of the high-security courts in London, Belmarsh is the most recent, with direct access to Belmarsh Prison through an underground tunnel. It is the first court in London to be built and designed with security in mind. The linking of facilities means the normally hazardous journey of top-security prisoners between venues is eliminated.

'The other initiative which has been pursued by the Home Office,' said Mr Moss, 'is the feasibility of conducting remand hearings by video-link, so that there is no need for the prisoner to be taken out of the prison at all. I'm not sure whether it will work a miracle or not,' he added, 'but it's being considered, and we hope that it will succeed.'

Eighty officers of TO10 are Coroners' Officers, and of that number approximately one third are civilians. A Coroner's Officer is appointed to help the coroner investigate deaths which might have been unnatural. On the Coroner's behalf, the officer collects evidence surrounding the circumstances of a death, interviewing relatives of the deceased, colleagues, doctors and other medical

Incidents Occurring at London Courts During a Recent One-Year Period

Escapes	9
Attempted Escapes	28
Assaults on Staff	24
Self-Inflicted Injuries	21
Damage to Property	8

personnel as necessary, and he will even deal with the arrangements for calling out an undertaker to remove the body. Throughout each enquiry a Coroner's Officer's first loyalty is to the Coroner.

PRISONER TRANSPORT SERVICE

This is the part of TO10 which transports custody prisoners from police stations to Magistrates' Courts. It is hazardous work and sometimes downright dangerous. In 1988 Ronald Easterbrook, sentenced at the Old Bailey to four life sentences for armed robbery and wounding, managed to smuggle Semtex explosive into the police van and attempted to blow his way out. In the event he was lucky not to die in the explosion. TO10 coped and the escape attempt failed.

When the Courts remand prisoners in custody or sentence them to imprisonment, it is TO10's further duty to deliver them to the local prison.

'Since before the war,' said Chief Superintendent Alan Moss, 'the Metropolitan Police have always transported numbers of prisoners in special buses which used to be called Black Marias. But now they're painted white. They hold fourteen prisoners at a time, and we've got a fleet of twenty-two.'

The vans are painted white to deflect sunlight and reduce the temperature inside – the roofs have been painted silver for the same reason. Now the Home Office requires that these vans, formerly known among prisoners as sweat-boxes, be air-conditioned. The compartments inside, each designed to accommodate just one prisoner, are tiny, and great care has been taken to control the temperature since a prisoner elsewhere in the country died from the heat.

'In the process of moving these prisoners around,' Moss said, 'and we move many thousands of them a year, we often pass the door of the prison. So for many years now the Metropolitan Police has undertaken the transport of prisoners from prisons to Magistrates' Courts, a job which would otherwise be done by prison staff, and we charge the Home Office sums of money for that service.'

TOIO also act as a holding and distribution centre for prisoners that the Prison Service should accommodate, but for one reason or another do not. 'At times this has involved us with well over a thousand prisoners,' Moss said, 'who have to be distributed to police stations within London and elsewhere. We've transported them as far away as Durham. It's a well-worn chestnut that the Prison Service got used to imposing this burden upon the police, which was resented by all other agencies.'

TOIO has a building at Lambeth where prisoners are transferred from prison van to prison van. 'Much as Victoria Coach Station operates as a transfer point, our equivalent is at Lambeth Holding Centre. We move prisoners from one van to another and the timing is absolutely critical.'

'To sum up the transportation of prisoners,' said Moss, 'taking them from a police station to a Magistrates'

Court is a police responsibility. From Magistrates'
Court to prison is also police. But from prison back to
Magistrates' Court is the responsibility of the Prison
Service.'

There are seventy officers in the Prison Transport
Service, the majority of them performing escort duties;
the van drivers are provided by the Chief Engineer's
Department. They undertake 150,000 prisoner movements every year, including women prisoners to and
from Holloway prison and the Magistrates' Courts.
Women travel in vans different from those used to
transport men: they are converted Leyland Sherpa buses
with bars on the windows. Detainees from Feltham
Young Offenders' Institute are also transported to Magistrates' Courts for normal remand hearings, and a few
other categories of juvenile transportation are carried
out on behalf of local authorities, which are charged a
fee for the service.

There are advance signs of TO10 being privatised.
Commander Clive Pearman, who is in overall command,
says the matter boils down to cost, and to getting the
quality of services provided by the police for much less
expenditure.

'The bottom line on this,' he said, 'is that you can run
something like the police service very much on a business footing, on a management footing . . . The question
is, do you get the right calibre of person if you pay a
certain salary?'

They have had experience of the problem at Scotland
Yard. The civilian grades are paid considerably less for
doing police work than they would get in, say, a computer bureau in the private sector. And if the jobs existed,
the civil administrative grades within the police service
would be paid more outside, too.

In releasing more police officers for the job of policing,

Pearman argues, there must be no sacrifice of a standard of service which tirelessly takes account of the rights of human beings.

TO14
Traffic

(1) ADMINISTRATION

Kevin Delaney is one of the bicyclists motorists curse as he cycles to and from work every day. In this case the motorists would be well advised to exercise restraint, as this cyclist runs the Traffic Department of the Metropolitan Police.

Chief Superintendent Delaney agrees that the functioning of TO14, viewed from a moderate distance, is pretty clear-cut. It is a three-phase operation involved first of all in policy making, then in consultation with the Areas, then in the implementation of traffic regulations.

'On the consultation side,' he said, 'I suppose I should say that we actually consult with Government, and with local authorities as well. We act as a sort of representative for the Metropolitan Police Service. So on traffic matters it is likely that the Minister for Roads for London will end up talking to Kevin Delaney rather than with the Commissioner. And as long as he's easy with that, it doesn't bother me.'

The administration department, TO14(1), deals with correspondence, expenses and the thousand details that make up the minutiae of keeping a busy department moving. On top of that there is a liaison role – TO14 chair a large number of meetings with Area Traffic Superintendents and with Area Traffic Management teams.

'Every month,' Delaney added, 'I go and talk to the Commanders, Operations – why shouldn't they suffer as well?'

The administration takes part in numerous other meetings and conferences, and all this involvement has to be recorded, reported and properly channelled for action.

'Down the corridor I've got a Sergeant,' Delaney said, 'who is probably run off his feet. There are occasions when the poor man has got so much work in terms of reports and minutes of meetings etcetera waiting to be done, that sometimes he only manages to get the damn things out a week or so in advance of the next meeting. So TO14 Administration's got that kind of a role – it's part administrative, partly a secretariat.'

(2) POLICY AND LEGISLATION

We are accustomed to doom-laden press reports of worsening traffic problems in the metropolis, and darker predictions for the future. But Kevin Delaney points out that people from abroad frequently consult TO14 because they believe the London traffic runs beautifully. 'We actually think we do badly in comparison to them, then they come over here and think that we do reasonably well compared to them.'

Nevertheless, Delaney thinks the amount of traffic legislation in Britain is horrific. 'It increases exponentially,' he said. 'It doubles and quadruples at a vast speed. Also there's policy. We make our own policy in London – how do we feel about Red Routes and so on, that kind of thing. And of course the Metropolitan

Police is a member of what we call ACPO, the Association of Chief Police Officers, and they, bless their hearts, also make policy, some of which we agree with, some of which we don't, and all of which we have to consider and file away, so that when some Traffic Patrol officer stops you or me at three o'clock in the morning because we've got a different tyre on one back wheel to the rest, he or she can come for an answer the next day, or the next week, to find out A, is it illegal, B, what our policy is, and C, what is the ACPO policy.'

When the Department of Transport decided to introduce Red Routes in London under the Road Traffic Act of 1991, they announced that the police would be expected to enforce the regulations. On the face of it that was a straightforward and unexceptional announcement, but Kevin Delaney said it caused a great deal of soul-searching within To14.

'Basically, it was because maybe nine-tenths of my organisation assumed we would give the red lines the same level of enforcement that we gave the yellow lines, namely almost nothing, apart from sporadic guerrilla raids.'

The feeling among Traffic Officers has been that if they enforced the regulations on yellow lines by penalising motorists who parked on them, it was a fast way to alienate a large sector of the public and a shortcut to ensuring a loss of respect for the police.

'It falls to me,' Delaney went on, 'to try and recover something from a situation that hopefully will form the basis of a traffic policy for years to come. I have to explain to the nine-tenths of the Metropolitan Police who believe that we should be doing nothing that this is an opportunity to show that we can provide value for money. And I'm hoping that in years to come I will actually shape the Met policy around the Red Route network.'

In response to the argument that traffic work would be best left to the traffic wardens, leaving police officers to do their proper work of preventing crime and catching villains, Delaney says that in many respects the job certainly could be done by the wardens. A problem would arise, though, he feels, from the current discrepancy of power. Police officers have powers to report people, and powers to require production of driving documents. Traffic wardens don't have these powers, they can ask to see documents but they cannot demand. More seriously, there is the power of arrest in offences like reckless or drunken driving – Delaney suspects that the public would not like to see that power handed over to a warden.

Far more important is the question of the expertise needed to deal with serious traffic accidents, expertise which can be decisive in claims often amounting to hundreds of thousands of pounds. That level of informed commitment, Delaney believes, cannot be expected from a warden. Nor does he think there would be much enthusiasm, politically, for changing the rules to broaden the wardens' powers without radically restructuring their training programmes.

'But I think that we within the police have got to recognise,' he said, 'that an awful lot of the functions we perform in Traffic don't require the level of training or justify the expense of a policeman. And so I would see that in time to come we would perhaps devolve a lot of functions to traffic wardens.'

In fact a number of London boroughs will soon be taking responsibility for all their parking and yellow-line offences. 'We, the police, will be pressing all of them to take it over, because I shall want to be moving the Metropolitan Police on to the Red Routes and leaving everything else to the local boroughs.'

When something goes wrong in the flow of London traffic, chaos swiftly sets in. There is no slack in the system, no capacity for absorption of breaks in the rhythm. If Vauxhall Cross, a major junction in the south of London, becomes blocked or the traffic lights fail, then within thirty minutes there will be a traffic jam two miles long in every direction, which in turn will block Victoria, which will block Westminster Bridge, which will then block Parliament Square, Trafalgar Square and the entire West End. Within one hour to an hour-and-a-half, London can come to a virtual standstill.

'There was a bad accident in Oxford Street,' Delaney recalled. 'At around noon a cyclist was run over by a lorry. The air ambulance arrived and landed in the middle of Oxford Circus. They hoped they could save the cyclist's life but sadly they didn't. Now, that ambulance was on the ground for perhaps half an hour, and the congestion it caused did not end until nine o'clock that night.'

(3) REMOVALS, WHEEL-CLAMPING AND CAR POUNDS

In 1991 the police in London removed approximately 135,000 illegally parked vehicles and wheel-clamped a further 125,000. A year later the figures were substantially lower. Fewer cars were being illegally parked, which was seen as a reflection of the recession, with penalty-conscious drivers taking more care where they parked and being sure they didn't overstay their time on meters.

Kevin Delaney believes the lower figures also reflect

the extent to which police officers no longer see wheel-clamping as a relevant procedure. Soon, revised arrangements will mean that the police will not sanction any wheel-clamping at all. Some councils, however, being newly responsible for parking offences, will probably have wheel-clamping programmes of their own. Delaney does not doubt it.

'Places like Westminster I believe will do so with great joy, for it will be seen as a means towards the overall end of raising revenue. I was at a conference recently where a very senior official from Westminster City Council said that Westminster regarded on-street parking as a valuable resource. So in those terms it would be surprising if they didn't farm that valuable resource to its ultimate level of productivity.'

Until now the Metropolitan Police, as the only authority removing cars in London, have operated all the car pounds. In the coming years it is almost certain that the local authorities will need car pounds, and at present the police are working to devise equitable means whereby the pounds can be shared. As to staffing, Delaney hopes that very soon all the police officers will be gone from the pounds – in fact he sees no reason why the facilities should not be totally privatised. People have told him the presence of a policeman helps when an irate motorist arrives, but Delaney is not convinced of that.

'I think sometimes a policeman or a traffic warden can make the situation worse,' he said. 'A motorist who's had his car towed away arrives at the car pound and finds a person who actually represents the organisation that took the car. The car owner's got an awful lot of frustration and anger pent up, and here is an individual on whom he can vent it. If, however, he was confronted by someone who worked for a totally different organisation, someone whose role in life is simply to collect the money, then I suspect the owner would pay his money, take his car, and write vitriolic letters to me.'

(4) OPERATIONAL SUPPORT

It is unusual for a policy department to have a training wing, but the Operational Support division of TO14 has one. Chief Superintendent Kevin Delaney said this is largely because no other part of the Metropolitan Police is prepared to offer continuation or refresher training for Traffic Patrols.

'They do a course when they become Traffic Patrols, and a lucky few of them go on to do an advanced course, probably a year or two years later. And that's it. Nothing else happens.

'We went out and blatantly stole two Traffic Patrols, who we've now welcomed into the fold, and they run continuation training. Every Traffic Officer – and anybody else who wants – comes twice a year for one day to be updated on legislation, policy and technical developments.'

There is also a team – a Sergeant and three Constables – who deal with offences committed by licensed cab drivers. Increasingly they have been involved in complaints raised against mini-cab drivers by the public, and by drivers of black cabs.

TO14(4) also advises on the use of Gatso cameras, which are traffic monitoring cameras usually positioned near traffic lights. In addition to photographing speeding vehicles they note the date and time of the offence together with the offender's speed. It is the responsibility of local authorities to ask for cameras to be installed;

thereafter the police will see to the running and maintenance of the installations, and where necessary they will
act on the evidence produced. The cameras are set
deliberately above the speed limit so that only blatant.
offenders are caught. In that way the public become
accustomed to the cameras without developing any mis-
placed sympathy for convicted offenders.

The cameras are proving highly effective against red-
light violations and speeding at intersections. When
they were first erected on the A40 a film lasted just one
hour, now it lasts up to three days, because drivers are
aware of the cameras and curtail their speeds.

On the public transport side at TO14(4) is an officer
who acts as a liaison point with London Transport, and
another who does the same job with private coach operators. Their role is to advise on re-routing of buses
during upcoming public events, and to negotiate compromises when there is the danger of conflict with other
bodies such as the Road Hauliers Association.

London is beset with thousands of tourist coaches
virtually every day of the week. They tend to park in
large numbers along Park Lane, by Westminster Bridge
and near Buckingham Palace.

'And so,' said Delaney, 'an officer from my department has to go and talk to the tour operators, to the
English Tourist Board, to all the major operators – he
even, from time to time, goes abroad and talks to foreign
operators and tells them where they can and can't park
in London.'

The officer, a Sergeant called Bob Pilby, produces
detailed tourist maps and information leaflets in a
number of languages. Many people write to Scotland
Yard thanking him for his help and advice.

'We get letters predictably from all over the UK,'
said Mr Delaney, 'and from France, Germany, Belgium,

Holland – throughout the EC in fact. In recent years we've had letters from Russia, from Belorussia, from the Baltic States, you name it. Sergeant Bob Pilby is certainly better known than any senior officers in the Met, and probably as well known as the Commissioner – abroad, I hasten to add.'

TO18
Public Order Training

The foundations of public order training were established after the Notting Hill Carnival of 1976, when rioting broke out on a scale that had not been seen in London for years. It was clear that the police could not contain such disorder, and strategically they were unequipped to bring it under control.

'The now legendary scenes of police officers running down the streets with dustbin lids and milk crates to protect themselves,' Superintendent Douglas Brand said, 'have become a vivid reminder of circumstances that existed not so long ago. And from there we springboarded into a more organised approach to the tactics and the equipment.'

Training for public-order assignments is carried out at the Public Order Training Centre, unofficially known as Riot City, a nine-acre site at Hounslow in West London. A variety of street and housing layouts have been built to simulate real-life settings. There are also two underground train carriages for practice in disorder-management in confined spaces, and the body of a Trident jet is used for training related to disorders on aircraft.

'We have a simulated urban street,' said Brand, 'modelled on parts of Clapham and Battersea, not because we particularly fear problems there, but because it gives us the best sort of street structure for training officers in the kind of flexibility we're looking for, with the railway arches, overhead walkways, crossroads and the typical street furniture. I find that the situations we create here are very realistic, and they do tend to stretch the competence of the young Constable, the Sergeant, the Inspector and particularly the senior officer.'

Training at Hounslow is at three levels: Level Three is basic coaching for police recruits, Level Two is graded for Police Support Unit (PSU) officers, and Level One is intensive training designed for Territorial Support Groups (TSGs).

Level Three Public Order Training gives recruits the fundamental tactics of crowd-control. At this level they learn no more than effective linking of arms to form containment barriers, the defensive method of using a riot shield and the right way to make a cordon. The course has no loftier purpose than to prepare new police officers for the possibility of being thrown into a crowd-control exercise without warning or experience.

The next stage, Level Two, is aimed at PSUs (known to other police officers as 'Broadway serials') and is given on a regular topping-up basis. Ideally, officers attend for a minimum of four days a year – two two-day periods – although there are constant problems of availability and many officers attend for only two days a year. This level of training is much more rigorous and detailed than Level Three. Officers work in teams, learning the tactics and manoeuvres of crowd intervention, making arrests in the midst of a riot, using shields efficiently, making formations and synchronised advancements, and working among officers on horseback.

Currently there are 2,400 officers trained to Level Two standard. 'These are the people who would be mobilised in the event of large-scale disorder in London,' Brand explained. 'They would be brought to the seat of disorder by police transport, and then deployed in groups. Although they learn to work in a team it's not always the same team; they just learn to work with other officers.'

The ultimate stage of public-order training is Level One, a comprehensive regime for TSGs, who attend the complex at Hounslow one day a month for training. These officers are the successors to the SPGs (Special Patrol Groups), formed in 1961 as preventive patrols and stand-by in breaches of public order.

There are eight TSGs, one for each Area, and their numbers vary between eighty and 100 officers. They are multi-disciplined and their training is geared to emphasise operational versatility. They learn evidence-gathering skills – photography, fingerprinting, basic forensic sampling – and members of POLSA (Police Search Adviser) teams train them in the fine points of active and defensive searching. Active searches are for drugs, firearms or explosives; defensive searching would entail making an area safe (police use the word 'sterile') for a particular event, perhaps a military gathering, and keeping it safe until the event is over.

'So what we have here,' Brand summed up, 'is an exercising and training centre where, at three different levels of competence, we can exercise most of the officers in the Metropolitan Police to some degree of competence in working together as a team.'

Individuality can be an obstruction to group-reaction training. 'We're always faced with the officer still accountable to himself in law, disagreeing with a command in public disorder and refusing to do as he is told. We don't have the military mentality, where there's a group decision and everybody follows orders, because each constable is accountable for his own actions.'

The Home Secretary has decided that police in Britain can now carry out trials with the PR24 side-handle baton, a weapon praised in some quarters for its efficiency and flexibility, especially in circumstances where police officers are outnumbered.

Then there is the issue of body armour. Brand knows it looks daunting, but he argues that isn't the intention. 'I certainly don't seek to have my officers looking fearsome, but the reality is that the way we equip is reactive, because what we wear is what we need, in the light of so many injuries in the past.' Not that he thinks the alarming appearance of officers in riot gear is entirely unfortunate. 'The psychological effect came along as an ancillary benefit rather than as a definite perk when we designed the equipment.'

A Public Order Review in 1985 insisted that senior officers' training should be thoroughly appraised and that those with proven competence in public order be selected on each Area for advanced training.

'In 1977, as a sergeant then commanding my little team of shield people,' said Brand, 'it was frustrating to find that the senior officers didn't really understand how to use shields, and senior officers did come in for a hell of a lot of criticism after Brixton and Tottenham in 1985.'

Brand was actually brought to Hounslow to set up the new public order training for what are known as cadre officers. In the advanced training scheme, each Metropolitan Police Area nominates two cadre (nucleus) teams of senior officers, made up of one Chief Superintendent, one Superintendent and three Chief Inspectors, to be the ground commanders in public-order situations. These officers would be backed by five more senior officers from each area, trained in control-room duties.

Brand described the general training regime at Hounslow. 'We use most of the site for the purposes of exercising the police officers in street craft when it comes to matters to do with public order. We also culminate each day's training with a mini-disorder so that the disparate parts of their training that day can be brought together and they can play it for real, so to speak.

'We also use a petrol-bomb exercise,' he added, 'because our experience in 1985 both at Brixton and Tottenham was that a determined attack by petrol bombs could have prevented the police from achieving their objectives.'

He recalled an incident where a female officer froze during petrol-bomb training. 'She said she couldn't go on. Before she joined the service she had seen friends die in a car crash where the car caught fire, and she just couldn't face doing that, and we had to say, well, fine. There's no shame in that at all.'

On a related issue, Brand believes there is no way that an instructor can weed out the officer who is going to freeze with terror, or lose control and start lashing out indiscriminately with his baton. 'Whether you talk about military training, or police training or any other training, somebody at some stage will do something unpredictable. That's because they're human and no two human beings are the same.'

As a crucial part of their training at Hounslow, officers are taught how to overcome obstacles to gathering evidence in riot situations. 'We've found that it's extremely difficult for an officer, who is perhaps fighting for his life, to try and gather the evidence that's required to prosecute somebody later on.' The training given to designated evidence-gatherers is now integrated with the general training at Levels One, Two and Three.

The training received by women at Hounslow is exactly the same as that given to men. Although there are occasions when women officers, according to Brand, would themselves agree that their presence is inappropriate, they are nevertheless to be seen, regularly, in the police front line at public-disorder incidents.

'They were in the front line at Wapping, at Trafalgar Square and the poll tax riots,' Brand said. 'They're in the front line in many places. There are those, and they're not the misogynists of the world, who would say it's the wrong place for women. I take a very open view.'

He acknowledges that the days of relying on a woman officer's femininity to defuse a situation are long gone. 'If we've got the sort of situation where the violence is such that the officers are really going to take a hammering, then I would probably pull out the smaller or slighter females, and I think that is common sense. But it's a dilemma.'

Although police horses are trained by Mounted Branch (TO27), they are brought to Hounslow to use the facilities for the later stages of their training.

'We don't put them through petrol bombs,' Brand said, 'and we throw tennis balls at them, since the effect is much the same as any other missile – the horse sees something coming towards it . . .'

Horses are a valuable resource in public-order incidents, where the sight of five or six of them side by side, coming along a street, can definitely deter rioters. Brand believes in using horses so long as the limitations are taken into account.

'Senior officers must understand what horses can and can't do. They can't suddenly stop. If you commit them to disorder, you've got to accept the risk to the animal and the rider.'

Those same senior men, Brand believes, now have a far more positive approach to public-order problems. 'There's certainly an awareness among a lot of senior police officers that wasn't there ten years ago. They're prepared to apply the appropriate interventions to deal with disorder.' In the future that may mean using baton guns, Brand says. 'Maybe, I don't know. But at least the preparedness is there. It's better than just dismissing an idea as being unconstitutional, as being not traditional, not Dixon of Dock Green.'

TO20

Public Order

The branch known as TO20 Public Order Events is responsible for assembling the manpower needed to police major events – ceremonial, public order or sporting – when they are large enough to need policing on a scale beyond the resources of the police area concerned. The Chief Superintendent in charge of Events, Mike Davies, also has administrative responsibility for TO20's Central Information Office and Forward Planning.

Marches and demonstrations always have the potential for trouble, and even the most respectable organisations can attract outside elements intent on disruption. So policing measures have to be tailored and orchestrated to take account of the ever-present possibility of disorder. To give an idea of the scale of preparation necessary, Davies cited the example of a proposed march involving many thousands of people.

'We would have a preliminary meeting with the organisers, look at what they were proposing, then set up a meeting between the authorities likely to be concerned in the event.'

On the day of a large march in Central London a ranking system – Gold, Silver, Bronze – is adopted for the police command structure. Gold commander formulates strategy; Silver commander implements tactics; Bronze commanders control operational functions.

Before the big event the officer designated Gold commander calls a strategy meeting. Officers attending will include Silver commander and the various Bronze commanders. Together they look at plans and strategies for the event and consider various 'what-if' scenarios. Broad tactics are agreed and put in the hands of Silver commander. At the end of the meeting, the individual Bronze commanders brief the staff operating directly under them.

If the event is on an especially large scale, the control point will be the Special Operations Room at Scotland Yard. This room, known to many officers at GT (from its radio call sign, 'M2GT') and to others increasingly as Met Ops, is not permanently staffed, but is ready for immediate use when it is needed. Normally it is used only in the event of outbreaks of public disorder, pre-planned demonstrations and marches, ceremonial events or major disasters.

During a major demonstration Gold will oversee events from Met Ops, where operational staff for the event are supplied by TO20; the Chief Superintendent in charge of TO20 Public Order Events will usually be Met Ops Controller.

'Our function,' said Mike Davies, 'is to coordinate all the resources available to Silver on the communications side, to ensure that staff are correctly booked on or off duty, fed and watered at the appropriate times, and moved around at the request of Silver or the Bronzes. We would also cover the what-if scenarios, providing appropriate responses if disorder breaks out. If things go to plan, Gold will have very little to do. He will leave it to Silver to get on with the job.'

Silver will normally stay close to the event, setting

himself up at any position he judges to be appropriate. It is important that he does not become entangled with any unscheduled action that might compromise his ability to implement strategy. Having been thoroughly briefed on tactics and procedure, he must operate largely on his own initiative without reference back to Gold. Even in the event of a breakaway march, Silver would be expected to execute measures to bring the situation under control. Whenever it is necessary, Silver can use a mobile control room to monitor the event closely and be in radio contact with his Bronze commanders.

Matters of direct involvement with the marchers or demonstrators must be left to the Bronze commanders. On a big demonstration, TO20 would divide the area into perhaps six sectors, each with a Bronze commander, who would be in charge of upwards of 100 officers.

The press and other commentators have raised the point that Central London is no longer a suitable place for a large-scale march or demonstration. Chief Superintendent Davies had mixed feelings on the point.

'It's open to debate,' he said. 'I think the problem with Central London is there's no suitable venue for a large crowd to stop and have speeches. For demonstrations, merely walking along the streets, I would have said it's as good as anywhere, really.'

(2) PUBLIC ORDER FORWARD PLANNING UNIT

The Forward Planning Unit prepares for the unthinkable. 'About two years ago a Russian satellite crashed,' said Chief Inspector Tom Pine. 'We knew it was going to crash somewhere, and the flight path was along the M4 and over London. Fortunately it crashed in the Andes, but this was a vehicle the size of two London buses bolted end to end, and it would have made quite a big hole somewhere.'

Following a spate of rioting across Britain in 1981, the Forward Planning Unit was set up as a joint Metropolitan–Provincial police venture, with the central notion of anticipating civil disorder and laying down plans to have public order equipment and vehicles ready for the next outbreak. The present department, run by a Chief Inspector, three Inspectors and an auxiliary staff of three, deals with major incident procedures and public-order forward planning, under the catch-all heading of the Public Order Forward Planning Unit.

Tom Pine explained the role of his office in the event of a major incident, right from the first alert. 'The first thing that happens is the 999 call comes in, and there's a Chief Inspector on duty in the Central Communications Complex who's got a great deal of discretion, devolved to him in the middle of the night, to actually call up resources and mobilise people. We have direct lines to all the other services, so what we need first is a police officer at the scene to report back and tell us what's happening. We have trained and equipped those officers to give coherent information, and there's a checklist of points they have to cover – it's actually stuck on the visor of the police car, and it's on a card in their pocket, and we hope it's also drilled into them.'

The *aide-mémoire* card lists the observations to be made and actions to be performed by the first police officer at the scene of an incident. First he has to ask himself if it is a major incident and, if so, he must declare it as such. Next he must make an assessment of the scene and pass it on to his control. He then follows the mnemonic word CHALET to guide himself through the next set of procedures:

C – – Casualties: approximate number
H – – Hazards – present and potential
A – – Access routes for emergency services
L – – Location of incident: exact
E – – Emergency services present and required
T – – Type of incident: crash, explosion, etc.

'The information is immediately relayed on direct lines to the other services,' Tom Pine continued, 'who have probably been mobilised already through the 999 system.' This is not simply a matter of alerting the fire and ambulance services. 'There are other police forces – there's the City of London Police, who are independent, with their own territory. British Transport Police are independent and relate to British Rail and the London Underground. Lots of other premises that are owned by those two are swiftly becoming private companies. The Royal Parks Police cover large areas of London. There's the Ministry of Defence Police as well. There's a lot of agencies we need to cover.'

When the information has reached all the relevant bodies and they move into action, a small command vehicle is mobilised from Scotland Yard, crewed by the control room staff who must be present at the scene of the incident. If he feels it is necessary, the Chief Inspector in charge of the Central Communications Complex can call up the Commissioner's Reserve, a mobile reserve of forty Territorial Support Group (TSG) officers, with their own vehicles, who are available at most times of day on a stand-by basis. They can be dispatched to the scene of the incident to reinforce local divisional officers already there.

'The initial police role,' said Tom Pine, 'is to try and avoid getting involved too much in the rescue work. There's an instinct of police officers to get stuck in doing rescue work. We don't have the protective equipment, we don't really have the training, it's better left to the Fire Brigade. So, apart from the initial saving of life – that's obvious, that can't be ignored – the job of the police is then to withdraw, form a protective cordon around the scene to keep the public out, and let the Fire Brigade and Ambulance Service get on with their job within what we call the rescue zone.

'We then take over. We have responsibility for the overall coordination of everybody else involved in the event, and we would set up rendezvous points, marshalling areas, rest centres for people who were evacuated, a whole range of functions like that, while the Fire Brigade and ambulances are busy taking care of the survivors.'

The dead, if there are any, are left where they are found until crime and forensic teams have finished.

The police will meanwhile have opened up a Casualty Bureau at Scotland Yard to cope with the rush of telephone calls which always follows the news of a major incident. Police teams are sent to the hospitals to list the identities and numbers of casualties admitted. Other teams in the rest centres make a record of the people who have survived uninjured; apart from providing reassurance to relatives and friends, their names have to be eliminated from lists of dead and missing.

'We then initiate investigation of the scene. There's a whole range of activity there – Railway Inspector, Health and Safety Inspectorate, CAA – and our own detectives are brought in at a very early stage to assume control of what becomes a criminal investigation.'

Detective work is begun by officers from the local division, but soon officers of an Area Major Incident Pool (AMIP), who are specialists in major crime investigation, will take over. Stage by careful stage, control and order are overlaid on the chaos of the incident, although it will be a long time before the matter can be set aside.

'Once all the fires are out, once all the living have been rescued, the Fire Brigade lose interest and the Ambulance Service lose interest, and they go back to base,' said Pine. 'But we're left with that incident for many weeks, investigating it, and the local authority is left with it for many years, because they're looking after the orphans.'

On average there are two major incidents a year in London. To be classified as major, an incident has to include any one of the following:

- Rescue/transportation of large numbers of casualties.
- Involvement of large numbers of people, directly or indirectly.
- Handling of a large number of inquiries from the public and news media.
- Mobilisation of the emergency services, boroughs and voluntary agencies to deal with the threat of death, injury or homelessness to large numbers of people.

The Forward Planning Unit recently arranged for every police manager in London to be put through an exercise in major incident response, carried out in liaison with the other emergency services.

Details of one major incident, however, the *Marchioness* tragedy on the Thames in 1989, show that existing policies and contingency plans, complex and comprehensive as they are, can be entirely irrelevant in circumstances that have never cropped up before.

Early in the morning of 20 August 1989, approximately 150 young people were at a party on the disco boat *Marchioness* when it was struck from behind by an ocean-going dredger, the *Bowbelle*. The *Marchioness* keeled over and sank in only a few seconds. A total of fifty-one people died.

'The problem was, there is no agency really equipped to do rescue on the river,' said Tom Pine. 'Fortunately we had police patrol boats close by. But the reality is that those patrol boats could have been half an hour to an hour away, on the far extent of their patrols. And they were never designed or expected to do rescue work in the true sense. The Fire Brigade had no facilities, and the Ambulance Service had no equipment. So, you've got this ribbon running through London on which nobody's really equipped to do rescue work.'

Communication on the river was a problem, because the marine police radios do not link up automatically with their land-based counterparts. The patrol boats could only talk to each other. When an air-sea helicopter from RAF Manston arrived at the scene it couldn't communicate with the boats and, worse still, its engine noise drowned out the efforts of others to communicate at river level. Eventually a police helicopter, not equipped for rescue, appeared and provided high-intensity lighting for the Thames Division boats as their crews worked at recovering survivors.

All forward planning is hampered to some extent by the fact that, in London, no clear structure for handling a major incident is possible. Each of the three services – Police, Fire, Ambulance – are independent organisations with their own budgets, their own equipment, their own culture and training. In London there are thirty-two local authorities, all independent, with their individual budgets and Chief Executives. There are numerous regional health authorities, too, which means that the hospitals act as independent agencies.

'And the problem is,' Pine said, 'when you get a

major incident across boundaries, how do you get all these groups to function together? That's really an area of confusion.'

In the event of a warning that some disaster, say a falling satellite, was about to take place in the West End of London, a decision on action would not be straightforward.

'Fortunately, when we come to potential disasters of that magnitude,' said the Chief Inspector, 'we're not alone. There is a Cabinet Contingencies Office that would be involved, and decisions would be taken at Ministerial level.'

Contingency planning in the Unit never stops. Reports are being drawn up on procedural measures in coordinating a pan-London emergency, a hypothetical situation where an aircraft explodes over London, just as the jumbo did over Lockerbie, and parts land all over the different boroughs and different police areas. There is also involvement in the Chemical Industry Major Hazard (CIMAH) sites, of which there are at least twenty-four in London, a cause for concern at any time.

On a smaller planning scale, the Unit is examining the design of specialised body-armour, a project arising from the wounding and killing of police officers in knife attacks.

'We have been trying to develop armour that protects against stab wounds and bullet wounds,' Tom Pine said. 'But it's been very difficult to get the two types of protection together, more difficult than you can imagine.'

Straightforward projects are not common in the Unit.

TO25

Central Communications Branch

A man in Golders Green called 999 and complained that a lamb had followed his wife home. It would not go away and now it was eating his flowers. Another man called, fearing for the safety of a woman he could hear screaming. Police rushed to an address in SW1 where they found an operatic soprano rehearsing. An ambulance request explained that the caller had cleaned her bidet earlier that day with acid. She had just used it and was now in great pain.

Amusing calls are in fact quite rare, but they help ease the stress at Scotland Yard's Central Communications Complex (CCC), one of Europe's largest, most modern police communications systems and arguably the busiest. In 1992 the Information Room, backed by the Met's Command and Control Computer Systems, answered and processed approximately 1.27 million 999 emergency calls. In the same year there was a daily intake of approximately 900 burglar alarm calls, a total of 329,211 for the year, of which a startling 317,131 were false alarms. Every weekday the Information Room takes nearly five thousand calls of all kinds, and the number is rising.

The Information Room is only a segment of the CCC. Previously every communications unit within Scotland Yard operated separately, but since 1984 they have been together in the headquarters building in Victoria, where five departments are housed on one floor.

They are the Information Room, Central Traffic Control, Message Switch Office, Central Casualty Bureau and Special Operations Room.

The Information Room, by far the largest unit within the Central Communications Complex, employs 111 police officers and seventy civilian staff. It has three main functions:

1. To take all 999 police calls made inside the Metropolitan and City Police Areas.
2. To provide communications to police mobile units through four main outgoing radio channels, support channels and a personal radio network linked to every Metropolitan Police Station.
3. To take all automatic and Central Station burglar and hold-up alarm calls occurring within the Metropolitan and City Police Areas.

Chief Superintendent David French is head of TO25. He explained that when operators (called Communicators) in the Information Room receive 999 calls, they have a number of immediate options. A call can be passed to a Despatcher (radio operator), who will send out a police car for a fast response. Alternatively, if the call isn't urgent, the message will be passed to a divisional police station near the caller's address and the local police will deal with the matter.

'Or the Communicator will do nothing at all,' said Chief Superintendent French, 'other than give advice to the caller, because about 30 per cent of the calls we receive should never really be made on the 999 system. These are calls where people have dialled 999 when they should have contacted the local police.'

Other calls may come from old people, or from people who suffer feelings of threat and insecurity and will actually believe a situation is an emergency when it is not. As a rule, the police do not mind receiving these calls on the emergency system, and are always ready to offer reassurance to the callers.

Whenever 999 is dialled the call is answered by a British Telecom operator in London, who will re-route the call to whoever is needed – Police, Fire Brigade or Ambulance Service. Police calls go straight to Scotland Yard, where an automatic distribution system, capable of handling up to four hundred calls at once, spreads the calls throughout the Information Room, ensuring that better than 75 per cent are answered within fifteen seconds. The system also contains an automatic archiving system, providing supervisors with information about the time taken to answer calls and details of particular calls handled by individual operators.

On receiving a call the Communicator gives the police reference number and the Telecom operator transfers the call; Telecom will only disconnect when the operator is sure the police are in contact with the caller.

'Although the situation sounds straightforward, there are probably several options available, depending on what the caller is ringing about,' said French. 'Our Communicators have to be trained to deal quickly with the emergency through operational procedures. For every type of call there's a procedure.'

Communicators are trained never to relax on a call, no matter how routine or pointless it may seem. French explained why. 'It could be somebody phones in, for example, and says very calmly, as actually happened, "You've got to send a policeman down, I think I've murdered my boyfriend." Now, the same day a call was received from a man saying, "Right, you've got ten minutes! I'm going to my mother-in-law's and I'm going to knock her f***ing head off!" You can imagine a Communicator coping with both calls, reacting but dealing with them calmly, professionally. In fact, the one we thought was perhaps the hoax, the one with the calm voice, turned out to be genuine. The one screaming and shouting was a hoax. The point is, the Communicator couldn't tell which was which. What's important is, the response in both cases was calm and professional.'

The Communicator's job can impose stress of a more affecting kind. French spoke of the case of Lawrence Brown, a PC at Hackney. 'He got murdered with a shotgun. And the murderer admitted making a 999 call, enticing Lawrence Brown to the scene, so he could shoot him. And of course our Communicator here actually dealt with that call, and somebody despatched PC Brown to the scene. There is stress in that.'

Then there are bomb calls. 'It could be a call about a suspect package, or a direct message telling us a bomb has been placed. There might be a coded message, or the call might be from a third party, for example a news agency giving a recognised code.'

There is always an element of doubt, even when the caller is a terrorist using an agreed code to establish his credentials. He might be lying, either about where the bomb is, or even about its existence – he could simply be making the call in order to cause disruption.

Alternatively there is the possibility that a bomb call is genuine even when it doesn't answer the criteria. A record is kept of all known codes, but the Communicator has to be careful when a call is made using an unknown code, because a procedural bungle among the terrorists is not unlikely. A man may identify himself with a code in the mistaken belief that the police already know it. So a situation arises where a bomb has genuinely been planted, but the caller giving the warning has no immediate credibility. Whatever the degree of doubt, the bomb experts have to be called straight away and given all available facts, even when there are dozens of calls like that in a day, a lot of them from hoaxers.

'The information from all those calls would go through to our SO13 (Anti-Terrorist) Branch,' French explained. 'It would also be sent down to the appropriate division or, in the case of a bomb in a railway station, it would be transmitted to the British Transport Police, who would liaise with the officials of British Rail to decide on the course of action to be taken.'

Communicators are given appropriately intensive training: in the case of civilians it lasts thirteen weeks, and experienced police officers who work as Communicators are trained for four weeks on Information Room operational procedures.

The mainframe computer system can very swiftly shortcut operations. For instance, as soon as the Communicator gives the address of an incident to the computer, the call will be automatically sent to the Despatcher who has access to the radio channels in that area. If the Communicator decides the call needs immediate action, a single press on a button will put the call at the top of the Despatcher's priority list.

As soon as decisions are in the hands of the Despatcher, he or she has the radio capability to call up area cars, police vans, dog vans, the Air Support Unit, Thames Division and other specific services. Major emergencies, such as explosions or outbreaks of public disorder, automatically become the administrative territory of the Chief Inspector supervising the Central Communications Complex.

A Chief Inspector is on duty twenty-four hours a day and is responsible for the running of the entire Complex. Most of his time is spent in the Information Room in an office unofficially known as the Wendy House (for reasons no one can recall), where he will take responsibility for organising the response to major incidents. He also has the authority to call out the Commissioner's Reserve (Territorial Support Group) and to authorise, in extreme circumstances, the issue of firearms. At all times the Chief Inspector is available at his post in the Information Room to guide and advise the various divisions. After midnight, he is often the most senior officer on duty in the Metropolitan Police.

Inspector David Lee has been involved with a number of major disasters in recent years, including the *Marchioness* tragedy in 1989, when he was criticised for calling out the RAF Search and Rescue helicopters, because the Met helicopter took so long to get airborne at night.

'The RAF said how many helicopters do you want? I said as many as you can spare. They rang back five minutes later and said there was one coming from Manston, another from Lee-on-Solent, and another from Norfolk.' The first few minutes of the operation were a confused period, when it was still unclear what had happened. 'We were getting reports of people screaming in the water at Putney, which is miles away . . .'

Lee went all out to mount a major rescue bid on the night the *Marchioness* went down, and he was careful not to underestimate anything – 'If somebody says there's hundreds in the water, you've got to assume there *are* hundreds in the water.' His determination was backed by twelve years' service with Thames Division. 'I'd seen lots of people drown,' he said, 'and I'd rescued lots of people myself, but I kept my mind off the horror and concentrated on what I was supposed to be doing.'

The horror did, nevertheless, get through to him, on the day the *Marchioness* was brought up from the bed of the Thames. 'As the vessel was raised bodies were all heaped up in one end, all nicely dressed ... That's when you appreciate the size of it, the horror of it.'

Lee remembered another dramatic occasion in the Information Room in December 1988.

'I was on late turn, and the duty officer at Buckingham Palace rang to say he'd like a major exercise first thing in the morning, an intruder alert, but do it for real with everything implemented.'

The exercise finished at approximately 7.55 a.m. David Lee decided he would like a cup of coffee. He rounded off what remained to be done at the desk and prepared to take a break.

'It was nearly ten past eight, if I recall,' said Lee. 'I was about to hit the Log-Off button when one of the girls who had taken a 999 call said "There's someone shouting about a rail crash." Then other calls began coming in at different sections of the room and somebody else shouted "I've got a rail crash!"'

When the first police unit arrived at the scene the assessment came through. It was Monday 12 December 1988. Two crowded rush-hour commuter trains had run into each other at Clapham Junction, the world's busiest rail junction. A third empty train piled into the wreckage shortly afterwards, adding to the carnage. It was Britain's worst rail disaster for twenty years, with thirty-six people killed and hundreds injured. Activity in the Information Room was frenetic.

'As well as the 999 calls on the incident, the other emergency services went into their procedures. We had to be careful what we did, so we didn't interfere with the other services. The only good thing was that the crash happened near a big green park, where the railings could be taken out. As the day progressed we got television pictures back from the helicopter and we were better able to organise emergency vehicle routes in and out of the disaster area.'

An underestimated function of the Information Room is that of monitor and general overseer. 'We're aware of any special schemes that are in existence,' said Chief Superintendent French. 'Any special operations taking place, a movement of Category A prisoners, bullion runs, armed Flying Squad operations, and so on, we monitor them so that, if anything goes wrong, we can be aware and send immediate assistance.'

Alarms Communicators, as their title suggests, attend to the thousands of alarm calls that pour into the Information Room every week. When an alarm company or a Telecom operator contacts the Information Room they give the Communicator a code number. When the code is fed into the telephone field of a CAD entry, the name and address of the premises are instantly generated, along with other data to speed the police response to the call. A number of alarm companies now take responsibility for calling up keyholders when alarms are activated, thus saving police time.

Several security alarms are linked directly to the Information Room for urgent response. In the case of a major break-in, the Information Room lays on additional radio channels and communications control. In those cases a Communication Control Van can be sent to the scene, if necessary, with a fully-trained operational staff on board, thereby creating a multi-outlet extension to the Information Room itself.

Central Traffic Control and Area Traffic Control

The flow of London's traffic and its associated problems are the responsibility of Central Traffic Control. The eight main areas of responsibility are:

1. Maintenance and monitoring of traffic flow.
2. Gathering traffic information for broadcast by the news media.
3. Supervising the attendance of specialist Units at major accidents or other incidents.
4. Liaison with Fire Brigade, Ambulance Service, and London bus authorities when roads have to be closed and diversions set up.
5. Contacting garages to remove vehicles involved in accidents.
6. Setting up and monitoring ambulance escorts once they have been authorised.
7. Monitoring of escorts for abnormal loads.
8. Acting as reference point for the police in matters of traffic legislation, and advising on the transportation and storage of hazardous chemicals; also advising hauliers on transportation and handling of special types of explosives.

Traffic information is collected from a number of sources, and, when it has been gathered, it can be passed to the media with a minimum of delay for broadcasting. There is a direct line to the BBC, and Greater London Radio have a studio in the Press Bureau on the ground floor in New Scotland Yard. On weekday nights Carlton – LWT on Fridays – transmit a television traffic report which also comes from the Press Bureau. Information supplied to the AA is used in their Roadwatch broadcasts and is passed along to several independent radio stations.

Serious accidents or other major incidents inevitably interfere with the traffic flow, and Central Traffic Control has well-tried procedures to cope with most scenarios.

'Word of a serious incident would come in to us

either by telephone, or by radio from a unit,' said Superintendent Jack Bunker. 'We would immediately assign resources to assess the situation. Once the situation had been assessed, we might assign a unit of TSGs. Also, we would normally send a Communication Control Van from here.'

Message Switch Office

The Message Switching System (MSS) replaces a network of 190 teleprinters and five separate Telex machines. It is a computerised store-and-forward message switching system using the same computer as CAD, but a different software program. It is linked to the international Telex Network and the Police National Computer. On average 6,400 messages are put into the system on a weekday, with a resulting 21,300 deliveries, 85 per cent of them within one minute of input. All messages are kept on file for twenty-eight days. Telex transmissions of messages are normally between police stations (all police stations will have MSS, replacing existing teleprinters), but the dial number is in the British Telecom Directory and messages are occasionally received from private companies.

Central Casualty Bureau

The Central Casualty Bureau (CCB) was opened up for the King's Cross fire, the Purley train crash, the Clapham train crash, the *Marchioness* disaster and the Victoria Station bomb blast. The Bureau was originally formed after a rail crash at Lewisham in 1957, when the local police station was so badly swamped with telephone calls that the work of dealing with the incident was severely hindered.

Now, after every major incident involving injury and loss of life, or those likely to cause widespread public reaction, the CCB opens up to handle the telephone calls from the police division controlling the incident. There are five main areas of responsibility:

1. To collate the details of everyone involved.
2. To collate and record details of casualties, injured and dead.
3. To record and collate information from callers about persons who might be involved, and to try to match these details to persons known to be involved.
4. To ensure prompt action is taken to inform next of kin about casualties.
5. To create a point of contact for both police and civilians.

'Normally we put Supervisors into the Casualty Bureau,' Bunker said. 'They may be Supervisors from the local area, or any area. There are twenty lines for incoming inquiries and other lines to communicate with the hospitals and mortuaries. So we could have a Liaison Officer and a Casualty Officer out at the hospital or mortuary, and they would be feeding information in to us about the names of casualties and their descriptions, and we would try to collate that information with the inquiry.'

The number of inquiries received can be overwhelming, even for a tightly organised team. Following the King's Cross fire in 1987 the CCB received 10,537 telephone calls resulting in 4,184 Casualty Inquiry Cards being completed. The *Marchioness* disaster brought in five thousand calls and there were eight thousand following the Clapham train crash, all within a very short period.

Special Operations Room

Like the Central Casualty Bureau, the Special Operations Room (SOR) is not permanently staffed, and is ordinarily only used in the event of spontaneous outbreaks of public disorder, for pre-planned demonstrations or marches, for ceremonial events or major disasters.

Staff for SOR are provided by the Information Room, Traffic Control, and the Public Order Branch (TO20). Liaison personnel are brought in as necessary from inside the police service and from outside organisations. The rank of the officer in charge of SOR is determined by the type or magnitude of the event, but he or she will normally be a senior officer from the Area where the event occurs, and will be assisted by a Chief Superintendent or a Superintendent from TO20. The Traffic Control Room is effectively a nerve centre, complete with advanced electronic communications, including integrated access to cameras on all systems used throughout the police service except those used at motorway control rooms. Anything viewed on this system may be videotaped.

These facilities, plus the specialised features of the Special Operations Room Computer System (METOPS), give the team in charge a formidable capability. It has been said that with good communications, SOR could be used to control an event happening anywhere.

TO26

Air Support Unit

The Air Support Unit has three helicopters: two Bell 222s and, since summer 1993, one Air Especiale Squirrel. The unit is based at Lippitts Hill near Epping Forest, north-east of London.

A Chief Inspector, an Inspector, two Sergeants and six Constables make up the permanent police staff, and trained auxiliaries – a Sergeant and three Constables – are available on call. Since few British police officers hold commercial flying licences, the four pilots are civilians, employed by Bristow Helicopters of Redhill and working under long-term contract with the Metropolitan Police. There is an engineering staff of fourteen.

Every week the Unit aims to run a schedule of six patrols of seven and a half hours daily. 'The only times we don't meet that criterion,' Chief Inspector Mike English said, 'is when the weather is against us, or when there's mechanical trouble. The single biggest impediment to our efficiency is the weather. We can lose a whole day's flying, not through any defect in the aircraft, or shortage of pilots, but simply by waiting for the weather to improve. At Lippitts Hill we're 343 feet above sea level, literally sitting in the clouds.'

The Air Support Unit performs two principal functions in the Metropolitan Police District. The first is to operate regular patrols, working in effect as a super-versatile radio car in the sky. The second embraces anti-terrorism and the preservation of public order.

'We may have to take arrested terrorists anywhere in the country,' Mike English says, 'or transport firearms teams and their equipment to where they are needed. Occasionally we pick up dog handlers and their animals. Dogs like the helicopter – it's a lot better than sitting in the back of a van.'

Crime-related surveillance from a helicopter can be very rewarding. A height of 1,000 feet gives officers a detailed view of the ground – premises, people, vehicles, incidents – without arousing much awareness of their presence. This holds especially true when the people being watched are in a car.

Under normal operating conditions the helicopters have three-man crews. In the left-hand seat next to the pilot sits a police officer known as Observer One. His job is to monitor the radios and take details of calls for assistance. He also decides the course they will take in response to a call, and he navigates the craft to the scene. It is important that he sets the helicopter on an approach that will put the scene of an incident on the right-hand side of the craft. When the incident is in view, Observer One will say to the man in the right-hand seat behind the pilot – this is the third crew member, known as Observer Two – 'You're radios,' which means that he is now in charge of the incident.

'Ranks have no part to play in the aircraft,' says Mike English. 'We are all trained to the same level.'

Helicopters in the air are under direct radio control from Scotland Yard's Central Communications Complex (TO25). More than half the calls answered by the Air Support Unit involve burglaries, usually when officers on the ground believe suspects are still on the premises or in the immediate area. Using a stabiscope, which is a monocular equipped with a gyroscopic base to cancel the effects of airframe vibration, officers in the air can pinpoint the movements of suspects and even make individual identifications.

Vehicle pursuits make up another large proportion of the calls answered. 'There are a lot of fast cars about,' Mike English says, 'but once we've located one, and as long as we've got fuel, it won't get away from us.'

Approximately two hours every week are spent in the air with a police air-to-ground photographer from SO3 (Scenes of Crime Branch). He brings a list of sites which, for a variety of reasons, have to be recorded photographically. Recently Chief Inspector English spent an entire working day with a photographer taking shots of properties from Portsmouth on the south coast to Clacton in the east. A paedophile ring was about to be broken and all the houses in the photographs were to be raided simultaneously; it was useful to know the layout of the properties in advance, so that any outbuildings or side or rear exits could be noted and their location incorporated into the planning of the raid.

Constraints exist against flying near Heathrow Airport, but in emergencies the Air Support Unit can negotiate clearance from Air Traffic Control, who will usually sanction police flights in specific areas so long as no conflicting air traffic is within the zone. Under normal patrolling conditions, the moment a Unit helicopter is airborne it is within the umbrella of Thames Radar, who deal with all low-level flights over London. Top patrol speed is 140 knots (173 m.p.h.), making it possible for a 222 to be over any spot in London within fifteen minutes, although the average response time is closer to five minutes.

A lot of the Air Support Unit's work is backed by advanced technology. Mounted under the tailboom of each helicopter is a Nitesun unit, a thirty million candle-watt searchlight, controllable from within the aircraft, which can illuminate an area the size of a football pitch from a height of approximately seven hundred feet. The light is focusable and can be concentrated to a beam narrow enough to isolate a solitary man on the ground. Also mounted beneath each helicopter is the speaker of a highly amplified public address system, known colloquially as Skyshout, which has a curiously powerful effect when the volume is turned up: people on the ground have been known to lie down when cautioned to stop.

An infra-red thermal imaging camera is available for night work or for locating people or property hidden from direct view. Thermal imaging is a highly dependable process which can be used at the helicopter's normal operating altitude of 1,000 to 1,500 feet. The camera provides the operator with screen images of heat emanations, principally from human beings, animals and motor vehicles, which stand out in stark contrast to their cooler surroundings. A stolen car being followed in the dark can be kept in view because of heat-images from the engine block and the tyres, and from strips of heat-transfer on the cold road surface. Should the thief park the car and try to run away he can still be followed, even on the darkest night, thanks to his distinct heat trace. The equipment is also useful for finding persons missing in the dark, or in areas of dense overgrowth.

GEC Avionics' Heli-Tele, considered to be the finest system of its kind, is a combined colour television camera and transmission unit that can be quickly fitted to the aircraft whenever it is needed. The unit attaches to the right side of the craft and is housed in a weather-proof stabilisation pod fitted with remote controls, including swivel and tilt for the camera body and a zoom control for the lens. The system's transmitter passes real-time pictures to Scotland Yard, or to the Air Sup-

Metropolitan Police Service Air Support Unit: Analysis of Operations During a Typical Month

Robbery	24
Surveillance	3
Search Person – Crime	202
Search Person – Missing	8
Search Vehicles	18
Escorts	18
Photographic	59
Speed Detection	1
Heli-Tele Operations	10
Thermal Imaging Operations	0
Other Assignments	32

Total Assignments	375
Total Assigned Time	97 hrs 13 mins
Total Arrests	31
Total Days Flown	24
Total Hours Flown	135 hrs
Planned Patrol Hours	146 hrs 15 mins

Analysis of Patrol Hours Lost

Inclement Weather	5 hrs 15 mins
Photographic Task	12 hrs
Surveillance	1 hr 15 mins
Speed Enforcement	1 hr
Public Order Tasks	10 hrs 20 mins
Security Tasks	14 hrs 30 mins
No Aircraft	7 hrs 55 mins

port Unit base at Lippitts Hill, or to mobile ground units, for instance at Epsom Downs, where Air Support always cover the traffic converging on the Derby.

Heli-tele is also used to make detailed security checks

before important occasions that call for high security, such as state visits, the ceremony of Trooping the Colour, the Remembrance Sunday service in Whitehall and the State Opening of Parliament.

TO27

Mounted Branch

The main duties of Mounted Branch cover traffic control, street crime, rowdyism, autocrime and theft. Their forte, however, is crowd control, and nowhere are they more effective than among the fans at football matches.

The man in charge of Mounted Branch is Chief Superintendent Peter Hayward, who is also responsible for Thames Division, Air Support and Police Dogs. He buys the police horses, oversees their training to operational standard, then allocates them throughout the Metropolitan Police Areas. He also supervises recruitment and training of riders to the point where they take up duty in their areas.

Day-to-day mounted patrols are the responsibility of the individual police areas, but in major commitments, such as Trooping the Colour, the State Opening of Parliament, public demonstrations and the larger football matches, Hayward's staff coordinate the mounted officers.

The Branch was founded over 220 years ago. In 1763 the Treasury granted a small sum of money to Sir John Fielding, the Bow Street Magistrate, for the establishment of a horse patrol to police the approach roads to London which, at that time, were infested with highwaymen.

The organisational structure of the present-day Metropolitan Police Mounted Branch was established in 1918 by Lieutenant Colonel Percy Laurie. After service in the Great War, he took on the reorganisation of the Mounted Branch and his principles of feeding, training and the general care of horses are still largely in force. Since 1920 the Branch's Central Training Establishment has been Imber Court, at East Molesey in Surrey, where training facilities and accommodation are provided for officers and their horses; there are also classrooms, a museum and the Mounted Branch administrative centre.

Mounted Branch has 201 horses and 237 riders, including the administrative and training officers. Most new horses come from Yorkshire, chosen from a number of breeders who provide animals with the right bloodstock requirements for police work. A new horse, which costs approximately £3,700, is usually no younger than three years old, since below that age it would be hard to train and would have difficulty carrying the weight of a policeman on its back. Finding just the right horses is vitally important and Hayward knows what he is looking for.

The types of horses selected may be anything from Medium Hunters to a cross between Irish Draught and thoroughbred. 'We don't worry too much about type, nor about conformation and looks, as long as they have the right temperament and the physical capability to carry police officers for long periods.'

In the early stages the trainer works on the ground, putting the animal through exercises in handling, lunging and driving, always remembering the rule of encouragement-and-reward that underlies the whole training programme.

For the next stage the trainer gets into the saddle. In the controlled school atmosphere he introduces the horse to simulations of its future working environments. Recordings of crowds and traffic noise are used and in time the animal learns to accept them without surprise or distress.

In the third stage the horse goes outside for special operational exercises including the 'sidling' movement into crowds, one of the safest, most effective forms of crowd control ever devised. Now the basis for later training is laid down: riot shields start to appear and raised voices are directed at the animal.

Full-scale public-disorder training takes place at the Public Order Training Centre (TO18), known as Riot City, at Hounslow. Here the horses are gradually introduced to louder noise and harsher discord; people in growing numbers move towards them and eventually missiles are thrown; they are tennis balls and the horses wear protective covering, so there is no danger of injury. As the course goes on petrol bombs are thrown, too, but never directly at the animals.

When a horse's training at Imber Court is done he goes to an experienced officer working from one of the area police stables, who carries out final training on the London streets.

'To have a novice horse with a novice rider,' Hayward says, 'is a recipe for disaster. You'll end up with one in hospital, or worse, and the other one being sold, or worse. After twenty-two weeks of training at Imber Court, a young rider goes up to an area stable and he's allocated his first horse, and it tends to be an old steady horse to begin with. After two or three more years he'll move on to something a little more demanding.'

In the Metropolitan Police District there are eighteen stables distributed through the eight areas. Mounted officers of each area are under the command of a Chief Inspector; overall responsibility for the horses remains with Scotland Yard.

Roughly 25 per cent of the officers in the Mounted

Branch are female, and this is higher than the average proportion throughout the Metropolitan Police. Hayward believes that in a few years the proportion in Mounted Branch will be nearer 50 per cent.

The inimitable 'presence' of a horse – its combination of bulk, grace and mobility – makes it a powerful force for calm when public order situations move towards violence. Few rioters, whatever their orientation, will believe there is anything personal in the actions of a horse.

At the height of the disorder during the much publicised printers' dispute at Wapping, when police regularly had to face crowds of more than ten thousand protesters, Superintendent Andrew Petter was in charge of the mounted contingent.

'On the night when things went particularly bad for us,' he said, 'and there was a hell of a lot of violence involved, the mounted police cleared a gap for the foot-duty serials to move in and get the crowd away from their objective, which was to storm the printers' building. The horses' part in that was to push the crowd back and make a bit of space. The crowd fell back as the horses advanced, and it wasn't a cavalry charge, they moved in a controlled way. You've got to make sure a crowd's got somewhere to go, it would be irresponsible not to . . . When we found they needed time we backed off before we moved in again, giving them time to disperse.'

On Saturdays Mounted Branch can have more than 100 horses on crowd-control duty at football grounds. It was at a football match in 1923, the very first Cup Final at Wembley between Bolton Wanderers and West Ham, that a police horse called Billy became a legend. Crowds of fans, nearly 200,000 of them, had stormed the turnstiles and clambered over the boundary walls, desperate to see the historic match. The stands were crammed and people were spilling on to the pitch. The organisers, anxious to avoid a riot, were about to cancel the match when PC George Scorey on his white mount, Billy, began riding back and forth across the pitch, exhorting the crowds to be calm and to return to the stands. The fans responded. With the support of a few more mounted officers they were brought under control. Order was restored, Bolton won the Cup and Billy entered the history books.

In recent years a number of police horses have been injured or killed in London in the line of duty. The case of police horse Echo is especially poignant. A few minutes before 11 a.m. on 20 July 1982, Echo and his rider PC John Davies were rear escort to a detachment of the Blues and Royals providing the new guard for the Queen's Life Guard on the way to Whitehall.

Just before the guard reached Apsley Gate at Hyde Park Corner, IRA terrorists detonated a bomb made from twenty-five pounds of gelignite enclosed in thirty pounds of four-inch and six-inch nails. The bomb was concealed in a parked car. The explosion killed three members of the guard and seven horses. PC Davies and Echo were at the rear of the guard and therefore on the periphery of the blast; even so, they were both seriously injured. Echo was deeply wounded on his abdomen and neck while John Davies had an incised wound on his shoulder. Before collapsing from pain and shock, he managed to lead the horse away into Hyde Park.

In hospital a nail was found in John Davies's shoulder; to remove it safely the surgeon had to excise a section of muscle. At the stables at Hyde Park Police Station several pieces of metal were removed from Echo's body.

In the aftermath John Davies received hundreds of letters and cards from wellwishers. Echo, for his part, enjoyed a seemingly unending stream of confectionery sent by members of the public during the period of his convalescence.

Although Echo recovered, he became noticeably stressed when he was in traffic or among crowds. In 1983 it was decided he should be retired to a home of rest for horses at Aylesbury. He remained there in quiet and contentment until he died in 1993.

The Metropolitan Police Horse Show is an annual event where the public, who attend in large numbers, are able to meet the officers and the horses. Relations between the public and Mounted Branch tend, predictably, to be good, without the help of public-relations exercises. But Hayward said there is more to the Police Horse Show than PR.

'We're actually testing our standards against those of other forces, and indeed against the military,' he said. Apart from the police show, Mounted Branch compete each year in the Royal Tournament at Earls Court. 'It is all about maintaining standards, about making sure that we keep up to scratch. And, by and large, we fare very well.'

TO28

Police Dog Section

In the eight Metropolitan Police Areas there are a total of 298 German Shepherd dogs.

'We've found German Shepherds the best breed for the types of work they have to do,' said Chief Superintendent Peter Hayward, head of the Dog Section. 'They also fit the image.'

There are also thirty sniffer dogs – Springer Spaniels, based at Nine Elms in Central London. Experience has shown that this breed is especially good at detecting drugs and explosives.

The use of dogs by the Metropolitan Police had a belated start. Dogs had been helping law officers in other countries, notably France and Belgium, since before the Great War; in Britain at approximately the same time there had been small-scale trials at local level with mastiffs, Labradors, Airedales and bloodhounds. (Bloodhounds had previously been tried by the Metropolitan Police in 1888, to poor effect, during investigations into the Jack the Ripper killings.) It was not until the 1920s that the Government began to show any serious interest in using trained dogs to augment the work of policemen. Beyond discussion, however, little else happened.

In 1934 the Home Office Detection Committee studied a report by a Metropolitan Police officer on the use of police dogs on the Continent, and as a result it was decided that an experimental training school should be set up to determine the best breed or breeds of dog to bring into service with the British police, and to devise a suitable training programme.

A small training school was set up at Imber Court, East Molesey, which was – and still is – the Central Training Establishment of the Mounted Branch. On the very first night of a test patrol using dogs in Hyde Park, one of the animals foiled an attempted purse-snatch. It is recorded that the crime rate in the park plummeted. In 1953 the Dog Section moved to Keston, near West Wickham in Kent, which is still the headquarters and training centre.

Today, a police officer wishing to be a dog handler must have completed at least two years of street duty as a uniformed Constable, and must have a demonstrably stable domestic life. A board of senior officers usually interview about ten applicants for every vacancy advertised. The successful applicants go on to a two-week course aimed at assessing their ability and temperamental fitness to work with dogs. If they pass the course they are each allocated a twelve-week-old puppy, which from that time onward will live with the officer and become an integrated member of the family. The closeness and day-to-day contact between dog and handler is designed to produce trust and kinship, both vital to a good working partnership.

At the time the dog is allocated, his handler is taught about care and welfare and the kind of problems that must be avoided – most important among these is poor discipline, which can seriously undermine a dog's temperament.

Until the puppy is ten months old he visits Keston with his handler every month for a check on his health and progress. At ten months, dog and handler go on a five-day course aimed at assessing the dog's general ability. Finally at twelve months comes the basic-training course and, if the animal gets through that satisfactorily, it will emerge as a fully-schooled operational police dog.

During the basic course at Keston an instructor trains the handler to train the dog, because dogs, by and large, only respond to one person, and it is essential that when the handler leaves the training centre he has full control of his animal.

The course prepares a dog for most of the situations it will meet in the line of duty. Obedience exercises cover the familiar 'heel', 'sit' and 'down' commands. The dog then moves on to the fundamentals of tracking; it learns to follow a ground scent over different terrain in a range of conditions. Search training is next, including searches of open ground, woods and buildings, seeking out people or property; at this stage the dog learns to bark as soon as he has found what he was sent to look for. An underlying feature of every stage of training, which also applies to the training of police horses, is a system of praise and reward.

At the end of fourteen weeks the dog is usually proficient in criminal work, which includes chase and attack, stand-off, chase under threat from a stick, from a gun and from other weapons, and the control of prisoners and crowds. At this prime point in its life, with a programme of care and training behind it, the average police dog is estimated to have cost the taxpayer £6,000.

The reliability of German Shepherds is regularly questioned by press reports of Alsatians (another name for German Shepherds) attacking people and occasionally inflicting serious injury. A milder charge, just as persistent, is that they can be unpredictable. Peter Hayward says that can be the case with any breed.

'If a burglar escapes from a house, and you know

which door he's left by and you get there fairly soon after he's gone, you can put the dog to work and he will track the burglar. If you're giving chase and there's a chance the man will escape, you can send the dog after him. If he stops and stands still when you tell him the dog is coming after him, the dog will circle him and contain him without taking hold. But if the man refuses to stop, the dog is trained to take hold of his right arm and stop him that way.'

At Keston there is a breeding scheme for German Shepherds, producing a strain which is genetically tailored to police requirements.

The sniffer dogs are regularly used by area drug units. A dog can locate cannabis or heroin more efficiently than a team of officers carrying out a hand search. In half an hour a trained dog will check an entire building with a degree of thoroughness to rival the efforts of several officers, and the dog will cause minimal damage to property.

Over the years some very brave dogs have worked for the Metropolitan Police. Early in the 1950s there was Rex III who made more than 130 arrests during his career, including one in which he was shot several times. A robbery at Petts Wood in Kent was thwarted by police dog Yerba, who continued to pursue the felons in spite of having been shot; Yerba died later in the arms of his handler. The Harrods Bomb incident at Christmas 1983 claimed the life of Queenie, who was posthumously awarded the RSPCA's highest award for gallantry. Queenie and Yerba are buried at Keston, where they were born.

The following account is based on an official report dated 6 January 1989.

In the early hours of 27 September 1988, at an

address in Battersea, a burglar stole several items including the keys to the occupier's Suzuki jeep, which he drove away. Details of the theft were radioed to all units.

At about 5.00 a.m. PC Steve Lehec was driving a police dog van along Effra Road, Brixton, towards Tulse Hill. In the back of the van was police dog Rocky, a four-year-old German Shepherd. The stolen Suzuki jeep turned left out of Kellett Road into Effra Road in front of the dog van. While on the move PC Lehec made a registration check on the jeep and confirmed that it was the vehicle reported stolen from Battersea.

The jeep driver increased speed and drove through the back doubles, eventually turning on to the Tulse Hill Estate. He had difficulty handling the vehicle, and eventually he slowed down, jumped out and left the jeep to collide with a car parked on the road.

PC Lehec stopped the van and got Rocky from the back. He shouted at the jeep driver, telling him to stop and warning him that a police dog was present. The suspect ignored the warning and kept running. Rocky was sent to stop him.

The man ran across a children's play area and into the back garden of a house in Medora Road, still followed by Rocky. PC Lehec, meanwhile, ran towards an alleyway at the end of the gardens. The suspect and Rocky reached the alleyway before Steve Lehec, who saw them both cross Medora Road.

The man managed to get into the front garden of a house; Rocky was having difficulty jumping the fence, which had a thick privet hedge growing at the front. Lehec went to the gate and challenged the suspect, who pulled out a knife with a five-inch locked blade. He lunged at PC Lehec, trying to stab him in the stomach. Lehec jumped back and fell against cars parked at the roadside.

Rocky now reached the front garden and grabbed the right arm of the man, who shook him off and turned to face him. As Rocky lunged again the suspect thrust the knife forward and slashed him across the chest, then ran at PC Lehec and tried to stab him. Lehec backed off and again Rocky sprang at the man, who was now changing the knife from hand to hand. The dog tried to grab his hand, then yelped as the knife was plunged into the side of his head.

In spite of being badly injured, Rocky continued to harass the man, who was again trying to stab PC Lehec. As Rocky distracted the attacker, PC Lehec was able to punch him on the face and knock him to the ground. Lehec stamped on his arm, making him drop the knife. He was then handcuffed and arrested.

PC Lehec was walking the suspect back to the dog van when he was approached by five or six residents of Medora Road. Lehec, realising he was in imminent danger of being attacked again, grasped Rocky's neck chain and told the aggressive-looking group to move away; the person he was detaining was a prisoner. The group continued to advance on him. Rocky, although bleeding profusely from the head and chest, began to bark savagely and actually held the group at bay until other police officers arrived to assist.

The prisoner was taken to Brixton Police Station. PC Lehec took Rocky directly to the Blue Cross Hospital, Victoria. His condition was stabilised and during the afternoon of 27 September he underwent surgery for two stab wounds on his head and one on his chest. The operations required numerous external and internal stitches.

The suspect was eventually sentenced to three years' imprisonment. He was convicted on a number of charges including assault with intent to resist arrest, and criminal damage to a police dog.

Rocky made a full recovery and went on to be awarded the National Action Dog of the Year Award, 1988, presented for the most meritorious action by a police dog.

TO29
Thames Division

The Thames River Police were in operation thirty-one years before Sir Robert Peel's Act of Parliament established the Metropolitan Police, so Thames Division has evolved from the oldest police service in London.

The present Division has a total of 140 personnel – 131 police and nine civilians. The Division has seventeen motorised vessels, known as duty boats. Six of these are fast patrol launches powered by twin turbocharged diesel engines, used mainly on the wider, rougher stretches of the river between Wapping and Dartford. Eleven single-engine boats patrol the shallower waters above the headquarters at Wapping.

All duty boats carry a range of emergency equipment, including lifebuoys, lifejackets, first-aid kits, drags, resuscitators and aspirators, as well as searchlights and echo sounders. They also have police and marine-band radios for contact with other river traffic and, whenever necessary, between river police and land-based units. They have come a long way from humble beginnings.

The Marine Police began as an experiment by the West India Trading Company in 1798. In 1800 the Marine Police Act put the river force on a statutory basis, and the Commons approved their financing out of public funds. In 1839 they were given the official title of Thames Division of the Metropolitan Police.

All present-day Thames officers are volunteers who must have served a minimum of two years' foot-duty with the Metropolitan Police. Before being accepted for training they have to pass an examination to determine their suitability. Swimming skill is tested, together with talent in the handling of rowing dinghies and the ability to tie basic rope knots. Successful candidates take a twelve-month course of training that combines river duty with classroom work.

They have to learn a lot in the space of a year: boat-handling and navigation skills have to be developed; they have to master the complexities of marine radio and get a thorough understanding of marine legislation. The training stresses Thames Division's operational links with other agencies which have jurisdiction on the river, mainly HM Customs and Excise, the Port of London Authority and the Thames Water Authority.

'Some of our officers have served in the Merchant Navy,' said Chief Inspector Clive Chapman of Thames Division, 'some in the Royal Navy, so they've got marine experience. Others are yachtsmen in their own right. But they do that in their private capacity, that's their hobby – they are policemen first, police officers who police in a marine environment.'

Thames Division's three-man crews police fifty-four miles of the river. Apart from this stretch, which passes through six of the eight Metropolitan Police Areas, they monitor twelve miles of navigable creeks. The patrol area starts in calm waters at Staines and moves on through turbulent currents in Central London; from there it passes into broader stretches south of the Thames Barrier, ending in Dartford Creek in Kent.

At strategic positions along the patrol stretch are specially equipped stations from which boats and their crews can operate. Beyond the Headquarters at Wapping there is Waterloo Pier, claimed to be the world's only floating police station, situated alongside Waterloo

Bridge. This is sometimes referred to as the Jump Station.

'That's a bit of Thames slang, if you like,' said Inspector Ray Bishop. 'We have an emergency boat crew there, and when the other boats are out on patrol and anyone jumps off the bridge, the boat will respond immediately. Two men are in the station all the time to man that boat.'

'I've had experience of people hitting one of the buttresses on the way down and being dead before they hit the water,' said Chief Inspector Chapman. 'And bear in mind, at Westminster Bridge there's only about five foot of water at low tide, so you can go right to the bottom and break your neck.' And the shock of hitting the water seems to change some people's minds. 'Unless you actually put weights in your pockets to make you sink, it's not the easiest thing in the world not to struggle, it's a natural thing to do.' Others don't want to be rescued. 'They react very violently sometimes,' said PC Clive Barnes. 'They just don't want to come out of the water. In their mind they want to die and that's it.'

A powerful arm of Marine Division is the Underwater Search Unit (USU). They are an eleven-man team (an Inspector, a Sergeant and nine Constables) who work from their own specially-equipped boat. Apart from working underwater in the Thames, the USU conduct diving operations in canals, ponds and reservoirs throughout the Metropolitan Police District and in other parts of the country.

'Ninety-five per cent of the time our searches are done in nil visibility,' one of the team explained. 'It's done with touch. Any visibility is a bonus.' A good police diver has what is called the piano touch, an acquired finger-sensitivity that enables him to detect and differentiate even small objects in the murky waters.

Locating corpses is different. 'With a body you're searching for a large object, charging up and down the canal, without too fine a touch. You're hoping to bump into it.'

As well as routine searches in cases of crime, accident and suicide, the USU does essential security work. For example, before the annual ceremony of Trooping the Colour, and prior to state visits and parades along The Mall, they make a security search under the bridge in St James's Park lake, the bridge being a possible escape route for a procession.

Typical recent figures show that over a one-year period, more than 200 operational searches by the USU yielded nineteen dead bodies, sixteen firearms, seven edged weapons, fourteen safes, forty-six cars and thirteen motor cycles.

Now that the working docks have gone from the Thames above Tilbury, leisure has taken over most of the old industrial and commercial centres. Marinas have sprung up and pleasure boats are thick in the water. The training of Thames Division officers keeps pace with the shift to recreation and the more sophisticated techniques of crime on the river.

Murders are rarer, but recently a woman was charged with attempting to kill a three-year-old girl, after witnesses saw the child thrown from a bridge into the river. Details surrounding some apparently accidental deaths make it clear that, with a little more evidence, the police would be investigating murder.

Most common are the accidents, some of them horrific. When the *Marchioness* keeled over after being struck by the dredger *Bowbelle*, four patrol boats of

Recorded Incidents on Thames Division During a Typical Six-Month Period

Persons Rescued by the Police	139
Persons Rescued by the Public	75
Persons at Risk Given Assistance	612
Occasions Advice Given	1,580
Vessels Assisted	448
Dangers to Navigation	326
Disturbances on Disco Boats	45
Verbal Warnings	720
Vessels Stopped	418
Searches of Vessels	33
Miscellaneous Incidents	3,262
Dead Bodies Recovered	36

Thames Division were swiftly at the scene and between them they rescued more than fifty people.

'I've been in situations where I've been in the dark,' said Chapman, 'searching for a couple of people that have fallen in the river. That was bad enough. But here they were faced with a hundred plus . . .'

Thames officers also carried out the operation to remove the dead from the river – fifty-one bodies in all. The weather was warm and the work, which took about two weeks, was increasingly unpleasant. Chapman remarked that it took the men roughly two more weeks to recover from the ordeal.

Other deaths can be taken in the officers' stride, especially when there is only a single anonymous body with no available history. At the Thames Division Identification Office at Wapping the officer in charge has to record the condition of each dead body pulled from the river and establish its identity as quickly as he can.

In the main, Thames Division officers are stoically

calm in their dealings with the unspeakable. The recovery of corpses is a service they perform methodically, arousing little or no outside attention, like most things they do. In spite of their central placement in the life of London, they are a low-key branch of the Metropolitan Police. As Chief Inspector Clive Chapman remarked, 'You very rarely read about the Thames Division.'

TO31
Community Affairs Branch – Vulnerable Groups

A prominent area of TO31's work is in Youth Affairs.

'We aim to prevent youths offending, prevent youth victimisation, and promote active citizenship among young people,' said Superintendent Ruthven Horne, who runs the group. 'The systems on the ground act as a filter to sift out casual offenders who will offend once or twice and then no more ... The more persistent offenders are channelled, initially, to diversionary projects, but then they go into the formal criminal justice system, where they are subject to court orders that address their particular problems.'

Three departments, TO30, TO31 and TO32, jointly make up the Community Affairs Branch. TO30, which is called the Community Involvement and Crime Secretariat, is the support for TO31 and TO32.

TO31 has a strength of ten police officers, three civilian personnel and one part-time civilian, backed up when necessary by support from TO30. Horne does not believe that the criminal justice system, at present, does much to tackle persistent offending. He would like to see the offenders' development influenced in a positive way, with efforts made through schools programmes to raise their awareness of the long-term negative consequences of offending. To that end, TO31 is already involved with 86 per cent of the schools in London, providing training systems, videos and printed material. Reports of some left-wing councils being obstructive may have been exaggerated. 'Hand on heart,' Horne says, 'I cannot think of any schools that have refused us admission on political grounds.'

A powerful youth-initiative scheme administered by TO31 is an annual five-a-side football match, which has been running for approximately thirteen years.

'It takes up a tremendous amount of time,' Horne said. 'It's funded to the tune of approximately £70,000 by the Midland Bank. That covers the costs of printing and publicity. The cost to the police is between £375,000 and £400,000 annually.'

A Junior Citizens Scheme, funded by British Telecom, is designed to alert children up to the age of eleven to everyday dangers and equip them with the expertise to cope with particular situations – accidents in the home, responding to an accident in the street (e.g., dialling 999), electrical and gas emergencies, rebuffing strange adults.

'A serious dilemma is that youth provision in London, in local authorities, has been cut back by 30 per cent,' Horne said, 'so the youth service is almost non-existent in some boroughs. There's a vacuum, and we have to be careful we don't get drawn in to fill it. We are going to have to prioritise our activities, and ask ourselves does it prevent victimisation, does it promote active citizenship? And the activities we run will be the ones that fulfil the criteria.'

Another vital function of TO31 is to devise policies on vulnerable groups for the guidance of local police divisions. The groups include the homeless, the elderly, the physically disabled, the mentally ill and gay and lesbian people. Each group produces its own problems for local policing, and TO31 tries to devise effective ways of dealing with these.

Relationships between the police and homosexual

groups have been tense in the past; at present they are not entirely cordial. Concerted efforts at improvement are being made, but a difficulty, said Horne, is that Inspector John Brown, the officer directly responsible for liaison with homosexuals, gets inundated with almost every call for help or liaison work.

'Homosexuals may have the odd contact in the police that they will trust,' said Horne, 'but by and large, a fair cross-section of the gay and lesbian groups know and trust Inspector Brown, so he's the one they contact.' This problem of trust centred on one person is a symptom of homosexuals' general distrust of the police. 'What has to be done now is to depersonalise it,' Horne says, 'so that they make contact with other people at grassroots level and build up relationships of trust, just as they have with Inspector Brown.'

Where the homeless are concerned, the Metropolitan Police does not have a defining policy. Horne says they are considering whether they should have one or not. The police do not believe they should be the lead agency dealing with homelessness.

'We have an important role under the Vagrancy Act and the Highways Act,' he said, 'but this is a central government and local government problem. Given the number of people who sleep rough in London, it seems purely short-term to arrest them for highway obstruction, or vagrancy, when they will soon be released and be back in the same position again. We would seek to work with central and local government in a coordinated approach of giving advice to rough-sleepers – for instance, telling them where they can get accommodation in cold weather.'

TO31 and the National Children's Home, jointly researching the plight of young people among London's homeless, discovered that most of them do not, as had been suspected, come from all over the country. The majority are native Londoners, with only the occasional one from elsewhere.

'What the research revealed,' Horne said, 'was that we were addressing the wrong issues. In the main we were viewing these youngsters as potential offenders, when in fact we should have been looking at them as potential victims and asking why, in fact, they had run away. The numbers involved are quite staggering. In one division, Hornsey and Haringey, we had approximately 1,320 missing youngsters – that's absentees from care and those genuinely running away from home.'

The Police Foundation are now working with the National Children's Home to devise a pilot scheme in one London borough to address the problem of missing children and find some means of tackling it with more sensitivity than previously.

Difficulties between the police and racial minorities tend to resemble those between the police and homosexual groups. There is still suspicion within certain racial groups that the police discriminate, or that they do not accept there are disadvantages to being a member of a racial minority in Britain today. As was apparent from events surrounding the case of Joy Gardner, a West Indian woman who died in August 1993 after a struggle with police and immigration officers, there are always people ready to fan the flames of potentially explosive situations.

'We have a system for monitoring racial incidents,' Horne said. 'These are submitted from the divisions to our Performance Indicator Bureau, and we oversee them, we interpret them, we develop policies, we try to integrate the whole into equal opportunities, into training, and generally we have an overview on all issues to do with race.'

The mentally ill are a special concern, since more and more of them are coming back into the community because of the steady closure of mental hospitals. 'There is a greater opportunity for problems,' said Horne, 'especially when they don't take their medication. If they become violent they have to be put in a police cell. But the time in that cell should be minimal. It is not the right environment, we are not doctors . . .'

Another TO31 function is that of Metropolitan Special Constabulary Secretariat. It means, in effect, that Horne is nominally the head of a secretariat which deals with the 1,600 Special Constables employed throughout the whole Metropolitan Police Area. Special Constables are unpaid part-time police officers who have permanent jobs elsewhere. They are expected to perform two four-hour duties a month on attachment to divisional stations.

TO32
Community Affairs – Partnership Branch

Superintendent Howard Driver has been in the Metropolitan Police for almost thirty years. 'I wasn't in Broadwater Farm at the time of the riots,' he said, 'but I was the officer in charge of the raid on Broadwater Farm in '89 when we went into the estate and arrested twenty-three drug dealers. I think if you go back to Broadwater Farm now, you will find it a safer place and a more pleasant place to live in. The quality of life has improved.'

Taking charge of TO32 is the first Scotland Yard job Driver has ever had, and it is a lot different from practical on-the-ground policing. He believes that if he had not had the long years of divisional experience, he would have found the decision-making and the exercise of influence very difficult. As matters stand, however, he is perhaps a little wistful and misses his days out on Division.

'The role of TO32 is to support areas and divisions in dealing with such problems as street crime, drug peddling and the special difficulties surrounding alcohol abuse,' he said. 'It's also to undertake functions that need to be performed centrally, to formulate policy and monitor departmental performance. We cannot dictate to areas and divisions, only through the policy committee and the executives, so consequently we influence in that way, and in the way that we are demand led.'

'The 'partnership' concept came from the Home

Office, the idea being that the police should work more closely with local authorities.

'But it isn't just local authorities that the police work with any more,' Driver said. 'We work with business, with the education people, with social services. So the bottom line is that we have to work together now in relation to crime reduction.'

TO32 has a staff of thirteen police officers plus support staff. Their work is carried out under specific headings, although there are occasional overlaps.

Inspector Dick Groves is a member of a Territorial Operations work plan which looks at future Metropolitan Police strategy related to the prevention of drug abuse. Groves is researching and helping to implement a coordinated drug strategy for the whole of the Metropolitan Police Service, underpinned through education and training.

Driver himself chairs the Police Utilities Working Party, put together to tackle burglary artifice, which is the ploy where bogus officials appear at people's doors and ask to be let in.

'People turn up pretending to be board officials,' Driver said, 'water, gas, electricity. We hope to produce a code of practice for the big companies on preventing or reducing the opportunity for bogus officials to enter houses, especially those of elderly people. This is one of the first times throughout the Met that all the utilities, from British Telecom to the Water Board, gas and electricity, and the regulatory bodies of these companies have got together round the table and produced a code of practice. It should have long-term repercussions for reducing crime in the home.'

The 'Partnership Approach' is described by Driver as 'an approach by those with influence, those who hold the purse strings, to provide a better quality of life within the London boroughs.' He offered an example.

'In the Elephant and Castle shopping precinct they're having problems, inside and out, with street robbery. We have been to the site, had meetings with local-authority officials and the people running the complex, and now, with the help of closed-circuit television, there's a major initiative going on there, coordinated to reduce crime.'

Inspector Shirley Tulloch supports the 126 officers in the sixty-two Domestic Violence Units on the divisions. She also chairs the Domestic Violence Working Party of the Metropolitan Police Service. Tulloch has an over-view of domestic violence, she formulates policy, and she gives advice and support to the domestic violence units.

'She is an observer on a pilot scheme in Islington at the moment,' Driver said. 'It's called Domestic Matters. This is different from a domestic violence unit, where there are only police officers. This scheme has family consultants, too. Once police officers have been to the scene of an incident of domestic violence, the family consultants will move in.'

Driver explained the idea behind the 'Design-Out Crime' scheme. 'Where there is a crime problem,' he said, 'you can design it out. Within the Met there are Prevention Design Advisors (CPDAs) and these officers are skilled enough to be able to say to the planners and architects, look, if you design this in a different way, this footpath, this alleyway, this car park, this estate, you will reduce the opportunity for crime.'

Driver said he believed the main problem with a department like TO32 is one of image, and it is a problem that is being addressed.

'Crime prevention has been an Aunt Sally to proactive policing. It is now realised that you can have proactive policing, but you can also have your 'designing-out' activities, too. There must be networking between the police and the community agencies, those with influence, those who hold the purse strings at a local-authority level. I can lend my skills and my knowledge of working in difficult, politically sensitive areas, I can lend those skills to the design-making process up here. Without my experience out on division, the decision-making process would have been very, very difficult.'

INSPECTION AND REVIEW
Introduction

Assistant Commissioner Peter Winship first joined the Metropolitan Police as a Chief Superintendent, having been a police officer since 1962 in the Oxfordshire Constabulary, which later became part of Thames Valley. During his time there he joined an accelerated promotion course and was sent to Oxford University on a Home Office Scholarship, reading English at St John's College.

'I think I was the first policeman to read English,' he said. 'There were various professional elements to the fast-track scheme, too – I spent four months in America, for instance, training with the FBI.'

He climbed steadily through the ranks at Thames Valley until he took the Senior Command Course in 1982.

'I came into the Met and went on to a division for just over a year. I then entered a department here at Scotland Yard, spending about two and a half years as part of the then Commissioner Sir Kenneth Newman's planning and policy team. Then I went back to Thames Valley as Assistant Chief Constable, and returned to the Met in '87 as Deputy Assistant Commissioner.'

For a little over a year he was Director, Complaints Investigation Branch (CIB), after which he took command of Number One Area (North and East London) for a further year. In June 1990, he was made Assistant Commissioner. Late in 1992, at roughly the same time that he was asked to coordinate the Yard's submission to Sir Patrick Sheehy's inquiry, he took charge of the new Inspection and Review Department.

During 1991 and 1992, in debate with the Home Office, Winship was very much the Met's spokesman on the matter of clearly defined standards within London's police service. The idea of developing a regime with a more positive and focused performance began to emerge.

'We were sitting down almost every week with the Audit Commission, talking about how one might monitor and measure police performance, what were the indicators of success, what were the standards that we might be setting – what, indeed, were the priorities. Having the inspection process in the same department was a natural way to bring those particular elements together. We had a whole raft of functions that helped the service determine what its priorities were, because initially I had the planning and the policy elements also working to me, determining what our corporate strategy was, starting at the very macro level, deciding what the five-year plan would be and what were the priorities within that.'

The setting of clear standards, alongside a mechanism for auditing their implementation and redressing failures or abuses, is central to the operation of Inspection and Review; the more so, Winship observes, since London tends to set the standard for the rest of the United Kingdom.

'The Met has been a leading innovator in policing,' he said, 'and so it should be. After all, we are the critical mass, we are nearly a quarter of all policing in the United Kingdom, we have the skills and the talent to lead the service in a number of areas. We have traditionally done it, with our policies on child abuse, on domestic violence, on screening of crime, on dealing with burglary and so on. Our capability to think through these ideas and develop policies comes from the critical-mass argument, that we have the opportunities here.'

The demand for competent policing is probably higher in London than elsewhere in Britain, Winship believes: 'We have a disproportionate number of success-ful, bright, assertive people who make a demand on their policing service which is a little different, perhaps, than in the rest of the country.' If that is the case, it reinforces the argument for the Met being a necessary source of policing standards for the rest of the country.

As Chairman of the Crime Report Information System (CRIS) Project Board, Winship is adamant that, in spite of a poor start and consistently glum predictions for the system's future, it will eventually flourish.

'The Met has the most antique way of reporting crime at the moment,' he said. 'It's a paper system – photocopying, sending it up to headquarters to have the stats prepared – it really is disgraceful. CRIS has been a long time coming, because it has the most exacting and complex specification of any crime report system, certainly in Europe and probably in the world. I happen to believe we're on the edge of getting it right, it's becoming more and more stable. It hasn't cost us any more money than we originally planned, some £21 million. It's cost the contractor and the supplier a great deal more, and it may have been too clever, too complex in its origins, but we're close now to delivering.'

Winship's belief in CRIS is as firm as his views on the creation and maintenance of high operational stand-ards, and his belief in Scotland Yard as a centre of excellence. He talks of the Yard's global standing, its reputation for integrity, and for getting results.

'A lot of that reputation derives from the Specialist Operations work,' he said, 'the old "C" Department squads who went out in the '40s and '50s and detected and investigated murder in the United Kingdom, and went much further afield, and still do. Today we have over a score of police officers from London working somewhere in the world, investigating very serious crime, at the invitation of various foreign governments. They ask us to do it because they respect our history and our tradition, and they probably know they're getting the finest.'

COMPLAINTS INVESTIGATION BUREAU (CIB)

The Police Complaints Authority (PCA) is an independent body set up in 1985 to supervise the investigation of complaints against the police. It has two roles: supervising the investigation of complaints, and considering the recommended disciplinary measures against officers below the rank of Chief Superintendent.

CIB1 is the force discipline office. They read the complaints reports and decide in each case if the evidence justifies a formal disciplinary hearing. The final decision is taken by Commander Eric Humphrey, Director CIB. If he decides on a disciplinary hearing, CIB1 will formulate the charges and make the arrangements for the hearing; if the officer in question is found guilty and makes an appeal to the Commissioner, CIB1 will prepare the appeal papers, and the response to the appeal.

CIB2 is the investigative arm, a much larger team than CIB1. They investigate more serious cases (especially those supervised by the PCA), and serious internal-discipline cases.

Although the most common complaints are those made against the police by members of the public, and internal disciplinary matters, there are other, smaller categories. 'You do get a number of cases where a judge expresses concern about the conduct of a police officer in relation to a trial he has dealt with,' Humphrey said, 'and those cases would be investigated.'

Each of the eight Metropolitan Police Areas has its own miniature CIB, known as an Area Complaints Unit, headed by a Superintendent. These units investigate less serious complaints and internal discipline issues. They pass on the more serious cases to CIB, especially those involving very large numbers of witnesses and perhaps a lot of travelling, sometimes abroad.

Detective Chief Superintendent Douglas Shrubsole is Head of CIB2. His department is divided into nine teams, each having a Superintendent, an Inspector and four Sergeants. Shrubsole said the process of investigating a complaint scarcely differs from an ordinary CID investigation. In his view CIB2 strongly resembles a divisional CID office in a small provincial town with a population of 28,000 – the population in this instance being the police staff of the Met.

'To constitute a Section 84, a complaint against the police, it has to be something a police officer did in his capacity as an officer. If an allegation of rape is made against a police officer and he was off duty when the alleged incident took place, then that would not be a Section 84 complaint. It is an allegation of crime against a member of the public who happens to be a police officer.'

For financial and technical reasons CIB2 do not have their own surveillance team, so they have to call on teams from SO11 (Criminal Intelligence). 'It's impossible to know always who's worked with who, so if it's possible during the briefing with SO11, we avoid mentioning the name or names of the people we are investigating.'

To illustrate a straightforward and largely typical CIB2 inquiry, Shrubsole outlined the case of a police officer, formerly stationed in East London. The officer, on a murder investigation, was initially questioned by CIB2 when it became clear that items of property – books, ornaments – were missing from the murder scene.

'He said he had authority from the bank, who were responsible for disposal of the property, to dispose of it himself, because it had no value,' Shrubsole said. 'His home was eventually searched and various items from the murder scene were found. He was charged with theft and eventually he was found guilty and sentenced to eighteen months' imprisonment.'

Alleged assaults form the bulk of complaints made against police officers by members of the public. Shrubsole thinks it is only to be expected, since every time a member of the public is arrested, there is a confrontation, and it frequently has a physical component. The majority of alleged assaults, on being investigated, turn out to have been no more than the application of force which, in the circumstances, was entirely reasonable. But even when there is evidence to suggest a police officer overstepped his legal rights to the use of force, juries show a tendency to acquit. Shrubsole believes they are reluctant to accept that police officers could commit assaults of the degree often alleged.

In March 1993 the Home Office published a discussion document outlining a proposed two-tier system to deal with complaints against police officers. The first tier, covering cases of serious misconduct, would continue to be determined by the PCA; a new procedure would be introduced to deal with cases of unsatisfactory performance. Officers who fell below required performance standards would face an internal management disciplinary procedure, allowing for access to industrial tribunals in appeals against dismissal.

The document also proposed:

- Chief Constables to be given the right of instant dismissal in extreme cases of discreditable conduct.
- Police officers to be required to resign, if necessary be dismissed, for patterns of unsatisfactory behaviour.
- A 'significant public interest test' to be applied in deciding which cases should go to the PCA and which should be determined internally.

PCA Chairman Sir Leonard Peach remarked in the PCA annual report that his authority had repeatedly complained at the number of police officers being granted early retirement before complaints could be heard.

Asked to comment on this, Assistant Commissioner Peter Winship said, 'The reform programme proposes that where officers are not fit to appear before a discipline hearing, the hearing can go ahead in their absence. That is important. Up till now, the regulations have denied us the opportunity to do that.'

On a Press claim that complaints of racism against police officers in London had risen by 13 per cent, Winship said flatly that there were sixty complaints of racially discriminatory behaviour in 1991–1992, and fifty in 1992–1993, so the number of such complaints appears to be falling. There has been concern in the press, however, that from a total of 4,258 general complaints recorded in 1992–1993, less than 3 per cent, in other words fewer than 130 cases, were upheld following investigation.

'That is not good enough,' Winship said. The problem, he believes, is a chronic lack of corroboration. 'One of the key issues is the burden of proof, and for all police discipline at the moment it is at the higher level, it is the criminal burden of proof, beyond all reasonable doubt, that lies with the complainant. Bearing in mind that most contact between police and public in an arrest situation is one-on-one, you will never get corroboration of what the complainant is alleging, unless there is exceptional medical evidence to support an allegation of assault, for example.'

Bringing down the level of the burden of proof would seem to be a step towards achieving balance. 'If a police officer assaults somebody, that is a crime and it must be investigated as a crime, as well as being an allegation or complaint. Corruption is another example. So, we cannot ask for a lower burden of proof in those serious complaints. But for many of the other matters that are complained of, such as incivility, oppressive conduct, neglect of duty – we could clearly, I think, look for a lower burden of proof.'

In spite of poor figures for complaints upheld, Winship believes the Met shows a very strong commitment to keeping its house in order. 'Our record for the ultimate punishment, dismissing officers and requiring them to resign, is very, very high compared to the rest of the country. In 1992–93 we sacked seventeen officers and we required a further seventeen to resign. That's thirty-four officers who lost their jobs as a result of the formal discipline process. I think that indicates our commitment.'

As for the police conducting inquiries into their own alleged shortcomings and crimes, Winship takes the view that a lot of police experience is needed to 'work through the wrinkles', as he puts it, of those officers who abuse the law. If there is a real problem, he says, it is convincing the public that the police are quite capable of being dispassionate in their investigations of their own kind.

'I can produce complaint files which, when they are resolved, are *feet* thick. Thousands of witness statements taken in some cases, scores in every complaint case, and yet we cannot persuade the public that we are unbiased.'

Winship repeated that he was aware of the shortcomings in the mechanisms for investigating complaints against the police, but indicated that determination to put the defects right was intense and widespread.

'I think we need to be doing better, and we need to demonstrate to the public that we're doing better,' he said. 'The process needs simplification, it needs speeding up, and it needs better outcomes. If we adopt a slightly lower burden of proof, that will help.'

INSPECTORATE

Deputy Assistant Commissioner John Metcalfe sees the function of the Inspectorate as twofold: to improve the overall service delivered by the Metropolitan Police, and to act as a line of assurance to the Commissioner and, via him, to the Home Secretary, that the police is being run effectively.

It is a small department. In addition to Metcalfe there are two Commanders, three Chief Superintendents (two of them detectives), and a small clerical support staff. Recently the Home Secretary decided that the

Complaints against the Metropolitan Police 1991/92 and 1992/93

TYPE OF COMPLAINT	NUMBER OF CASES OF COMPLAINTS RECEIVED *		TOTAL NUMBER OF COMPLAINTS COMPLETED†	
	91/92	92/93	91/92	92/93
Incivility	546	553	1,378	1,356
Assault	2,061	2,107	2,710	2,581
Irregularity in procedure	97	88	505	445
Traffic irregularity	23	13	47	39
Neglect of duty	240	298	811	845
Corrupt practice	36	37	23	31
Mishandling of property	94	109	253	253
Irregularity related to evidence/perjury	128	137	465	441
Oppressive conduct or harassment	355	382	792	902
Racially discriminatory behaviour	60	50	189	210
Unlawful arrest or detention	303	266	785	740
Impropriety in connection with the search of premises	108	127	260	292
Other crime	34	50	180	175
Other	36	41	115	85
Total	4,121	4,258	8,513	8,395

* Counted by the main allegation known at the time of receipt
† Includes all matters of complaint, not only the main allegation

Inspectorate should come under Her Majesty's Inspectorate of Constabularies.

'They've been invited into the Metropolitan Police to do two inspections a year for the last four or five years,' Metcalfe said. 'If we read the Home Secretary right, he's going to give them full responsibility for inspecting the Metropolitan Police, so I don't think this department will continue to exist after the next eighteen months or so. The Met will come under the same form of inspection as the rest of the country.'

Metcalfe, formerly an Area DAC, said he did not want to join the Inspectorate at first. 'When I was asked to do it I prevaricated for quite a long time until the Commissioner, Sir Peter Imbert, called me up and asked me if I'd do it . . . So I finally gave in and came, under one condition, that what we did was going to be effective.'

The London Police Areas vary in size between eight and ten divisions, and each year, under the present arrangements, there are four full Area inspections and four interim inspections, so all of the Areas are covered. A Commander and a team of Chief Superintendents examine one division for three days, the others for one day each. Inspections of headquarters departments are also carried out, whenever the time can be found.

'On Area inspections, we start off by writing to the DAC, get his approval on which divisions we spend three days at, and which ones we visit for one day,' said Metcalfe. 'Covering a division in three days is difficult, and in one day it's impossible . . . So, as soon as the background work has been done, we focus as a team on what we're going to look at during three days. At the moment we're highlighting things like equal opportunities, success in terms of crime prevention and crime detection, how well they are achieving their objectives in training, and what their plans are for the future.'

Metcalfe makes sure that after an inspection, the follow-up recommendations are restricted to major steps that can realistically be taken, and avoid trivial fault-finding that could be applied to practically any situation.

'I suppose they do find us a bit of an imposition,' he said, 'and as an Area DAC I felt a bit imposed on. But I was always hopeful the Inspectorate would find something I didn't know, and *needed* to know about.'

Staff Inspection Unit This is a group of officers who examine specific posts in the Met and try to decide, first, whether there is a need for the work to be done, and, if there is a need, whether it is being done at the right level and by the right persons, i.e. police officers or civilians.

Headquarters Review 'It was necessary to re-examine our spending,' Winship said, 'and I think we recognised, over a year ago, that our management overhead was too high. In addition to that, we probably had too many people working at headquarters. We can't buy any more policemen, much as we need them, so we've looked long and hard at what is done at the centre, and the result of that is John Metcalfe's work, undertaken for Sir Peter Imbert.'

The work in question, a Headquarters Review known as the Metcalfe Report, has recommended substantial transfers of officers from headquarters to the divisions. The repercussions on police officers and civilians working in Scotland Yard were enormous.

'We indicated that we felt there were about a thousand posts that could be dispensed with,' said Metcalfe, 'without major effect on the service. The idea was that the staff would go, but the work wouldn't, it would not be devolved with the staff. This was a thousand jobs out of a total of approximately five thousand.'

Predictably, there have been complaints and objections, but Metcalfe believes the moves are simply a response to obvious priorities.

'When you're talking about the rises in crime that we've had, and the rises in public disorder, it is true that out on division they are strapped for people,' he said. 'I don't think the same pressures have affected Scotland Yard.'

Devolution always carries the risk of damage to centres of excellence, and Scotland Yard, being rich in talent, stands to suffer particularly from reductions of personnel in its specialist departments. Metcalfe believes some things ought to remain at the centre, and he is sure that during the last devolution, in 1985, assets were transferred which might have been better kept at Scotland Yard. This time no such serious damage will be done, he is sure. Besides, he thinks it is possible to be sentimentally unrealistic about the Yard.

'The tourists come and look at it, and they think of Scotland Yard as the Murder Squad, which hasn't existed there for yonks. I think of it as headquarters.'

Metcalfe admits that he has learned more about the Met in eight months at the Inspectorate than he did in the previous thirty years. But now that he has completed the Headquarters Review, he would love to go back to Area.

'But none of my friends out there look like giving up and letting me have their job,' he said.

PLUS PROGRAMME

Shortly after his appointment as Commissioner of the Metropolitan Police in 1988, Sir Peter Imbert dropped the word 'force' in favour of 'service', a sign of his concern for the image of the Met, which people believed was losing the trust and confidence of the public. In the same year Imbert commissioned the corporate identity consultants, Wolff Olins, to report on the state of London's police service.

The Olins report, *A Force for Change*, was released in September 1988. It said, among other things, that the police in London operated in an 'atmosphere of shabby confusion' amid crumbling buildings, with only a muddled notion of their group identity. The report cited social, legal and administrative changes as contributing to a loss of public faith and private self-esteem, and it criticised underlying stances and policies, some of them official, some not. Emphasising that the Metropolitan Police lacked corporacy, the report identified six areas for remedial action:

- sharpening the sense of purpose
- healing the divided organisation
- tightening management practice
- promoting a service ethos
- improvement of internal and external communication
- improved visual appearance

The impact of the report was profound, since it came from a firm of unbiased professionals unconnected with the Press or with any group having a grudge or prejudice against the police. Responding to the report, Sir Peter Imbert commissioned another study on how best to implement Olins's recommendations. The result, a booklet entitled *The Plus Programme – Making it Happen*, was published in April 1989. It outlined several vital components, a prominent one being adoption of the *Statement of Common Purpose and Values*, which reads:

> The purpose of the Metropolitan Police Service is to uphold the law fairly and firmly; to prevent crime; to pursue and bring to justice those who break the law; to keep the Queen's Peace; to protect, help and reassure people in London; and to be seen to do all this with integrity, common sense and sound judgement.
>
> We must be compassionate, courteous and patient, acting without fear or favour or prejudice to the rights of others. We need to be professional, calm and restrained in the face of violence and apply only that force which is necessary to accomplish our lawful duty.
>
> We must strive to reduce the fears of the public and, so far as we can, to reflect their priorities in the action we take. We must respond to well-founded criticism with a willingness to change.

It was unfortunate, from a public relations standpoint, that on the day the Plus Programme was launched the Metropolitan Police was ordered to pay £30,000 to a man wrongly convicted on the basis of confessions fabricated by detectives.

Imbert's proposals for change triggered heated debate inside the Met, mainly between those who believed change was essential to their survival as a credible organisation, and those who believed the Met was swinging too far in the direction of social work.

To win the hearts and minds of the forty-four thousand people working in the Met, a huge programme of seminars was organised. It lasted for over sixty weeks, at a cost of £5.5 million.

'Seminars ran five days a week at eight centres,' said Commander Tony Rowe, who runs the Plus Team. 'Each person was expected to leave with an entirely notional but personal contract about what he or she was going to do to make things better. There followed a debrief with a member of each person's management team. In May 1992 we did a staff opinion survey, and almost 40 per cent of the people in the organisation said that the Statement of Common Purpose and Values was something they used and related to every day.'

Rowe explained how Wolff Olins's main recommendations for change were addressed.

'Developing a common sense of purpose was really the need to look and see what the core business is. What we did was to develop and issue the Statement of Common Purpose and Values. As for fragmentation within the organisation, we were very much two organisations, the police side and the civil side, and now, increasingly, people will say we are an organisation of 46,000 people. Improving poor management – we reviewed that bottom to top, looking first at the policy-makers, and setting up a whole different system for determining and improving the policy of the organisation.'

In general terms, Rowe believes, the Plus Programme has advanced a lot of ideas and reinforced awareness of a need in the service for improved leadership, and for quality service externally and internally.

'The AC said to me when I took up this job, "You know why we need the Plus Programme? It's because people aren't taught good manners any more." We have to teach people in the organisation and remind them that there is a standard, and that standard is very much part of old-fashioned values and old-fashioned good manners.'

Now there is Charter, launched in October 1993, which purports to be just what its name suggests, a written declaration of principles. Peter Winship was asked if Plus had done its job and was now winding down and being replaced by Charter.

'Three-and-a-half years on, we think Plus is now flourishing,' he said. Now, Winship believes, Plus is at the stage where it must be integrated into the main stream of the organisation, and that is being done.

'We see Charter as the natural corollary of Plus. Charter is a stated declaration to customers of what we will do on their behalf. It takes the Statement of Common Purposes and translates it into practical values.'

PERFORMANCE REVIEW AND MANAGEMENT SERVICES (PRAMS)

In an age when women's stereotypes are being over-turned, Mrs Sue Merchant admits there have been a few giggles over the fact that she is the Director of a department known throughout the service as PRAMS. Assistant Commissioner Peter Winship explained that it is part of the history and tradition of the Met that departmental titles are reduced to acronyms.

'I remember Sue coming to me in the planning stage and saying, "Do you realise that it could emerge as PRAMS? Look at the implications for me, a woman, acting as leader of this ..." And we actually had a serious conversation, lasting about forty seconds, about whether we should try and come up with another title.'

Leaving university with a physics degree, Merchant

worked for a few years with the Ministry of Defence, engaged on defence and naval operational studies. She joined the Metropolitan Police as a Senior Scientific Officer in 1975 and has been there ever since.

'Nearly everything we do is pointed at trying to improve the effectiveness and efficiency of the Met,' she said. 'It's quite simple, really. We collect information and do a variety of studies. We collect the information to be able to show how we're performing, and then we carry out a range of studies designed to improve that performance.'

PRAMS is subdivided into a number of units, including:

Performance Information Bureau (PR1)

Merchant says the job of PR1 is to take the temperature of the Met. The Bureau's ninety-five employees collect Crime statistics, magistrates' court statistics, traffic accident statistics and a variety of other data which add up to a performance-related picture of London's police service. They also collect public-attitude-survey information.

Work Study Projects (PR2)

This is a small department employing nine people to carry out assessments of working methods within the Met. Usual work studies involve people with stop-watches measuring the time it takes to do something, usually with a view to improving efficiency. Merchant said that PR2 have tended to widen the scope of work studies.

Blueprint Suggestion Scheme (MS15)

The traditional staff suggestion scheme. Police officers or members of civil staff can make suggestions for improving conditions or procedures within the Met.

Management Science Projects (MS12)

Five people in this group are engaged in designing mathematical formulae aimed at improving efficiency. One example of what they have done is a Manpower Allocation Formula, which works out ways of allocating manpower across the entire Metropolitan Police Service.

Occupational Psychology (MS14)

'There are three people in the group, and they do a range of things,' Merchant said. 'They have expertise in questionnaire design – putting the boxes in the right place, keeping the questions unambiguous, things like that. They do a variety of psychosomatic testing for a number of branches, like Obscene Publications for instance.'

At present, MS14 is mainly occupied with psychometric testing of police recruits. 'Psychometric testing is things like intelligence tests, or tests which show how well a person is matched to the job on offer. They have used these techniques in the past to recruit scientists for our department, to make sure they have the correct intellectual and communications skills.'

Other sections within PRAMS provide support for various police computer systems, produce clearer police forms and arrange access for people who wish to see details held by police on computers.

DEPUTY COMMISSIONER'S
EXECUTIVE
Introduction

'I never refer to a Deputy Commissioner's Department, because it really isn't that,' said Deputy Commissioner John Smith. 'It's an executive. This organisation needs to decide a range of things which are not of the highest order, but they're important decisions that can only be decided by all of the prime players reaching agreement – such things as who gets what in relation to resources, both manpower and money. Issues of that sort tend to be determined in my Executive, so we don't bother the Commissioner with them.'

Three departments work to the Deputy Commissioner: Central Staff, the Department of Public Affairs and the Solicitors Department. There is also a small scrutiny section. 'That's an accident of history,' Smith said. 'It would more logically have fitted into the Inspection and Review Department. But the Deputy Commissioner has become, over time, the scrutineer-in-chief.'

For a time John Smith was tipped to succeed Sir Peter Imbert as Commissioner of the Metropolitan Police. He is currently President of the Association of Chief Police Officers (ACPO), a post which makes him the spokesman for all senior police officers, representing them to the public and to the Government.

Curiously for someone of such high rank, Smith does not have the power of arrest. His position is special: like other officers of the rank of Assistant Commissioner upwards, he is a holder of the Royal Warrant, an indication that he was selected by the Queen on the recommendation of the Home Secretary. He is not a police officer in the strict sense, does not have the extended powers of the police constable, and in relation to criminal matters he has only the rights of the ordinary citizen.

It was decided some time ago that the Deputy Commissioner should have an over-arching responsibility to ensure the effectiveness and efficiency of the organisation. The Value For Money Committee was the outcome of that decision, and it is headed by the Deputy Commissioner.

'It gives me the ability to ask appropriate questions of the most senior people in this organisation in relation to the service that they're providing,' Smith said. 'So it does give me a certain influence. Value For Money is a Government thrust. There is a central Value For Money Committee at the Home Office and it is reflected in every police organisation – soon they will all have one for the whole force. It's all about the thrust for efficiency, making more of what you have, providing a better quality of service. Quality of service and value for money can't be separated.'

Smith agrees he has something of a roving brief. The role, he said, is partly trouble-shooting, partly public relations. 'In getting around and talking to people in a way that perhaps others can't, then I can help bridge the communication gap that will always exist between those people out there, and these people in here.'

CENTRAL STAFF

Central Staff is an example of an important department high in the structure of the Metropolitan Police which many people, police officers among them, do not know exists. It is staffed by thirty-five people, including three

Superintendents, five Chief Inspectors, three or four Inspectors and civilian administrative staff. All of them, with the exception of one female civilian, are graduates, most of them MBAs. The department is headed by a Yorkshireman, Commander Michael Briggs, who admitted that one of his reasons for joining the Metropolitan Police was to get a change from his life in Leeds.

Central Staff is, in effect, the Civil Service for the Policy Committee. 'One of our functions here is environmental scanning,' Briggs said, 'which is an elegant way of saying we keep an eye on the world around us. We look at emerging socio-economic trends, and at times we make predictions – at times we're actually better at predicting the movements in the economy than the Treasury economic model.'

He cited the issue of AIDS and how, in 1986, the Government's Chief Medical Officer was denying it was a particular issue, or even a problem of any significant proportions.

'We actually looked at what had happened in California,' Briggs said, 'we talked to virologists, experts in the field. And we made predictions, although we got the numbers wrong. We were looking to more exponential growth, but interestingly, many of the things we said would happen have happened in the last few years.'

It is a major part of Central Staff's responsibility to warn the Commissioner and the Policy Committee of any major changes that are likely to occur in the political climate. But it is no part of Central Staff policy to make value judgements on the decisions or actions of any political party.

'In my view we would be doing a great disservice to London and to the people who pay the bill for policing if we didn't have an eye on the future, and also have an eye professionally on how government thinking, translated into legislative action, will actually impact our resources. It's all about getting ready for the future.'

Under the heading of Performance Review, Central Staff is required to provide a survey of performance, in specified areas, to compare with the corporate policy.

'For example,' Briggs said, 'some of the material we have offered has been on how minorities are treated both within the organisation and outside, how they do as candidates for the organisation, how black people, how women are doing in relation to promotion, and in relation to selection for specialist branches. With ethnic minorities, we've taken a look at our case-disposal arrangements to see how black people coming into custody fare when it comes to being charged, to being cautioned, to having no further action taken, etcetera.'

Briggs agrees that in servicing the executives and the associated bodies, Central Staff's role is, again, similar to that of the Civil Service, providing the necessary analytical back-up.

Briggs is proud of his department and believes it has been a serious force for change within the Met. His only misgivings lie in the direction of changes which may mean, among other setbacks, a reduction in the numbers of his staff.

'One does worry that with all the changes going on, fundamental changes to our structure, we'll still have to maintain the thrust to deliver a service to an increasingly sophisticated customer. We will probably get there, but it ain't going to be easy.'

DIRECTORATE OF PUBLIC AFFAIRS (DPA)

'Whenever you see or hear the phrase, "A Scotland Yard spokesman said . . .", 99 per cent of the time it is something that has come from here,' said David Jervis, Head of the DPA's Press Bureau. 'We have nine shift workers who work round the clock, and during the day there's anything up to five press officers on duty. Nights and late evenings, there's usually an officer on alone. Sod's Law says that if a bomb goes off, or there's a multiple murder or a train crash, it's going to be when there's only one person on.'

The DPA employs more than 100 people, among them fifty Government Information Service staff whose collective specialities are journalism, broadcasting, marketing, public relations and advertising.

The DPA is divided into five branches.

Corporate Communications Services has three sections who report to the Deputy Director. The first is Internal Media, which offers a range of publications for relaying information to members of the service. Number two, Briefing and Parliamentary, produces briefing papers on various issues – police, media, Parliamentary, judicial and social – which are likely to affect the Metropolitan Police Service. The third, Consultancy and Development, gives general advice on communications, helps other parts of the service to develop communications strategies and runs pilot projects.

The news branches deal with local, national and international media. They cover the eight Area press and publicity offices and the Press Bureau, as well as three teams working for headquarters departments. Each branch works to an Assistant Director.

Each of the eight Area headquarters has a press and publicity office and its staff, the Area Press and Publicity Officers (APPOs), deal with the media at the scenes of serious crimes and major incidents.

The ambitious aim of the Press Bureau is to answer every question about the Metropolitan Police put to it by the media. It has been claimed that this is Europe's busiest press office, working around the clock every day of the year. They deal with an estimated 350,000 questions a year.

The two main operational departments, Specialist and Territorial Operations, and the smaller support departments, have their own DPA teams.

David Rangecroft, Assistant Director, DPA, said that nowadays they spend more and more time briefing journalists on what they can and cannot say; 'And on how far they can and can't go. It's amazing how, as the number of journalistic outlets has burgeoned, the level of journalistic basic skills has gone down. One of the staff got a phone call from a fellow journalist who didn't know what a coroner was, or what an inquest was – he or she had heard of them, but didn't really know ... You have to be very careful that people understand what you say, and the language you use.'

The Director of the DPA, Sarah Cullum, joined the Met from Inland Revenue in 1993.

One of the first matters the Commissioner raised with Cullum was his strong wish to see a narrowing of the gap between what the Metropolitan Police do and what the public believe they do. He felt that the service needed to shout more loudly about its successes. Charter, Cullum believes, goes some way towards doing that.

'It's not the same as the Statement of Common Purpose,' she said. 'That's about us, that's not about the service we give to the public.'

Charter is a document with two key parts: one sets out the role of the Metropolitan Police, the other is a declaration of performance standards.

The word 'charter' has arguably been devalued, not least by the poor reception that greeted John Major's promotion of a citizens' bill of rights under the same title. Cullum accepts that the name could be an obstacle, but not a serious one.

'We're facing a lot of cynicism, but the Commissioner's view is that we've just got to prove that our charter is going to be different.'

Keen to generate incentives in support of Charter's image, Cullum believes the Met could benefit from more economy in the area of complaint. 'Our way of trying to achieve change sometimes is by moaning. We ought to be looking for the more positive things, rather than lashing ourselves in public.'

A pall drops over DPA whenever press publicity is given to cases of misbehaviour or criminal activity by Metropolitan Police officers. Cullum agreed that a recent case, where three police officers were jailed for making a drunken attack on a family and trying to frame one of the victims, was profoundly disheartening. But it would be wrong for the DPA to refine the facts to make them more palatable to the public.

Early on the morning of 3 June 1993, more than 2,000 police officers swooped on 617 houses across London in an anti-burglary operation codenamed Bumblebee. It was a successful raid: 400 arrests were made and property worth many thousands of pounds was recovered. That morning journalists and camera crews joined police units, by invitation, on many of the raids.

'I was very keen on this,' Cullum said. 'I was coordinating that campaign across London. It wasn't easy to get done, but the operational people wanted to do it, and I wanted to do it in terms of publicity because I didn't see any other way to do it. I'd like to do much more of that.' It was the first major example, under Sarah Cullum's regime, of the Met making the news, rather than simply reacting to it.

At a time of profound change within the Metropolitan Police, internal communication is crucially important. Cullum, accordingly, has embarked on the creation of an Internal Communications Department. If they get the internal message right, she believes, it will help get the external one right, because they should not differ very much.

'If we tell staff that we're performance related, that this is our focus and this is how we're going to work, that should also be the message going outside.'

DPA CRIME MUSEUM (THE BLACK MUSEUM)

The curator emphasises that the purpose of the Black Museum is to instruct, but it is hard to ignore the melodramatic impact. It would be hard to play it down, too, since the exhibits are relics of more than 100 years of sometimes grisly crime, presided over by the death masks of several murderers.

There are no windows and the lighting is low-key. The temperature is kept surprisingly low – 62° Fahrenheit – while the humidity is high, to minimise the processes of decay on the exhibits, some of them old and fragile. There is a funereal hush, which is particularly odd at the heart of a modern office building.

The name 'Black Museum' has stuck since it was used by a journalist in 1877 to describe the first crime museum on the top floor at Great Scotland Yard. The museum was originally an instructional facility where policemen learned about burglary, but within a year it expanded to cover most other kinds of crime.

Unique in its scope and in the concentration of exhibits, the present museum occupies two rooms on the first floor at the headquarters building in Broadway. There is a visitors' book with the signatures, among many others, of Gilbert and Sullivan, Laurel and Hardy, Harry Houdini, E. W. Hornung (author of the *Raffles* stories), Jerome K. Jerome, and Sir Arthur Conan Doyle.

The museum is not open to the public. Entry is by invitation. 'What we cannot have is people who come in here just gawping and looking at various bits and pieces,' said the curator, Bill Waddell. 'Policemen form a percentage of our visitors, of course. Then there are magistrates, judges, pathologists, doctors, criminologists – people who have a direct interest in crime and the solving of crime. We also, as far as possible, try to perform a public relations exercise, so sometimes we have community groups coming round.'

The constantly updated collection of specialised weapons is one of the most remarkable exhibits in the entire museum. In their wide variety they demonstrate both the distorted ingenuity of criminals and the steady evolution of their weaponry. The classic crimes depicted in the museum are also of special value, Waddell believes, to the student and the concerned layman.

Among the exhibits are the bath Denis Nielsen used to dispose of some of his victims, the gun used by Ruth Ellis (who was the last woman to be hanged in England), a bomb that killed bomb-disposal expert Ken Howorth, the shattered helmet of a member of the Household Cavalry killed by an IRA bomb in Hyde Park, and many other exhibits in dedicated displays under such headings as Abortion, Bank Robberies, Drugs, Murder of Police Officers, Poisoners, Vice.

One ingenious exhibit is a pellet, no bigger than the head of a pin, that was used to kill Georgi Markov in 1981. Markov, an exiled Bulgarian broadcaster, had been standing on Waterloo Bridge when he felt a sudden sharp pain in his leg. He turned and saw a man pick up an umbrella and get into a taxi, which quickly moved off. That night Markov became ill and the following day he was admitted to hospital, cyanosed and semi-conscious. Doctors believed he was suffering from blood poisoning, but, in spite of intensive therapy, he died a couple of days later.

At the post-mortem a tiny metal pellet was removed from his leg near the spot where he had reportedly felt pain. The pellet was found to be hollow, with holes on its surface, presumably to allow the escape of a poison. A later study pointed to the probability that he was killed with a plant-poison called ricin, derived from the outer covering of castor oil seeds. No one established what mechanism was used to administer the poison, but the tiny pellet remains, mounted under a magnifier in the Black Museum, as a persuasive reminder that, with enough will, especially ill-will, practically anything is possible.

To qualify for exhibition, an item must have instructional value, or historical value. If an item is instructional but has no historical worth, then it may be taken into the museum, used for a time, then thrown out. On the other hand, if it has both historical and instructional value, it will be kept.

One group of items – among them a handkerchief, an earring, and a piece of rope used for strangulation – make up an exhibit of special historical interest: they were clues to the murder of twenty-two-year-old Lorraine Benson, whose killer was the first in Britain to be caught by the use of DNA profiling.

In his twelve years as curator of the Black Museum, Bill Waddell has had some amusing moments, most of them connected with people's shocked reactions. He recalls a woman magistrate who got as far as the door but would not step inside. On occasions people are overcome by the combination of humidity and the sight of the pathological exhibits; Bill Waddell says that on average three people faint in the museum every week. One visitor, dazed, sat down on the edge of Denis Nielsen's bathtub and gently slid down inside.

'He knew what he'd fallen into,' Waddell remarked. 'Getting him out was the problem.'

DPA BAND OF THE METROPOLITAN POLICE

'We're a public relations vehicle, really,' said the Director of Music, Lieutenant Colonel Duncan Beat. 'We go into schools and play for children. We play for senior citizens in old people's homes and in day-centres and theatres. We play in hospitals, too. We play for the public in general, really.'

The Metropolitan Police Band, based in a converted garage at Bow in East London, has a busy – some would say hectic – schedule of engagements that calls for a regularly-revised repertoire and plenty of rehearsal. Their fifty-three-seater coach is not only their transport, but a travelling instrument store and a changing-room. There are thirty-one players in the band, four of them women.

They average ten performances a week and during a recent year they played at sixteen police passing-out parades, six medal ceremonies and six dinners; they gave seven bandstand recitals in St James's Park, three performances at Metropolitan Police Horse and Dog Shows, one for the National Day of Music, one memorial service, ten full-blown concerts, and fulfilled 148 community engagements.

A performance reappraisal in 1986 recommended that

the band should be civilianised, and the first civilian members were recruited in 1987. Since then the official feeling has been that the Metropolitan Police Band has become more musically professional, and it now costs far less to run. The current salaries bill is £611,320; this figure is a saving of £363,297 on the salary total for the period 1986/87.

Beat explained that recruitment of new band members has been from the Services. 'They are all ex-members of staff bands, the top-class bands in the Army – the Guards, for instance, and the Royal Engineers, the Royal Artillery and so on.'

Beat spent forty-one years in the Army. He began as a bandboy in the Royal Artillery Band in 1947 and eventually became Director of the Band of the Black Watch, the Royal Army Ordnance Corps and others; in 1982 he was appointed Director of Music and Chief Instructor of the Royal Military School of Music at Kneller Hall. He has been Musical Director of the Band of the Metropolitan Police Service since 1989.

Although the band is strongly associated with the police in the minds of the public, the Musical Director and his colleagues are aware of a sense of distance between themselves and serving officers.

'There is a separation,' he said; 'there's no doubt about it, and we can't argue against it. Strangely enough, very few of them come into contact with us, and we don't play for the police, apart from when they pass out at Hendon.'

The band's biggest event is the annual January concert at the Barbican, which for twenty-five years was introduced by Shaw Taylor, and is now presented by Richard Baker. Recently the band reached a much wider audience with the issue of a compact disc and cassette of their music entitled THANKS FOR THE MEMORY.

Superficially, the Musical Director's rank seems to be a matter for confusion. In speech and in writing he is addressed as Lieutenant Colonel Duncan Beat, but on his coat he wears the crown and pip of a police Chief Superintendent. The rank of Lieutenant Colonel, he explained, is a courtesy from his Army career. The police rank is another matter entirely.

'When I first came to the job I was interviewed by a Chief Superintendent who asked what rank I thought I should wear, if any. I said, well, I think it would be nice if I wore the rank that I previously held – the police equivalent, that is. He said there was a slight problem, in that the Superintendents' Association are not too happy about musicians wearing badges of rank since they wouldn't have earned them. I said fair enough, I appreciate that, but it's a bit immature; I did after all do forty-one years' service, I would have thought some effort could be made to accommodate me. He said, "Look, I'll tell you what, why don't you just put the crown up?" which is what I did.

'Come the annual concert at the Barbican, I was invited for drinks later with Sir John Dellow, the then Deputy Commissioner, who after talking to me and saying how wonderful the concert was, asked me why I was wearing that rank. I thought, well, I'm in for trouble now, I shouldn't be wearing it, and I told him the story. And he said, "Ridiculous! Put up the other pip!" And that's how it is, and nobody's questioned it since.'

SOLICITORS DEPARTMENT

The Solicitors Office was a prosecuting department until 1986, then the Crown Prosecution Service was created and took over all police prosecutions. When the present Solicitor to the Commissioner, Chris Porteous, took office in 1987, he was handed the job of choosing staff and shaping the new department to the form in which it exists today. He heads a team of twenty-seven solicitors whose job, broadly, is to deal with civil actions brought against the Metropolitan Police, which account for roughly 75 per cent of their work, and to act as advisers to the Met on general matters of law.

'We also deal with inquests, the ones held on people who die in police cells when we wish they hadn't,' Porteous said. 'We deal with dangerous dogs, because they don't all get done by the CPS; we deal with objections to the renewal of liquor licences; we deal with firearms appeals. We deal with police discipline law and we represent the prosecuting officer in discipline appeals, and in appeals to the Secretary of State. We also instruct and prepare counsel in discipline cases – that law is almost identical to criminal law. We used to advise Interpol, so we still get involved a little bit in EEC law and cross-border law. We also sometimes advise the Press Bureau on defamation, confidentiality and things like that. In fact we deal with whatever we are asked to advise on, which can be almost anything.'

Public-order work would typically mean giving advice on the use of force by police officers, and advising on the extent of their powers to restrict certain movements, such as a route march.

'We will get cases under the Riot Damage Act, where the owner of premises wrecked by riots can claim damages under the Act against the police,' said Porteous. 'We had one or two, in fact, relating to the Poll Tax Riots ... The Notting Hill Carnival is a particular event which we advise on every year.'

A typical race-relations case involved Sarah Locker, a

woman of Turkish descent employed as a WPC with the Metropolitan Police, who claimed that she had been subjected to racial and sexual abuse by her colleagues; in such a case solicitors advise the police and, where necessary, represent them in court.

'Racial discrimination cases vary,' Porteous said. 'Sometimes they relate to racially motivated behaviour by other police officers in the police station where somebody is excluded from something; for example, where an officer claims that he should have been allowed to go into the CID and wasn't, and claims that it was because he was black. We've also had to advise, in the past, on the Alison Holford case in Liverpool, because she did, at one time, work in the Metropolitan Police, and either she or the other side wanted evidence, and the question arose as to whether it should be given and by whom.'

A duty solicitor is available every day, and on Bank Holidays, including Christmas Day, there is a service available to advise the police on any legal matter that might come up. Everything, no matter how seemingly trivial or bizarre, is given consideration.

'We have quite a number of people who are mentally ill who bring cases against the Commissioner,' Porteous said. 'We have people who are probably suffering from schizophrenia who believe that we've got a machine inside Scotland Yard, and that that machine is governing their actions. They try to take civil actions against us, asking us to turn it off. We've had one or two of those.'

Another case involved the Force Firearms Unit (SO19), who mistakenly arrested an entire family having a quiet weekend in a boat on a canal. The boat had been wrongly identified by a member of the public as one on which a dangerous robber was hiding. Technically the police could have put up a case blaming their informant for the distress and inconvenience caused to the family, but they did not. They paid compensation. While Porteous would not discuss precise figures, he did explain the method he used in this case to reach a determination.

'I had each of the police officers in and I said, "If you were the person who was arrested in these circumstances, and you wanted compensation, how much would it be?" Interestingly enough, the figures they gave me – and there must have been seven or eight of them – were exactly the range of figures over which we actually argued. And I can say that we started at a thousand. The sums for which we settle cases that don't actually go to court, where the settlement figure isn't mentioned, are confidential. But I will say that we gave this family what we believe was reasonable compensation, and they must have thought so, because they accepted it. And the figures were actually consistent with what the officers themselves thought they would want if they were in the same boat.'

The Solicitors Department advises TO9 on the grey areas of the Police and Criminal Evidence Act (PACE), where there is some doubt as to how the law is to be interpreted. Section 78, dealing with evidence which must be ruled inadmissible because it has been unfairly obtained, is one example. Porteous explained.

'In Operation Herring, in North London, a bogus jewellery shop was set up to which thieves brought stolen jewellery and credit cards, and it was all televised and everything, and the case eventually went to court. In court the accused argued that the evidence was inadmissible, because it was unfair. Their lawyers must have thought up that one. I don't think it was half as unfair as what these robbers were doing, and the Court of Appeal thought so as well.'

The fact that wealthy clients will use expensive

defence counsel, even in trivial cases, is not a source of concern for Porteous. 'If you are a rich crook you can employ an expensive counsel to defend you, and some of them do . . . Once, when I did prosecutions, I prosecuted Mick Jagger, and they only had me to present the prosecution, but he had Havers, who became the Attorney General, to defend him. I may say I won the case.'

Unfair and unethical tactics in the courtroom tend to give the police the feeling that the system is slanted to their disadvantage. Porteous cites the defence tactic of blackening the reputation of prosecution witnesses, which not only weakens the case being tried, but will often deter the witness from ever coming forward to help the police again.

'I'm not sure that some of the responsibility for this doesn't actually lie with the lawyers that do it, and with the judges who allow them to do it,' Porteous said. 'I am not sure there shouldn't be a change in the way such cases are conducted.'

Porteous's principal role is Solicitor to the Commissioner, and while he will give advice and assistance to a broad range of people within the service, his client, and the client of his entire office, is the Commissioner.

'Our client is not the police,' he said. 'If a police officer is sued personally in an action where he arrested somebody unlawfully, you normally have the action against the Commissioner, because he's vicariously liable under Section 48 of the Police Act. But you can sue the individual police officer. In those cases we normally represent the police officer, too. The only occasions when we don't is if, for example, he's gone to prison for what he did. Then we don't represent him because there's a conflict of interests.

'We do have a role in policy making at the Yard, as

well,' Porteous said. 'We also serve on a lot of commit-tees – we have lots of roles to play, and I certainly have to do quite a lot of representational work. Occasionally I have to pin rosettes on winners at the Horse Show.'

SCRUTINY

A scrutiny, explained Charles Reeves, the Scrutiny Liai-son Officer, has three main thrusts: to improve value, to examine concerns in the areas of management and organ-isation, and to improve the quality of service.

'The objective of the Scrutiny Team is to produce recommendations which will improve the current situ-ation,' Reeves said. 'They have a brief to be as radical as they need to be, but they must be sure at the end of the day that their recommendations are practicable and capable of being implemented.'

A scrutiny, customarily carried out by one police officer and one civilian member of staff, usually lasts for ninety days. It takes two years, however, to produce a final report. As to the reason for the Scrutinies unit being under the direct authority of the Deputy Commis-sioner, Reeves pointed out that Deputy Commissioner Smith chairs the Value For Money Committee, and obtaining value for money is the underlying reason for scrutinies.

A couple of past scrutinies illustrate the work of Reeves's group.

The Metropolitan Police Band was progressively civil-ianised to minimise its call on the duty time of serving police officers. The phased procedure, coupled to a reduction in the number of members, cut the cost of the band by more than £400,000 a year. Further savings were made by cancelling band engagements outside the

Metropolitan Police District. Minimum-entry standards were imposed on new recruits, which resulted in a raising of the band's musical standard. A central engagements panel makes sure the band is used effectively in its community-relations role.

A scrutiny of Metropolitan Police Overtime resulted in an improved system for recording and monitoring overtime and examining its operation. This produced a continuing saving of approximately £3 million a year.

RECEIVER'S DEPARTMENT
Introduction

The Receiver is equal in rank to the Deputy Commissioner. He is chosen from senior officials of the Home Office and is an independent finance officer with important powers. For example, when the Commissioner has proposals for new spending he must take them to the Receiver, and, if the Receiver should oppose them, the Home Secretary is not likely to approve, either. The present Receiver of the Metropolitan Police is Graham Angel, a man with wide experience in the Home Office, who has been private secretary to three Home Secretaries – Callaghan, Maudling and Carr.

In official terminology the Receiver is a corporation sole, which means that in his official capacity he owns all the property of the Metropolitan Police, an arrangement which simplifies the transfer of documents and the handling of property issues.

Defining his job in simple terms, Angel says he is the Commissioner's chief adviser on administrative and financial matters; 'I am accountable to him in the sense that he does my annual report, but it's counter-signed by the permanent secretary of the Home Office, so both are involved.'

In a hypothetical case, where the Home Secretary decided to spend a lot of money on a big anti-terrorist effort, but the Commissioner, for his part, felt that the money should be spent elsewhere, the Receiver would suffer no conflict of loyalties. He would be a member of a policy committee, participating in the Commissioner's decisions on operational priorities, and he would back the Commissioner. 'I don't have an independent position on operational matters.'

Most of Angel's predecessors have finished their careers as Receivers. Being younger than they were, Angel has come to the job with, as he puts it, a return ticket in his pocket, and one day he might go back to work in Whitehall as a civil servant. While he is Receiver, however, he is technically not a Civil Servant but a Crown Servant, appointed directly by the Queen. The difference means little in practice, he says, but he does have a very splendid warrant signed by the Queen, and he has the ancient seal of his office.

'It is a very grand means of impressing on documents my status as corporation sole,' he said. 'Actually the implement looks rather like an old-fashioned mangle, but the results are quite impressive. We seal lots of documents; it's a very practical way of transferring property.'

An important part of the Receiver's function is to meet with the London Boroughs to settle the precept; in this connection, a precept is an order for collection or payment of money under a local rate. Meeting with the Receiver gives the local authorities a chance to probe police proposals for expenditure, to question details of the estimates and to find out if the public are getting value for money. When the issues are all settled, or at least when workable compromises have been reached, the approximately £1.8 billion payable annually to the Metropolitan Police is sent directly to the Receiver. All financial arrangements for the Met go through the same channel, and all cheques must be made payable to the Receiver of the Metropolitan Police.

A Receiver's Liaison Officer is on call twenty-four

hours a day. During emergencies when large numbers of police are alerted, the Liaison Officer will be alerted, too; his job is to provide meals and technology in quantity, and at short notice.

'He takes one call,' said Angel, 'and on the basis of that he makes sure that the technology people, the caterers, the property services people, and anybody else that might be needed, are available.'

The Receiver's Department covers four large, very diverse areas – finance, property services, technology and personnel.

'They naturally fitted together,' Angel said. 'We had a very intensive study starting with ten or twelve separate departments, and the resulting reorganisation not only grouped four departments under the Receiver, but created four new departments where previously there had been twelve. It did things like bring together in a single finance department all the range of financial services. In a single personnel department it brought together the personnel function for police and civil staff, which is a very major step.'

FINANCE

The Director of Finance, John Crutchlow, gave the figure for the 1993–94 Metropolitan Police budget as £1.8 billion. 'And that is gross expenditure,' he said, 'before we take account of miscellaneous receipts, which are not the receipts where the money comes from Government and local government, but where it comes from things like football clubs and major public bodies where we provide policing.'

In the broadest terms, 52 per cent of the money comes from the Government as a specific police grant.

Theoretically the other 48 per cent is provided from the council tax. A precept (which is an order to collect money under a rate) draws revenue from the thirty-two London Boroughs within the Metropolitan Police District, plus eight others whose boundaries are partly within that area.

From 1829 until 1987 the Met had no control over its budget, because it was thought that it should concentrate on operational priorities and leave the bureaucratic jobs of providing services and managing money to the civil staff.

'Inevitably, as resources became tighter, concentrating on the priorities needed a management style that took account of the financial resources,' Crutchlow said. 'The organisation kept the very clear distinction between money and the provision of resources and operational policing all the way through to about 1986, 1987. When I came into this job I was asked to do a review of financial management, and that's what started the local-budget approach. It had been becoming obvious that something was missing, and what was missing was a police connection with the money.'

At approximately the time Chief Superintendents were given overtime budgets, Crutchlow introduced a scheme which gave them, at divisional level, control over limited-spending projects like local building repairs and local redecorations. Officers from the rank of Inspector upwards, Crutchlow says, have become senior managers.

An important new development affecting the management of budgets is a computer system called FINESSE (Financial and Enquiry Support System), which is a standard financial database for use throughout the Metropolitan Police Service. During 1994–95,

FINESSE will also introduce a full cost-centre accounting (CCA) and resource-budgeting system.

As with any large organisation, every year there is powerful competition between the departments of the Met to gain as big a piece of the annual financial allocation as they can.

'There is certainly healthy debate every year,' Crutchlow said. 'And we have the complication of putting the bids together, then we debate how they should be split, then we put them to our paymasters, the Home Office, who have to go through the public expenditure survey with the Treasury. Predictably we don't get everything we bid for, and when the results of our bids come back we have the uncomfortable process of deciding what has to go, what has to be kept in, what has to be scaled down.'

The pinch is felt strongly in the area of capital equipment. Crutchlow pointed out that the Metropolitan Police have a very low level of investment in new equipment, relative to the total budget. The annual allocation for items like vehicles, plant equipment and computers is only £30 million.

'Thirty million pounds is a lot of money,' he said, 'but in that size budget, given the sort of revolution there's been in the computer world, let alone in vehicles and plant and so on, thirty million is not a lot to keep the service properly equipped with new developments. After all, the criminals spend a lot on computers and other new equipment, and if we are not careful we can lag behind developments.'

PERSONNEL

The Personnel Department has five units: Police Personnel Management, Civil Staff Personnel Management,

Manpower Planning & Personnel Policy, Catering, and Occupational Health.

Police Personnel Management

After more than thirty years as a police officer, Acting DAC Colin Couch now finds himself in his first desk job, in charge of Personnel Management. The main differences between running the Personnel Department in the Met and its counterpart in industry, he said, is that police officers are not subject to employment legislation; they cannot sue for unlawful dismissal, but at the same time the terms of the Police Act make it very difficult for the administration to sack even incompetent officers.

'That's mainly the issue. I can't suddenly make a police officer unemployed or redundant.'

At present there is no shortage of recruits. Couch said there are so many applicants that those holding O and A levels could be ignored entirely and a selection made from graduates – not, he added, that he would dream of doing that.

'We don't want all chiefs, we need rather a lot of Indians, because 20,000-odd employees have got to remain constables, otherwise the service doesn't work properly. So we have no recruitment problem at all. Recently we advertised in the *Evening Standard* for recruits to fill about 400 jobs. We had 6,000 applications.'

For about two years it has been policy only to recruit people with London addresses. There has also been an emphasis on attracting members of ethnic minorities, although this has not been as successful as was hoped. Couch said the situation is improving. He believes the service is more attractive to smaller ethnic groups now that the workings of the police are less opaque to outsiders. Efforts are made to minimise barriers to recruitment, including recruits' educational shortcomings.

'When we go out on our positive drive to get ethnic minority officers,' Couch said, 'if people are suffering from the inability to pass, perhaps, the written examination and general knowledge examination, then we encourage them to go to a different site of learning – not that we provide it, I must be honest – to get up to that standard. We give them that way forward.'

There is a tendency among critics of the police to hark back to a time, Couch says, when the 'canteen culture' reflected the underlying attitudes of diehard thief-takers who conducted themselves by rules founded on 'them-and-us' prejudices.

'If you went into the canteen now,' Couch said, 'you would probably find that the oldest police officer in the place was twenty-five or twenty-six years old. The canteen culture people talk about was what we used to have thirty years ago, when it was an entirely different police service. The frontline officers of today are young people, and their attitudes are very different, they understand the issues and the problems.'

Couch acknowledged there have been occasional reports of black and Asian police officers being harassed by white officers. 'I'd be silly to say it doesn't happen, but I have faith that a combination of the training we give people, the changing culture, and the education of the type of individuals who are joining us now is making a vast improvement. Racism won't be eradicated, it's never eradicated anywhere – let's be honest, you can see on television every day the way people behave. None the less, I'm positive it's getting better.'

A sense of detachment among ethnic minority officers is being combated, he added, by making sure that, if there are only a few of them at one station, they will be put together, operating in twos and threes, rather than in isolation.

Women are still notably a minority in the Metropolitan Police Service, and, although 30 per cent of applicants are female, the proportion of serving female officers in May 1993 was only 13.2 per cent. Couch is adamant, nevertheless, that women are welcome within the service, and that energetic measures are being made to recruit the right kind of people.

'I can think of no other organisation that makes so public its equal-opportunities policy. I think we still get bad press, but the public must realise that if they read bad things about the police, it's because we're dealing with it, it's not because we're ignoring it and brushing it under the carpet.'

Alison Halford, a former senior police officer, recently alleged in her memoirs that as a young recruit she had to present herself bare-breasted before a Metropolitan Police recruitment board. While few if any people at Scotland Yard could have found such a claim credible, the story nevertheless stimulated the interest of the press, and as a result the image of the Metropolitan Police must have been damaged.

'The trouble is,' said Couch, 'that whatever the media says is believed by the majority of people. If it's in the paper it must be right. We can do ninety-nine great things in the police service, but we only need one untruthful item in the press to undo all the good we've done. I get extremely frustrated.'

By the normal route, an officer can take fourteen years to rise from the rank of Constable to Chief Inspector. There is now a High Potential Scheme, aimed at getting officers through the ranks much faster.

'For example, an officer can join as a graduate,' Couch

said, 'then do two years on the streets as a Constable, after which he can sit the exam to become a Sergeant, and if he passes that he can go on the accelerated learning course. That is seven or eight weeks at Bramshill, after which he comes back to the real world to prove his ability as a Sergeant.'

Bramshill in Hampshire is a Home Office training establishment. Apart from running the Met's accelerated learning course, they provide the Junior Command Course for Chief Inspectors, the Intermediate Command Course for Superintendents, and the Senior Command Course for Chief Superintendents.

'Within either a year or two years,' Couch went on, 'if the officer is considered to have made a good Sergeant, he will go back to Bramshill for Inspector training. Then, as before, he comes back to prove himself in the real world, as an Inspector this time.'

Recruits who are not graduates can join the High Potential Scheme by going before the Met's Central Selection Committee, where their aptitude is tested. It is possible to reach the rank of Chief Inspector, which is as high as the scheme takes anyone, within seven to nine years. Individuals who begin well but under-perform at a later stage are removed from the scheme.

After reaching Chief Inspector, the 'fast-stream' officers are not really on their own as far as future promotion is concerned. They are still regarded as being special. Senior management keep an eye on their careers, making them presentable to bodies that can continue to accelerate their movement up through the ranks.

'Most people from the High Potential Scheme – not all, but most – rise pretty high in the ranks. It's unusual for anyone on the fast stream to get stuck anywhere.'

Notable successes from the fast stream are Bill Taylor,

who is ACSO, David Veness, DACSO, and Colin
Coxhill, Assistant Commissioner of the City of London
Police.

Manpower Planning and Personnel Policy

Increasingly, personnel policy for police and civil staff
is being developed through policy guidance and strategic
frameworks, rather than by blind prescriptive rules.
The man coordinating these measures is John Steele,
Director of Manpower Planning and Personnel Policy.
He is also responsible for employee relations and manages consultative procedures with the civil staff trades
unions.

Prior to the creation of the new Personnel Department
in August 1992, there were two equal-opportunities
units, one for civil staff and one for police, but now they
have been merged. While Steele is responsible for
equal-opportunities policy in the Metropolitan Police,
the policy is executed by the line managers.

The Met's success as an equal-opportunity employer
has been variable, so special corrective training is being
introduced for middle management, both police and
civilian. The aim is to improve understanding of the
equal-opportunities law and its implications for staff
relations.

The Personnel Policy Branch produces the framework
of personnel policy. 'We do it for things like appraisal
systems, for example,' Steele said, 'working out how
we're going to appraise people, producing the documentation and the forms, arranging the initial training. Civil
staff are all on performance-related pay now, so you've
got to have a structure that integrates the appraisal
system with the performance-related pay, so people are
given their objectives, they are assessed on those and it

goes through to their pay. All that sort of thing is arranged by this branch.'

Steele believes that nowadays recruitment policies and organisational structures within the Met ensure that, in most cases, the best people are chosen for the most important jobs.

'Prior to 1979,' he said, 'or around then, the quality of people coming in was not as high as we would have wished. Some of those are still here. The quality of recruits in recent years, on the other hand, has been exceptionally high. Very bright people are finding their way through the ranks, and they are being helped along by the introduction of Assessment Centres.'

Turning to ethnic minorities employed as civil staff in the Metropolitan Police Service, Steele said that recent statistics indicated the figure was between 13 and 15 per cent.

'So we were able to say, "Pat on the back, we're not doing badly, are we?" But there are two caveats to that. First, the civil staff ethnic minorities are over-represented in some areas and tremendously under-represented in others. They are over-represented in the poorer-paid jobs, areas like catering for example. Secondly, we now know that the ethnic minority population in London is around 20 per cent – previously we had been using old benchmark data. So, by any standards, it's a lot better than it is on the police side, but it's still not good enough.'

In Steele's view the police service, until recently, was an intrinsically racist organisation. 'Because it used racist stereotypes. That's not blaming anybody, I think society until fairly recently has been pretty racist, it's been a white stereotypical society. We've made tremendous efforts in the police service nationally to overcome those problems, and I don't believe it's the case now. So

I think it's a matter of time, and convincing people and winning trust.'

Civil Staff Personnel Management

Roger Gregory, Director of Civil Staff Personnel, is responsible for the management of 18,000 civilians working for the Metropolitan Police.

'There's no doubt about it,' he said, 'it's different. Comparing the civil staff with the police officers, in broad terms there are a limited number of roles for police, but on the civil staff side there are literally hundreds of different specialisms. Each one has its own specification of the kind of people we are looking for – the personnel requirements for kennel maids are a lot different from those for forensic scientists, or radio engineers, or whatever. The job is enjoyable and fascinating and various. There's a lot of it, in the sense that with eighteen thousand people, all with their own special difficulties, there's a never-ending queue of people needing to solve problems of one sort or another.'

'In big organisations, traditionally,' Gregory said, 'there has been a feeling that the personnel department should deal with all personnel matters, and the minute a line manager finds one of his or her people having difficulties, what he does is send them to talk to the personnel department.

'I am hell-bent on devolving as much as is possible of what traditionally has been central personnel department responsibility to the line managers and to the individuals to get on with.'

One of the biggest changes taking place within the Metropolitan Police at present is civilianisation. Gregory said it had been a part of life in the Met for many years;

Proportion of Serving Female Officers

YEAR	TOTAL SERVING	FEMALE OFFICERS	FEMALE %
1981	25,161	2,315	9.20
1982	26,350	2,464	9.35
1983	26,806	2,483	9.26
1984	26,844	2,484	9.25
1985	26,783	2,528	9.44
1986	27,005	2,637	9.76
1987	27,438	2,932	10.69
1988	28,009	3,211	11.46
1989	28,267	3,408	12.06
1990	28,364	3,551	12.52
1991	28,455	3,714	13.05
1992	28,230	3,834	13.58
5/'93	28,269	3,877	13.72

Ethnic Minority Officers

YEAR	TOTAL SERVING	ETHNIC MINORITY	FEMALE %
1981	25,161	137	0.54
1982	26,350	182	0.69
1983	26,806	238	0.89
1984	26,844	253	0.94
1985	26,783	287	1.07
1986	27,005	334	1.24
1987	27,438	418	1.52
1988	28,009	426	1.52
1989	28,267	441	1.56
1990	28,364	483	1.70
1991	28,455	552	1.94
1992	28,230	594	2.10
5/'93	28,269	662	2.20

'But only in a minor way, until about five years ago, when the previous Receiver and I, and the people in the personnel department, realised there was scope for getting more police officers out on to the street. There was scope for civil staff doing things that we had never ever dreamt they might have done before. The best example is that in almost every police station one goes into in London these days, the station reception officer is a member of civil staff, whereas traditionally it has always been a police officer.'

Gregory believes that in five years, as civilianisation proceeds, sectors of police work currently undertaken by, say, ten police officers, will be done by six police officers and four members of civil staff.

The competence of civilians doing jobs that used to be done by police officers is not reflected in the remuneration. In many cases the amount being paid to civilians is roughly half that earned by police officers. Gregory addresses the disparity by observing that a police officer is paid for being a police officer, whatever job he may be doing, and if a member of civil staff wants the same money as a police officer for doing the same work, the staff member should have become a police officer in the first place.

Gregory agrees that some members of civil staff feel like second-class citizens, but not because they lack the police uniform and warrant card. 'It's more to do with the way people are valued by others, and not valued by others, and so on,' he said.

Gregory has a responsibility to develop management and leadership skills across the whole Metropolitan Police organisation, among both civilian and police personnel. In his view, the quality of managers and leaders is one of the major concerns. He quotes the business dictum which says that modern managers are paid not to manage the status quo, but to manage change; the Metropolitan Police, he says, have not been very good at that.

Turning dyed-in-the-wool thief-takers into modern management figures is quite a challenge, he agrees. A large part of the answer is aggressive re-training of existing personnel, and recruitment of new people.

'It's inevitably a three-way thing,' he said. 'It's picking out the people that can already do the things, picking out those without the skills but who perhaps have the potential for learning them, and bringing in new people who already have the skills built in.'

Catering

In 1988 the London *Evening Standard* quoted Alastair Thompson's predecessor as Director of Catering, Bob Downing, as saying there was nothing in the country to compare with the Met's Catering Department, operating at such a scale, twenty-four hours a day, fifty-two weeks a year. That is still true, Thompson said.

'Running the Met, I've got all the facilities on tap, because wherever the police go, we go afterwards. If somebody pushes the button now, I won't know about it; I don't need to know, it would just happen.'

Staff involved in the twenty-four-hour call-out system are equipped with electronic pagers. 'They're all drivers,' Thompson said, 'and they've all got their own vehicles. We've got a scale of response and I can get people into the centre of London very, very rapidly – we will be in our emergency kitchen within twenty minutes of being called.'

Responding to the Napoleonic adage that an army marches on its stomach, Thompson said, 'I don't think policemen would move more than a few hundred yards from a cup of tea, a cheese sandwich, a Mars bar and an all-day restaurant.'

Thompson trained as a chef and worked in hotels before joining the catering staff of the Home Office, where he worked for a number of years before moving to the Prison Service, and then, two years ago, the Metropolitan Police.

'We provide catering to a customer base of 30,000 people, that's police and civil staff, through 171 catering units across the Met,' he said. 'Some of the units, like Scotland Yard, Brixton and Croydon, are open twenty-four hours a day.'

There are 1,060 staff in the Catering Department, which is organised in two groups, Operations and Support. The catering units serve nearly nine million meals a year in headquarters buildings, police stations, residential section houses, training centres, traffic warden centres, garages, workshops and magistrates' courts. The net cost of the operation for the year 1992–93 was £10.5 million.

Officers on duty at ceremonial events often have to be fed at the site. About 1,500 breakfasts will be laid on at 5.30 a.m. during rehearsals for Trooping the Colour; at Cup Final matches approximately 900 officers receive an afternoon meal. During the two-and-a-half days of the Notting Hill Carnival, school kitchens taken over for the event are used to prepare between 25,000 and 30,000 police meals, which will be served in school dining rooms.

'Ninety per cent of our work is routine feeding of personnel,' said Thompson, 'the other 10 per cent is emergency-response stuff. If there was a Provisional IRA attack in London this afternoon and we had to support the police in the aftermath, I could be on the scene anywhere within half an hour with hot cups of tea

Catering Department: Annual Consumption of Selected Items

Eggs	400,000 plus
Rashers of Bacon	600,000
Sausages	1,000,000
Portions of Baked Beans	1,000,000
Cups of Coffee	2,000,000
Cups of Tea	3,500,000
Butter Pats	2,000,000
Flora Pats	600,000
Portions of Chips (fried in oil)	1,300,000

and Kit-Kats. We have a kitchen with boiling water available twenty-four hours a day, and we've got two emergency-response vehicles. We compete with the Salvation Army to see who can get to the scene first – they're an excellent service, probably the most professional catering operation after us. We race each other across London. We usually win because we get a police escort.'

The Catering Department's emergency response vehicle is known throughout the met as 'Teapot One'.

Occupational Health

'If you spend your life looking at victims of child abuse,' said Dr Alan Johnson, Director of Occupational Health, 'you can get the distorted view that every child is being abused. There are also problems produced by being in the vicinity of bomb incidents and shootings, and other forms of direct violence towards the police. I often try to provide a rehabilitation service for traumatised officers, on similar lines to what I was doing in the services.'

Johnson, a consultant in Occupational Medicine, joined the Metropolitan Police Service two years ago, after retiring as Principal Medical Officer, Strike Command, at the end of the Gulf War. At the time of his retirement he held the rank of Air Vice Marshal.

'I am the only doctor employed full time,' he said. 'There are four part-time doctors, three consultants and a general practitioner. We don't take the place of an officer's GP, he must remain the primary deliverer of health care. But I have two full-time physiotherapists, for example, who can provide an immediate service to the police, and perhaps get officers back to work faster than might be the case if they were receiving treatment from the National Health Service alone.'

The surface calm of many police officers conceals an underlying strain that can lead to a number of complaints grouped under the heading of Traumatic Stress, or 'burnout', where physical and emotional exhaustion, sometimes physical illness, is brought about by job stress. Officers working in child abuse units are susceptible to stress ailments, and have been known to become incapable of everyday acts like driving a car, or even making a cup of tea.

A build-up of traumatic incidents challenge a person's ability to accommodate stress. The Directorate of Occupational Health tries to increase awareness of the dangers of stress by organising workshops to examine the causes, the consequences and a number of strategies for coping. The aim behind the workshops is to help officers identify stress factors and deal with them. Post-trauma intervention is organised to make sure that groups and individuals receive appropriate assessment, support and referral after traumatic incidents.

'We must educate senior officers to adopt the approach that the police officer who does show his feelings is not weak,' Johnson said. 'He is human, and perhaps he is demonstrating his ability to discharge his duties towards the public *because* he has these human sensations and feelings.'

Since November 1992, ten Occupational Health Advisers (OHAs) have worked full time for the Directorate of Occupational Health. They are Registered general nurses, each with a post-graduate qualification in Occupational Health, and at least three years' experience in commerce or industry.

The work of the OHAs is to encourage managers within the police service to develop health-care programmes for their staff. The aim, over all, is to promote a healthier and safer working environment, where possible, and to stimulate awareness of fitness and health among police officers generally.

Healthy diet is an area of direct concern for Johnson and his team. 'We work with the Catering Department to provide and promote healthy dietary alternatives in all our food outlets. Of course, we are fighting the fish-and-chips outlook which believes nothing is wrong if you eat indiscriminately for many years and remain healthy – that's what puts us fairly high up the league for cardiovascular disease. We do what we can, but it has to be done by persuasion, by offering a suitable and attractive alternative.

'There are a lot of officers whose level of fitness could be better,' Johnson said. 'I could say cynically that my responsibility as an occupational physician finishes at retirement, but as a physician I have a responsibility to each patient. From the health point of view I would like to promote a higher level of fitness among police officers, to enable them to live longer.'

The Director of Physical Education is a member of the Directorate of Occupational Health, working directly under Johnson. Approximately forty Physical Training Instructors (PTIs) provide a service at Area and Divisional level. 'The PTIs are an Area resource,' said Johnson, 'but I have functional control in how they work and what they do; it is the responsibility of myself and the Director of Physical Education.'

Johnson emphasised that the bulk of work done by the Directorate of Occupational Health does not lie in the direction of the extreme or the exotic. It is the ordinary daily work of general and occupational medicine.

'Things like the injuries people get falling down the stairs in the station, like whiplash injuries in police vehicles, and so on. I realise there are psychologically traumatic situations, but one has to keep these in context. They are still, thank goodness, the smaller part of the work we do, but very important, and, although we perhaps haven't managed them well in the past, we're getting better at it.'

TECHNOLOGY

Nick Boothman has been described by the press as 'The Metropolitan Police's Mr Fixit'. He is Director of Technology, the head of a department with a mission, in his words, to amplify the effectiveness of police officers by providing technical equipment to support them.

'We are responsible for pretty well all of the technology that the Metropolitan Police use,' he said, 'with the exception of building services, air conditioning, things like that. The department covers almost every area of the engineering industry.'

'The Metropolitan Police are actually bigger than the

New York Police,' Boothman said. 'There are cities with larger populations, but the way they are policed is different to London. New York is the only comparable city, and that's reflected in the scope and number of technical projects we handle.'

A complex telephone network is run by 250 telephonists, while approximately 100 operators manage computer and data-transmission installations.

'We also have one of the most complicated radio systems anywhere. It's concentrated into the Greater London area, with a sixteen-mile radius, with over 100 radio channels in use, and something like 15,000 people using the radios. We also operate Scotland Yard's Central Communications Complex.'

A commercial approach has been adopted in the area of transport. Traditionally, the Department of Technology operated like other Government departments, deciding from a central position exactly what would be provided, and supplying it free at the point of use.

'That isn't very good, and we've always been uncomfortable with it,' Boothman said. 'It means the end-user doesn't have a choice in what's provided, and tends not to value it, and often dislikes it. So now we give the user the choice, and we behave as a very closely-associated supplier.'

The department buys between 800 and 1,100 vehicles annually, depending on the pattern of replacement year on year. They are bought direct from the main manufacturers. The discount is usually more than 25 per cent, because not only are the vehicles bought in quantity but also, according to Boothman, the manufacturers and suppliers like to see their cars bearing the badge of the Metropolitan Police.

There is a policy of buying British vehicles. In particular, there is a long relationship between the Department

of Technology and the Rover Company, which Boothman would like to see continue.

When they think it is necessary, Technology Department engineers adapt existing models of motor cars to
suit police needs. Brakes from Vauxhall Cavaliers have
been put into Vauxhall Astras, for example, because
police drivers are tough on brakes and the Cavalier's are
bigger than those fitted as standard to Astras. Handling
characteristics are improved where possible, and extras
like flashing lights, police horns and special speedo-
meters to measure speed violations are fitted as a matter
of routine. But engines are not 'souped up'.

The Technology Department is also responsible for
the helicopters of the Air Support Unit (TO26) and the
boats of the Thames Division (TO29).

The position with boats is governed more by changes
on the river than by technical considerations. Compared
with the amount of industry and traffic on the Thames
in the 1950s, the river today is virtually deserted, and
the need for patrol boats has dropped. There are fifteen
police boats on the river at present and two rigid inflat-
ables have been bought for use in rescue work, but,
apart from that, the fleet remains stable. 'What we
have done recently,' said Boothman, 'is reorganise the
maintenance procedures for boats, so that the resources
we're using are much less, and our efficiency is a lot
higher.'

The Met's cars used to be serviced in thirteen workshops by 130 fitters and a large support staff. 'The
people in the workshops thought they were doing a
tremendous job, but the cars looked a mess and their
availability to the police was very poor,' said Boothman.
'Now we have only eight workshops and we don't have
any overtime at all, whereas previously there was about
£4 million worth of overtime. The number of fitters

will drop below 100, and the availability of cars has gone up from about 70 per cent to 96 per cent.'

For some time the police in London have been unhappy about the quality of their radio communications, and a long-term project to replace all of the police radio systems is almost half completed. All mobile radios in police cars have been changed and a start has been made on replacing hand radios, although the changeover has been faltering. The problem is not a technical one, Boothman says.

'There isn't enough money, that's the difficulty. We could only do it by drastically sacrificing the vehicle fleet and our computer systems and data systems, and it's been decided we really daren't do that.'

The root of the communication problem with hand radios lies partly in the design of the current handset, partly in the allocation of airspace. Within a police division, only a single radio channel is available, so it is often congested and officers have to struggle to use it effectively.

'Another problem is that every officer is forced to listen to absolutely everything that's going on even when it has nothing to do with him,' Boothman said. 'This is distracting, and it also encourages officers to chase after things that they shouldn't.'

Criminals who listen in to police messages with radio scanners are being combated with radio sets which can hop frequencies, making it difficult for the intruder to follow the signal. Encryption is being used, too. Boothman explained.

'We take the voice signal and turn it into a string of numbers, like the digital telephone network does now. We then scramble the numbers through an arithmetic unit and we transmit a scrambled set of numbers, and then the receiving end unscrambles the numbers so we can decode the speech and hear it. The scrambler is a random sequence generator. Both the transmitter and the generator are in synchronism, and the idea is that it would take a very big computer a very long time to identify the series of random numbers that the arithmetic unit applies.' Encrypted radios are issued to specialist groups. Because of the cost, there are no immediate plans to supply them to police officers on patrol.

The ideal radios for general police work would give improved coverage and allow controllers to be selective with the officers they speak to. The channels would also be less congested. Approximately £50 million is needed to buy the equipment, but only £34 million a year is available for purchasing in this sector. The Government is unlikely to grant any more.

Boothman said his department is stuck between officials and politicians. 'I think one of our difficulties is that the politicians have felt – wrongly, in my opinion – that they've been getting bad value for money from the police. I think that view is entirely too simplistic and unsophisticated.'

Another area of communications beset with problems is the Crime Information System (CRIS), which was introduced to replace the crime book. When a crime is recorded, a comprehensive entry is made in the crime book, which contains every available detail of each crime recorded. The system is unwieldy, repetitive and time-consuming. A computer database, on the other hand, allows a single set of records to be searched under a wide range of criteria. CRIS, a database computer system customised for criminal record work – the biggest of its kind in Europe – was originally brought into service in the late 1980s.

'It ran into trouble when the company who supplied the system discovered they had underestimated the size of the job,' Boothman said. 'The problem was particularly sticky, and it's gone along for four years, but it looks as though we might soon be able to introduce the system successfully.'

When it is operational, CRIS should allow crime reports to be entered from any of 1,500 terminals across London. Data on criminals, crimes and patterns of crime should be available instantly to any police officer needing the information.

Everyday communications statistics from the Department of Technology include a telephone bill for 18,000 lines which has risen to £18 million a year; they are responsible for maintenance on 16,000 radios (12,000 of them hand-held), and similar support is provided for everything from generators and video cameras to mobile canteens and road barriers.

The Department of Technology was responsible for equipping all custody suites in London's police stations with audio interviewing equipment. 'The programme took four years to complete,' said Boothman. 'We had some presentational problems early on, because we need a low-noise background so that the recordings can be played back without any distracting sounds. As an early idea, we ended up with a very expensive soundproof room. We went away from that because we simply couldn't afford it. We finally arrived at a package which works, with a mike in the prisoner's lapel and some deadening of background where it is needed. The spec is much less expensive than before.'

Facilities are now being arranged for the routine video-recording of interviews. 'There's no decision yet that every interview will be videoed,' said Boothman. 'Some say they should be, others say you can hide as much malpractice outside the room as you can prove didn't happen inside the room. It's difficult to manage a situation like this. You have to keep track of all the tapes, keep a master tape, make a requisite number of copies, seal everything up properly, do transcripts from the tapes and so on – it's a very expensive business.'

The Bomb Squad get their special equipment, such as remote manipulators, from the Technology Department. Engineers concerned with Bomb Squad equipment experiment regularly with new and possibly better ways of carrying out standard procedures. A recent idea was to fit a stereoscopic camera to the Bomb Squad's remote handling equipment – the device they call the 'wheelbarrow' – so that Explosives Officers would be given an impression of visual depth. The idea was worthwhile, Boothman said, but again cost got in the way, and for the moment the stereo camera is not being used.

The Technical Support Unit (TSU) is a department of approximately sixty people, engineers and technicians, who devise and develop gadgets of various kinds to help operational officers combat crime. Being careful not to betray any of the techniques and technical strategies employed by the unit, Boothman did reveal that they design and manufacture tracking units, surveillance equipment and monitoring devices. In South London there is an unnamed establishment, run by the Department of Technology, which supports the TSU.

'Many convictions are obtained through surveillance,' Boothman said. 'This department's support makes sophisticated surveillance possible. It's also involved in trying to break kidnap cases. We have advanced audio and video equipment designed for surveillance. We also have the capability to verify that tapes from our video equipment are evidentially sound, which means they are what they appear to be.'

This department also has equipment and technical

ability which puts it in the forefront of image enhancing techniques, often used to improve the quality of pictures taken by security video cameras. The technicians' working-image quality is high; they start from broadcast standard and work upwards.

'We've used our technique for enhancing images for years,' said Boothman. 'We have techniques which are, if anything, better than those offered by IBM. Their techniques were used for enhancing images coming back from spacecraft, ours are for "noisy" images on tape.'

Boothman did not hesitate to explain why this department is so covert.

'It's secret because the criminal doesn't realise how much we can do, and that's one of his weaknesses. We don't want him to know how much we can do, otherwise the sophisticated criminal would start protecting himself against us. We want him to underestimate us.'

PROPERTY SERVICES

The stated purpose of the Property Services Department (PSD) is to manage the Receiver's estate efficiently and economically. They spend half a million pounds every working day on building, estate maintenance and estate development. The properties in their care include police stations (over 180, the exact number changes from year to year), major office buildings, warehouses, training establishments and a large residential estate. In total, approximately 500 buildings and sites.

'We've got about eleven hundred staff, all civilians,' said Mr Trevor Lawrence, Director of Property Services. 'We do all the jobs you'd expect from managing a mixed-property portfolio. About sixty of our people are architectural, both trainees and qualified staff. They deal with much of the new building work, part of which goes outside each year to private consultants.'

Property Services buy and sell property, and they are lessors as well as lessees. They develop police stations and properties as they acquire them, both through buying existing units and by building new ones.

'We maintain them, we furnish them, we clean them, we guard them,' said Lawrence. 'We provide operational support services as well. We have forced-entry teams who help the police gain quick access through doors when they go on certain covert operations, against drug dealers for example. They use ram mechanisms which fix to the frame and force out the door. They are disappointed if it takes more than four seconds to get in.'

The broad total value of the Metropolitan Police Estate is £1.25 billion. It is a mixed domain, with some of the newest and oldest buildings of any police service in Britain. The new Charing Cross Police Station has recently been opened on the site of the former Charing Cross Hospital; at a cost of £19 million it is probably the most expensive and certainly the most up-to-date police station in the country. A move towards general modernisation is hampered, however, by financial obstacles. There are hopes to reduce these with an operational building strategy coupled to a reduction in the size of the estate, so that the money will go further. By the year 2020, the old buildings which have been retained will be improved to an efficient modern standard. The policy is to dispose of properties or improve them on a 'worst first' basis, arriving eventually at a point where the average maximum age of buildings within the estate will be sixty-five years.

One headache for the PSD, in Lawrence's view making Britain unique among European countries, is the fact that the Victorians, with the benefits of money from Empire, put up splendidly durable buildings. Bricks and mortar continue to do their job, but functionally the buildings, many of them police stations, are dark, obsolete rabbit warrens urgently in need of modernisation. In all, nearly half of the police stations in the Metropolitan Police District are considered to be below desirable standards.

The PSD are not required to go through the standard procedure of planning permission with local authorities. However, there is a planning consultation exercise which has most of the same features, and allows for an appeal. At the design level attempts are made to keep new buildings harmonious with their surroundings, at the same time incorporating all the requisite security mechanisms. At Stoke Newington police station, for example, there are defences built in which can cope with a siege if necessary.

'Without saying too much,' said Lawrence, understandably reticent about station security, 'at Stoke Newington we could seal off the entrance and isolate the building as a whole. There are steel shutters over sensitive windows, and certain protections behind the windows where they would otherwise be vulnerable. So, there are a number of features we do build into stations, but, as far as the design side is concerned, the fundamental philosophy is that they do not reflect a prison mentality, are not austere Civil Service blocks, and they must look like part of the community.'

It is believed, now, that the pendulum of improvement swung too far in the case of privacy screens for the lavatories in police station cells. These can be seen in some very old stations, but in recent times they were abandoned, so that a full view of the cell would be possible from the communication panel in the door.

'Now the screens are actually returning,' Lawrence said, 'though it's not a simple matter of just building screens. They have to be very robust, you're talking about reinforcement and careful design. Nevertheless, they have to be included if you are going to build a modern station which has to last for sixty years.'

When building and improvement strategies were being drawn up, one of the foremost questions was whether the New Scotland Yard block in Victoria should remain the headquarters. It is an unattractive building, distinguished only by the famous revolving sign outside.

'The locality is important,' Lawrence said. 'It is well sited for access to the Home Office and the Cabinet Office. That was part of our consideration, but also we have a shared equity in our building, so, as a consequence, it is one of the buildings which has a better value to us. We've looked at the various options, but we've come down in favour of New Scotland Yard, despite its somewhat limited architectural value. It does its job adequately, no more than that, but we have a lot of sophisticated equipment installed in there, and the cost of re-location is, of course, always a consideration.'

Within the Metropolitan Police there exists what Lawrence calls a 'high-churn' factor; that is, the rate at which office moves take place. Lawrence believes that the Met probably has the highest 'churn' factor of any organisation in Britain, public or private.

'Given that scenario, there's a big advantage in us adopting more open planning than we have at present. There's no less reluctance to the idea in the Met than there is in other organisations. But there is a greater need to maintain a secure office environment within the Metropolitan Police Service, and that's always going to affect the extent to which we can have open-plan. But that said, I would hope we will be able to go ahead, anyway.'

Lawrence believes his number one concern coincides with that of the Met as a whole: above all other considera-. tions, the 999 service must be sustained. That depends on a well-maintained supply of electricity and electrical services, plus standby generators, and all of those are the responsibility of the engineers at the PSD.

Back-up measures are built into most facilities, particularly 999. If the back-up were to fail, generators would have to be moved in, and the consequent delay in restoring power could have serious consequences, even if it lasted no more than a few seconds.

Standards of hygiene in police station charging areas get special attention. Specialist cleaning contractors are employed to eliminate vermin and clean up blood spillage, the latter an area of special concern now that the risks associated with AIDS and hepatitis are understood.

EPILOGUE
THE FUTURE

The changes about to take place in the Metropolitan Police Service will be the biggest and most far reaching in its history. They will come about in response to the Sheehy Report, the report of the Royal Commission on Criminal Justice and the new Police Bill; they will come about, too, because of public opinion and a strong motivation for change from within the service. The Commissioner, Paul Condon, has a personal agenda to develop and improve the Met.

'There will be significant, substantial, prolonged change during my Commissionership,' he said. 'The reason I wanted at least a seven-year term of office was that it takes a long while to change a big outfit like the Met. I believe I've got the stamina and the commitment to see it through.

'What I am absolutely determined to do is make sure that all the change comes together in a way that is manageable, that's in the public interest and is fair to the men and women who I believe heroically serve the Metropolitan Police. It is a very heavy burden, to steer the Met through that change process, partly induced by me, but also responding to all these outside events which are changing around us.'

Scotland Yard itself is going to be very different. There will be changes in its size and in its overall role. Condon hopes it will be seen as evolution rather than revolution.

'Technology gives us a whole range of choices to do with putting people in various locations around London. I want to give real autonomy and freedom to police stations in a way that they've never had it before. I want to put as many police officers back on the streets as I can, but at the same time I want to retain the notion of the Yard as a centre of excellence.'

Not all the changes are coming from outside. Some of the biggest changes are the work of a group led by Bob Hunt, Assistant Commissioner, Territorial Operations, who has been freed of his main operational duties to lead the Service Restructuring Team (SRT). This team, some of the most able officers in Scotland Yard, has the job of introducing a new structure and management framework to the Met, which, in turn, Hunt believes, will deliver benefits to policing and the general services provided to the public.

'We're going to reduce the number of what are now Divisions from seventy to something just under the sixty mark,' he said, 'and have a smaller number of Areas, probably five or four, instead of the present eight. Whether we call the heads of those Areas Assistant Commissioners or Chief Constables remains to be decided, but they will actually be in on the Policy Committee, which is a very substantial move forward. That's the starting point.'

Key objectives which have already been defined include improved decision-making, effective delegation of power to local levels, more effective use of resources, improved communication, increased accountability and better involvement of the public in the day-to-day work of policing London.

Hunt emphasised that the SRT is only the catalyst for change; as a body it does not incorporate enough knowledge to draw up all the preferred options. It will use the expertise in existing specialist units at Divisional, Area and Headquarters levels.

Like the Commissioner, Hunt is aware of the importance of Scotland Yard's prestige, and he is keen to see that the coming changes do not in any way impair its character and standing.

'The international reputation of the Metropolitan Police has largely been built on the excellence of some of the specialist departments based at Scotland Yard,' Hunt said. 'It's important that we don't lose that expertise and experience, and the reputation that we have built up on that experience. The restructuring that I'm doing will be looking to build on the strengths and remove some of the weaknesses of the organisation, rather than to erode what we're already doing well. So Scotland Yard may look slightly different, and will operate perhaps within slightly different rules, but substantially it will be the same important centre of excellence as far as policing the whole of London is concerned.'

One vision of the future of policing Britain is that of a national police force.

'I suppose in a truly British way, we're trying out the best of all worlds,' said Paul Condon. 'If there is a need for a national response then we tend to set up a national unit – there's NCIS, the intelligence unit. We have started with drugs; we have the Serious Fraud Office; on terrorism the Met has a national coordinating role. So on big thematic issues we do form national units. Then we like to think, and I sign up to this, that there's great pride in local policing, in local police stations, in local cap badges and so on. I have no doubt that over time we will go from forty-three police forces in England and Wales down to a smaller number, and maybe eventually to a single national force.'

The interim measure, he said, would be to reinforce the national specialist squads. He believes there is a 'critical mass' factor related to the number of police forces. So, if the number of individual forces dropped below twenty or twenty-five, then in his view it would be wise, at that point, to move quickly to a national force.

'I think there is an inevitability of us moving, at some stage, towards a national strategy,' he said. 'I'm not going to be running screaming in the opposite direction, but I do believe that, having commanded a provincial force of over 3,000, there is great strength in the model of policing that we have at the moment, with local identity, local pride, different centres of excellence, people trying different things. I think that's to our advantage.'

Any discussion of change within a huge structure like the Metropolitan Police must always take account of foreseeable difficulties. One of the biggest, Condon believes, will be trying to do more in the Met with the same or even less financial resources than before. But that problem, huge as it is, will be simply one among many. The next few years will be a very tough time, Condon says.

'As Commissioner I've got to find the best way through it, to lead the Met through it so that at the end of the day we give the public the best service we possibly can. That's the challenge for me. What I have to put to one side is that I'm Chairman and Chief Executive of a big organisation. You're going to have enough problems looking after an organisation with 46,000 people, with a revenue budget of £1.8 billion. If you add to that the process of change we've got to go through, that's quite a challenge. So I anticipate being fairly busy.'

Asked what he believed the Met would be like at the

end of his seven-year contract, Condon said he hoped the change would be invisible.

'In other words I don't expect police stations to look fundamentally different. I don't expect police officers to look different. I don't want them to be different sorts of characters to what they are now. They are a very high-calibre, brave, loyal set of people. I want more of the same people doing more of the same, but in an even better way than they are now. In seven years I would like to think the Met would be providing an even better service than it does now. I'd like to think that public confidence would have held up, or even improved. I would like to think that our performance against crime would be as good if not better than it is now.

'Along the way there will be crises. There will be moments of great anguish, moments of great sadness. I have to recognise that Metropolitan Police Officers will be killed on duty between now and then. I can anticipate that there may be outbreaks of serious disorder for whatever reason. I can anticipate that terrorism will continue to be played out. But if I have delivered in the way that I've spoken about, I would feel that the Met is in a healthier shape than it is now, and that I'll be handing it on to the next Commissioner who, he or she, will come in with their own plans and take the Met forward.

'There's a great sense of carrying on, a sense that, even if it turns out to be ten years rather than seven, I am only the guy who is doing it at this point. There's a sense of history, of continuity.'

Bibliography

Begg, P., and Skinner, K., *The Scotland Yard Files*, Headline, London, 1992

Cox, B., Shirley, J., and Short, M., *The Fall of Scotland Yard*, Penguin, London, 1977

Geraghty, T., *The Bullet-Catchers*, Grafton, London, 1988

Goodman, J., and Waddell, B., *The Black Museum*, Harrap, London, 1987

Gould, R.W., and Waldren, M.J., *London's Armed Police*, Arms & Armour Press, London, 1986

Graef, R., *Talking Blues*, Collins Harvill, London, 1989

Gurney, P., *Braver Men Walk Away*, HarperCollins, London, 1993

Howe, R., *The Story of Scotland Yard*, Arthur Barker, London, 1965

Kelland, G., *Crime in London*, Bodley Head, London, 1986

Northam, G., *Shooting in the Dark*, Faber & Faber, London, 1989

Waddington, P.A.J., *Arming an Unarmed Police*, The Police Foundation, 1988

Waddington, P.A.J., *The Strong Arm of the Law*, Oxford University Press, 1991

Index

Published or forthcoming

THE SAS: SAVAGE WARS OF PEACE

Anthony Kemp

Founded in 1941, the SAS is still the most feared and respected elite fighting force in the modern military world. Anthony Kemp's definitive history – the sequel to *The SAS at War* – penetrates the cloak of secrecy that has surrounded the SAS counter-terrorist activities, including those in the Falklands and the Gulf War.

With each new offensive – Northern Ireland, the Iranian Embassy, the Falklands War, the attack on the IRA in Gibraltar – speculation about the SAS has intensified. This is the fullest picture yet of a brave and astonishingly successful regiment, never far from the glare of the limelight.

Published or forthcoming

SIGNET

Atlantis of the Sands

Ranulph Fiennes

For 2000 years Arabian legend has spoken of a fabulous lost city of Ubar, buried under the immense sand dunes of southern Oman ...

For twenty-four years explorer and adventurer Ranulph Fiennes searched for information that would give him the exact location of the city. Finally in 1991, armed with new photographic evidence from space shuttle 'Challenger' and a fascinating series of clues from ancient documents, Sir Ranulph began his epic journey into the Empty Quarter.

EAM TORNADO

RAF Flight Lieutenants **John Peters** and **John Nichol**

Gulf War heroes John Peters and John Nichol wrote about their ordeal as prisoners of war in the bestselling book *Tornado Down*.

Team Tornado tells the story of what made John Peters and John Nichol become airmen, how their lives have been affected by the Gulf War and what life is like in the Royal Air Force.

Packed with real-life situations they tell of split-second decisions that can make death a real possibility, the thrill of manoeuvres and the pressures of training for nuclear, biological and chemical warfare.